PENGUIN BOOKS

RECOVERING FROM THE WAR

Patience Mason is the wife of Robert Mason, author of the best-selling Vietnam memoir *Chickenhawk*. A survivor who has lived with Post-Traumatic Stress Disorder (PTSD) for twenty-three years, and a trained crisis-line phone counselor, she lives with her family in High Springs, Florida. This is her first book.

Recovering from the War

A Woman's Guide to Helping Your Vietnam Vet, Your Family, and Yourself

PATIENCE H.C. MASON

PENGUIN BOOKS

PENGUIN BOOKS
Published by the Penguin Group
Viking Penguin, a division of Penguin Books USA Inc.,
40 West 23rd Street, New York, New York 10010, U.S.A.
Penguin Books Ltd, 27 Wrights Lane, London W8 5TZ, England
Penguin Books Australia Ltd, Ringwood, Victoria, Australia
Penguin Books Canada Ltd, 2801 John Street,
Markham, Ontario, Canada L3R 1B4
Penguin Books (N.Z.) Ltd, 182–190 Wairau Road, Auckland 10, New Zealand

Penguin Books Ltd, Registered Offices:
Harmondsworth, Middlesex, England

First published in simultaneous hardcover and paperback
editions by Viking Penguin, a division of Penguin Books USA Inc. 1990

1   3   5   7   9   10   8   6   4   2

LIBRARY OF CONGRESS CATALOGING IN PUBLICATION DATA
Mason, Patience.
Recovering from the war : a woman's guide to helping your Vietnam
Vet, your family, and yourself/Patience Mason.
p.   cm.
Bibliography: p.
Includes index.
1. Vietnamese Conflict, 1961–1975—United States.   2. Vietnamese
Conflict, 1961–1975—Psychological aspects.   3. Vietnamese Conflict,
1961–1975—Veterans—United States.   4. Veterans—United States.
5. Women—Mental health—United States.   6. Adjustment (Psychology)
7. Self-care, Health.   I. Title.
DS558.M314   1989
959.704′3373—dc20   88–40422
ISBN 0 14 00. 9912 3

Printed in the United States of America
Set in Century Expanded
Designed by Victoria Hartman

To Bob and Jack

In memory of
Sarah Haley

Contents

Foreword

Patience and I are both survivors of the Vietnam War. To some degree, all war veterans and their families suffer from the trauma of the war the veteran fought. Most of them don't know it. We didn't.

As vets, we ignore the fact that we have been changed by denying that the war had an effect on us that we can't control. As family, we expect the vet to put the war behind him and don't want to hear about it. John Wayne movies and most popular fiction instill within males the notion that they *can* cut through hordes of people, slashing them down like so much wheat, without suffering a moment's regret. It's part of the culture to believe that people, unpathological, everyday people, can—on the battlefield—kill other people who have been defined as the enemy with moral, legal, and psychological impunity. They can watch their friends being blown to bits, left dead or horribly maimed, with a shrug—or if the character is portrayed as a thoughtful man—a shrug and a couple of manly tears. After Joey gets it, Johnny leaps into the fray and makes the bastards pay. Everything is okay when Johnny comes marching home.

The facts, of course, are completely different. Every war produces permanently maimed—physically and psychologically—veterans who will never be anything like they were before they experienced combat. And neither will their families. No matter how long everyone waits, Johnny is *always* going to be different. The pain and injury inflicted upon our warriors and their families are an often-ignored part of the actual cost of waging war. In the case of the Vietnam War and World War I—both wars fought for nebulous ideals or political belligerence—all the pain and injury were probably completely unnecessary, which only exacerbated the pain felt by the survivors and added to the turmoil, anguish, and grief within their families.

Problems can only be solved when they are understood. For years, Patience and I sort of blundered around, confused—knowing something was really very wrong with me and our relationship, but we hadn't a clue exactly what or why. After all, the war was over. I was home. So what was the damn problem?

I was a warrant officer pilot who flew assault helicopters in Vietnam in 1965 and 1966. The job, one of hundreds of other bad combat jobs, was extremely stressful. When we flew troopers into landing zones under fire, there was no way for the crews of these helicopters to duck or dodge the machine-gun bullets coming up at us. We just hung on and kept flying. Many of us were killed and wounded. A year of this *impotency* will *mess* you up. Naturally, as I neared the end of my one-year tour, I began to think I might actually live through the experience, and that became the most stressful period of my whole tour. They called it the Short Timer's Blues. Part of every day was spent daydreaming about how great it was going to be to get home, get back to ordinary life, with ordinary problems; get on with a career, leave the war behind.

The first night home, I leapt out of bed in a panic. And again the second night. *Eventually, this will stop,* I thought, *as I get used to being out of the war.* But it didn't stop. And because it didn't, I quite naturally believed that I was somehow defective or weak, lacking the proper moral fiber to force myself to be normal again as John Wayne or Ronald Reagan would've on the silver screen. The acknowledgment of this kind of deficiency is something people want to keep to themselves.

I'd been assigned to teach pilot candidates to fly helicopters in combat at the army's helicopter school in Texas. A year later, a year out of combat, and I was still leaping up when I tried to sleep. Patience and my son, Jack, just thought of it as "Dad's jump-ups." We all tried to ignore the problem. When I had been back a month, I went to the flight surgeon and told him I was leaping up all night and he repeated the myth: It will go away in time. When it still hadn't a year later, I was unwilling to go back and admit that I was a freak. I slept less and less each night to avoid the nightmares and feelings of panic. I wandered around the house for hours until I became exhausted enough to sleep a few hours before I went to the flight line and tried to teach people how to fly an extremely complicated and potentially dangerous flying machine.

Lack of sleep was taking its toll. I was fuzzy-headed every morning and exhausted by early afternoon. One night, I opened one of the bottles of whiskey my students had given me at the end of a cycle. I'd kept these gifts in a cupboard, unopened, because I didn't drink. I had a pretty stiff drink, and fell asleep. It was a great relief.

Within a few weeks, I had to drink nearly half a bottle to get the same relief. It wasn't helping. It was masking a problem. I still didn't know what the problem was. I thought I was going crazy.

I had a dizzy spell in a helicopter with a student one morning. He never knew it because I had him take the controls—instructor pilots are always telling their students to take over to see what they'll do. I went to the flight surgeon and was immediately grounded.

I should mention here that the reason I joined the army in the first place was to become a helicopter pilot. I wanted to do this professionally when I got out of the army. Being grounded eliminated flying as a career. My weakness was costing me everything that mattered to me.

I was also extremely difficult to live with. Patience and I fought often. Our home life was seldom happy. Jack could probably count on one hand the number of times he and I played together.

Being grounded made things much worse. Determined not to lose my career, I went back to the flight surgeon a month later and lied. I told him I felt fine—"musta" been a bug or something. I was checked out again and returned to flight status.

No improvement. A month later I had another dizzy spell while flying and turned myself over to the doctors. Grounded again. This time they had a diagnosis: severe combat anxiety. I was given what was called a million-dollar ticket: a medical profile that stated that I could not serve in combat or be assigned duty in a combat zone. I was assigned to the academic section to lecture incoming Vietnam veteran pilots on how to be instructors at the flight school.

I did this for about a year, until my military obligation was up. I could not, even when offered a direct commission as a captain, stay in the army without being a pilot. I left the army and returned to college. I was convinced that this change would finally do it—get me back to normal.

I was wrong. The flight surgeons said that my anxiety would probably disappear when I got out of the army, but if it did not, I should go to the Veterans Administration and continue to get the Valium the army had been giving me.

In school, I was showing up at my eight-in-the-morning classes after having had two very stiff whiskeys. No one but Patience knew. My consumption of alcohol was then up to a full quart a day just to stay "normal." Finally, I went to the VA and asked for the Valium. They gave me a two-hour psychological examination and didn't give me the drugs. A month later, I got a letter saying that I had been declared a disabled veteran. I suffered from "nervousness," said the letter. It wasn't the kind of disability one would like to mention in public, but I did get the Valium, and it did help. Armed with alcohol, the pot I'd learned to smoke at the university, and now the Valium, I appeared almost normal. Inside, however, the storm still raged.

We were still fighting in Vietnam. Americans watched the debacle on television as if they were watching the weather reports. For them, it was a background irritation, a kind of Muzak war; a hateful tune that wouldn't go away. For me, it was a senseless and horrifying mass murder of brave young Americans, Vietnamese, and Cambodians. I felt physically ill when I saw the news programs casually interlacing the staccato blasts of a Vietnam firefight and the exposed intestines of an American boy on a stretcher with Budweiser jingles and Marlboro men. Meanwhile, the students at the university were demonstrating against the soldiers—not against the people who sent them.

Patience knew she was married to a guy who drank a lot, but it was almost something to be proud of: Bob drinks a bottle a day and can still walk—what a man. She spent a lot of time cooking gourmet meals, placating me during my bleak moods, attempting to be the perfect wife—also in the grand movie tradition. After three semesters trying to be a student and barely succeeding, I made a run for it. I dropped out and took Patience and Jack to Spain.

Spaniards also like to drink a lot, and almost never talked about Vietnam. I tried writing a story in Spain. A writer friend, Martin

Cruz Smith, read my story and said it was good. It just needed a few rewrites was all. I took this to mean that in addition to not being able to fly, I also could not write. I was a basket case of doubts, a fury of completely unfocused energy. Meanwhile, Patience was putting up with my dark moods with great understanding. She learned to cook Spanish cuisine and let me hang out with the Spanish guys, drinking and playing barroom games. The perfect little woman.

That lasted seven months.

I kind of careened through life for the next few years, driving Patience crazy with me. We worked at an electronics factory for a while. I started having an affair with a girl I met in the factory cafeteria. We went back to school. Eventually Patience and I graduated, but not before we broke up for a couple of months.

When Patience started to read books, especially self-help books, things got better. She spent less time trying to repair me, and more trying to help herself. This gave me a break. I had to bottom out, I guess. I did. Eventually I gave up drinking because it was giving me horrible hangovers. I read one of Patience's books, *Your Erroneous Zones*, which made me think about helping myself. In that book, Dr. Wayne Dyer asks, "What would you do if you had six months to live?" Almost everybody says they'd go on a trip around the world, live in Tahiti, you know, all the fantasy stuff. Almost none of them wanted to keep doing what they were doing. When I asked my writer friend, Smith, that question, he said he'd speed up a little and finish the book he was working on. I decided then that my goal would be to get paid to do what I wanted.

Not so easy. We had to take some gambles and they didn't always work. But we were trying.

I built a house, our first, by hand in the woods of Florida.

I started writing a book about my experiences in Vietnam. And rewriting it. I think going back through my experiences helped me in the long run, but it was painful.

I stupidly tried to smuggle marijuana to make enough money to live on while I wrote.

I got caught.

A publisher, Viking, bought my Vietnam memoir, *Chickenhawk*, while I was waiting to go to jail.

I spent two years at Eglin Federal Prison Camp completely defeated and unable to write. When I was released in May 1985, I started writing at home, full-time.

Putnam just published (March 1989) my first novel, *Weapon*, and 20th Century-Fox bought the film option. I've been very lucky.

With my success, I can feel good enough about myself that I sleep okay. I still have problems sometimes. I wake up in a panic occasionally. I still take Valium, which seems to help. I limit my drinking to weekends. I know I will probably always suffer some effects from my experiences in Vietnam. So will we all.

Some aren't so lucky.

Recently, here in Gainesville, Florida, a Vietnam veteran, John Frederick Barlog, was trying to get into the VA hospital for treatment of his alcohol addiction. He had to wait three days, so the VA let Barlog sleep in his van in the hospital parking lot, a common practice. On March 4, 1989, he had been there for a couple of days, sleeping in this van, when two hospital security guards peeked inside and saw that Barlog had a sheathed hunting knife next to him. Having a hunting knife next to you in a camper while you're sleeping in a parking lot doesn't seem so strange to me, but to these two guards, apparently it was one of the more exciting events of their lives. Maybe they were just bored. They called the local police and told them there was an *armed veteran* in the parking lot. When the police arrived, they banged on the van to wake Barlog. He was so drunk he didn't wake up. The cops rocked his van back and forth. Still Barlog slept. Finally, like kids worrying a hibernating bear, the cops slid open the van's door, pulled Barlog's blanket off and shook him. Shaken out of a drunken sleep, Barlog leapt up yelling, brandishing his knife, and came after them. He refused to stop when the cops told him to, and was shot. Three times. Dead.

The grand jury exonerated the two cops—self-defense.

The hospital director, Malcolm Randall, announced that the VA's internal quality-assurance review "confirms that all the VA personnel acted appropriately," but that the VA wasn't allowed to make their internal report public. No one at the hospital had done anything wrong. No one was at fault.

The VA has a tremendous work load, but I think shooting the patients in the parking lots is a bit extreme.

Maybe if Barlog had had better help along the way, he'd still be alive.

Patience is trying to help. By interviewing many veterans, she describes what they went through, what the veterans' natural reaction to combat trauma was, and what changes that kind of trauma can cause.

She devotes much of her book to telling you how you can help your veteran by helping yourself. You and your veteran can get better.

It works. Patience speaks from experience. And she cares.

Robert Mason

Acknowledgments

I'd like to thank my husband, Bob, and my son, Jack, for their support and encouragement, and for putting up with me when I thought I was perfect. My mother, Constance G. Hartwell, M.D., for modeling intelligence, growth, courage, strength and faithfulness, and for her interest in veterans and PTSD, and my father, the late John J. Cincotti, M.D., for expecting me to have a life of my own. Wallie for supporting me, needing me, listening to me, valuing my advice and actually following it—which meant I had to follow some of it, too. Patti and Mike, Joe and Nikki, Jim and Eileen, Joe and Gay, Larry and Edie, Mugga and Poppa, Nancy and Erik, and Paula for their support and friendship. Zubi, Lovey, Sarah, Preston, Wink, Mack, Kyle, Breena and Amanda for helping me feel special. Patti for showing me you didn't have to put up with so much from your vet. Mal for organizing my first vacation ever, the wild trip to Maine. Leslie for sharing it. Molly, Ruth, Sha, Jean, Sarah, and Marsha for sharing and support. Marci for hearing my Fifth Step the first time and her friendship and support. Suzanne for taking me to my first meeting, and a friend and Bobbe for showing me the 12 Steps in action and leading me to another 12 Step group.

My editors, Gerry Howard, Pam Dorman, and Ashton Applewhite helped me more than I can say with advice and encouragement. Bob and Jill Sharkey kindly let me whoosh out the manuscript on the *High Springs Herald*'s laserwriter.

I'd also like to thank the guys in New Missions 'Nam Vets at UCI for giving me the idea for this book in the first place: Mike T., Frank, Willie, Jerry, Louis, Guy, Colon, Steve, Keith, Mike N., Dwight,

Craig, "KC," George ("Lucky") B., John G., Bill F., Big Bill, Mongoose, Eugene, Larry, Tom, Ken, George R., Mike M., John S., Ray, James, and Eric. I'd also like to thank the prison administration and the group's sponsors, Linda Ryder and Richard Hinkle, for caring about veterans.

I'd like to thank Clant, Larry, Ric, Marty, Chuck, and the rest of Nam Vets of Alachua County for being there, and all the vets who wrote, called, or talked to me, especially Doc Jack for giving me my first interview, and the guys from Nam Vets of Marion County and Vietnam Veterans of Brevard County who heard me speak and volunteered to be interviewed. You guys mean a lot ot me.

I'd also like to thank various Vet Center people who hung up "Help" notices for me, David Harrington and the VVA *Veteran* for mentioning in his column that I was looking for information, and Molly King-Gilpin for putting a notice in the Vietnam Veterans of Oregon Memorial Fund Newsletter.

The members of the Society for Traumatic Stress Studies welcomed and supported my project, shared information with me, and encouraged me to go on. John Wilson, Charles Figley, Yael Danieli, Erwin Parson, Sarah Haley, John Russell Smith, Ray Scurfield, Tom Williams, Pat Sheehan, Bruce Webster, Ross Mayberry, Joe Gelsomino, Alan Brett, John Krystal, Linda Reinberg, Mary Moyers, Linda Carole, and many others gave me information and support and by their example helped me keep working despite the pain and anxiety which I experienced over the material in this book.

I'd like to thank my therapists over the years: Dr. Yozgat for asking the question that changed my whole life: "How does Bob feel? Is he sorry?," Steven Schoenhaut for telling me I didn't have to be perfect over and over for six months until I could hear it, Kathrin Brantley for many insights, and Pat Sohler for many more.

Finally I'd like to thank the Vietnam veteran nurse at the Society for Traumatic Stress Studies meeting in Denver, Colorado, October 1986, for asking me, "Who is taking care of Patience?" because without her, the help-yourself part of this book would just be directions on how to be co-dependent. Thanks.

Recovering
from the War

Introduction

Recovering from the War is a book for women who have relationships with Vietnam veterans. Its subject is the problems that arose out of the Vietnam experience itself, and what we can and cannot do about them.

I needed to deal with a Vietnam combat veteran, my husband. His experiences created problems that almost destroyed our marriage, but no one had anything to offer except Valium. I needed to know that his problems were not my fault and that I could not cure them, but nobody could tell me that either. I'm writing the book I wish I'd had back then, in the hopes that my experiences and those of other women and of our vets will help you.

Perhaps you've picked up this book because you have to deal with a Vietnam veteran, too: son or father, husband, lover, or friend. One of the problems Vietnam veterans face is the incredible ignorance of the rest of the population about what went on in Vietnam. I hope to help fill that gap. I also need to know about Vietnam so it won't happen to my son. Perhaps you do, too.

Since the publication of *Chickenhawk*, a memoir of the year he spent as a combat helicopter pilot in Vietnam, my husband, Robert Mason, has received countless letters. Vets have thanked him for telling it like it was, and non-vets for helping them understand what it was like to be in Vietnam. Mental-health professionals have told me repeatedly how helpful *Chickenhawk* has been to other vets. If they aren't feeling anything it helps break through their numbness, and if they are having problems it helps them to know that Bob did, too. Bob will tell you that he did no more than the other helicopter pilots in Vietnam. He will also tell you how lucky he was that he was not a grunt. Grunts went through hell.

"You'll never know what you guys meant to us grunts," Greg Cook wrote Bob from Cleveland, one of the first fan letters he ever got. If you're saying "What's a grunt?" and you're involved with a vet, you need to know. A grunt is an infantryman, the guy with the rifle in his hand out humping the boonies. Humping the boonies? Going out on patrols, pack on back, ammo clips, grenades, and canteens hung all over him, walking. Helicopter pilots took them in and brought them out when they were wounded, or done with that day's, or week's, or month's sweep.

In another of Bob's fan letters, a woman wrote Bob that he was a hero for flying into all those hot LZ's (landing zones under hostile fire). Her husband had been "just in the artillery," no hero. You probably know that being *"just* in the artillery" could have been pretty hairy, along with a lot of other jobs. As a matter of fact, lots of vets have told Bob they had no idea being a helicopter pilot was so much work. "I always thought you guys dropped us off and went back, got drunk, and fooled around with the nurses," admitted Mike Costello, author of *A Long Time from Home* and a LRRP (long-range reconnaissance patrol) in Vietnam, when he first met Bob. "I had no idea that you went back and got another load, and then another, all day long."

"Hey, that's what we wanted you guys to think." Bob laughed. "We used to lie about it all the time."

Men.

Two million eight hundred thousand men is a conservative estimate of the number who served in Vietnam. The U.S. Department of Defense doesn't know the exact figure, which may surprise the reader but will not surprise any veteran of the Vietnam War. They don't expect much from the government.

Recently, Bob and I talked to a history class at the University of Florida. One of the students said, "I thought with all the recognition and the Memorial and all that Vietnam veterans would be okay now."

"You are laboring under a misapprehension if you think the United States government built that Memorial, or organized the parade, or anything else," I informed him. "The Vietnam Memorial was paid for by money the vets raised themselves. Vietnam veterans gave the Memorial to the government." My eyes were flashing, and I was trembling, and suddenly I felt really badly for this young guy who was only trying to understand.

I'm glad he was trying.

Vets do need and want to be understood, yet for a number of reasons they have a hard time talking about Vietnam. When they came back no one wanted to hear what it was like. We all know the feeling of starting to confide in someone who turns away. We never try again.

Vietnam vets are also afraid that most people can't face what they had to face. Some combat vets fear that no one could love them if they knew what they had to do to stay alive. They also feel that talking about it will bring it all back. They'll crack. They'll go crazy. They'll cry and you won't respect them anymore. Or they'll experience flashbacks to Vietnam or to the years when they first got back and felt violent and self-destructive. They're afraid to set off a volcano of feelings. It's safer to forget.

Many men don't feel that they were combat vets, so they have no way to understand why Vietnam still bothers them. They don't want to talk about it, because they think it *shouldn't* bother them. What about the guy who was in the rear, who was greeted with "How many babies did you kill?," when all he did was run a forklift at Cam Rahn Bay and endure the occasional rocket attack and the daily harassment of the lifers? He doesn't know that rocket attacks are traumatic stressors whether you're hit or not. He doesn't know that every human being on the face of the earth has to talk out traumatic incidents with *someone*, not necessarily a psychiatrist, or the incidents go on hurting and hurting and coloring everything else in life.

Other veterans succeeded in forgetting Vietnam and are annoyed by those with problems. I hope this book will heal some of that split, as luck is the only thing that sets them apart. It is not their strong character, their guts, their morals, their good family background, just the same blind luck that kept a bullet from adding their names to the names on the Wall. Many of them do not realize that workaholism and lack of emotional connection can be symptoms of stress just like substance abuse and other more visible problems.

I'm not saying that all Vietnam veterans have problems, but that if a vet does, he should see himself and be seen by his family, friends, and society as normal, not defective. As John Wilson, Ph.D., and Gustave Krause, M.A., two respected researchers in the field, put it: "If conditions are favorable, especially if there is a supportive recovery environment, the individual may gradually assimilate and 'work through' the trauma. . . . If conditions are not favorable, the survivor may need help in the working-through process. . . ." Or to put it in my terms, luck.

"At least 250,000 and possibly as many as 500,000 Vietnam veterans who need various forms of help in order to have a productive life . . . unhampered by problems of adjustment . . ." exist in this country. These vets display some or all of the symptoms of PTSD (Post-Traumatic Stress Disorder), a *normal* reaction to the stress of battle.

People with PTSD symptoms are hard to live with, and more have killed themselves since the war than died in the actual conflict (according to several reports, starting with one by the National Council of Churches in the late seventies). Living with traumatic experiences buried inside is difficult. Sometimes it's impossible. A lot of the guys credit their wives or girlfriends with keeping them alive. We love them and we want them to be happy. We can't stand it when we see them in pain. Why does it hurt so much? I'm hoping this book will give you some of the answers.

My husband, Bob, went to Vietnam as a helicopter pilot with the 1st Cavalry Division in August 1965. Jack, our son, was a year old. Bob and I wrote each other every day. Once he wrote that he was surprised to be alive, but usually he told funny stories about the army or just said he loved me. In one letter written after he'd been there eight months he counted up the days he hadn't flown—ten. He was sent to the 48th Aviation Company three months before he came home. The stories got funnier, but he wrote that they had to start giving him tranquilizers so he could sleep.

We moved to Texas, where he taught at the U.S. Army Primary Helicopter School. For a while he even flew two shifts, training guys in the H-23 in the morning and the TH-55 in the afternoon.

Bob began to have dizzy spells at Fort Wolters. He was grounded twice and finally sent to Fort Sam Houston to be evaluated. He came home with a million-dollar piece of paper that said he had combat fatigue and could never be sent back to a combat zone. He also came back with a look on his face that I will never forget as long as I live.

"There are kids there, Patience," he said—Fort Sam was the burn treatment center for the army—"eighteen-year-old kids with their faces burnt off from napalm. They aren't ever going to look any better, and they have their whole lives in front of them."

When his obligation to the army was completed, he left—a grounded and, in his eyes, useless pilot. We went back to school at the University of Florida. He studied fine arts, I worked and took English courses. Bob went to the VA for the Valium the army had started him on and was declared a 50 percent disabled veteran for "nervousness." He had all the symptoms for which he would have been rated 100 percent disabled for PTSD, except that the diagnosis didn't *exist* until 1980. The next few years were chaotic. Although we both finished college, we moved almost every year, and we played musical jobs. If he had one, I didn't, and vice versa. For some of those years, Bob drank a quart of whiskey a day, smoked pot, and took a lot of Valium—and he was still *wired*. He couldn't sleep, he had nightmares, rages, constant anxiety attacks (with irregular heartbeat, chest pains, dizzy spells, and incapacitating weakness), intrusive thoughts, deep depressions. He alternated between thinking he was nuts, telling me I was nuts, driving like a wild man with me and Jack in the car, riding his motorcycle like a madman. Often he was cold and critical, or angry and critical. He was unfaithful to me. He left various jobs for both reasonable and unreasonable reasons. Neither of us knew what was wrong. I screamed and raged and enabled and took care of the family stuff while he suffered, I suffered, and Jack suffered. Jack became a very tense little boy, and he took care of me when Bob couldn't. Most of the time Bob just *wasn't there*, emotionally. But sometimes in the midst of all this chaos it would be okay between us, and sometimes it would even be beautiful.

After a few years, the most intrusive phase seemed to pass. Bob developed a manufacturing process for decorative mirrors and became vice president of a mirror-manufacturing company in Brooklyn, New York. I was his assistant. We worked long hours under a lot of stress. Bob got two hangovers in a row, his first, and stopped drinking. He also stopped Valium for a while, but the arrythmia and chest pains put him in the hospital. Something had damaged his heart, but no one knew what.

After a few years in New York, we quit our jobs, bought a school bus, loaded it with everything we owned, and drove to a piece of land we'd bought in Florida on the Santa Fe River. We cut a road down to the riverbank, and sat, exhausted, for a week. The three of us lived in the woods in the school bus, a pup tent, and a screen tent while Bob built a house by hand, and mostly by himself, because he got so annoyed when I'd ask for directions that I'd end up leaving. Bob became extremely depressed. To this day we still find tools he threw into the woods.

We lived cheaply on a settlement from the mirror-manufacturing company and both started writing. Bob wrote the first third of *Chickenhawk*, while I worked on a science-fiction book. Bob decided to try to sell his book on the basis of the completed third and sent it off to New York. We both took up driving paper routes—a hundred miles over dirt roads every night starting at 2 A.M.—so we could continue writing during the day. Yet we became so focused in on the seven-day-a-week rat race that it was impossible for us to write. A few months later Bob's car, a 1954 VW, blew up. We faced financial ruin. A friend offered him $30,000 to sail to Colombia for a load of marijuana as a deckhand on a thirty-five-foot sailboat. As Bob put it, he found out he could be bought. So did I. We lied to everyone about where he was, but after forty-four days at sea, the boat sailed up a creek in South Carolina right up to a U.S. Customs boat.

A month after his arrest, Viking bought *Chickenhawk*. We were afraid to tell the publisher he'd just been busted, so we didn't. He had to complete the story of the worst year in his life, out on appeal, with a five-year jail term hanging over his head. It was an exercise in courage that I will never forget. He wrote and I supported us by working as a cleaning woman. By the time he finished the book, he was so thin that he went to the VA one day to check out this lump in his abdomen, and it was his kidney. As soon as the book came out, it got rave reviews and he lost his appeal. He was on the "Today" show on Wednesday and reported to Eglin Federal Prison Camp in Florida's panhandle on Friday, August 19, 1983.

I asked him what he would want people to know about what he did: "I'm not proud of it. I knew it was a crime when I did it and I was willing to take that risk, and I've paid the price. It had nothing to do with Vietnam except in the sense that I looked on it as a mission. I knew it was a bad idea almost from the start but I stuck with it."

We stuck it out too, worked on our problems, and now we're closer than ever. Therapy helped us both at times. Other times, especially at the VA in the early seventies, it was the wrong therapy and didn't help. Self-help books have been the other, greater factor in our learning to get along.

I've also read everything I could about Vietnam that was written by veterans themselves. No histories. I don't care what happened when Kissinger went to Paris. I wanted to know what it was like for the guys who were there. While Bob wrote *Chickenhawk*, we read *The Killing Zone*, by Frederick Downs, and Phillip Caputo's *A Rumor of War*. Downs's book made me realize a lot about the war, about booby traps and anger. At the end of it, I was ready to kill the Vietnamese villagers myself. Caputo's book had a different effect on me. Although the writing was excellent, he couldn't remember his men's names. It made me mad. (I'm letting you in on what a jerk I am sometimes.) George Washington and Robert E. Lee knew their men's names. Even Harry S. Truman in World War I, the officers in *Battle Cry*, and *Those Devils in Baggy Pants* in World War II knew their men's names. That's as it's *supposed* to be, I thought. I was mad at Caputo for a long time before I understood and realized he wasn't indifferent, and it wasn't his fault. I still feel guilty about it, though.

I read *Nam*, by Mark Baker; *The 13th Valley*, by John Del Vecchio; Michael Costello's *A Long Time from Home;* the unpublished poems of medic Jack Strahan; and Mike Geokan's unpublished memoir of the tank war in Vietnam, *Aces of Iron*. Every guy had a different war. When I finally put down Larry Heinemann's *Close Quarters*, I understood fear. He's one of America's greatest living writers, but even after winning the National Book Award, too few people know it because nobody wants to know about Vietnam. Heinemann never pulls a punch. Every ugly thing about Vietnam is there. *Fields of Fire*, by James Webb, opened my eyes further. I remember saying something angry to Costello about "that coward Braverman, 'the Professor,' the only one who lived," and the look Costello gave me. Who was I calling a coward?

I cried my way through Rick Eilert's *For Self and Country* and Lynda Van Devanter's *Home Before Morning*. By the time I heard some nurses were claiming *Home Before Morning* wasn't true to their experience in Vietnam, I knew everyone had a different war. When I read a vile review in a small-time Vietnam vets' newsletter saying Lynda Van Devanter wasn't a real American woman, another problem struck me: divisiveness. The newsletter was put out by a guy who actually admitted to being a REMF (rear-echelon mother-fucker) in Vietnam, chief enlisted publicity man or something. I suppose he felt like the guy 1st Cav grunt Marty Rogers once decked in a bar for saying "You grunts spoiled it for everyone."

Someone spoiled it for everyone, but it wasn't the grunts. Nor was it the people who told the truth, however ugly. We the people sent eighteen-year-olds to die in a foreign country we had no intention of conquering, as cogs in a military machine run on principles that guaranteed we couldn't win. And when we couldn't win, we left.

The idea for this book came to me on March 18, 1986. Bob and I went to Union Correctional Institute at Raiford, Florida, to talk to a Vietnam veterans' self-help group called New Missions Nam Vets. Raiford has a wall, towers, barbed wire, a series of electrically operated gates that groan and rumble as you pass through. Linda Ryder, the sponsor of the group, met us at the entrance and led us through the complexities of getting in. We walked through a tree-shaded compound past a couple of old pale green buildings with barred windows. We passed through a checkpoint. The newer buildings looked more like dorms than sinister state prison cells. Inside the psychology classroom were twenty men who were going to be in Raiford for a long time. Raiford is the only prison in the state that has to take violent or disturbed prisoners, so it's the roughest. I felt like crying. These guys had been through Nam and somehow had wound up in another dangerous, hard place where any one of the population could suddenly turn out to be your enemy, and where each man's life is controlled by the government, represented this time by the prison system.

"What went wrong?" my heart cried.

Bob had been out of Eglin Federal Prison Camp less than a year. He'd accepted the invitation to speak to these guys because they were vets and in a much worse prison than he'd been in. He told them right away that it made him nervous to come inside. He wasn't sure they'd let him out. Everyone laughed. Bob talked a little about *Chickenhawk*, which many of them had read, about making something positive out of the experience, and about the wimp prison he'd been in, which made them laugh. Then we opened it up for questions. Eventually one of the guys asked how I'd felt when I found out Bob had been unfaithful to me in Vietnam. "By the time I found out it was a couple of years later," I said with a smile. "I realized people had been trying to kill him so I felt he deserved whatever he could get his hands on." That made them laugh, too. We also talked about Vietnam and the pain of remembering it, and the similarities between Vietnam and prison.

Afterward several of the guys came up to me and said, "I wish you could talk to my wife."

I cried in the car on the way home. Bob looked bleak. I kept thinking all the way home, *What can I do? I wish I could talk to their wives. I wish I could talk to the wives of all vets. Bob and I are happy now but we went through really hard times. I want to do something!* Somewhere on U.S. 121 between Raiford and Worthington Springs, the design of this book appeared in my mind. I could share what I'd learned and find out more.

I have to admit that when I started I thought I knew the answers. Now I think I know the questions you might want to ask and places you can look for your own answers. I've worked and read and studied how to be happily married. At first, I thought all our problems could be solved and were my fault. Then I got to the point where I could see that they weren't anyone's fault, least of all mine. Life had dealt us a hand and we had to go from there, but I still thought eventually we'd reach unalloyed happiness. Now I realize that Bob was damaged in Vietnam and will never be the way he was before. Some days he will wake up and the world will be a black pit of depression. Some days he won't want to see people. Thoughts of Vietnam or violent death will intrude sometimes no matter how hard he wills them away, and he won't tell me. He'll just be hard to live with. It has nothing to do with me. It's not my fault, and I can't cure it. All I can do is be there for him. That's all anyone can do.

So part of what I want to offer in this book is how to make the good times better and how to make it through the bad times. Veterans of Vietnam and combat veterans of any war have been through a fire that women, unless living in a combat zone, will never see. They have seen and done things for which the human psyche is not designed. Damage was done. They will never be the same.

Combat vets can't *get over it*, because those images of dead, burnt bodies and exploding friends will never leave them. They can never forget the friends they lost in the A Shau Valley, at Dak To, or Khe Sanh, or a thousand other places in Vietnam, nor in other wars, on the Anzio beachhead, D-Day, in the Ardennes, on Guadalcanal or Iwo Jima, at the Chosin Reservoir. They can never forget that they themselves were expendable. And Vietnam veterans lost their friends in a war our country wasn't trying to win.

I don't think we should be asking men to forget what war is. We should be listening to what they have to say about war, and never have another unless we follow the original intent of the framers of the Constitution and declare war. Remember, those framers had *experienced* war on our own soil, and they felt war was not to be lightly entered into on the will of any single human being, even that of the president.

We can also help our vets to live with these painful experiences, perhaps better than the generation of World War II, the men who never talked about it, and the wives who never asked. All the heroes trying to forget The Big One at the bars of countless VFW's and American Legion halls in all the towns across America. The generation that let Vietnam happen.

The three main sections of this book deal with Vietnam itself (Part One. Vietnam: What It Was), the problems that naturally arise out of such experiences (Part Two. The Aftereffects), and what we can and cannot do about them (Part Three. Help Yourself).

The first part of this book is about Vietnam because that is the experience that changed our men.

Maybe you want to learn more about Vietnam.

Maybe you don't. Maybe you're just desperate for help. Living with a Vietnam vet who is having problems can make you desperate. I know; I've lived with one for twenty-some years.

If you feel a great resistance to reading about Vietnam because you feel that your vet uses Vietnam as an excuse for everything, take your resistance to reading about Vietnam and see how hard it must be for him to do anything he doesn't want to do.

What I offer in Part One is a broad range of personal stories to give you an idea of what it was like over there. I've tried to give an idea of the varied experiences and different points of view vets have. My coverage is by no means complete. My original idea was to detail the dangers of *all* jobs by year and service. After I went down to the army recruiter to try to get a list of all the army's jobs, I gave that idea up. The army's book of jobs was four inches thick. Then there were the marines, navy, and air force. What I hope you will get out of the stories I tell is that there is no *"just"* in Vietnam, as in "just a truck driver," or "just an artilleryman," or "just a clerk," because as was said in *Gardens of Stone*, the movie about a Vietnam-era burial detail at Arlington National Cemetery, "There is no front line in Vietnam."

If you have to deal with a Vietnam veteran—son or father, husband or lover, or friend—one of the problems he may face is the incredible ignorance of the rest of the population about what went on in Vietnam. One vet whose tour made *Platoon* look like a cakewalk returned to a mother who asked him what kind of girls he got to *date* in Vietnam. Another veteran of a dangerous, bloody tour was still angry that his mother wouldn't send him booze in Vietnam because "it was bad for him."

The exercises you'll find in Part One are meant to help with *comprehension*, not *comparison*, a point I can't emphasize too strongly. Don't compare anyone's experiences to your vet's. Even yours. It will only make him think you don't understand, especially if you say, "I got over it. Why can't you?" Never, never, never say that.

In Part Two you will read about the problems that naturally arise out of being in combat or in a combat zone. They are normal, your vet is normal, and the difficulty you may have coping with him is normal, too. Some of the stuff vets do seems deliberately designed to hurt us, but that is often the last thing on their minds.

In Part Three you can read about where to get help and how to help yourself.

In the back of the book there is a list of Suggested Further Reading, and Some Further Sources of Help.

Don't get me wrong. I'm not saying that because your vet had a hard time in Vietnam and now has a hard time doing things that you need him to do, you should let him off the hook. But if you can see in yourself how hard it is to change, then you can support his efforts, however imperfect. He needs your support and respect, but he probably can't ask for them.

Men.

Later on, when you read about what he went through in Vietnam and do some of the exercises to understand, you may find yourself crying in corners and vowing that his buddies may have died on him in Vietnam, the brass may have tried to waste his life, the country may have turned its collective back on him, but you will never desert him. He needs you. Whether he can say it or not, whether he can act like it or not, he needs you.

Part One

Vietnam:
What It Was

1

Who Went

The Draft

"When people ask me why I went to Vietnam, I just tell them my mama and daddy didn't have the money for a bus ticket to Canada. Besides," he continued, "I never thought of it." Clant Clayton did take the bus from Lulu, Florida, up to the induction center in Jacksonville. A tall, handsome, broad-shouldered country boy, he laughed. "I said I had flat feet. The doctor took my trigger fingers and said, 'Son, as long as you got these, we're taking the blind, the crippled, the lame, and the lazy.' "

Bobby Smith is a soft-voiced Southern black man. "I was eighteen. I felt like if I hung around too long I was gonna get into a slump. You know, you finish high school, you want to become a man, you want to get away. I said, 'Hey, I'll take the Army.' Like I say, I was a stickler for patriotism. I wanted to get in the Army. I just wanted to feel like somebody."

"I was afraid I was going to miss the war," George Hill recounted. "I'm from Pasadena, Texas, and the recruiter told me later on—he's retired now and sells furniture there—that that area of the country was one of the highest for Marine volunteers during Vietnam. It seemed like everybody—I know ten or twelve just right off—in the few streets around me that joined the Marine Corps in '64–'65–'66. They were coming back and telling us, and we were afraid we was going to miss it. And I didn't like school anyway so I quit and joined the Marines when I turned seventeen in April."

"I joined the military," Archie wrote. "Some of my friends came

15

back hurt and I was going to kill 'em all for that. I went to the recruiter on a Wednesday eve and left for Parris Island on Saturday."

Do you know the story of why your vet went? Was he one of the ones who felt "my country right or wrong"? Was he a reluctant warrior or was he gung-ho? What year did he go? Did he get drafted? Did he go while there were student deferments or during the lottery? How old was he? Was he in the military already? Did he plan to make a career of it? Was it a way to get out of a dead end economically or a way to leave a bad family situation behind? You need to know.

I've seen some automatic anger at the question "Why did you go to Vietnam?" Now I prefer the phrase "How did you wind up in Vietnam?," accompanied by a commiserating grin. Somehow it doesn't come off as judgmental. When these guys came home a lot of them were blamed for having gone to Vietnam. "Why *did* you go?" was an ugly question thrown at a lot of them as if it had been a crime, or even a choice for most of them.

If you don't know the story, don't just ask bluntly. Be prepared for an eruption if your vet was blamed for having gone, or spat upon and called baby-killer when he got back. It is important, however, to know how, why, and at what age our vets got into the military. If idealism motivated your vet to join at a young age, the problems he has may be different from those experienced by a cynical older draftee.

"The VC violated the Christmas truce one hundred and twenty-seven times in 1966, so I joined up to stop them," a former marine told me.

"I was an admirer of John F. Kennedy. 'Ask not what your country can do for you, but what you can do for your country.' So I went when they asked me," another guy said.

"I loved my country." I can't tell you how many guys said this.

"I volunteered because I knew I'd get drafted." Another common answer.

"I simply wanted to serve my country," Jim wrote. "My father was in the navy in World War II. I felt I had to do better." He served sixteen months in Vietnam with the 9th Marines, a unit that saw so much combat they were called The Walking Dead. "Both my ex-wives say I have too much marine in me, too much Vietnam. I've been ruined."

"I grew up in a small mill town, working-class folks," Tim Beebe told me over the phone. "Everybody went. We felt it was inevitable. . . . I didn't particularly want to go to war, but we felt 'It's our turn now.' All the fathers were veterans." Tim trained as a radio repairman. In the 1st of the 9th Cav, where he wound up, "even the cooks took off their aprons to fly door gunner when they were needed and so did I."

"I was the right age in 1966," Bill Hutchinson told me. "My dad was in World War II. When I went, my dad looked at me, holding and shaking my hand, and said, 'Remember, don't be a hero. Fuck the Army.' I enlisted for the band and they put me in the infantry."

Marty Rodgers, a grunt in the 1st Cavalry, said, "One of my buddies, Billy, had been to court that day. The judge told him to go to jail or go in the army, but Billy didn't tell us that. He said, 'We might as well get it over with. We're gonna get drafted anyway. Let's go together.' So we volunteered for the draft. I guess he didn't want to go alone."

"I was idealistic," Scott Camil said. "I signed up in the 120-day plan [which gives the new recruit 120 days of seniority over the other recruits for pay and promotion purposes] when I was in high school and was at Parris Island three days after I graduated. I didn't question Vietnam. I needed positive reinforcement from my teachers and parents. They'd be proud of me. They and I believed I was right. I also wanted to find out who I was. A coward? Brave?"

"I joined up because a school buddy had gotten killed over in Vietnam and I wanted to fight the people who killed him," Franklin Gale wrote.

"Do nothing and you'll be drafted," the army recruiter in Cocoa, Florida, told Charles Demchock. "Enlist for a three- or four-year tour and you get a guaranteed long-term training program in a noncombat job like computer operator. Or you can gamble: enlist for two years and apply for a short-term training program. Can't guarantee you'll get it, but we'll put you at the head of the waiting list." Demchock gambled and became an 11B, rifleman. His luck changed in Vietnam and he actually served as a clerk.

"I worked one summer as a DJ at a radio station." Ron Livingston laughed with just a trace of bitterness and said, "Got my FCC license.

The recruiter told me if I went in the army I could get the same type of job. 'I got just the place for you,' he said. 'Field wireman, 36K20, climbing poles.' I took it because I knew it wasn't the infantry."

"I was drafted!" A former grunt in the 1st Cav grinned down at me from his six-foot-something height. Amazement and amusement lit up his face that I should even ask. He played football at Lincoln High, a segregated black high school in Gainesville, Florida. He's big and strong and smart. "The day I left, they had one of the first big antiwar demonstrations. People were laying down in front of the bus." He shook his head, remembering. "They wouldn't' let *us* off the bus, though." A wry smile crossed his face. "This was 1967, and the whole busload of us, all draftees, was black. Four white guys from ROTC were on the bus with us. They had volunteered to go. Miz Duncan was on the draft board then."

"Are you saying she just drafted black guys?"

"Well, that's the way it looked to us."

"I was drafted from Puerto Rico in June 1966." Angel Quintana, who served as a point man (the guy out in front) in the 4th Infantry in 1966–1967, has a thick Spanish accent. His next words surprised me, though. "I couldn't even speak English. The first months, Basic and AIT [Advanced Individual Training], were terrible. I couldn't have an English conversation with nobody. My sergeants thought I was faking when I say *'No comprendo.'* They think all Puerto Ricans speak English because the ones from New York—but in my home we don't speak English. They don't understand that." How the hell could they draft someone who can't speak English? How would he function in combat? "They do it all the time then in Puerto Rico," Angel said.

"Yeah, they did that all the time, drafted Puerto Ricans who couldn't speak English," one Chicano vet from L.A. told me. "They always put 'em in the field, too. All the Puerto Ricans who didn't speak English got sent to the field. I was drafted when I was twenty-five, had four children. I didn't have to go but I saw it as a way to get out of the fields, being a farm worker, so I went."

"I'd just missed being a marine when I was drafted," Mike Geokan wrote. "They had us count off in two's. One's were army and two's were marines. The guy on either side of me went to Pendleton [a marine boot camp]."

"I had just graduated from college and had been accepted in graduate school when I was drafted." Joe Haldeman writes science fiction. *War Year*, his Vietnam novel, is one of my favorites. He served as a combat engineer, carried an axe and a demolition bag along with his M-16 rifle, humping the boonies with the grunts in the 1st of the 22nd and other infantry units working the Central Highlands.

"Didn't they still have graduate deferments then?"

"Yes."

"Then why were you drafted?"

"My draft board had run out of blacks." He laughed at the shock on my face, but he didn't take it back, wouldn't clean it up for publication. "I guess they had run out of whites, too. Everyone at my third induction physical was in college, a junior or senior. This was Bethesda, Maryland, a rich suburb." It was also the summer of 1967, when we were building up to our highest troop levels in the war.

"But with a degree—what was it in?"

"I had a triple degree in math, physics, and astronomy—"

"How come you wound up in combat?"

"My recruiter told me I could sign up to be a scientific assistant in the engineer corps. A two-year enlistment."

"And you believed him?"

"Yeah."

"Why did I join the Marine Corps?" Larry Raskin was an RTO (radio telephone operator) in the 4th Marines. "I punched my teacher in the face for calling me a goddamned Jew." Larry laughed. "I was suspended, but I didn't want to go back to high school. I tried working for a while but found out work was not for me, and then I joined the Corps because I figured the uniform would get me a lot of dates. I never got the dress blues, though—they don't issue them—you have to buy them." He grinned.

"So did you get a lot of dates?"

"Yeah. When I got back the first time in 1966 people still supported us."

"And the second time?"

"I was wounded and spent a lot of time in the hospital."

"So what do you think about the guys who got out of going, the protestors?"

"I think they were just afraid."

According to *The Vietnam War Almanac*, 8,720,000 men enlisted in the military during the Vietnam era. Draft boards called up 2,215,000. Of the 15,980,000 men who did not serve, 15,410,000 were deferred, disqualified, or exempted. Randy Martin reported that of these, 483,000 were occupational deferments. Millions had student and graduate-student deferments until the lottery was instituted in 1969, and then those who already had student deferments, as David Curry reported in *Sunshine Patriots*, kept them until they finished their studies. Millions of kids with money and connections got exempted for physical or mental medical reasons. According to *The Vietnam War Almanac*, high-school graduates were two times as likely to serve as college graduates.

How did the draft work? Men were required to serve our country in the armed forces unless they were mentally or physically unfit or had a deferment. Those who couldn't afford to go to college were drafted unless they qualified for a medical, hardship, or conscientious-objector deferment. According to Randy Martin, "Whites received twice the medical deferments of blacks." There was an art to getting deferments and books were written on how to do it, how to dodge the draft. As Myra McPherson put it in *Long Time Passing:* "[antiwar protestors] bought into the very system many of them professed to despise by going along with the discriminatory rules that favored the privileged."

Draft evaders starved themselves, took drugs, developed psychiatric symptoms, went to divinity school, produced proof that they were the sole support of their widowed mothers, developed or discovered convenient back and knee problems. I remember laughing at the cleverness of a guy from Gainesville who secreted a Hershey bar between his buttocks and got rejected by the draft when he reached into his pants and whipped out a handful of brown stuff and began to eat it in front of the doctor. It's hard for me to believe now that I once thought of this as brave.

The social and economic inequalities of the draft were recognized by Senator Edward Kennedy, who worked tirelessly for the lottery system. Unfortunately, when the lottery was instituted in 1969 to solve the inequities, it became even more important to become ineligible for medical, psychological, or hardship reasons or reasons of conscience.

People who didn't go are often defensive. "I had my own war," one protestor said to me. In one sense this may be true. Still it seems insensitive to compare the possibility of being whacked on the head with a nightstick during a demonstration with the daily possibility of stepping on a mine in Vietnam and being blown to bloody bits.

It is hard to admit you haven't been brave, as James Fallows did in his essay "What Did You Do in the Class War, Daddy?" I quote: "He wrote 'unqualified' on my folder . . . I was overcome by a wave of relief, which for the first time revealed to me how great my terror had been, and by the beginning of a sense of shame which remains with me to this day." Fallows went on to say "the boys from Chelsea [a working-class neighborhood in Boston] . . . walked through the examination room like so many cattle off to slaughter."

Contrast Christopher Buckley's Esquire article "Viet Guilt." How badly he felt that through youthful folly he lost the chance to *witness* that rite of passage, war. What he (and David Stockman and Elliott Abrams and 15,000,000 other men and most of the young women) evaded was the chance to come home in a body bag, or with his nice face burnt off, or his legs blown away, or having lost, as my friend Steve put it, ". . . according to scientific measurement by the VA, 50 percent of my mind."

For seven years, people watched young Americans dying on TV until the body count became just a tiresome statistic on the nightly news. Politicians were willing to let the protestors sit out the war with college deferments. It kept their parents quiet. Most of the protestors weren't willing to go to jail to stop the war. Only 8,750 out of 209,517 accused draft offenders were convicted, and of them only 3,250 went to prison rather than be inducted. Most of them served less than a year. Civil disobedience, which had proved so effective in the civil-rights movement, was replaced during the Vietnam War by draft evasion, not draft resistance.

Recently Bob and I spoke at the University of Wisconsin, Eau Claire. When I made my point about the damage done to vets by individuals spitting on them and calling them baby-killers, one former protestor stood up and said we were trying to justify Vietnam and he had spit on vets and would do it again. The war was wrong and killing was wrong. We asked him if he'd gone to jail to protest the war.

"No. Why should I let the system ruin my life?" he replied.

In a way, that expresses the heart of why your vet is pissed off. Other people's lives were being ruined, those of Americans and of the Vietnamese they professed to care about so much, yet it wasn't worth this protestor's time to do anything but go to demonstrations, talk, smoke, get laid, and keep his grades up. He wasn't about to let the fate of his own countrymen who were *dumb* enough to go in his place, or the fate of the Vietnamese, ruin *his* life, yet he still calls veterans murderers for not letting anyone *take* their lives in Vietnam. Lives were at stake, but not his.

In 1970, I thought the student protestors were against the war out of principle. Now I wonder how the same guys who had such principles could let the poor and the powerless and the minorities be drafted in their place. Was it easy to have principles with a student deferment? Even easier as a girl? With twenty-twenty hindsight, it's easy to see that if more people had resisted (rather than evaded) the draft, the war would have ended sooner. Col. William Corson, USMC (Ret.), thought so, but when he told the students at the University of Kansas that they should all turn in their 2-S draft cards, become 1-A, and refuse induction, "I was practically run out of there on a rail," he told Myra McPherson.

John Chambers, who spent a year in combat with the 199th Light Infantry Brigade, told me, "I don't have much respect for the guys who went to Canada. Now, I have friends who went to jail, and they suffered for their beliefs. I respect them."

Near the middle of the war, the military began offering enlistees guaranteed programs that would keep them out of combat. Draftees went into combat units. In 1965, 16 percent of the guys killed in action were draftees. By 1969, draftees were 54 percent of those wounded in action. This rose to 57 percent in 1970. In 1969–1970, 60 percent of the army killed in action were draftees. When you consider that 8,720,000 guys enlisted and 2,215,000 were drafted, it becomes clear that the draftees were bearing a disproportionate share of combat.

With so many people finding ways to keep out of the draft, in their desperation to supply the bodies the armed forces came up with a new program in 1967, which continued until 1971. Project 100,000 supplied the armed forces with a total of 240,000 men who had scores of between ten and thirty on the Armed Forces Qualification Test. Before this program, David Curry reported, a score below 30 percent (IQ about 80) disqualified the person from serving in the armed forces. Under the program, a man scoring as low as 10 percent (which meant his IQ was about 60) could enlist or be drafted and be sent to fight in Vietnam. What a boon to desperate draft boards.

Not only was this not fair to the inductees, it wasn't fair to the men who had to serve with them. One of my informants told me, "I tried to get this one guy to play Russian roulette with a forty-five automatic. It took him fifteen minutes to decide not to. . . . This guy woulda had to take his pants off to count to twenty-one."

The rationale for inducting these guys was to give them training that would ensure their future in civilian life. Seven and a half percent of them received remedial education. What were the rest trained as? Riflemen. There's not too much call for that specialty in civilian life. Phillips reported: "Thirty-seven percent of these Project 100,000 men were sent to the infantry units in Vietnam. . . . By the time they were an average of 18 months into their period of service, [they] had been decimated—10 percent were either killed, wounded, or received less-than-honorable discharges."

These statistics give you an idea of why many vets get angry at being asked, "Why *did* you go?" The implication is always that they were too dumb to evade the draft, or that they were suckers to believe the government, or that they were the kind of people who wanted to go kill women and kids. If your vet went for patriotic reasons and found the reality of Vietnam very different from a noble crusade against communism, his feeling of betrayal may be even stronger.

So asking your vet "Why did you go?" or "Were you drafted?" may be a simple request for information from your point of view, but from his it might be a loaded gun, more proof that people just want to get close and then kick him in the teeth. It may simply be more than he can bear to talk about if he lost someone he enlisted with along with his innocence and faith in this country. Or he may feel he was a fool to go. He may hear a sneer in your voice where none was intended, an echo of past experiences and other women. "Sometime, when you feel like it, I'd like to hear how you wound up in Vietnam." There's a nice neutral opening, which gives him a lot of space.

Another reason not to ask him in a phrase also used by the hippie protestors—"Well, why did you go, (baby-killer, monster, murderer)?"—is that you will tap into how he felt then, and that was pretty angry: the kind of anger we all feel when we can't explain, can never get a fair hearing, never be understood and are falsely accused, judged by standards that are unrealistic and unmeaningful. Judged by people who not only have already made up their minds but who also have never been hungry, or thirsty, or covered with sores, never been splashed with the blood of a friend, and never had to kick someone in the face in order to live.

Your vet may not want to talk about Vietnam or how he got there. I wouldn't press him. You can figure enough of it out for yourself from what you know of him by trying to put yourself in his place. I suggest doing the following exercises in a notebook. I was amazed at the things I thought of the second or third time around.

Exercises

Think back to when you were eighteen. What were your interests? Your pressing concerns? Boys? Hair? Clothes? Music? A car? World peace? What your friends thought? Your education? Politics? Were you more mature than the boys your age? What were their interests? Think back to an eighteen-year-old boy you remember. What was he like?

After you've thought about it for a while, close your eyes and try to think of yourself as eighteen and a boy. How would you feel to know that you had to go to war? Scared? Proud? Will it prove you're a man? Do you want to get out of it? You don't want to look chicken, do you? Can you do it, though? Will you be brave? What if you're a coward? What if you can't make it through basic? What other thoughts and concerns, hopes and fears, do you think an eighteen-year-old boy might have? Will my girl wait for me? Will I be crippled for life?

How does it feel to know you might die because you can't afford a lawyer, or aren't willing to do whatever it takes to get out of the draft, or can't get into an all-white National Guard unit? How does it feel now for those who survived Vietnam?

Look at an eighteen-year-old and ponder the fact that most Vietnam vets, especially the grunts, were over there at that age. And the current crop of eighteen-year-olds is much less naive than our generation!

The Training

Step two in the process of getting to Vietnam was basic training (boot camp for marines):

> Another day in the Corps, Sir,
> For every day's a holiday
> And every meal's a feast
> Pray for war
> Pray for war
> God bless the Marine Corps
> Pray for war
> God bless the DI of 353
>   [Drill Instructor and group
>   number]
> Pray for war.

Marines recited this litany every night for eleven weeks of boot camp at Parris Island in 1965. (To really get the feeling of basic training, I recommend watching the first half of Stanley Kubrick's movie *Full Metal Jacket.*)

Basic training is intended to remove the constraints of civilization and turn a normal person into one who will kill when he's told to or when he feels it is necessary. Basic training has to be rough, tough, and ugly, or the soldier is likely to get killed when he goes into actual combat. If your vet was seventeen, eighteen, nineteen when he went into the military—the years that Erik Erikson called the *psychosocial moratorium* during which young people are finding out who they are—unless he was very mature and very cynical, basic had a profound effect on him.

In basic, teamwork is emphasized: Don't let your buddies down. Killing is the job. How easy it is to glide over the fact, ignore it, forget it, miss it, drop it from consciousness. For the kid in basic during the Vietnam War, it was not easy to forget that he was expected to be able and willing to kill people in Vietnam. This meant that he had to put aside some of the most closely held beliefs of civilized Western society about the sanctity of human life. He had then to adopt the set of values of the military-warrior code: Killing is my job; not just a duty but an honor. We kill *them*, whoever *"them"* is. We are a team, and we don't let one another down. We obey orders without question.

When Bob went through basic in 1964, he had to charge a dummy with a bayonet, screaming "Kill!" By '65, the marines were already using the litany of racist names: *gook, slanteye, slope, dink, zip.* A shift from political enmity (killing commies) to racial enmity was taking place. Due to the guerrilla nature of the war, this spirit intensified as more and more of the instructors were Vietnam vets themselves, who knew what it was like over there. Returning vets wanted to save the recruits from dying at the hands of some woman or child or old man or the barber in the village, so they taught them, very understandably, to trust no one. To toughen up the recruits, to prepare them for the insanity that was Vietnam, they began to dehumanize the enemy. "They are all gooks. You can't trust anyone in Vietnam. Kill them all and let God sort them out. American lives are worth more than Vietnamese lives. Gooks don't have feelings like we do. Shoot first. Ask later." The *cartoonization* of the enemy, as Dr. William Gault called it in "Some Remarks on Slaughter," published in 1971 and one of the first scientific papers about the exceptional problems caused by conditions in Vietnam for returning veterans, was an attitude that eased many young men into actions that would later haunt them.

At eighteen, resisting the thinking of your drill instructor is really hard. Can you remember how naive you were at that age? Do you know that this was also the youngest army we ever fielded? The average age of the Vietnam combat soldier was nineteen. That means that for every forty-year-old in Vietnam there were more than ten eighteen-year-olds. Some of the older recruits managed to resist thinking of all Vietnamese as the enemy, but many couldn't. They believed. They identified with their instructors, with the military, with our noble cause in Vietnam. Everything was clear and bright to them: why we were there, our goals, our goodness, the enemy's badness. Simple patriotic duty took them to Vietnam. They went there willing to die to do their duty. More than 58,000 of them did.

Older recruits like Charles Denchock, twenty-two, were harder to mold: "Fort Polk [Louisiana, where many men took Advanced Individual Training] was a hell-hole, made Fort Benning look like the Hilton. It felt like Vietnam: dirty, oppressive. The cadre [lifers] was stupid. I hated it. Guys told me you don't want to go as an 11B [grunt]. It's a death sentence or a maiming sentence. . . . My Dad [a former air force officer] was against the war because it was being fought wrong and he did not want me wasted, so he offered me money and a car when I was home on leave. I felt it would be cowardly. I wanted to see what Vietnam and the war were like. It was a once-in-a-lifetime opportunity and also might be the end of my life. I showed up five days late at Oakland to go to Nam. They asked how many of us were AWOL and three-quarters of the room raised their hands. They only took out those who were more than five days AWOL. . . ."

Our vets faced a lot of double binds: heads-I-win-tails-you-lose situations. One of them was the training they received. In most programs standards had been lowered. The training Bob was allowed to give in flight school was substandard compared to what he'd had. He was required to pump students through. I remember his coming home really upset because one particular student would panic when Bob spoke to him while he was flying. When he panicked, he couldn't remember the radio frequencies. I had a lot of sympathy for the student because Bob made me nervous when I was just driving the car. He epitomized the instructor-pilot, always watching like a hawk for mistakes.

"Maybe you just make him nervous, Bob."

"Patience, he can't be nervous. If he's nervous here, how do you think he's going to be in Vietnam when they're shooting at him? He's going to fuck up and kill himself and everybody on the helicopter with him."

Put that way, I could see why Bob wanted him washed out, but he wasn't. Standards were lowered all through the military because of the need to fill slots in Vietnam with men, however ill-prepared. The fact was there was no training for what Vietnam was actually like. A lot of veterans will laugh bitterly about OJT, on-the-job training, but it wasn't much fun at the time. "I'd never thrown a grenade before. I was raking leaves or something that day," one vet told me.

Okay, so here we have our seventeen-, eighteen-, nineteen-year-old recruit. He has joined up or been drafted, but basically he has put his faith in the United States government. He hasn't gone to Canada. He may have doubts about the war, but he figures the politicians know what they're doing. He's entitled to believe that. The grown-ups are supposed to know what they are doing. One grunt put it this way: "I was doing what was expected of me. At nineteen I was not mature or interested enough to be able to have a mature opinion. Now I feel like I was taken advantage of."

The recruit goes off to boot camp and is taught how to kill people in various ways. He gets a lot of positive reinforcement if he's good at following orders, if he's a good shot, if he can be meaner and tougher and better at pretend-killing than the others. "The Marine Corps makes men," or at least larger, meaner, and more dangerous boys, but the military is telling him, eighteen-year-old impressionable, human him, that this training is making him a *man*.

If he's not sure he agrees with what they are teaching, it's still going to take an amount of character that most eighteen-year-olds don't have to protest or resist the conditioning. Because that is what it is—a well-planned program to break down the recruit's normal reactions and train him to do things without question that will often get him killed, or make him wish he had been killed. If he resists, they come down heavier on him. Piss them off and you *will* wind up an 11B in Vietnam, a rifleman, a grunt.

The boot also assumes that his instructors are training him as much as he'll need. He assumes he's learning how to stay alive. He assumes they are telling him the truth about the character of the war. He assumes that they won't waste him, that his life is of some importance. He doesn't assume that he's just a number aimed at filling a slot in Vietnam.

"Eleven-B's were like tissues," Bill Hutchinson told me. "Use 'em up and throw 'em away."

The future tissue doesn't know this. He assumes they want him to survive. Imagine Jerry Gilbreath's feelings at eighteen when his colonel (who never goes out into the bush) gets out of his chopper one day and says, "I don't care if you *can* do it or not: Do it. How you feel is not important. It's your ability to do your job that's important. I personally don't give a fuck about any of you. What I do care about is your ability to do your job. You get a higher body count or you will go out longer."

He went on to describe the contrast between the colonel and the men: The colonel had on "a nice green uniform, shiny boots, a haircut, crisp hat, bloused pants. Our fatigues were bleached by the sun and washing. We'd get clothes back to wear with bullet holes in them."

Our conversation covered an incident in which his patrol blew up a bunker full of VC wounded, including two nurses. I asked how he felt about it now. He gave a heavy sigh. "Uneasy, if I had to pick a word, in that those people were killed just because they were there—more than anything else. We called in and told them what we'd found. 'Whaddaya want us to do?' They sent us a LAW [light antitank weapon, a disposable bazooka] out on a chopper, and we blew it [the bunker] up."

"I get the feeling you feel responsible," I said.

"I am responsible." He looked at me. The painful answer. "I am responsible for everything I did. I was misled." He flushed. "I was expected, if necessary, to give my life. 'Do what you're told,' is what they wanted from us. 'Everything's been figured out. Just do what you're told.' Why the fuck are we here? 'The reason you are here is to do your one year and get out.' Not to fight communism, not to save South Vietnam, to save your ass. Realistic paranoia. If you don't develop that kind of attitude, you are gonna *die*."

These kids grew up on World War II movies, on John Wayne and Audie Murphy. A lot of them wanted to be just like those guys.

Exercise

First of all, rent a videocassette of *Full Metal Jacket* if you can, and think about going through basic. Imagine yourself charging a dummy with a bayonet, screaming "Kill!" Play the game, get with the spirit, brainwash yourself. Think about those influences on you at eighteen. Think about how important it is for men to do well, how at that age they hassle one another at the slightest sign of weakness. Think of how our culture values being the best, being brave, being strong, being tough. At eighteen, wouldn't you have wanted to excel? Now think about what you are going to excel at.

The Career Military Dilemma

If your veteran was older and already in the military when he went to Vietnam, the habit of subordination, of obeying orders, of not questioning authority was already ingrained in him. He had chosen this life because it met a need in him to be useful, to work in a structured and worthwhile job. Societies need soldiers. Societies have to be very careful how they use them and whom they tell them to kill. Soldiers don't get to pick the wars they are sent to fight.

I talked to several officers who wrestled with their consciences about going to Vietnam and killing people. One said: "I consulted with my pastor and he said, 'You have to understand, you're not the only one responsible. You're representing those who are standing back, the whole country.' " It surprised me that a person in the military should have such strong feelings about the evil of killing, and I realized to my shame that I do a lot of stereotyping of men. One of the things I learned in these interviews was that men care about things that women don't even know they think about. Another thing I learned is that there's a big difference between talking and doing.

For many career men the conduct of the war in Vietnam, the body counts, the lack of unit cohesiveness, the inability to win due to the rules of that particular war and the political situation (most of the Vietnamese who were willing to lay down their lives seemed to be on the other side), combined sometimes with the desire for military glory and sometimes with simple patriotism, made it impossible for them. They ceased to think. It was too painful. They ceased to feel; that was also too painful. They were careful not to question, because what could they do? They could resign, which would not stop the war, or they could fight, which would not stop the war. All roads led to losses, but if they stayed and fought, at least they could save some lives. Choices like that don't make 'em easier to live with.

I'm trying to put things in the best possible light. There is another view: "Some aggressive commanders were willing to get their career tickets punched by leading troops into the right kind of combat action, even if this entailed a needless expenditure of their own men's lives." William Mahedy was a chaplain in Vietnam, but he doesn't pull any punches in *Out of the Night*. He isn't the only one who felt that way about officers and lifer NCO's. Mahedy wrote further: "Lifers tended to 'buy into the bullshit' in Vietnam. They planned and executed the strategy that cost lives, and even worse, they seemed to do it without question. . . . They often seemed perfectly willing to sacrifice the lives of their men to get their career tickets punched. One former grunt told me that while he was in Vietnam he 'hated lifers more than the enemy.' This was not an uncommon emotion."

"Officers," Mike Morris said. "You had some good ones and you had some real bozos, the real gung-ho gentleman that would do anything to further his own career. We had one lieutenant . . . puts a couple of M-79 rounds into this hooch and a piece of shrapnel comes back and grazes him on the cheek, drew blood. He was the type of guy that went back, put himself in for a Purple Heart, and they gave it to him."

Jon Anderson, an operations officer who went to Vietnam in 1970, had this to say: "By then the NCO's that were still alive—they took those guys and they would do one year in Vietnam and one year back and one year in Vietnam and one year back, good sergeants. These sergeants who could do everything. They started going to Vietnam in '65 and '66 and invariably they were platoon sergeants, you know out there in the thick of things and you just didn't live that long, or if you made it through your tour in '66 did you make it through in '68? 'Cause you were back. The ones who were left, the old sergeants had done two tours there or maybe three and they knew what was going on. It wasn't gonna be won." He went on to say, "The young kids had no illusions about it. The officers had studied warfare and knew that we had lost it. Everyone knew at different levels and in different ways that the war was really over but stay alive and kick ass when you can."

While senior officers lived in air-conditioned trailers and fussed about painted rock borders for their flower beds or custom-camouflaged jeeps, their men sweated and died in the jungle. In *The 13th Valley*, John Del Vecchio sarcastically mentioned an officer who gets a Silver

Star for remaining on alert in his quarters while his men fought a major engagement. One marine told me about rear-echelon officers up to the rank of colonel—including two dentists—going on one patrol with his outfit and receiving medals for it. Bob's unit broke ranks and left when the operations officers were given medals that they'd put themselves in for, although they had never flown more than the four hours a month required for flight pay, nor anywhere but in the traffic pattern at An Khe.

"The medic was useless, a lifer, such a wimp. To advance his career he had to go to Vietnam to get a Combat Medic badge. After we got in a firefight, he had the Combat Medic badge and re-upped for six years to get out of Nam," one vet said.

In the Peninsular War (Spain, early 1800s, against Napoleon), Wellington's British troops divided officers into two categories, either *come-on*'s or *go-on*'s. Why were there so many go-on's in Vietnam? I don't have an answer.

"I think the war was fought all wrong," Steve wrote me. "I think the enlisted men should have shot the lifer dogs, and then come back and shot a bunch of Congressmen and General Hershey Bar. . . . It was definitely 'Us vs. Them,' with them being the lifer dogs."

Exercise

How would you deal with this kind of double bind? You want to serve your country. Your ideas and ideals revolve around courage and glory and service and sacrifice. Or maybe you joined the military for the retirement benefits. How do you deal with the lives entrusted to your care? How do you win? What are you winning?

On the Way

After training, how did your vet get to Vietnam? Did he go over on a boat at the beginning of the war with a whole unit, like Bob with the 1st Cav in 1965, or Joe Pearson on his second tour with the 25th Infantry in 1966? That was rare, but it did happen. Did your vet go over alone in a civilian airplane with stewardesses serving drinks and fear sitting on one shoulder? That's the way most of them went, lucky if they knew even one guy on the plane. Alone. Eighteen. Facing the real possibility of death.

Maybe your vet was older. Maybe, like Jules Goetz, he went back into the military at thirty-seven because he had critical technical training and wound up driving a jeep and manning a machine-gun bunker at night for five months before being assigned to a specialty which reflected his training as a calibration technician.

When he arrived in Vietnam, what did your vet see and feel? "We flew into Long Binh," Frank Hewitt remembered. "It was clear that day, picture clear, and I can see craters and junk. Arc-lighted areas [bombed in B-52 raids and always described as looking like the moon, cratered, dead] looked weird. When we're letting down, seeing all this, I wondered what am I in for?"

"We came in on a Pan Am flight." Joe Pearson recalled arriving at Tan Son Nhut Air Base in July 1965 for his first tour. "They rolled steps up to the airplane, and halfway down the steps, there's a heavy mortar attack. A truck came running up to the airplane, and they threw M-14's and M-60's at us—'Charlie's trying to overrun the perimeter!' We're in Class-A khakis and qualification badges. They put us in a truck and take us to the perimeter of the airport, spread us around the bunkers and machine-gun emplacements . . . It was a rude awakening. I was petrified. And I got wounded. I always thought I was shot in the right leg and got shrapnel in my left arm but last month at the VA, a doctor told me he thought it was the other way around, shrapnel in my leg in two places and a bullet in my arm . . ." He shrugged, bewildered.

"How long were you in the hospital?" I asked.

"Oh, a medic came around and gave shots and bandaged up wounds. He sent me to the hospital." He stopped for a minute. "I felt guilty when I got there. It really didn't hurt—I was too scared to feel it, I think—so I went into the dispensary. I'm *walking*—" He looked at me to be sure I understood. I nodded. "There are gurneys running around—one flew by—I remember the injury, but not the color of the guy. I saw the remains of a charred leg hanging off the gurney, and I'm walking in under my own power. He may not *live*, and I'm walking. I was seventeen. I wanted to get out as fast as I could. There was a tremendous feeling of guilt at being there with my little scratches . . ."

"The plane landed under fire." Ron Livingston arrived in August 1968. "I was petrified because I was so green—never been in anything like that. As soon as we hit the door, they're yellin' 'Squat and run! Keep down! Keep down! We're under fire!' We ran to the closest bunkers and stayed there six–eight hours, thinking any minute we're gonna get blown to pieces. A couple of guys got shrapnel from mortars, about six people, not real serious." The last words were from the perspective of a vet, calm and casual.

"I flew into Tan Son Nhut, came in on World Airlines," Lynn Whittaker recounted. "Coming in and landing, we started getting airbursts [enemy fire] and went back up. Came in for a second landing. Got off fast. They threw our seabags off. They took us in jeeps to hotels in Saigon with sandbags all around them and we had to walk a half mile to an Army chow hall through Saigon traffic. Three days later I was chief engineer on a patrol boat."

"I got off at Cam Ranh Bay," Joe Haldeman told me. "It was huge. There was fighting all around the perimeter. Gunships, Puffs [C-4's equipped with Gatling guns that sent down a solid column of fire] all around. It was night. I had to go to KP and shoveled mashed potatoes for hours. Lots of people showed up. Afterwards I sat on the back porch of the mess hall and watched the war going on—with a beer."

Not everyone flew into a literally "hot" situation of bullets flying when he landed. "As we got off the plane," Tom Comiskey, a Seabee who landed at Da Nang in 1965, wrote, "the hot humid air hit us in the face like a slap. I was stunned. It was hard to breathe any air. As we stood in formation the sweat was running down our bodies. My God, I thought, how can human beings stand this heat! One doesn't get used to this heat, one only endures it one day at a time. *Every day* was 95 to 110 and humid. The only exception was the monsoon season—the temperature went down, but it never stopped raining for six weeks, day and night."

"Heat. I couldn't believe it. The heat hit me. I'd entered a sauna. I couldn't believe it. I could hardly breathe . . . and I'd been in Florida and Louisiana," Charles Demchock remembered.

Even if his arrival was peaceful, did your vet see a pile of body bags on the runway? Smell death? Bob says it's a smell you never forget and one that you know immediately. This is not a dead dog. It is a man. It could be me. "If you've ever smelled human flesh burn, you never forget the smell." Frank Hewitt shook his head. "I was raised on a farm. We killed five–six hogs at a time. Smelling hog blood didn't bother me . . . It smells sweet. Human blood—there's no other smell like it."

Did your vet see a line of men with haunted eyes getting on the freedom bird, the plane back to America, back to the world? "You get off the plane feeling like you'll get shot, catch the clap or malaria right away after the indoctrination they give ya." John Dexter laughed. "After twenty-six hours on an air-conditioned plane, it's sweltering—heat and humidity. You're seeing people leaving—catcalls, jeering—'FNG's [fucking new guys]—We're going home! You're staying!' I had sixteen weeks military training at that time."

Maybe your vet was pretty scared.

"We got off at a big hot huge military base," Mike Costello said. "Got on buses with the heavy screens and wire on the windows and drove." Why did the bus from the airport have wire screens over the windows? Your vet realized it was to keep the random grenade or satchel charge out. Gives you pause, eh? Someone got it, someone was blown up on one of these buses. Maybe a lot more than one someone. It meant that here in Saigon, Tan Son Nhut, Da Nang, Cam Ranh Bay, wherever, here in the rear, he isn't safe. The whole year here, 365 days (395 if you're a Marine), people will want to kill him, plan to kill him, try to kill him. Them. The people out there with the little bodies and inscrutable faces.

My God, she just squatted down and went in the street!

What kind of people are these?

What have I gotten myself into?

Exercise

Picture yourself landing in Vietnam, the heat, noise, smells, maybe a rough landing, and running for cover. How would you feel when you realized why the buses have screens on the windows? Aren't we here to protect this country? How would the sight of returning vets affect you, grunts thin and sunburnt with haunted faces, fat colonels sweating in the sun? How about body bags or piles of coffins? Would you think about death? Would you be afraid and try to hide it?

2

In the Rear

People arrived "in the rear," as opposed to the bush, where the worst fighting often took place. American GI's weren't safe even in Saigon.

Vietnamese culture was a shock to most Americans. Finding yourself in a place populated by people who look different, act differently, have motivations you don't understand, is difficult even for mature and well-traveled people. For eighteen-year-old Americans, just the jabber, jabber, jabber of the language was weird. "Unidentifiables and rice" is how Bob described their food in *Chickenhawk*. They ate it with a sauce made of rotted fish heads. They were so poor, they didn't even know how lousy their lives were. They didn't appreciate our efforts on their behalf, didn't even seem to care. Med-CAP's (medical combined action platoons) gave them soap, and they sold it instead of using it. They went to the bathroom in public. They chewed betel nut and had black teeth. They smiled all the time. Nobody told our guys how important the village of his ancestors was to the average Vietnamese, so that when we moved villagers to save them from the VC, we destroyed what was most important to them. Our guys couldn't speak Vietnamese, so they couldn't find out what the people thought. Paid interpreters naturally produced information acceptable to the brass hats who were paying them.

Being an enlisted man in a big rear area was "worse than stateside duty," George Hill said. Spit and polish. Heat and dirt. Bunkers that rustled with rats and big cockroaches. Waiting for that attack that may never come can be hard. As a matter of fact, many guys who were in the rear volunteered for the boonies (what would have been the front if there had been one) because if they were going to have to put up with Vietnam, at least they wanted the excitement of the real thing.

For every combat trooper there were between five and nine non-combatants (depending on where you get your statistics). Many of these noncombatants risked their lives, although neither they nor I want to compare the problems they faced with those of the grunt.

Some Americans never fired a gun. Men built bunkers, barracks, runways, and roads in the fierce sun or monsoon rains. They drove forklifts in the big depots. They drove convoys over roads that were always mined. They stood perimeter guard. They helped carry wounded and dead off helicopters. Men and women labored over the wounded, trying to keep them alive through nights and days of hellish pain. Guys burned shit, defended our garbage from hordes of hungry Vietnamese, did the paperwork that keeps the military going, endured fear because no place was safe, and got none of the glory. Some of them saw signs of the Tet Offensive of 1968 coming through their analysis of intelligence information and were ignored. (Back in Washington, General Westmoreland was presenting Congress with figures showing enemy weakness in the south.) In their "safe" jobs men and women died in rocket or mortar attacks. Few of these vets will claim to have had it as bad as the grunts, yet for every participant in that war there was the constant threat of sudden death. The barber on the base could turn out to be VC, and often did. People died in senseless attacks in downtown Saigon. A base that was untouched for months could be rocketed one night and lose thirty men. The element of unpredictability was one of the most stressful aspects of Vietnam and, as we will see in Chapter 7, "So What's So Different About Vietnam?," it was also unique as far as most American fighting men were concerned.

Many vets feel a sense of guilt to this day because they did not share the sufferings of the grunts. Granted, some men with safe rear-echelon jobs, REMF's (rear-echelon motherfuckers), pogues, fat cats, Remington (the typewriter) raiders, could lead the life of Reilly after work, drink and whore and stay stoned. But not all of them did. They still had to keep their boots spit-shined. Some had to brownnose day in and day out for fear of getting sent out. Sometimes they were sent out to the field for such infractions as failing to salute a superior officer, or wearing an Afro and resenting being called a nigger. One vet I met was told, at nineteen, to withdraw his complaint to his congressman about racism at Cam Ranh Bay or he *wouldn't make it home.*

We come back to the main question: What was *your* vet's tour like? When I've interviewed vets who don't consider themselves combat vets, and can't imagine why I want to comprehend their experience, I discovered that they often had extremely painful traumatic experiences or entire tours, but feel that by comparison with the grunts, it was nothing—so they have no way to deal with the pain except to discount it, and, by discounting it, bury it.

From the point of view of the man who spent his whole tour in the bush, everyone else was a REMF, but as you will see, some were more rear-echelon than others. Some people lived on firebases in holes in the ground. Some people lived in air-conditioned comfort and traveled back and forth to office jobs: real estate officers, clerks, intelligence, public relations, guards and drivers for VIP's. Somebody had to run all the officers' clubs in Saigon and man the big PX's and push the papers that proved we were winning.

City Life

As long as your vet didn't travel the same route every day and stayed out of certain areas, he was pretty safe in the cities unless he happened to be in a bar when someone rolled in a grenade or took a taxi with a satchel charge in the briefcase someone had left on the seat. Keep an eye on the Vietnamese at all times. If they disappear, the vet had better, too.

One guy I talked to said his year in Saigon was the best year of his life because of booze and broads.

Steve also spent his tour in Saigon, working from June 1967 to June 1968 as a still photographer at the 9th Med Lab taking photographs of autopsies. "An easy day was when the body bags were very light and they rattled when you carried them. That meant that the guy inside it had been out there a very long time and all that nasty flesh had been eaten off by the birds and bugs and beasts, and all that was left were some nice clean bones that didn't smell and weren't crawling with maggots, and didn't have a green iridescent color to them . . . Once I saw the first Pile-of-Hamburger-with-a-Face, which was Day One at the morgue, they were all the same," he wrote. "So figure if that's a good day, what's a bad one? Maybe the day I opened up the body bag with the Man with No Face . . . Actually he did have a face. As I pulled the zipper down and opened the bag, I could see that the front of his face was nothing but meat. His face had been sliced off by the tail rotor of a Huey, and the guys who had put him in the bag had laid his face out on his chest. His mother would have been able to recognize him. Now maybe that was a bad day. But it's hard to say. What's bad? I didn't puke. I never puked. I did get the feeling that my ass was writing a check my brain might not be able to cover."

He added, "The Wounded Data Medical Evaluation Team (WDMET) was working in the same place in the morgue . . . They were studying the effects of weapons on human meat and bones . . . 'Here's a picture of what our new bomb can do. See how it blew away his whole arm, along with half his ribcage. More mutilation for the money.' Nice work if you can get it.

"The guy I replaced was considered nuts when I got there," Steve wrote. "One time they sent me to the hospital to photograph a couple of live casualties, guys that had been napalmed. At least dead guys were dead. You couldn't hurt them. These guys were awake, holding their arms in the air, shreds of flesh hanging off of them. They radiated pure pain. I had to use flashbulbs to take the photos. I know they were hardly aware I was there, but I had the feeling I was burning them all over again."

Steve had never been in danger, *not like the grunts*, but, "One of the guys [at 9th Med Lab] was from someplace in western Mass. Real quiet, mild guy, you hardly noticed he was there. One day he wasn't. He missed the bus the first day of Tet and some dink nailed him in the chest with an AK-47."

When we first met, Steve told me, "Did you know people who have burned to death are so black—" His voice ground to a stop. With an effort he continued: ". . . that you have to open the lens aperture on the camera two extra stops to get any detail at all? I had an easy tour. I just had to look at dead bodies all day and watch them cut them up to find out how they died. I mean here's this guy burned black. You have to open the lens up two extra stops just to get any detail in the picture. And they want to know details. He fucking burned to death!" His voice dropped. "And you know what? They made me do that for a fucking year, take pictures of dead men till I never want to see another dead thing as long as I live, and when I left, they didn't replace me." His eyes searched my face to see if I understood. It was all for nothing.

Gerald F. Dooley wrote home to his wife, Pat, in October 1967, that he was quartered in Cholon, "right in the heart of VC territory, or at least where they have most of the single killings . . . I live at the Virginian . . . but there is no mess there, and we must eat at the Hong Kong BOQ [bachelor officers' quarters] . . . That place gets hit at least once a week . . . This is my first OD [officer of the day] watch here at the headquarters, and I got exactly two minutes of instruction before assuming command of U.S. Naval Support Activities, Republic of Vietnam . . . We have double watches set tonight, as it is the eve of the elections . . . The whole time I have been on watch since darkness set in, we have been hearing claymore mines going off—those are the ones with 900 double 0 buckshot in them along with glass, cut-up wire, steel chips and anything else they can put in them. They sure do make one loud noise, and create havoc when they are cut loose in a market place, or against the front of BOQ's . . ."

Peggy Rohror was a civilian executive secretary for the navy in Saigon from June 1966 to November 1968. "We were told not to walk alone nor in a group . . . My duty day was 12 to 14 and 16 hours per day and also Saturday and sometimes Sunday . . . We always had to be very observant of what was going on around us. During the TET offensive we were taken to work in armored cars or trucks . . . There were rockets all around and small arms firing also. I saw rockets coming in, and there was no place to hide . . . We got used to watching all around us when we were out, plus we never rode in a cab that might have a package in it nor did we ever pick up a package from the street. I saw two children pick up a package from the street, and it was an explosive that blew them up . . . There was nothing to win. There was no country that we were going to get . . . no nothing. I returned home after 2½ years because I was sick of it, and the Vietnamese always had their hand out . . . I also did volunteer at the 3rd Field Hospital [where] I saw many men who were brought in from the field and were terrible to look at."

Don Sherry was a data-processing machine operator in Saigon from April 1966 to April 1967. First, he lived in a smelly green tent and then in an open-sided screened hooch in a camp southwest of Saigon. "There was a lot of VC terrorist stuff in III Corps, upheavals in the government, claymore, mortar, sniper activity . . . We were trucked into this big building, a fish market. They pulled the guts out of it and renovated it and made air-conditioned rooms for the computers and keypunchers. We had some Vietnamese keypunchers so the VC knew what it was. The unit was fifty–sixty people. We did twelve-hour days, seven days a week, sunrise to sunset. Trucks were never on the road after dark. It was a long stretch from the fish market to the tent city and there were always mines and sniper fire. Once in a while you'd take a cyclo back to the tent city, drunk, and they'd take pot shots. We pulled perimeter guard sometimes . . . I was scared from the time I hit Tan Son Nhut till two years after I left Vietnam . . . One night, I was talking to my buddy and bullets started going through the tent. We hit the deck . . . A bullet landed six–seven inches away from my head. I remember that distinctly— looking at the spot when it hit. I thought six inches and my head would have been gone."

In the other cities, things were also dangerous.

"They were short on MP's in Da Nang so we worked for the Marine Provost Marshal," Stephen Hatfield told me about his seven months in that city. "We lived in barracks with marine MP's, and also patrolled with AP's [Air Police] and SP's [Shore Patrol] . . . We patrolled Da Nang East at night . . . I never was ambushed but others were. Da Nang was a crazy town. On a slow night, this VC section had a lot of whorehouses and we'd go raid that—hear all these boots hitting the floor, cussing and shrieking, jumping out windows, chasing across rooftops and alleys . . . Often one army MP and one marine MP would have to arrest one or two guys in the midst of twenty of their friends . . . One marine was stopped by a Vietnamese National Policeman and he picked him up above his head and smashed him on the pavement four times and killed him.

"The Provost Marshal decided to have ceiling fans installed upstairs [in the barracks]." Stephen grinned as he began the story. "Two gooks came in and wired them up, and it burned down that night. Fifty-caliber machine-gun rounds were going off upstairs while we were taking cases of grenades and C-rations out of the basement. The fire was roaring like it was going to come right through the floor onto us, but we got out." The memory shadowed his face.

"That must have been scary as hell," I said, thinking *traumatic stressor*.

He nodded and continued. "After that we stayed in a ratty hotel in Da Nang. I hated it. I couldn't get to sleep. No guards, no watches. We could've got bombed or had our throats cut anytime, but I was so tired, I'd just say, 'Fuck it,' and go to sleep. If you're alive the next day, you go do what you have to do . . ."

"Weren't you scared?" Again, I asked the obvious.

"When I had to go in the middle of the night to some little village outside Da Nang, I figured I had time to do it, or I didn't, and I would never worry again. So I went about it. I didn't fret, but I was always very wary. I didn't want to die. I did my job. I did it well." I was to hear this phrase often. "My worst moment," he went on slowly, "was a marine gave these kids a ride in his supply truck. One of the boys pulled the trigger of his M-14 which was butt on the floor aimed out the back window. Another kid was looking in the window. The round went point-blank through the kid's face and blew the back third of his skull away. I had to go investigate that and take pictures." He paused. "The marine felt about the same way I did. He loved those kids. The little boy's body was in the back with brains and hair all over the back of the truck. You could smell it. His mom and dad came up as I was doing my stuff. She just jumped up in the air and landed on the ground on her side, screaming."

"The main thing I did was read reports and orders and sign them," wrote a vet who was an intelligence officer in 1971–1972, who lived in several cities. "I was talking to a guy in Phung Hoang, the new name for the Phoenix Project after the U.S. press found out about it. If a report went out, people from Phung Hoang went and killed somebody— It was then that I realized that by signing all these reports and all these orders, I was a big part of that whole process legitimizing murder and imprisonment. Most atrocities seemed to be

It's Easy To Sell Your Books To Us.

"What about the black market?" I asked. "Was it active when you were there, early in the war?"

"Working around supply, I seen a lot of black market going on too . . . Officers, they'll come in they try to pay me under the table, but I'm always thinking 'CID [Criminal Investigation Division], this guy could be CID.' This one guy wanted to pay me to get money orders for him but I was always scared to do it. He was selling all kind of things, Air Force survival kits, all kinds of things. They'd get it and sell it, and you'd see it uptown.

"Guarding Long Bin ammo dump," Bobby recalled, "they had this big guard stand. You had to climb up the ladder. You could see all over the field, but if you had a direct hit, you're gone. I didn't like that at all. I used to love to see that sun come up . . . [On perimeter guard], you couldn't see nothin' at night . . . just keep sweeping your eyes over and just listen for sound. My alarm—you hear these bugs and crickets going off, and if you hear them stop, that's when you see the flares jumping off and the firefights going on. It was a psychological thing, and I was going to be ready."

Bobby wasn't sure if I'd really want to interview him because he was rarely in firefights, but I figured that was the experience of most of the rear-echelon people, so I got him to describe one: "Well, I had come in one night and I was laying across my bunk, and all of a sudden—I try to describe it like the Fourth of July, but it wasn't like the Fourth of July—it was like mad fire hour, every weapon you had was going off. I jumped out of my bed. We kept our rifles in a conex [a locked shipping container] because they didn't want guys coming in drunk shooting up the place. This one guy had the keys and he just froze. I threw on my helmet and ran to the bunker, and I had my M-14, and I saw at the time the fire was so intense I didn't even try to look. I felt that if I were to try to get up and get some vision, I'd get hit. I didn't get a shot off that night. I was ready for hand to hand . . . It lasted for ten to fifteen minutes. Somebody called cease fire. It must have been a hit-and-run attack. You just don't think, and then when it's over, you have a lot of guys freaking out."

Tom Comiskey of the Seabees' Mobile Construction Battalion #5, in Vietnam in 1965 and 1966, sent answers to the questionnaire I passed out at the Chicago parade: "My work on the first tour of Nam was mainly at the 3d Marine Division Field Hospital in Da Nang (Charlie Med). We built OR's [operating rooms] and other service buildings for the Marines. Sometimes during mass casualties we would put our tools down and lend a hand to the corpsmen carrying stretchers and holding IV's and getting the wounded Marines from the choppers to the OR's . . . Why does God pick some to die and many to lose legs, arms, body functions, and then allow some to return with no physical damage? I don't understand. It's so unfair . . . My worst moment in Vietnam? After a major operation and mass casualties at Charlie Med, when the excitement was over, my buddy Bob and I surveyed the helicopter pad. The dead Marines (forty-seven or forty-nine by our count) were neatly laid out along the pad. We looked at each face. Only five or six needed a shave. The whole group were pinned down under fire for two days. They were so young. A few looked to be in their twenties . . . Bob and I said nothing, looked at each other, and cried . . ."

Tom is a big, tough-looking man, yet time after time, I saw the same pain. I saw men caring not just for something that happened to themselves, but for what happened to others. It didn't even have to be someone they knew.

Combat vets were also hassled in rear areas and I've heard a lot of bitterness about it. Vets have told me of not being allowed in rear-area mess halls and clubs because they looked and smelled so badly when they got in from the field. A rebellious cook in the marines told me his solution to this phenomenon: "I was only supposed to cook enough chicken for the guys who were in the camp, but I knew a company was coming in from the field. So I got out a bunch of boxes of frozen chicken, and I just kept cooking. When they caught me, I'd fried up all but seventy-five pieces, so I kept frying. Said it's no use stopping now. They were mad as hell, yelling and screaming about all the extra chicken. I said, 'A line company is coming in.' They said, 'They're not here so we're closing the mess hall.' I said, 'Go ask. I know they're coming.' They went and asked and came back to shut the mess hall down and I argued and finally the line company showed up and I had all this fried chicken ready for them and they could eat all they wanted." His face is lit up with pride.

When you read about life in the field, you'll understand what this must have meant to those grunts.

John Ketwig's . . . *and a hard rain fell* gives a picture of his rear-area life as a mechanic at Pleiku, working long hours in the rain and mud, cannibalizing parts off battered and blown-up machines, getting an occasional shower and then slipping in the mud on the way back to the hooch, listening to the rats fighting over crumbs, boots, books, and soap in the dark. John got used to working eighteen-hour days and never being clean, but "you never grew accustomed to working on trucks with bloodied seats and giant holes torn in their floorboards . . . to the chatter of a nearby machine gun . . . to the fear . . . The lifers in Qui Nhon, our supply depot, sold our rations to the black market . . ." Parts had to be cannibalized from the junkyard of broken and blown-up vehicles, yet the colonel who "received a Silver Star for directing operations at Dak To from a helicopter safely riding thouands of feet overhead" had them paint his jeep glossy green, slip-cover the seats in tiger camouflage for use around Pleiku, and then sand it down and repaint it olive drab like all the other jeeps every time he wanted to drive to Dak To.

People worked hard in Vietnam and not just the combat jobs were risky. "I was an enlisted man in the Corps of Engineers," a man told me over the phone years ago when *Chickenhawk* first came out. "I ran a bulldozer attached to a lot of outfits wherever they needed me. We were sitting ducks, and we knew it. Infantry was always there to protect us, and we were supposed to run for cover when they opened up . . . The infantry looked for trouble, but trouble found us." He laughed. "Infantry did not like to ride on the equipment, felt exposed. I remember hiding under the bulldozer. I felt guilty. One day melted into the next. I couldn't bear to count days, I was in limbo, in stasis. I was not a human being. I was something to use, equipment. I'd get back to my outfit after a month, and they'd say, 'Who are you?' No one knew me, just my name.

"One time we were working on hospital tents and a helicopter strip for the Big Red One [1st Infantry Division]," he continued. "That morning the choppers had took off with the infantry. It's chow time, six o'clock. I'm washing in a steel pot, washing the dust off my face, listening to the GI station on my transistor radio. Casualties light to moderate. At the same time looking up at the sky, choppers with the red cross landed and they're taking them out, taking them out, taking them out, half the battalion."

"I spent most of my time in basic construction, minesweeping roads, and the Phuc Vinh minefield," John Dexter told me with a grin. "We were building an airstrip at Phuc Vinh. They needed men to go out and work with Special Forces and Cambodian mercenaries to clear abandoned areas: demolition. I was experienced with minesweeping and liked it . . . Sure, I volunteered. I sat on two hundred pounds of TNT in boxes in the chopper. We had three or four on the team. Wore jungle fatigues, boots, socks, green underwear, one dog tag in boots, one around our neck, [so that if they were blown apart, one tag or the other would be found]. Whatever we didn't use, we went fishing with before we left. It was bad enough flying out with two hundred pounds of TNT on your ass without flying back with it when a tracer will set it off. I volunteered for anything to get out of building the airstrip.

"We had a jeep minesweeper, the latest thing. Had a big extension in front which would stop the jeep automatically if there were a mine. It either stopped every five seconds for shrapnel or it never stopped at all—we said the hell with it after the first or second week. One time going down a road doing a sweep near the Song Be Bridge we found something big. We thought, 'Did somebody bury a jeep?' We found a bamboo detonator, split bamboo with two tacks with wires, mud in between. If a man walks on it, that's not enough pressure to squeeze the mud out, but if a truck or tank went over . . ." He finished the idea with a gesture: Boom! "We're digging away and digging away till we find the firing device. Took that off. It was a five-hundred-pound dud [American] bomb with two pounds of C-4 [plastic explosive] on the nose with a blasting cap and a battery. It would *gut* a tank." He laughed reluctantly and said, "They were merging the modern with the old. They did it in *one night*, too . . .

"For three and a half months straight," John continued, "I cleared American minefields. We lost eleven guys in the American minefield. When Phuc Vinh got overrun the first time, maybe 1966, the military filing cabinets had a thermite charge in them which dropped down and burned everything. Anyhow, the minefield plans were destroyed, the map of all their locations, antipersonnel mines mostly. We had a Zippo, a tank with a flamethrower, come in and burn off six feet of grass and shit first which blew a lot of ammo and grenades. Then we used mine detectors. A Bouncing Betty is two pounds of TNT in a half-inch-thick, two-pound coffee-can-sized container. It comes up out of the ground three feet and blows waist-high. We couldn't find one of them. Thought it was under this termite mound. This first lieutenant asshole and the platoon sergeant, a black E-7, came over to help. The E-7 found it with his *foot*. Five of us were standing within five feet of them at the time. We were lucky because we had about one and a half seconds to live. The mine top had rusted shut but the initial charge went off and shoved the firing device up through his foot. I heard that *poof* and ran out into an uncleared minefield, realized, and froze. Didn't move. They had to sweep their way out to me and another one or two guys. The best bet would have been to hit the dirt, but you don't think that way . . . After one incident we realized we should only have two guys in the minefield: a prober and a minesweeper. We switched every thirty minutes. After we spread out the accident rate went down. That was after one and a half months."

"So how do you probe for a mine?" I asked.

"You go in at an angle into the dirt slowly till you find the metal . . . One guy caught a trip wire . . . All we found was his flak jacket. His head, arms, and legs were missing. The biggest part of him was in the flak jacket. The shrapnel killed two or three other guys and five or six were wounded. It happened just before I went on. I saw the medic carrying in the flak jacket with his torso in it."

"How did you feel?" I asked.

"I figured he fucked up." He looked down and filled his glass with beer. "I didn't have no problem with it. Just made me more determined not to fuck up. It was either that or heavy work." He laughed. "I didn't want to do heavy work. I'd do about anything to get out of basic construction . . . They were doing basic construction of the airfield, laying PSP [perforated steel planking] and PAP which was not perforated. It would tear your ass up in no time. Heavy work. It was a lot easier to stick a blasting cap into TNT or wrap with det [detonation] cord. We put a pound of TNT on each mine and run det cord, wrap it around with a demo [demolition] knot and go to the next one. Blow up four–five acres with one blasting cap. It's a goof to watch five acres blow up in one shot. The airfield was a twenty-four-hour project, high priority, seven days a week. They worked three companies. The biggest matted airport in the world . . . You carry the sections out and lay them down so they interlock. Take a Johnson bar and drive the pins in to hold them together, bend the tabs down. Your skin falls off, blisters, calluses, open sores on your hands."

I talked to another seabee who spent three and a half months on a bright yellow dredge on a river near Da Nang. They dredged day and night, using lights at night. They got shot at a lot. Of the thirty-five marines guarding them in that period, almost all were wounded or killed.

Maybe your vet had a tour like that of Jimmy Shields of the 13th Signal Battalion, 1st Cavalry Division, in 1967. Trained as a radio operator and a radio communications specialist with cryptographic skills, you'd figure he was as likely a candidate as anyone for an uneventful tour. With two other guys he operated a radio-relay station set up in a temple near the intersection of highways 1 and 19 at a hill called Bagi. "Three of us did our own security and perimeter. One guy ran the radio, one guy slept and one guy was security. We had this huge antenna pointing out where we were, and it was not a secure area. We got to be real close. We depended so much on each other. It was a real high hill. There was also a two-man radio team from the 27th Transport which did radio-relay work for the convoys. Five men total. We got fire every night . . . Then I was sent to Kon Tum and got malaria. When I got out of the hospital I hitched a ride on a convoy back to the Cav. We got hit. The first jeep was wrecked. I was in the fourth vehicle back—a deuce-and-a-half [two-and-a-half-ton truck]. We were shooting and saw VC fall as we drove on . . . Then I pulled perimeter guard at An Khe and ran a radio at DTOC [divisional tactical operations center], where I saw the SITREP [situation report] and the INSUM [information summary] for the 1st Cav every day and got to see what was going on. I was sent back to Bagi for a week, then pulled out to the field to be a gunner on a courier. The pilot was a warrant officer, made a joke out of everything: try to bounce [the helicopter] off Vietnamese people, head straight for the trees and bounce up over them. You get so you like excitement.

"Then for a month or so I flew in a C-7A Caribou over Vietnam running relays. Some unit encounters enemy fire, we coordinated support, took ground fire and hits often. Then I went back to Bagi again. I made friends with a family in the village. We traded cigarettes for rice beer . . . When I told them I was going to Dak To they started crying and saying 'Dak To, number 10! Number 10!' We loaded up a jeep trailer with a radio, fuel, ammo, claymores, etc., and flew to Dak To, unloaded, and drove the jeep off the Chinook to the area and put up a tent. A sergeant told us to sandbag the tent. There was an NVA [North Vietnamese Army] regiment in the area. The 173d Airborne was out there taking casualties, and the 1st Cav, the 1st Special Forces and the 4th Infantry were all coming in to help. We laid two or three courses of sandbags, and the sergeant said, 'Get it higher because the rockets will get you.' There were air strikes all around, Navy Phantoms coming down to treetop level and dropping napalm all around the perimeter all day. I was getting worried. I mean we were a three-man radio team in a tent. About seven that night, I was standing by the tent eating C-ration peaches. An explosion about one hundred feet in front of me blew me to the ground. I looked up, and it looked like the A-bomb. Guys were yelling and screaming. Guys were on fire. A C-130 on the runway was on fire. Stuff was falling all around me. My arm was burning from a six-inch piece of shrapnel that hit me. Rockets were coming in everywhere. They told me to get out to the perimeter between two pom-pom tanks. There were gooks in front of us everywhere, flares, people yelling, guys moaning, tanks firing close in front. It looked really hopeless. I saw a medevac chopper come in and take guys out, shooting. A guy yelled, 'We're pulling out. Take what you can.' We ran to the Chinook with what we could. There were more air strikes."

I think of how I want to hit the floor whenever the jet jockeys from the Jacksonville Naval Air Station go over my house at low level, fooling around on their training flights. I can't even imagine the noise level that night at Dak To.

"There was ARA, aerial rocket artillery—those big rocket pods on a helicopter—and artillery fire everywhere," Jimmy continued, "things burning all around. The Chinook took off. After we'd been up ten minutes, it fell about a thousand feet in three seconds. Things were flying around. I thought this was *it*. Then we landed. A sergeant came by, told us to pitch a pup tent and try to relax. Half an hour later they dropped in Budweiser by parachute and we drank all night. The next day we went back to An Khe. I felt sick, bad, nauseated, hyper . . . I went into booze to relax me down. I felt for the first time it was really real. They sent me back to Bagi. There I found one of my Vietnamese friends' heads cut off and put on a bamboo stake just for being my friend. The VC were merciless. One night me and this other guy decided to drive to Qui Nhon for booze. Shows you how hard up I was. We left our guns for the other guys to cover for us. All of a sudden this Vietnamese runs out in the road, and we hit him. He went up the hood of the jeep and hit the windshield and splattered." He stopped speaking for a minute. I could see the horror of the moment in his face. "There was blood and pieces of him on me. We made a fast U-turn and hit him again." The pain in his voice was audible. "We were really scared. Who was he? There was stuff on the jeep, and it was dented, and the windshield was cracked when we got back. We listened to the radio and a convoy reported finding a VC run over by a five-ton truck, he was so mutilated.

"After that my nerves really, really got bad. From there I went to the Tiger Division [a Korean division] to a place called ROK [Republic of Korea] Valley. I stayed with them and saw them kill a bunch of kids and stuff like that. I was so numb it just seemed to me like getting even. I got an emergency leave for my grandmother dying. I was in a daze, a walking zombie . . . I had anxiety attacks, sweating, felt like a heart attack. I woke up yelling and screaming. When my leave was up I told them, 'I can't go back. I'm done. I'll get killed. I know I can't take care of myself over there.' They didn't care. I did a good job. I couldn't sleep. I couldn't take care of myself, and they said I had a critical MOS [Military Occupation Specialty] and had to go back. So I went AWOL . . ."

"I went to Vietnam in July 1965, to MACV, as a communications specialist," Joe Pearson (whose arrival in-country was described in Chapter 1) continued. "When I got close to eighteen, I got sent back. We were dragging wire [for a telephone line] high and dry through

elephant grass when I stepped in a punji pit and had a punji stake
go through my left foot and out the top . . . It hurt really bad. It
was barbed. When I was shot, it was instant. When I stepped on
the punji, it went on. It made me mad. The pain was excruciating,
slow, and agonizing. They're pulling. I'm watching. They cut my
boot off and tried to pull it out first, but it was barbed. I felt it
catching on the cartilage and bone in my foot. I've got *time* to feel
this pain. So they pushed it back out, and a guy shot the end off it,
and then they pulled it back through. Gave me an anesthetic and a
bandage and we walked out three or four miles. They'd called a
medevac, but it was shot down about two hundred and fifty–three
hundred yards from us. I think we would have walked into an ambush—the guys who shot down the medevac—if I hadn't stepped
on the punji. When we got to Tan Son Nhut, we're walking across
the airfield with my arms around a couple of guys. A captain runs
up with orders with a big red seventeen marked across them assigning me to the 25th Infantry in Hawaii. They took me to the
dispensary, then to the plane. I didn't even get to get my stuff, past
field grade officers and up the steps, still in fatigues, covered with
mud and blood . . . One minute my foot is torn apart. Then I'm
thrown on a Pan Am. I'm trying to recover from the fear *minutes*
before. Am I dreaming or is this really happening? I smelled, I was
dirty, my leg was bloody, and I've got no boot on one foot, still
waiting for the mortars. If someone'd come up and tapped me on
the shoulder, I'd go right through the ceiling.

"After I turned eighteen in Hawaii, the 25th Infantry got orders
for Vietnam, and I got orders, too. I didn't serve a full tour so I had
to go back. Talking about it is a *lot* easier than living it. The larger
portion of that tour was sometimes boring or dull, always dark un-
certainty and you knew the people out there would love to put a
bullet between your eyes . . . Why are we here? What are we accomplishing? We were in neutral or reverse. B-52's are dropping
bombs all day long on Hobo Woods and Charlie still comes out at
night and sets booby traps. We're not accomplishing anything with
all our firepower and sophisticated equipment."

After I talked to many guys with rear-echelon tours like these, I
knew the difference between this and being a grunt, and believe me,

this was better than being a grunt, but it was still awful. Filled with fear and pain like I've never had to face. Most of them had never told anyone because they weren't combat vets.

"I never thought of myself as a combat veteran." Steve G., a big guy who looks as if he's been in a lot of fights, smiled warmly. "I was a gunnery tech on B-52's. Once in a while, I was still fixing something while they took off, and I'd fly the mission as an extra crew member. For the Christmas bombing in '72, for eleven days we ran twenty- to twenty-four-hour shifts. One mission there was no sweeping action in the pulse sweep generator. The new one arrived as the AC [aircraft] got to the taxiway . . . and someone threw it up to me. I secured it, crawled up with the gunner, and we took off. Then I go back and fix it, go through a small three-by-three-foot door back out into the unpressurized part of the plane. Out over Haiphong harbor we got a lot of SAM's [ground-to-air missiles]. Night missions you could look down and see a bright orange-colored flash and a black object with a fireball at the tail . . . The cell [formation of three B-52's] behind us, the lead aircraft, went down, hit in the bomb bay prior to release. It just *disintegrated*. I was in the truck for eight of the eleven days of the Christmas bombing, flew six missions. I was afraid," he said in answer to my question, "but I didn't want to let anyone else know it. Everyone just *did* it. The next three missions, it was the same problem, SAM's at Hanoi and Haiphong. It got to be competition, who counted the most SAM's. There was no time to think about it, just count and call out break right, left, or climb. The gunner sees everything to the rear. Me and him are leaning against the window looking out, see 'em coming . . . Early in the bombing run, fifty or sixty planes, you'd see 'em coming and would know who would get hit 'cause you couldn't break. There'd be 300 to 400 SAM's coming up, a forest of SAM's . . . On the fifth mission I flew, Kennedy got a MIG kill, and we took rockets off to the left side which knocked out the number-one far-outside engine. We had no communication with the rest of the crew. No one can eject till the pilot says. We don't know if the bail-out alarm system is out. We're scared shitless, but when we see we're still flying straight and level, and we don't see any parachutes, we stick it out . . . On the sixth mission, a friend, Little Buddha, went down. Took a hit and couldn't release bombs or make it back. Too low to jump so he rode it into Hanoi."

I asked if he was ever wounded.

"I took some shrapnel in my head," he said casually, "that fifth mission. The aircraft was breaking up as we came in. A piece of the AC itself hit me so there was no Purple Heart. The compartment broke up as we landed. I had eighteen stitches."

"You mean the plane was falling apart as you landed?"

"Yeah." He shrugged. Nothing to brag about or even remember. Nothing important. As I said, he never considered himself a combat vet.

Support battalion life ought to be easy, right?

"You do what they tell you, fill sandbags, build bunkers, motor pool, body bags, switchboard." This former soldier grinned at me. "I was in the 75th Support Battalion at Quang Tri up near the DMZ [demilitarized zone] until they disbanded it in '71. I had five months left so they transferred me to Chu Lai to the Americal."

"Body bags?" I asked. "How was that?"

"First time I ever saw dead, I had to go through their pockets to get personal effects and I.D. them . . . For two months, I packed body bags in Khe Sanh. When the chopper came in, we carried the WIA [wounded in action]. After that, we went back and got the KIA and got their tags, packed them in the bags for Da Nang . . . One of my friends volunteered for a detail, and I packed him the next day. The chopper came in. I grab the ankles and look up and it's my buddy." He was quiet for a while, then looked up, and continued. "We lived underground in Khe Sanh. It was dirty, like sand on you at the beach, twenty-four hours a day, and hot and muggy. We dug holes, filled sandbags, laid PSP [perforated steel planking] on top, sandbags, more PSP, more sandbags. Three–four–five guys lived in each bunker, and we had trenches from bunker to bunker . . . One night I pulled guard duty, second night in a row, and I was *pissed*. We got hit with rockets, a direct hit on the bunker where I would have been playing cards. They were all killed. Big rockets. They shoot 'em from a long ways. You hear 'em whistling in . . . I packed 'em, my friends." He stopped for a minute, then continued in a calm voice: "One had part of his head and neck blowed off. One had both arms and his chest cavity gone but still had his head. One lost both legs and most of his groin, but he lived a while." He shook his head. "Bunkers are mostly for shrapnel. A rocket goes right through.

"High-school dropouts from the support groups took a lot of shit for not being combat infantry: 'Losers! Gofer soldiers!' " His voice changed so I could hear the taunts. "We never had clothes to change. We never got to wash at Khe Sanh unless we got lucky with a patrol to the lake . . . The shower and john got blown away. We burned shit for other companies. When they were wounded, we carried them; when they were dead, we bagged them; and when they shit, we burned it. That's the job in support."

"What was the worst?" I asked.

"At Khe Sanh, one time an APC [armored personnel carrier] hit a mine, and these guys burned inside the tank. I grabbed one by the hands and the skin came off like barbecued chicken." He looked sick. "But one time I carried this guy, both legs blowed off, his belly open, we had him on a stretcher and were running him to the hospital tent and one of us tripped. His guts bounced out and I grabbed 'em and put them back. 'Am I gonna die? Am I gonna die?' he asks, so I said, 'Nah, you're gonna be fine.' And he lived!" He looked at me with pride on his face. "I saw him a few years ago and he said what I said helped . . ."

Medical personnel were especially likely to have had painful tours because of the nature of their jobs. Triage is a military necessity that is not mentioned by the recruiters. In battle, often someone has to say, "Put him aside. He's too far gone to save. Bring in those three guys because we have a much better chance of saving them." The person who does triage is required, literally, to play God. People who have done it have a lot of problems with the memories—or with having *no* memories at all—of their year in Vietnam. Don't ever let anyone tell you medics or nurses didn't have the authority to do this. Whether they had the authority or not, they did triage when they had to, just like everyone else in Vietnam did what he or she had to.

"Standing unspoken order," Marc S., who worked as a triage area medic in Da Nang in 1968–1969, recalled, "was 'Don't send any vegetables home to mom.' Head injuries were held for evaluation by neurosurgeons—if they died waiting for this so much the better."

After a while he learned not to follow up on patients after they went through the surgery doors. "Men and officers operated in two modes—either full throttle or full stop. Switched suddenly from 'give a shit' to give 150 percent at the sound of a chopper. Never saw anyone recover from a 'dead drunk' faster than when they heard the word 'incoming.' Think this was due to hyper adrenaline level that was a constant part of being there."

"I went to the 71st Evac," one soldier said. "The first almost five to six months are like they don't exist. You did what you had to do and went to bed, did what you had to do and went to bed. You're young and naive, and it's incomprehensible till you finally adjust.

"The hospital had a lot of 'C-4 ingestion cases.' " I could hear the quotes in his voice. "Their records stated they'd eaten plastic explosive to get high, [more CYA, cover your ass, by the officers] but it was heroin. I couldn't stand to be cooped up [with them tied to the beds, detoxing cold turkey] so I volunteered for the ER as an added 76-G-20 Medical Records Specialist. When helicopters came in, I unloaded and did triage. I used to compare with my mom, and the number of new wounded at my hospital was always more than what they said for the whole country on TV at home."

"Does one of these guys stick in your mind?"

"Yeah. This guy got hit in the face by a flare. His whole face was flapping on and off as we carried the stretcher." He flipflopped his hand. "Face, no face, face, no face, spurting blood." He stopped talking. After a minute he continued: "I didn't feel nothing. You had to let it go through you because it would hurt. You couldn't be personal with people . . . The worst thing was helicopter crashes and burnt bodies. One time, a helicopter had crashed and burned: There were these three bodies on a litter. Each one was about the size of a chocolate box." He made a square shape with his hands. "I had to pick out the colonel. That was all they were concerned with, that and the stink. The bird colonel [hospital chief] goes to the section chief, who goes to the lieutenant, who comes to me [a sergeant] and says, 'You do it.' I wouldn't tell the PFC, a new guy, to do it, so I got a gas mask and went in: did eenie, meenie, miney, mo"—he stabbed his finger—"real fast and looked at that pile and found his dog tags. I lucked out. It was the colonel. The private and corporal, who cares?" From the look on his face, I could see that he does.

"That was the worst. I wasn't in there thirty seconds but it turned my stomach. I went and threw up . . .

"We were hit every night." He drew me a map of the various bases at Pleiku. The 71st Evac was between an air force base, "where they had steak and air conditioning," and a radar installation. "One day they nailed us. The end of the hooch is gone and I'm laying in there. The first one hit the end of the building, blew it up. I rolled off and under the bed. I was in a corner, sandbagged on the outside, and I'd sandbagged the inside. I'm shitting in my pants and going 'Mother.' " He laughed softly. "They were always mortaring, missing the radar and the air force base and hitting the hospital.

"One big firefight, we worked five days straight eatin' 250 dex, Army issue, and Valium later to calm us down. You have to triage on the landing pad." He stopped a moment, drew me a diagram of the ER, the landing pad, and the ditch, then went on: "You look at them, check their pulse and respiration and put them in a ditch if they were gonna die. That's one of the hardest—all day graves registration's pickin' bodies out of that ditch. If it got real crowded, they'd lock the wheels of the gurney and work on that. Gurneys were stainless steel and easy to clean. We cut their clothes off and got their name, unit, both draft number and Social Security number, asking them these stupid questions. Sometimes they were unconscious and their dog tags were elsewhere. You clip the dog tags to the A&D records and stop the bleeding, get the person stabilized. If there was a medic where he came from [in the bush] he'd have a compress, and if he was seriously wounded, he'd also have morphine. Some come in screaming with pain. No morphine was better for the patient. On morphine you can't get so many symptoms from him. I mean shrapnel could hit him in the ass and be in his toe or his belly." He shook his head and muttered something about still "waking up in cold sweats and talkin' to yourself at night." There was a pause and then we went on.

"There was a guy with his legs pretty much gone, one leg gone, the other one's hanging there—He was *covered* with yellow-reddish mud, all over, on his face, all beat up and dirty. He'd been crawling on the ground. There was this nub—pulsating—blood oozing—His other leg fell off the gurney. I picked it up and put it back on. The

scream he let out . . . You can never forget. He passed out screaming
. . . That scream is still echoing in my mind."

"At the 196th Aid Station," Dave S. said, "my first time off-loading
wounded, the first guy is not that bad, the second I had to off-load
by his femur which is sticking out. The third, they hand me a burlap
sandbag. 'What the hell is this?' I said. 'A body,' they told me. Two
inches in the bottom of the sandbag is ground-up gristle, meat and
flesh that used to be a GI. I remember going back to the tent and
smoking about five cigarettes in three minutes and drinking three
beers to stop shaking." He had transferred from the 95th Evac.
"Working in a hospital, all you saw was people tore up every day
and night. All you saw was wounded. One company of marines was
bombed with our own napalm. *One hundred percent* death rate,
screaming for their mothers. The last one died two weeks later. I'd
had it. I asked for a transfer."

Here's a final quote about rear-echelon life. During the "Vietnamization" period when we were pulling out and turning the fighting
over to the Vietnamese, Larry Smith was a Psychological Operations
Officer in Bien Hoa in 1970–1971. He was told, "Don't do *anything*,
because if you do it, the South Vietnamese won't." The South Vietnamese were supposed to be able to take over. The worst part for
him was that morale was slipping. He worked closely with South
Vietnamese and "the close contact led to the realization, 'What the
hell are we doing here?' Buddhists were burning themselves in the
streets. We're fighting for an inept and unpopular government. The
majority of South Vietnamese didn't seem to care one way or another . . . The craziness of it all changed me in a sense. I mean Nam,
King's death, Watergate. I had a growing sense of distrust of our
leaders. Serious mistakes were being made by well-meaning leaders,
but nonetheless big mistakes. Cynicism and mistrust made me question everything . . . I never saw casualties, a few body bags, but
my world views and trust in authority took a battering, but I think
it was healthy questioning."

Exercises

Think about what the rear in Vietnam was like compared to here,
compared to our lives. Think about being mortared, rocketed, sniped

at, harassed by officers, bored by some stupid petty job, or terrified by a dangerous job like guarding an ammo dump, or traumatized by a particularly gory job such as hospital medic, nurse, or, worse, graves registration specialist. Think of guarding the perimeter of a large target, of doing it without much experience so that every noise scares you, feeling guilty about not being in combat, feeling guilty about feeling glad not to be in combat, piddling regulations, frustration at the way the war was mismanaged and at the corruption and black-market activities visible around you, blatant racism on both sides, drug use, constant fear of attack, heat, smells, seeing people killed. How would you deal with those problems?

Think about never having cold water to drink or a place to get clean.

Think about doing heavy, boring physical labor in terrible heat day after day.

Think how you'd feel if your life was at risk and the people you're trying to save tell you to go home, or always have their hands out. Go on to imagine that some of these people want to kill you. You can't tell which ones, though. They all smile. How does it feel? Now see two innocent little kids pick up a package. See it blow up. See the kids dissolve into red rags of flesh. How would you feel about people who could do something like that to their own people? Or to you when you're there to help? How would you deal with seeing two kids die? How would you deal with the realization that it could have been you? What do you think you would feel? Would you express your feelings or bottle them up? Do you think you would feel the same thing if you were a nineteen-year-old guy? Express it as easily?

Think about how you'd feel in a black-market situation. At eighteen would it have horrified you? Would you have been strong enough to protest, or would you have tried to appear cool by going along with it? Suppose later you heard about the line troops and hospitals being short of supplies. How would you feel? How would you feel living in the grunge and scunge of a big base and knowing your beer and soda rations were being sold to the black market in *your* rear? How would you feel if you came in from the bush in rags and found all the rear-echelon types wearing starched jungle fatigues?

How would it feel to be judged by your skin color? Suppose you were fighting for the people who exclude you? How would you feel?

Think about officers and lifers making your life miserable or doing stupid things to risk your life. Think about being an officer or lifer and feeling that you have to do your duty. Can you see both points of view? If an officer/lifer had caused deaths, could you ever forgive him? Could he forgive himself?

Stand outside at night and listen. Imagine someone out there wants to kill you. What do you need to check? Are you silhouetted against the light? What was that noise? Why have the noises stopped? Are you afraid of the dark, or just afraid of the imaginary enemy? How would you have stood up to this at eighteen?

Go to a pistol range and fire a gun. The noise is unbelievable, inhuman. See if you can ignore it, get used to it. At the range, all the guns are aimed away from you. How would you feel if the bullets were coming at you? Guns are the quietest thing in a firefight, too. Explosions are louder. Do you think it would be a strain?

Rent the movie *The Stuntman*, an excellent Vietnam-vet movie. In one of the war scenes, half a man is shown on the beach. Rent *Platoon*. One of the guys staggers out armless after a booby trap goes off. Take those images, if you can bear to, and think about seeing someone who "got blowed to pieces with a 122-mm rocket. All that was left you could put in a 12-lb. paper bag," as Franklin Gale wrote me. Think about carrying a stretcher from a chopper, about trying to keep a wounded man alive, or about having to let him die, or about packing him into a body bag for the trip home. How would you feel? Would you ever get over it, even if it happened only once?

Think about the moment when you realize that someone you don't even know is trying to kill you. Think of the shock, the change in perspective. *Doesn't that person know it's me, that I'm a nice guy, that my mother loves me? Doesn't my own government care that I'm gonna get killed here?* The answer to those questions is *no*. Suddenly you realize for perhaps the first time that instead of making you invulnerable with all that training, all the government has done is make you expendable. The person who does not die in those moments is going to spend the rest of his life either going over and over that moment and trying to understand how it could be, or blocking out the realization that it happened because it is too frightening to realize that the world is not safe, that there is no set of rules to follow that will get you out alive. The person who has a year of those moments is changed forever.

Think about having moments like that without the close support of buddies, moving from unit to unit as needed, like the bulldozer man or Jim Shields.

How would you feel if you saw mass casualties, and the GI radio station (the military, the government) was lying about the casualty figures?

Adapt this exercise to your own closest call: I have been afraid for my life only once, when an out-of-control van swept to within a foot of my 1954 VW Beetle. If it had hit me, I would have been dead. Have you had a similar experience? Do you remember the emotions after a close call? The fear of getting back in the car? The conviction that everyone on the road is out to get you? Spending a year in that sort of atmosphere would be hard, don't you think? How about trying to carry a case of grenades while fifty-caliber bullets are cooking off upstairs, or trying to keep up with a convoy on a bulldozer that won't go fast enough?

Why is it so hard to talk about Vietnam? Angel Quintana explained, "When you see a movie or talk about it, you *see* the people with no head, your friend killed, wounded people crying, people running to find a safe place." Feel what that must be like, to see, to remember real deaths, real fear, real bodies, real blood. I bet your mind darts away from the thought. So do our vets' minds.

A lot of vets may never be able to talk about Vietnam. We should not press them. Read the stories and information I've collected. Read other books on what it was like to be in Vietnam. Think about the difference between our experience and theirs. Unless we've had some violent tragedy in our life, what you and I picture as death is not an eighteen-year-old person with a big chunk out of his head and brains splattered all over, not a guy our age screaming "Mama! Mama!" with his legs blown off above the knees, or the lower half of a body with the belt still around his waist and the top half suddenly, instantly, horribly gone. We've never seen a friend step on a booby trap, seen his leg blown off, groin blown away, one arm and half his face gone, and had him beg us to shoot him. We also know if our friends are alive or dead. Most of our vets don't even know that because of the individual rotation system, and they are afraid to find out. "We have things to tell each other that you don't want to hear, like who died," Chuck Emerson said, explaining why he doesn't want to see old buddies.

What we hear, they lived.

3

In the Pipeline
and Forward Bases

The Pipeline

Vietnam became more dangerous the farther you got from the big bases and cities. Supplies and men were moved all over the country by guys whose jobs sounded safe: truck driver, mechanic, supply-boat operator, pilot, crew chief, loadmaster, weatherman. But in fact the roads were not safe, the sky was not safe, and the rivers and canals were not safe.

Following are some stories of the everyday dangers.

On the Road

"When you drive a truck day in and day out you know how the clutch is, the brakes, steering, know what needs to work." Phillip Morris is a big, second-generation trucker. His wife offered me cake as he began his story. "We ran seven-hundred-and-fifty-pound bombs and napalm from Vung Ro Bay to Tuy Hoa. It was twenty-eight or twenty-nine miles. We sent out three trucks with five-minute intervals between groups of three so that if they [trucks] got hit, they [VC] would only get three." I'm thinking about what kind of explosion a truckload of seven-hundred-and-fifty-pound bombs or napalm would make if it hit a mine. My respect for him goes up about a hundred notches. "We ran every day, as many times a day as we could, twenty hours a day most days. At the time you never think about it, just do it. They gave us Bennies, pink tabs—do two pills and two joints and boogie on. I wore the same clothes for ten–fifteen days. Didn't have time to wash 'em. Got a bath at the ocean in Vung Ro. If you had Palmolive soap, the only kind that lathers in salt water, y'know, that was heaven. You had to change your own tires, get your own fuel, grease the truck every day, trade for parts or steal 'em. Used to trade the canned milk from the mess hall, came in gallon cans, tasted like it had been strained through shit—you could always get what you needed."

"You did your own maintenance? After driving twenty hours?"

He nodded.

"Took about an hour a day to check your truck." He used an imaginary hammer. "Bump the tires with a hammer. If it bounces right, you know by experience they're right. Check the funny noises, crawl up under the truck and grease everything if you've got grease. If not, do it tomorrow. They were three-axle trucks and all three axles were pulling axles. We could put it in low and drive through a rice paddy and go on. I bet I could drive one of them things up the wall of this house." He laughed. "Max, they went forty-five–fifty miles per hour. We ran at about forty. Sometimes at ten or fifteen, depending on how bad the roads were. Sometimes you had a gunner with you. When we drove bunches of three, the lead truck and the rear truck had a fifty [caliber machine gun] and a gunner. The guy in the middle had his own raggedy ass. Sometimes we had a quad-fifty [four fifty-caliber machine guns on one mount] mounted in back of a deuce-and-a-half—swivel-mounted right in the bed on a five- or six-foot ring, went up, down, around." He imitated the motions of a gun turret.

"A lot of nights I slept right in the truck." Phillip leaned forward in the chair, serious. "After you been there five, six, seven months, green guys are like kids, more likely to get killed. If things don't look just right when you enter a ville, you catch that. Mama-sans aren't by that hooch picking lice out of each other's hair. People aren't huddled around that pot of fish stew or out planting rice. Or you pass the engineers working on the road, putting in a bridge, and there's no gook kids out around the GI's, you know something's fixing to happen or done happened up ahead. Gets to be an instinct. And you know when you gotta do it, you gotta do it and do it *now*. The first person I ever killed, I cried for an hour. Fourteen days after I got in-country, I'd been up four days, I seen a guy running for my truck, and I thought he was gonna throw a grenade, and he did have one. I blowed him away. After the first time it was like a disease, I wanted to do it again. It was not fun watching him die, but it was fun killing him." He looked to see if I understood, and I nodded, trying to figure it out.

"If it's your time to go"—he looked me right in the eye—"you're gonna go. I've seen trucks behind and in front of my own get blowed up. I've been blowed up out of a truck. *Every day* was close . . ." Phillip was really bothered by a woman's saying to him that she didn't like *Platoon* because of the swearing and marijuana-smoking. He didn't say this to her, but he did to me: "What are you supposed to do when you are put in a situation where no one cares if you live or die, if you can't smoke a little dope and talk shit? You don't have no one to hang on to, no mother. You do not have a lifetime. You may not have a single day. Eighteen of us were on a convoy to Phan Rang one time. When it was over, there were eight left out of the whole company."

After a while, trying to be funny and also genuinely curious, I asked, "What did you wear, and did you get hemorrhoids [the trucker's nemesis]?"

"I didn't get hemorrhoids." He cracked up. "I wore a helmet and flak jacket, T-shirt, pants—the flak vest wore big open sores on the end of my spine, I guess from bouncing up and down on the seat. I had my M-16 and my ammo belt with the clips in the truck, and grenades, and, for a while, an M-79 grenade launcher."

In . . . *and a hard rain fell*, John Ketwig takes us inside the experience of volunteering to be a convoy driver:

> I was getting the hang of the ponderous truck . . . We passed ragged Vietnamese . . . Roared through Kontum and beyond, across a pontoon bridge, past a devastated American armored personnel carrier . . .
>
> We were on a straight stretch with heavy jungle on both sides threatening to engulf the road. The engine roared. Clumps of mud clattered against the undercarriage, and the canvas top clattered against the wind. Shotgun was telling me about ice fishing in Minnesota, when everything disappeared. There was a giant confusion up ahead, a curtain of mud, a blinding flash, a roar unlike anything I had ever heard. I

couldn't see. I couldn't hear. I existed in a slow-motion world turned upside down. The great barrier grew, fire and smoke and noise, and the earth heaved, and I thought I had been shot in the head and what I was experiencing was the final spasm of torn and shattered brain tissue. The wiper cut through the wash of mud, and I glimpsed a dark hole and went for it . . . we were stopped. I sat deflated and baffled. Frozen. I became aware of frantic activity. I became aware that I was alive. Like a surreal movie, a face appeared to my right, a distorted anguished face, obviously screaming, but I couldn't hear what it was saying. Where was Shotgun? I didn't remember him leaving. I couldn't hear! My hands went to my head, to my ears, and I realized I was hearing the most enormous crushing, howling, roaring noise of my life. Little noise among the great noise. Crackling. My eyes were okay . . .

I lay across the seat to look out the door, to see where Shotgun had gone. There was a guy, lying in the mud, with a stick or . . . and an abstract swarm of golden insects flew away from his head, and I concentrated on the crackling sound because it must be a clue: the stick was his rifle, and he was shooting, and the insects were shell casings, and the roar was a lot of explosive, and we were hit. I was alive and everybody was down there . . . Gotta get down with those guys, gotta shoot. Can't see anything but muddy splotches on dark green leaves, and vines, and grass . . . My head aches . . . I don't see anybody to shoot at. Big dark noisy shadows overhead, the roar again, the mud is shaking and none of it makes sense.

Suddenly it was quiet. Bodies stirred around me. I rolled over, lay on my back looking up into the gray rain. My head hurt . . . There was a roaring sound that wouldn't go away . . . What had happened? . . . I stumbled past the dark form of a truck . . . There was a crater, a huge bowl-shaped hole right square in the middle of the road. Wider than the road, stretching the jungle walls back. Twisted shredded dark forms, probably metal, a set of wheels, a grotesque steel ladder. Fireworks or gunpowder. I smelled gunpowder. What was going on? Why hadn't I seen that great big hole? . . .

Suddenly Shotgun was there, screaming, hugging me, slapping my back, raving at the top of his lungs. '. . . motherfucker had our name on it, and you fuckin' drove that fuckin' truck and we fuckin' made it, and . . . and . . . Fuckin'-A! Fuckin' Christ, man. You fuckin' did it, you fuckin'-A did it . . .'

The flatbed just ahead of us had hit a mine. The whole load of ammo went off. Somebody said we went through it on two wheels, just from the force of the concussion . . . The guys in the truck? They were looking for them, for something to send home."

Ketwig got back in the truck, shaking and stunned, and drove on to Dak To, where a battle had been raging for four days in the mud and rain, the roar of air strikes all around, frantic gunners short of ammo, almost mad with fear but still serving their guns under that rain of mortars and rockets. John, still too stunned to function, was the quintessential FNG [fucking new guy] till one of the gunners knocked him down and pointed out that he shouldn't stand up in this shit, nor should he keep his truck near their gun, as it made a better target. John spent that night in the rain and mud in an artillery gun pit, watching the wire, the 105's (artillery guns) loaded with beehive rounds aimed point-blank in case of human-wave attacks. He saw an APC [armored personnel carrier] drive out through a hail of bullets and tie ropes to twelve dead Americans—a patrol killed on the way back in—and drag the bodies back through a hail of fire. Shotgun, a hardened short-timer, spent the night helping with graves registration. When he got into the truck the next morning for the ride back, he was crying. John asked if he was all right. "I don't think I'll ever be all right again, but let's get the fuck outta here."

. . . *and a hard rain fell* went on to relate Ketwig's reactions to his further adventures. Ketwig was a *mechanic*. His book, like other personal narratives, builds up, piece by piece, a picture of Vietnam. Read enough of these personal narratives and you realize that the experience was often incomprehensible. As we'll see in Chapter 7, "So What's So Different About Vietnam?," nothing in America's past wars had prepared these guys for destroying villages to save them, for having civilians try to kill them, for taking places again and again at great cost in human lives and then abandoning them, or for the questions that would haunt them for the rest of their lives. Why did I live and they die? Why were we there? Why? Why? Why? A split develops here among veterans. Some begin to question, like Bob and John Ketwig, even as they continue to do what they have to do, and some shut down all questions and *do it*, whatever *it* is.

Here's a third look at convoy life from medic Dave S., who volunteered to get away from the hospital. He was serving on a track with F Troop, 17th Armored Cavalry.

"Escorting a convoy of NVA prisoners to LZ Ross, a road called Death Alley. The road had been swept. Didn't matter. Boom. A two-and-a-half-ton went up. There were bodies everywhere. The MP's, one was five meters away from the road. His hand gone, three fingers, his knee, and jaw, too. The other one was fifteen meters away, in really bad shape too, but with more chance of making it, so I worked on him, then went back to the other. Still alive. You put a plastic hose into their throat when their jaw is gone. He died on the chopper. When I threw him on, I realized he was a friend, twenty-eight days short [of going home]. The other guy was in a wheelchair wired together when I got to Japan [when he was wounded himself]. The truck looked like a twisted, ripped beer can."

Not everyone convoyed around Vietnam. George Hill was with the marines for twelve months and twenty days during his first tour, August 1967 to September 1968. "They sent me to Da Nang, to a motor pool." His voice sounded pleasant and Southern on the tapes he sent me. "It was worse than stateside duty. I mean, ever' morning shine your boots. You may get a rocket round shot from a distance once ever' week or two. I was there about two weeks, and they called me in . . . 'You goin' out to replace a driver who's rotatin' back to the States, Hill 55: Dodge City.' As soon as I got out there, I knew this was the real deal. Hill 55, Echo Battery, 1st LAAM [an antiaircraft missile battery]. Shared the hill with platoon of Kilo Company, 3rd Battalion, 7th Marine Regiment, a rifle company. My job was a truck driver, and that was our lifeline. I made all the rounds, got food, got some ammo, got the mail, take a different guy every day off the hill . . . Also I had a water buffalo, a two-hundred-and-fifty-gallon water trailer, which you filled up at the river at the bottom of the hill. The first evening we was down there, two–three rounds, y'know, pow-pow-pow, everbody gets down. A Mexican corporal just got knicked in the arm. The water point had mortars. They opened up and they wiped this whole ville out with mortar rounds and everything else you could think of over one sniper not even really in the ville. I knew it meant business then.

"That old truck didn't have no top." His voice was full of affection.

Camaraderie was what he remembered most about his tour. "Didn't have no canvas, didn't have nothing, no sides, the wooden benches were ruined.

"There was mines in the road," George said. "I seen vehicles in front of me going to Da Nang hit a mine. I seen vehicles in back of me hit a mine [after he'd driven over it]. When they hit a mine— the driver—their head is always gone and their legs. One time I saw this Vietnamese bus with people hanging all over it like they do— It went over a spot I'd just driven over and blew up. The biggest piece left was about the size of a steak and it landed on the hood of my truck. It got to where it didn't even bother me. Matter of fact, in the morning you was supposed to wait for the engineers with the minesweeper. A lot of times I'd tear out before they'd even go."

Ron Livingston, of D Battery, 2/40th Artillery, 199th Light Infantry Brigade, told of seeing "a deuce-and-a-half truck driven by an eighteen-year-old boy run over a little girl. She ran out and got killed. He held her in his arms. He couldn't see [that] half her face is gone— He's trying to do CPR, sticking his mouth into her bloody, gory face— If people could visualize that sight, see an eighteen-year-old kid trying to revive a six-year-old girl with half her face and body squished— Then he starts pounding himself in the face with his fist till he's a bloody pulp— That's the things you try to forget, throw it in the back of your mind and *forget* it."

"We drove all over Vietnam in a pickup and two big white trucks." Jules Goetz had another job that sounds innocuous. Calibrating radio frequencies so that transmitters and receivers were on the same wave length, calibrating torque wrenches so that the blades stayed on the helicopters is hardly a job you'd expect to be dangerous. "No convoys. No protection. Really on our own. Someone rode shotgun with an M-79 grenade launcher with shotgun shells. Up near the DMZ you'd see two columns coming at you on this dirt road wearing black pajamas. The home guard has a little red triangle sewn on their shirt. Whose gonna stop and look? We just put it to the floor and zipped right through. We didn't bother them, so they didn't bother us."

On the Water

Lynn Whittaker served on a YFR patrol boat. "We'd anchor out at night and move every two hours because they'd go up river and get under some reeds and float down with them and put a grenade or some C-4 on the boat. We'd throw concussion grenades all night. Our boat was different than based boats. We had built-in tanks for water and fuel, a small refrigeration area for meats which we sometimes filled with ammo. We had two M-60 machine guns, two fifties, one M-79, a shotgun, one M-16, and a couple of .45's.

"We had thirteen crew," he continued, "but it averaged nine, usually. We'd get a bunch hurt at once, and it would be a while before we got replacements. We got ammo in Saigon and Nha Be, where there was a PBR [patrol boat, river] base, a minesweeper base, and converted landing craft for hauling stuff . . . I was a twenty-one-year-old E-5, second-class diesel engine mechanic. In three weeks I was chief engineer. On the boat we had an electrician, a storekeeper, chief engineer who was second-in-command, three enginemen, and a chief bosun's mate, an E-7, who was the captain—we didn't have an officer—and five–six seamen and a cook. It was the old type of engines—you ring for changes. Two guys were in the engine room, and the other engine guys ran the fantail guns: two fifties and two sixties. Seamen ran the guns in the front on the top, two sixties and maybe a fifty clear up on the front. The shotgun was for standing watch. There were friendly villages on both sides. We couldn't shoot into them so we took a lot of rounds. We used the M-16 to board their boats to check I.D.'s, little junks smuggling weapons. In a firefight we used the higher-power weapons. The river was up to two thousand yards wide. We had more trouble where it was narrower.

"We saw PBR's turned over to the Vietnamese [remember Vietnamization?]. They had the big ammo boxes in the back full of fishing nets. They gave *no* support. They ran from fights.

"We had twin props on that boat. We had one shot off one time, and the boat curved right up into the contact." He made a path with his hand. "They [the enemy] ran, but we went right up into the mud, stuck. The engine and steering were both knocked out. A tug had to come up from fifty miles south and tow us back. The whole time towing us, a guy stood by on the tug with an axe to cut us loose if there was any shooting . . . One time the strainer for the generator cooling got clogged, and when I cleaned it out, I found a finger. We always went around bodies. One time a PBR grappled one and his head fell off."

Men also served on oilers off the coast, handling supplies and fuel. Mike Morris told me on tape: "My first [tour] was eight months and I was on an ammunition ship. We resupplied destroyers, cruisers, and carriers with ammunition and supplies—not only ammunition but also mail, movies, personnel, that type of thing, off the coast of Vietnam, so each time they ran short of ammunition or short of fuel they wouldn't have to go into a port somewhere and refuel or rearm. The second tour was a six-month tour on a fleet oiler and we did basically the same thing—that was in 1968—as a fleet ammunition ship but we transferred fuel oil for the main propulsion of most of the big ships, some ammunition for the five-inch guns on destroyers and cruisers, and also we had fuel for jets on the aircraft carriers and the helicopters and the propeller-driven aircraft."

Other men like Greg Brown served as naval advisers (skilled electricians, machinists, gunners' mates) to the Vietnamese, training them to work on the boats we'd given them. At Binh Thuy they had a little base on the riverside, two small piers, and about seventy Americans working in a big line of garages for the boats. "In '71 and '72 in III and IV Corps," Greg said, "there were lots of massive troop movements. We heard that they'd hit people three, four, five klicks [kilometers] out. On the pier we'd watch, fire pop-flares and shoot at anything a sapper could be behind. Our strength was in air support. ARVN commitment was a joke. It was said that they shot up a boat themselves, though this was wise—to be hooked up with the VC."

In the Air

One workhorse of the air, the twin-rotor Chinook helicopter, known as the Shithook, served as part of the pipeline. A Chinook could carry thirty troops or several pallets of ammo and supplies inside, and it could slingload even more, including artillery pieces. It made a really big target as it came in, and it often came in under heavy fire, but it could land in places no airplane could. The blades whipped up a lot of sand and debris as it came in. Jimmy Shields was rescued from Dak To under fire by a Chinook. Wayne Milles, who went through flight school with Bob, told me, "The first six months in Vietnam, I was more afraid of the Chinook than I was of the VC. They were coming apart in the air and nobody had any idea why."

Hueys were the most common helicopter. Without the armament—pilot-operated machine guns and rocket pods—of the gunships, Huey slicks like Bob's flew ass-and-trash [people and supplies] everywhere, every day. Took people out to their units, including nervous FNG replacements. Resupplied grunts and firebases. Brought people in to base to do paperwork or to go on R&R. They flew courier missions, gave people rides, flew in hot meals, mail, and VIP visitors. They took people on the first leg of the trip home, carried back captured weapons and prisoners, whatever. On top of that they flew combat assaults and medevac as required.

One week after Bob left the 1st Cav for the 48th Aviation, the pilot sitting in his old seat was shot through the head by a sniper on a peaceful ass-and-trash mission. Gerald Towler, Bob's buddy and flying partner for most of the tour, landed the slick, jumped out, ran around to help the guy, pulled his helmet off, and the top of his head came off with it.

Fixed-wing aircraft also played an important part in the pipeline. Of the various aircraft used to ferry stuff around Vietnam, I've heard the most about the Caribou and the C-130, both of which could land on short runways.

Among other exploits, C-130's dropped 12,400 tons of supplies to the defenders of Khe Sanh during the 1968 siege when the landing strip was too dangerous to use. The method for doing this involves flying low and deploying a parachute out of the back of the aircraft. The parachute jerks out a pallet of ammo or food. Hard, skilled flying. Everyone is shooting at you, but you have to fly slow and low so you won't drop the supplies on the defenders. The guys who did this were "*just*" transport pilots. I can't repeat often enough, there was no *just*, no *only*, in Vietnam.

"At the 92nd Aviation Company," Gerald Bussell, an Air Force pilot who flew Caribous for the Army in 1966–1967, told me "there was a sign over the door: 'The infantry is the Army and everything else is support.' If I was in a foxhole, I'd want an Army pilot. If I was a Theater Commander, I'd want an Air Force pilot. Army pilots fly anything, anywhere. The Army used aircraft like another kind of jeep. The Army pilots landed on runways less than one thousand feet routinely, the Air Force never wanted less than fifteen hundred. In the Air Force, an accident means no more promotions. For instance, two five-hundred-gallon fuel bladders weigh 6,500 pounds. The Army always hauled two in a Caribou, which made you slightly overweight. Air Force pilots would not fly with two bladders because if there was an accident, blew a tire, whatever, they'd be grounded. The Army attitude was different. I saw a Special Forces guy go out and shoot up an airplane once to make it a combat loss. That's the Army . . . 'Magnet ass' was the Army's explanation for why I got hit forty-five times in one week." He laughed.

"In the Air Force, there's something sacred about flight crews. Air-conditioned quarters, eight hours' uninterrupted crew rest. If you don't get it, you don't have to fly. Twelve hours after you land until you have to fly again. Sixteen hours straight is the longest you could fly without command approval. Many times after a sixteen-hour day, everyone in the Army is ready to go. They [the Air Force] would just say, 'We don't have any pilots available.'

"We were supporting Special Forces camps and Marine artillery units, dinky little places—nowhere, no nav [navigational] aids. You had to rely on having been in and out in good weather." He pointed outside at the street. "It'd be like flying down Main Street here and knowing you had to get above or below the train-crossing thing. The Air Force would say the weather's too bad, but guys under fire need food and ammo. The Air Force would say 'suppress the fire and we'll come in.' " He shook his head. "We got up at dark-thirty and take off at the first hint of day. We'd fly for fourteen, sixteen hours. One time we flew from Da Nang to Ha Tahn with a load of bulgur from U.S.A.I.D., were unloading, and heard a mortar round. It hit their mortar pit and cremated the guys in the pit." I noticed the familiar look on his face—*seen too much*. He continued: "The next hit is beside the plane. We cranked. Flight engineer said 'Get us up or I'm leaving.' Taxied out. A Birddog [smaller plane] landed over top of us, turned around, and took off, and I beat him over the end of the runway." From the grin on his face I could tell he was really moving. "Had twenty-one holes from the mortar—got a DFC [Distinguished Flying Cross] that day—got on the horn and told 'em these people need a mortar, and flew recon to see where the VC were . . . Often, Navy A-4's flew supporting rocket, machine-gun, and napalm passes beside you as you'd land.

"We used to take the artillery rounds out of the boxes and strap them on the deck because we could haul more faster. Do that all day long. Shuttle as required . . ." He said it so casually, as if it were nothing, but I was thinking *as required*, so if some little firebase in those jungle-covered hills needed him, he would come even if it meant flying eighteen-hour days.

"One three-day period," he continued on a sadder note, "we hauled dead and wounded out of the DMZ, two days' wounded, filled up every hospital down to Chu Lai and then two days' dead stacked on the deck like cordwood. We were not supposed to stack 'em, but we did."

The crew of the Caribou included two pilots. A guy called the loadmaster was responsible for securing the load on the aircraft so it wouldn't move in flight and change the center of gravity, causing the pilots to lose control of the plane. The flight engineer, a flying mechanic, serviced and maintained the Caribou and helped the loadmaster. Aloft, the flight engineer helped keep an eye on engine instruments if a problem was developing, or helped observe, looking for enemy fire. The loadmaster and flight engineer helped load and unload supplies, too, and finally, when one of these out-of-the-way places was under attack, an aircraft could be literally mobbed by Vietnamese. Then the flight engineer and loadmaster would have to kick and push them off to be able to close the doors. There was a lot of work to being in Vietnam, and if you didn't do your job, people could die because of it.

Paul Bicknell, an air force navigator, told me, "I flew medevac out of Travis Air Force Base in '69–'70, hopping across the Pacific and picking up burn victims in Da Nang and up and down the coast and returning them to the burn hospital at Travis . . . I was a navigator. My mission was basically to pick the AC through the thunderstorms and make it as easy as I could . . . A C-141 Starlifter [could] carry about twenty litters and the nursing station." The anguish of that

job, knowing every move was agony for the burned patients, trying
to avoid rough air, could still be seen in Paul's face as we talked. I
think of all the other people who flew or drove or ran the rivers on
various *non-combat* missions over there, of how much they cared,
and how some had to learn not to care to protect themselves.

One final interview, about a job that sounds really safe. Jim Good-
year was a weather observer for the Air Force in 1965–1966. "My
job was to sit out in the control tower and watch clouds and make
an observation every hour, or every five minutes, depending on the
situation." Resupplying the grunts by air depended on the weather.
At first he was at Pleiku, working shifts and drinking and fooling
around in town every night. "Pleiku was a Wild West town. We
couldn't carry a weapon to town because a Special Forces C Team
had had a big shootout with Vietnamese red berets [our allies!] a
few months before." When Pleime Special Forces Camp was under
siege in October, Jim volunteered to throw flares out of a plane so
the fighter planes could see to strafe and bomb the perimeter. "There
were fifty-caliber holes in the plane afterwards." I love the way he
said that—sheer luck kept him from having fifty-caliber holes in him,
too. "Then I flew up and down the border in an L-19 [airplane] real
low and slow with the FO's [forward observers]. We'd try to see if
it had rained or not—looking for tracks. I did that for about a month,
eight or ten missions, got an Air Medal, got shot at a few times."
He laughs. "Then I got gung-ho. The Air Force formed a combat
weather team to be sent out with Army units . . . We went to Phu
Loi first, the 1st Aviation Battalion, 1st Infantry Division.
Scrounged, stole, borrowed, and bought materials to build a weather
station there. Four-man teams to a brigade . . . I got sent to Lai Ke
with the Third Brigade. We scrounged and built a hooch, and when
the brigade went on a field operation we went with them, especially
in the wet season. Weather observations out in the sticks would help
the weather team in Phu Loi to make a good forecast for the infantry—whether they could get resupplied or whatever . . . We
went out to LZ's, secured LZ's . . . sometimes further. LZ's got
mortared a lot, medium- and small-arms fire every night . . . I filled
thousands of millions of sandbags . . . It was hot, dirty, nowhere to
bathe, C-rations, drudgery, heat, insect repellent, green cans of food.
I don't want to compare it to the infantry guys," he said, like every-

one else. "It was just burning-hot monotony and we drank a lot . . . I volunteered to fly backseat with FO's fifteen or twenty times to beat the monotony . . . When I went with the 1st Division and went out with smaller units, I saw how screwed up it could be."

"For instance?" I asked.

"We go out on an operation. The 1st Infantry Division and an Airborne unit captured weapons and rice but found nobody. The day we pulled out the VC artilleried the runway as we left just to show us they were there. Another instance—they brought in an air strike too close to a position. The pilots said, 'The [napalm] cans tumble too much. We'll hit our own people.' The general said, *'Do what I say.'* They hustled all the krispy Americans [napalmed] to all different field hospitals so there wouldn't be a bunch of them come in, no publicity . . . It was a normal thing, fuck-ups. We got cynical about it."

Forward Bases

What was the pipeline supplying? Firebases (artillery units), LZ's (landing zones), Special Forces camps. "Dinky little places. Nowhere. No nav aids," as Gerald Bussell said.

What were they like? Heaven to the grunts, places where not every step threatened a booby trap. Still, from our point of view and probably that of the guy in Vietnam who'd never been a grunt, they were dangerous, filthy, ugly places. Pictures of them show bald spots in the Vietnamese landscape, raw dirt, mounds of sandbags, rolls of concertina wire. Not inviting.

Firebases or LZ's—where the infantry could come in for one or two days to take a break and fill some sandbags—were the home of many artillerymen, officers, company clerks, cooks, mechanics, and other support personnel. The big guns could shoot only so far, so the firebases had to be out in the jungle or swamp near the grunts, where they made a nice big stationary target. LZ's were also located close to the AO [area of operation] of the unit the helicopters were supporting to cut down on the time it took to get them and prevent interruptions in resupply caused by the weather.

"We started out in the A Shau Valley," an artilleryman told me. "They couldn't take us out to our unit for four days because there was too much fire. We got there, the guys we replaced showed us around. They didn't try to scare us, tried to make us feel good . . . Two 105 howitzers were set up on top of a mountain and the other four guns from the battery were on top of another one. We had five men to a gun although we had trained with more in the States." Rockets and mortars were a constant threat. So was being overrun. Infantry units were stationed at each little firebase and LZ to defend it. The infantry went out from these bases, just as they did from the bigger bases on patrols and search-and-destroy missions.

"I guarded the road coming out of Dong Ha," Ric Hill, of the 2nd Battalion, 9th Marines, 1968, told me. "Every morning we swept two miles of road for mines and rode back on the truck. We went on rinky-dink one-day patrols all around Camp Carroll. Every four or five days, we went on a two- or three-day operation."

Meanwhile on the firebases, artillerymen spent long days and nights running fire missions, sweat running off their bodies, hot casings piled up around their knees, burdened with the responsibility of rescuing guys they couldn't even see from an invisible enemy. The fear of shooting short and getting our guys bore down on them. The worry of a short round, a defective charge that falls short and kills you, was there, too. Lifting the round, slamming it into the gun, checking the elevation and range and pulling the lanyard and setting it off, "on the way." The roar of the explosion, the powder smoke thick in the humid air—quick, another; quick, another; quick another. How'd we do? Arms aching, faces black with smoke, no glory, no high points, a grinding job. Cheering when they save someone. Desperately angry when they don't. At night, rockets, mortars, long weary watches on guard, fear. And sometimes the human-wave attacks, overrun, fighting for your life. And yet, someday, someone is going to say, "Oh, he was just in the artillery."

Some artillery units were permanently stationed in one place. Some moved every few weeks or months in order to support the infantry closely. Some guns were towed or airlifted. Others were self-propelled and made long, slow convoy moves on their own. In the early years they even tried to use self-propelled 155 howitzers to run convoys, but they were too vulnerable to mines. That knowledge must have made the convoys even more of a strain.

The artilleryman has to know exactly where he is on the map so he can fire accurately. Lives depended on it. Shells don't recognize nationality. After each move, in a hundred-and-twenty-degree heat or in the monsoon rain, artillerymen dug, leveled, and tamped down the gun platforms. Big guns have to be level, anchored, and surrounded by revetments of sandbags to protect the crew and the piles of live ammunition from enemy fire. Often the gun platform had to be releveled and retamped after each fire mission, because the ground was soft in different areas. I met one guy whose job was called artillery survey. That's what he did, measure to see if the guns were positioned correctly, and, if they weren't, level and fix them with a shovel. Artillerymen filled sandbags and stacked them around the gun, nonstop, until the gun was ready to fire. Others unpacked the ammo. Their own lives depended on getting revetments up and bunkers dug and sandbagged before Charlie zeroed in and the mortar and rocket attacks became a part of daily life. "Sometimes we started getting fire coming in before we knew our own coordinates," Ron Livingston, of D Battery, 2/40th Artillery, 199th Light Infantry Brigade, 1968–1969, told me.

"Filling a lot of sandbags, a lot of work, steady work, constant work," an artilleryman who served in A Battery, 1/21st Artillery, 1st Air Cavalry in 1968–1969, told me. "We even practiced one hour a day on top of the missions we had to fire. The sections tried to outdo one another: how many rounds you could fire in how many seconds . . . You clean it and you fire it and you clean it and you fire it. You don't want to need it and not have it . . . First I worked in ammunition [as a bearer]. We put a towel around our head and go out and unhook the water blivets and the ammo pallets from the Chinook. The sand blows up like a windstorm, y'know . . . We cut the straps on the pallets and take out the boxes and throw them on the jeep or the mule. Two shells to a box. Take 'em out of the box and out of the tube they come in and take 'em around to the guns. Got to keep them supplied." He smiled and shook his head. It wasn't so bad, not like being a grunt.

"What about mortars and rockets and being overrun?" I asked.

"We only lost one while I was there. Places got hit before we got there. Places got hit after we left. We were always waiting to get hit, which was hard. We got rockets and mortars all right, but we only lost one boy. He was young. We were training him. He got hit by a 107 rocket, I believe it was a 107, right at the entrance to the bunker." He didn't say anything for a while, and I thought how peculiar it was that his grief for this unknown kid killed twenty years ago on the other side of the world should surprise me. "I became assistant gunner later," he continued. "We had bunkers and concertina, pulled perimeter guard. The guys that slept were the ones who had to get up and do the fire missions, but we never minded. We took pride in it, doing it as fast as we could. They needed us. We liked it . . . There sure wasn't any sitting down, though, and they were hot miserable days. No trees where the artillery was . . . B-52 strikes used to knock us right off the sandbags if we slept out at night." He laughed at the memories. "We were sore all over. You're gonna get sore if you're in the artillery."

How did they know where to fire? A three-man team out in the bush with an infantry unit or on a hill where it could observe enemy movements called in the coordinates for artillery fire to an FDC [fire direction controller]. The FDC "put a pin in the map, got the distance and the azimuth and the weather and figured the elevation and deflection and quadrant," so the guns would deposit the high explosives in the right place.

Think about this: "I remember one night," George Hill recalled, "we was in a bunker. Artillery rounds was walking right up the hill, and the next set of rounds would of hit our bunker, man, and we climbed in a corner, and they quit. And it was the *wrong* army! Our U.S. Army had the *wrong* coordinates, man." He still couldn't believe it.

The gunner stood to the right of the gun, getting coordinates from the FDC on his headset and relaying them to his assistant gunner, who crouched beside the gun, frantically turning dials and wheels on a contraption attached to it. Meanwhile, the loader took the prepared round and threw it into the gun, closed the breech, listened for the click that meant it was closed completely, and moved quickly back to the corner so he wouldn't get hit by the recoil. The gunner pulled the lanyard. After the roar and the recoil, the loader opened the breech and threw the hot, empty shell to the side. The bearers got the rounds, took them out of the tubes they came in, set the powder charge in them, stacked them in piles by their charge (enough to shoot it 1,000-meters, 800-meters). During a fire mission, bearers handed them to the loader if there were enough bearers. Sometimes there weren't.

"I was a wireman," Ron Livingston told me. "They assigned me to a gun after I'd been in Vietnam four months—after they lost a lot of guys . . . They used you for what they needed. I never saw a gun [meaning an artillery piece] before. Guns are fascinating. I love them. It intrigued me how they could make something out of steel go that far and do that much damage . . ."—he made a gesture—". . . level this house with one shot. I was a bearer first, carried rounds. I worked a one-oh-deuce [102-mm howitzer]. It had this big gear on the ground and just cranked around three hundred and sixty degrees. The rounds weighed forty to fifty pounds, two to a box, a wooden box with handles. We had three bearers per gun, plus one guy with a headset checking coordinates, one loading, and one pulling the lanyard . . . When the lanyard was pulled, the ground shook like a small earthquake. It jars everything, teeth, head. We were issued earplugs, but we never wore them. Sometimes we were on eight-hour shifts, twelve-hour shifts, sometimes twenty-four-hour shifts. Depends on the intensity—I've gone as high as three days and three nights. In that period out of six men, we could let one guy get two hours' sleep."

"Did you run short of ammo?" I asked, thinking of being overrun.

"Yeah." His voice died and I looked up. "Frightfully so. One time we got down to eighty rounds for six guns. [Divided among the six guns, that would be *one and one-half minutes* of continuous fire on the 102.] It was scary. You had your personal weapon with you even when you went to the latrine, but when you got down that low you send a guy to supply for bandoliers of magazines for your personal weapons. I always carried two M-16 magazines. We got six more bandoliers. We knew if we run lower on the big guns, we're gonna have to shoot M-16's on either side of the gun. We were under fire from a hundred and fifty yards away, mortar and AK-47 and some rockets ever' once in a while. It was a small band, less than fifty of those people, but frightening, very determined, very vicious. We were firing almost direct fire, knocking trees down this big around"—he made a circle with his arms—"so you can see more than fifty yards out . . . We got down that low maybe three times.

"One man from each gun pulled perimeter guard," Ron continued.

"You can't fall asleep—so boring—listening so hard for that sound that you don't want to hear—a stick breaking, leaves rustling—your heart drops down to your toes—should I report it? One night Corporal John P. Seawright and I were walking perimeter. We heard leaves and a stick breaking. He was black as the ace of spades, but he turned white. We stopped and looked at each other. He blurted, 'I hear a goddam Cong out here.' Over the radio, no call sign or nothin'. They called us back in and started firing before we got over the wall. I felt bullets passin' me. A VC bullet hit a sandbag by my hand, a 102 round went right over my head—at times I think your own men will kill ya to keep themselves from getting killed . . .

"We wore what we felt comfortable in out in the field, do fire missions in flipflops, shorts, and bush hats." Ron grinned. This seems reasonable in the 100-degree-plus heat of a firebase with no shade. "This one new LT [pronounced ell-tee, and meaning lieutenant] wanted us to wear boots, socks, pants, belt, T-shirt, and fatigue shirt. He jumped on Seawright and me. Seawright was as close as a brother to me. He was blood. They was no better individual than him. This LT was a Southerner like me, and he hated 'Northern niggers,' and he hated Northern nigger-lovers like me, and he told us so. I told him, 'I hope nothin' never happens to you that you need an honest-to-God friend because you won't have one—I hope you get your ass blowed off the mountain.' When I said that, he said, 'Well, all I can say for you is you're a nigger-lovin' son-of-a-bitch.' At that point John says, 'Man, let it drop.' I knew if I done anything, I'd get in trouble, but I didn't care so I walked into my hooch and got a bar of soap and a sock and didn't really expect him to be there when I came out. He'd done jumped our case, and he'd leave. So I come out and swing the sock and soap and hit him right in the mouth, busted his mouth and knocked two teeth out, and I got an Article 15 [administrative disciplinary action]. He got miraculously shipped out, and I got busted one rank and fined $96 a month for three months, and my services were needed with the Forward Observers."

How common was this kind of racism? In his memoir, *Almost a Layman*, Chaplain Samuel Hoard reported: "A delegation of two black soldiers came to me . . . Black men in their company were not being given fair consideration on promotions and were not being assigned to jobs in the resupply or rear areas when they had only

45 days left before rotating back to the States. They told me that the next time they were scheduled for a 'search and destroy' mission, every black soldier in the company was prepared to stack his arms and refuse orders to move out . . . I went directly to the Battalion CO. I did not think it fair to single out the company CO, so I told the colonel that the problem existed with 'one of your company CO's'. . . . In a conference with all his commanders and their first sergeants, the colonel made it very clear that he would not tolerate any actions or treatment of black soldiers that would give the semblance or suspicion of unfair treatment . . ."

"Yeah, there was lots of racial stuff," a white guy told me. "Soul brothers had their own group. We had a fragging incident against a white sergeant from Mississippi who was a really vocal racist."

"I went to Alpha North [a firebase] on March 31, 1966," Scott Camil told me during our first interview. He drew me a map of the rectangular little base, bunkers around the edge, tents here, guns there. "On April 18, we were overrun. The compound was a rectangle with four-man outposts on the corners which were bunkers made of sandbags and empty ammo boxes full of sand. Each had an M-60, a fifty-caliber machine gun, two guys with automatic M-14's, and boxes of grenades. Claymores set up facing out. We had trip flares and concertina all around the compound. On the outposts two slept inside and two were awake on the top. The first thing I know, trip wires went off *inside* the wire. I was on top of one bunker. As soon as the flare went off, all these people stand up *inside* the fence." All the horror of that moment was in his voice as he said *inside*. "Machine guns open up on us from the mountain behind me, and rockets blew up one of the other posts. I had friends in there." Scott turned away for a moment. "They [the VC] were hitting the other side, too, and coming in the front. They blew up four howitzers and the ammo dump and ran through the tents shooting people. Our post was the first one to open up. Eight and Ten [two other bunkers] waited for permission but no one was there to give it. I guess the sergeant of the guard was grabbed by VC sappers because there was no one in the guard shack." He turned away again, then continued after about a minute, his voice quiet but full of anger. "The *rules* were we couldn't fire without permission, but as soon as I saw them, I started shooting.

I had a fully automatic M-14. The guys down in the bunker started to shoot, too. I saw enemy soldiers on top of Eight, standing over my friends and shooting them." Once more he had to look away. "I had to shoot to keep people off *me*. There must have been two hundred of them. They left thirty bodies. I jumped off the bunker and fought from the ground trying to kill as many as I could . . . The next day we were out on patrols following the blood trails . . . I killed this person. I cut his throat with my knife. At the time I was so mad it didn't bother me at all. I just wanted to kill as many as I could." He looked away again.

"It looks like it bothers you now."

"It all bothers me now," he said. "I made a promise to myself that day that I'd never smile again. I was real bitter." He turned back toward me. "One, because people died following the rules of engagement and trying to get permission to fire. Two, the grenades had tape around them as a *safety precaution*." His voice became a knife. "It had melted in the heat and it wouldn't come off. Four KIA [killed in action], twenty-eight WIA [wounded in action]."

Vietnam was dotted with these little firebases and LZ's. They had names like LZ Two Bits or Firebase Gold. Sometimes they existed a week, sometimes a year, sometimes for the whole war. "Flying in over an LZ once"—Bill Hutchinson looked sad as he spoke—"I could see the jagged French revetment, the Japanese two-man foxholes, and the three-man American foxholes all scarring the hilltop."

Forward bases weren't nice clean places. When your vet tells you he lived in a bunker, don't see a clean concrete German bunker from World War II. In the dry season, everything was covered in dust, and in the wet season everyone was knee-deep in mud. The bunkers started out as foxholes. Even if it was 110 degrees, if a guy was smart he spent every spare minute digging the hole and filling sandbags to pile around it and over it. Roaches, scorpions, centipedes, and rats shared the bunkers with the troops after they'd been there for a while. "I filled so many sandbags. I hated those sandbags. Plastic woven crap. They wouldn't even hold the sand," Bill Hutchinson said.

"They shoulda had two hours of filling sandbags and then five minutes of action. Woulda been more like Vietnam," I heard a guy say as we came out of the movie *Platoon*.

FNG, by Don Bodey, pictures the grim life our grunts endured, detail by detail, the feeling of what it was like to be there. Here's his description of digging a bunker:

> I get hold of a shovel stuck in a mound of mud and jump into the hole that has an inch of water in its bottom . . . The first shovelful causes a sound like the last bit of water leaving a bathtub. My shoulder aches when I lift the shovel and I can feel some of the scabs of my rot break loose. The rain is almost friendly. By the middle of the afternoon the hole is as deep as I am tall . . . and we start filling the bags in the bottom of the hole. Peacock sits on a pile of full ones with an empty one on his head as a hat.

After the digging, the grunts took axes and weapons and went outside the perimeter to cut logs for cover, being careful not to cut down a tree harboring an ant nest or a snake or big banana spider. Then they heaved the logs up on their shoulders, which already ached from all the digging, and humped them back to their hole. They put the logs across the top of the sandbagged walls and then put more sandbags over that to make a roof. One that wouldn't keep a mortar or rocket out. Keep shrapnel out, though, and bullets. "A B-40 RPG [rocket-propelled grenade] would splinter a log eighteen inches in diameter," one marine told me.

Each foxhole, as it graduated into a bunker, had a field of fire that someone cleared, grunts with machetes, engineers with explosives, tanks and APC's by busting the brush. The fields of fire were supposed to overlap so there were no gaps. Rolls of concertina wire made it harder to crawl up and kill someone in the night. Harder, not impossible. The VC could and did crawl through them. Flares and claymores were set out to be triggered when attackers crawled into the trip wires. Claymores also could be set off electrically. Sometimes thunderstorms set them off. Trip flares and claymores had to be checked every day to be sure the VC hadn't crawled up and disconnected them or turned them around in preparation for a surprise attack. "Charlie was always trying to slow us down," Joe Pearson said. "Mines. Stolen claymores. Mortar attacks at night, small arms. They sneak up at night—we had claymores about twenty-five yards in front of us—and turn 'em around and then make a noise, and you set it off and hit yourself. We got wise to that and painted the back white. Charlie would crawl up and paint the front white and turn it around so you'd still blow yourself up. There are two prongs on the bottom which you shove into the ground, so we took a grenade and pull the pin and shove the claymore down to hold it. When Charlie picked it up to turn it around, boom, dead Charlie. That worked for a while. When we moved them, you'd slip your hand under and hold the grenade— So Charlie starts putting an extra grenade under ours."

If there was a latrine, the barrels of shit had to be hauled out, doused with fuel, and burned. Sometimes there were cooks making do in a tent. Clerks worked in the HQ tent or bunker, depending on how hot it was on that particular forward base, and I don't mean temperature. Sometimes there was an aid station. Since all the trees were cut down, it was as hot as hell. In the dry season everything was coated with dust: food, clothes, men. When the helicopter re-supplied the forward base, that brought a dust storm with it. During the monsoon the place was a sea of mud. The one good thing about it was there was a perimeter between you and the enemy.

Some small units lived right in with the Vietnamese. The CRIP (combined reconaissance and information platoon) at Ho Nai, where Michael Costello spent the last part of his tour, was one. "We lived in a French fort in the middle of Ho Nai." Earlier, when the 199th had arrived in Vietnam, Costello recalled, "We lost some guys right away for the CRIP in Ho Nai. A lifer sergeant who acted like the toughest motherfucker there was, but was scared shitless. CRIP pacification force looked like good duty . . . livin' in a town . . . three of them re-upped to get it. When I was a LRRP [long-range reconaissance patrol] we walked into Ho Nai a couple of times and had to deal with those assholes with clean uniforms in the CRIP team. We had twenty guys in the CRIP at Ho Nai, three to five back at the 199th base fucking off at our barracks . . . The CRIP officers changed a lot. They were mostly incompetent. They sent us the worst they had. Naturally, they wanted the competent ones with the line companies. The CRIP sergeants were lifers about thirty days short so they stayed on base. The LT and the platoon sergeant only came out in the daytime. They never spent the night at the bridge. We were on our own . . . When the brass came out to visit, they'd bring in a line company to secure one end of the village, and we had to wear our steel pot and flak vest, get all the PF's [Vietnamese Popular Forces] to go out on a mission. It pissed the gooks off because they all had day jobs . . . We had a bunker with a big radio and generator in this old French fort. Every night we went out of the fort to each end of the village. At the north end was a small bridge, and every night Americans went down there with the PF's [called ruff-puffs for their fighting abilities] . . . They had fights every now and then with the VC . . . The whole town got blasted in August, a major fucking attack. They killed the first chief and his whole family—women, kids, pigs . . . His balls and pecker were sewn in his mouth and his eyes were cut out . . . They hanged some PF's and burned them."

Special Forces also had small bases out there in the boonies, where an A Team, twelve men, trained the natives to fight the VC or NVA. Dennis Le Sage was stationed at an A-Team camp at Polei Kleng in 1967–1968, training three different groups of Montagnards. "A camp on top of a hill. There was a triangular emplacement, barbed wire, concertina, claymores, toe poppers." In answer to my question, he explained toe poppers: "A tiny explosive device, a mine which blows a piece of your foot off. The VC used bullets and nails. We had manufactured ones. It's cheaper, and as good as blowing a foot off. The camp was on the hill, the airstrip on the bottom, and the ville across from the airstrip. There were three triangles within the camp: outer, inner, and inner-inner. The Americans lived in the inner-inner [where they had toilets and refrigerators]. Five or six Vietnamese Special Forces, the Montagnard strike force, ranking NCO's and officers, Tomstocks, the elite guard, and scouts lived in the inner triangle. The Montagnard grunts lived in the outer one, three hundred soldiers and about two hundred family members . . . Families lived near the door of the perimeter bunkers facing the inner trench. The gunports were facing out. The trenches inside each triangle were interconnected but we could block between the triangles. We figured ten percent of our people were VC. We provided good training." He laughed and shrugged. "They were all mercenaries except the Vietnamese Special Forces. Ky had agreed the Montagnards were not citizens of Vietnam so they didn't have to do military service and also couldn't vote, so they moved from camp to camp. We had three tribes working and living in the camp . . . Every Sunday a guy dropped mortars on us at twelve o'clock and five o'clock. He never hit the camp, always long or short. We'd always find the baseplate mark. Finally one week he landed a round in camp in the doorway of a bunker and five little girls got shrapnel wounds." Dennis was the medic so he took care of them.

"We'd send two Americans out on patrol with fifty to a hundred 'Yards [Montagnards]. Every four to five weeks you go out on patrol for a week. We continued on out for three or four days and came back in a circle sweep. Last day out we camped on top of a hill and next day went back down the same trail. We got ambushed on the way back down the hill. They shot the Vietnamese, not the 'Yards: 'Yards never hurt each other." He laughed again. "We'd go out on ambushes, some 'Yard would drop pots and pans or set off a claymore by accident. We very seldom had a good ambush or got ambushed. Anyhow, they shot two or three Vietnamese. We called in Medevac, chopped bamboo and put them on an extractor, called in a FAC [forward air controller, a pilot in a small observation plane] to spot for us. We're getting ready to go when someone says, 'You know what? Safest place in the world for those VC is on top of the hill we came down,' so we went back up the hill and surprised them eating . . . My chogey boy—"

"Chogey boy?"

"A chogey boy was a guy from the ville, not a mercenary. For one dollar a day he'd carry your backpack and dig your hole and cook your meal . . . I always hired the village coffin maker because he couldn't die until he'd made all the coffins for the village. Anyhow, he was leaning against a tree eating a banana watching the war . . . The FAC's finally flew over and dropped grenades on the hill, which ended the battle."

Another kind of small unit designed to win the hearts and minds of the Vietnamese was the marine CAP (combined action platoon).

"After 6 months in the bush," Marty Comer, a navy corpsman with the marines, told me, "I left 2/4 and went to the 3d Motor Transport Battalion in Quang Tri. My first experience with civilians, shit burners, hooch maids. We paid them. That was when I got a real grasp of what we were doing over there. We *were* their economy. Medical CAP (Civic Action Program): Two times a week we go to Quang Tri and treat civilians. Kids come in with little cuts and sores to get it washed, iodined and get a Band-Aid. One in fifty had something serious. We'd treat one to two hundred people in an afternoon. The Medcap consisted of a gunner, a driver, an interpreter, two or three corpsmen. We gave out three or four hundred bars of soap for impetigo and other skin diseases. We taught them to bathe and how to take pills. Next time we came back we'd see the same four hundred bars of soap for sale. No progress. No feeling of accomplishment. Just see what you'd *given* to help them up for sale. Money was more important to their parents than the kid was. Occasionally a real doc would go and give complete physicals. He found more but unless we took 'em to a field hospital . . ." He gestured helplessly. "One girl had an ear caked with pus which would have gone to her brain and killed her. We took her to the hospital and irrigated her ear, cleaned it out. We used injectable antibiotics because if you left them with oral penicillin or tetracycline they sold it to the VC or local doctors."

Archie was in a Mobile Combined Action Platoon from June 1969 to March 1970. "The later years," as he put it. "Out of 5,000 CAP marines, only 800-plus are left. A CAP was supposed to work with the ARVN to train the PF . . . The PF was equipped with new M-16's, grenades, helmets, flak jackets, and the K-bars [knives] we never got." (Much different from the Puffs of 68, of whom Le Sage said, "Out of three hundred people in the Ruff Battalion, there were five with automatic M-16 rifles. Less than one dozen M-1 carbine automatics. All the rest were M-1 carbines. They had two thirty-caliber machine guns, two sixty-millimeter mortar teams, one M-60, and one M-79.")

"We worked close to, but not with, the Vietnamese," Archie's letter went on. "The older villagers, if they had an opinion, didn't want us around. As a percent, it would be about one of the adult population that we could trust enough to call friend. A typical day: If you weren't on patrol, you had a 4-hour perimeter watch and sleep came accordingly . . . The CAP was supposed to be 3 fire teams (12 men), a grenadier (M-79), a squad leader and corpsman. We usually averaged around 8–10 people. [Marine policy was not to take people with minor wounds who would be coming back off the roster, so most

marine combat units seem to have been chronically undermanned.]
We were to move to a different part of the village each day. We
usually moved every 2, 3, 4 weeks. A village was a bunch of straw
hooches planted next to a river surrounded by paddies . . . just
paths, no grass, no street lights, no electricity, no bathrooms (except
for the pathways). A foot of dust in summer—a foot of muck in
winter.

"The day may be spent sleeping, exploring, mingling, practicing
our Vietnamese, teaching weapons use to the PF's, getting high,
getting laid, getting beer, getting back to the big city, writing letters,
sleeping, eating, taking shots at the rats, visiting friends in other
units, waiting for a chopper if it was mail/hot-chow day (once a week
if all went well), sleeping, checking I.D. cards, looking for a new
place to move, insuring our present locale is safe, playing volleyball
(Red Cross sent a set), cleaning/checking our weapons and radios.
We as a unit carried two M-60's with replacement barrels; 3 radios
(PRC-25) with batteries; 60-mm mortar with a box each of HE [high
explosive], WP [white phosphorous] and illumination rounds; indi-
vidually: M-16 or M-14 with more than 400 rounds (mandated), more
than 4 grenades, 1 claymore, a week's worth of C-rations and clothes
and any personal belongings (camera, radio, food from home, etc.).

"This was an easy day. When Charlie would call us on our classified
freqs and threaten us, the day would take a turn for the worse. When
the Capt/1st LT would call and say he was coming out to visit, that
made for a bad day. When reporters/VIP's visited, that was bad.
(They'd issue new "camo" uniforms to be turned in when the VIP's
left.) Whenever the people didn't go straight out to the paddies or
were fidgety, things weren't good. Charlie could be sitting in our
CP [command post] and we wouldn't know, but the people inad-
vertently let us know we should move. When the monsoons come
and you wake up to 4 feet of water and no boat, the day's going to
be rough. Things aren't going well when a man picks up a propaganda
notice and uses his flashlight for a better view. He was blown in two
by a rocket. That was probably my worst experience, as it happened
so soon in-country. It also taught me a lot. I don't feel we were
fighting a war. We were just trying to stay alive in one little piece
of Vietnam for 12 mos . . . The VC organization was improving rapidly. They would work the paddies by day and fight at night. I

probably rubbed elbows with the same persons who would try to kill me. The ARVN's were supposed to be the equivalent of the NVA, but as with anything American money touches, they too were spoiled. If they didn't want to fight, they just went AWOL. If you wanted artillery, they would give you every round they had, without effect. Their shooting was that bad.

"I spent 9 mos 10 days in Vietnam. 23 days in CAP school, 7 hosp. (dysentery), 10 days for R&R, 2 days in rear when we were flooded out. The rest was spent in the 'bush,' the 'village,' the 'hamlets,' etc. Combat is great. It's like playing war until you realize it's deadly. But with a small unit such as the CAP, one is afforded a chance to challenge on a one–one basis, to out-think the enemy, and in the spirit of that great American tradition give the other guy the edge, a head start, if you will, because you know you can still beat him. I peroxided my hair blonde, almost white, and would sit in the open while the full moon lit me up . . . simply to draw Charlie out. They thought I was dinky dao (loco plus) and therefore some spooky spirit to be shunned. Combat in the right frame of mind is child's play with grown-up toys."

"After my R&R," Ric Hill told me, "I volunteered for being in charge of eleven marines, two outposts at a refugee camp on the Qua Viet River. Corporal Ric in charge." He laughed. "We hung out in this watchtower during the day. The LT in charge of us was five miles away. We watched during the day, and the Civilian National Guard from the ville was supposed to stand guard at night. They had an ARVN commanding officer. I made a zig-zag path to the bunkers with concertina so they couldn't run away; at least they couldn't run straight. I buried claymores at every angle. If they ran, I was going to kill them. I got up the next morning and all the claymores were facing the door of my hut. After six weeks, I got a message with the mail to come back to the outfit, me and a black guy with three days left. It was a new CO [commanding officer]. I had seventeen months in-country, and this new captain wants to make me a squad leader; says the same to the black guy. I said no . . . He said, 'Be a squad leader, or be a rifleman.' I left on the chopper and went back to the outpost. Three days later I was made a supply sergeant, but they fined me $52 for being AWOL."

Ric's story illustrates something about the war between the lifers (career officers and NCO's) and the non-lifers. Ric's new CO wanted to put him back in the field, although he'd been in the field for more than a year, and was wounded, too. Ric was not afraid of the field; he was pissed. The established practice in Vietnam was that people who had "paid their dues" and had seniority got jobs in the rear. What was the officer thinking of? Was he going to win the war by sending Ric out again?

Let me repeat, not all officers were like that, but I've heard and read about this type more than the other. How were they dealt with?

One answer was fragging: "The men tried to kill the captain two times," one soldier told me. "They rigged a grenade in his mailbox and blew up the orderly room, and they rolled a grenade off the roof. He was gung-ho."

Another guy said, "My roommate had been in sixteen years, a green beret, had a Ku Klux Klan flag up on his wall. The enlisted men tried to kill him regularly because he was always fucking them over. Before I left Vietnam, he told me, 'I would have been killed this year if it wasn't for you. None of those enlisted swine would throw a grenade in this room while you were sleeping between me and the door.' "

Exercises

We've gone a little further into what Vietnam was like this time. Think about what you have learned. Here are some ideas.

The next time you drive anywhere, imagine that there are snipers along the road. Imagine that the road may blow up at any minute. Look at the passing cars. Will one blow up? Could you try to rescue the occupants if it did? Could you wrench open the door of a burning car? What if you lose your legs? Or just think about having to drive all day, every day, with a sore rubbed raw at the base of your spine.

You can do the same sort of exercise by placing yourself in an imaginary aircraft. Go to an air show. All the ones I've been to have various military aircraft open to the public. Getting inside them gave me a lot to think about. All those instruments to watch. Look at how thin the skin of an aircraft is. Get someone to show you where the guns were. Imagine shooting one. Think about flying with people shooting at you. Think how hot it would be loading and unloading; think of the maintenance; think of being responsible for one of these.

The next time you are in a boat, look for all the places onshore from which you could be ambushed. Think about sinking. Think about the fuel igniting like the ammo in Vietnam. As you pass another boat, think how it would be if someone on it opened fire.

Go sit on a treeless hill or in a field in the middle of summer. Sweat. Think how visible you are. Try to scare yourself with the idea that someone is watching you and planning to kill you. Think about a bullet coming toward you, or the roar of a rocket coming out of the bush. Do the same thing in the middle of a rainstorm if you are ambitious, or at night. Think about being overrun, about savage little men hacking your body apart after you're dead. Think about thinking about this for a whole day, or a whole week. How would you feel after a month? A year?

Think about doing heavy physical labor for a year in a place where there isn't enough water to wash, only an outhouse to use, and you have to live in a hole in the ground.

I suspect you can make up any other execises you need for this section, because if you've read this far you're beginning to understand that Vietnam was a hard place to be.

4

Going Forth: Aviation and Mechanized Combat

Beyond the pipeline and the forward bases, your vet was *in the bush, out*. This chapter is about people who got to go out and fight in vehicles: helicopters, planes, tanks, armored personnel carriers, and patrol boats. Fighting from a vehicle has advantages and disadvantages. Whatever armor there is offers a sense of protection, at least until the first time it stops working. Mobility gives a sense of security, too: I can get out of here. A nice feeling to have in a hot situation. Balancing these feelings is the knowledge that fighting vehicles are targets. Tactically, they are bigger than a single grunt, which makes them easier to see and hit. Strategically, they are an attractive target because they represent an investment in time—to build and repair them—and money. Riding or flying around in a big target can wear you down.

Fighting from a vehicle, particularly from the air, also distances you from the results of your activities. Perhaps that makes it easier to do.

Helicopters

The helicopter symbolizes the Vietnam War. Landing zones and firebases could be located anywhere because the helicopters could go anywhere. Guys like my husband flew troops into hot LZ's where bullets flew up at the helicopters like rain, into cold LZ's where there was no fire, into LZ's where an ambush was sprung only after all the ships were on the ground. Then they came back with supplies, more troops, flew the wounded out, and flew in replacements and

94

more ammo and supplies. Bob flew a slick, meaning a Huey transport, in contrast to a gunship. Slicks could carry about ten armed and supplied troopers. The best way to shoot down a helicopter was to shoot the two pilots. Behind the pilots, the door gunner and crew chief manned M-60 machine guns pointed out either door.

"First, I went to the 283d Dustoff [medevac]," one medic told me, "and flew with them . . . I loved to fly but it was no fun flying into LZ's. You find that out the first day: You don't want to be there. 'What are you doing, you idiot?' " He grinned. "I was loading a guy on a chopper on an LZ with a rope tied to my ass. A round went off and hit the ship. I thought to myself, 'This guy's heavy.' I thought I'd pulled my shoulder. [Shrapnel had hit him.] It was wet and burning. No big deal, but it hit the nerve so I couldn't open my hand."

When Bob was in the Cav, medevacs couldn't go in if an LZ was hot because they lost too many aircraft to ground fire, so the slick pilots went in instead. When he first got back, I asked Bob about what made people brave, what made them risk their lives to go in under fire to get the wounded when they didn't have to. I figured it must be some glorious feeling. I still remember his answer: "You're tired all the time from flying too many hours, and someone comes up on the radio needing help. You don't think about it. You just do it. It's not courage. It's your job." He looked at me to see if I understood.

"What about all those medals, then?" He had been recommended for two DFC's, and had a Bronze Star and a lot of Air Medals with a little V on them for valor.

"Yeah," he said. "They should have called them 'Too-tired-to-give-a-crap with V-device.' "

I'm not going to go into a lot of detail about flying a slick. If you want to know more, read *Chickenhawk*. Your library probably has a copy.

Please note that flying is strictly a voluntary activity, and an elite one, because not everyone can do it. Talking about helicopter pilots, Jon Anderson, an operations officer with the 4th Infantry Division, told me, "Because of where I worked and the Officers' Club, God, I used to see helicopter pilots all the time . . . They actually had silk scarves and they were the loudest and the funniest and the most endearing and they drank the most and they stayed up the latest and they still got up the next morning and they flew, and they flew admirably. You know they'd give their nuts for you, you know, they really did . . . They were just priceless people."

Hueys, turbine-powered marvels, were the workhorses of the war, but other types of helicopters were used, too. I could hardly believe that while Bob was flying his Huey in the Central Highlands in 1965 to 1966, marine pilots up north were trying to do the same thing with antiquated CH-34's, which look and fly like a large tadpole. Some marine pilots used to go to the Primary Helicopter School at Fort Wolters, Texas, where Bob taught. I remember them sitting in the Officers' Club at the bar with their short hair and straight spines, offended because they were getting the best helicopter training there was—*from the army*—not even able to relax over a drink. If I'd known they were going to be flying CH-34's, I would have cried.

"All we had was two CH-34's," one marine told me, "which could each lift four troops at a time, so we took LZ's with eight men. As FO [forward observer], I always went in with the first eight so I could call in artillery and secure the LZ for the rest. 34's only had one door so the VC knew where to shoot when you were getting off.

"I was hit [wounded] on Nov. 4, 1968," he continued, "and med-evaced on a 34, and the gunner was holding me in the chopper and shooting. We went down." Pause. "When it crashed, I was lying —" He stopped, then finally said, "The deck was the side and the door was the roof. It was on fire. I *gave up* and watched it burn." He sounded guilty when he said *gave up*, as if he blamed himself. "My own leg was flipped up on my chest, strangling me with my own boot. The corpsman came back in and shoved me up over the deck and down. Another one flew me to Da Nang . . . You can't give up," he explained. "I remember the nurse screaming at me that I had no blood pressure. I remember they were trying to cut my jungle boots off and I was fighting them."

"In 1967–68, I flew OH-23 Raven Helicopters," Thomas Barnes wrote me. That reliable old workhorse helicopter was the trainer in Primary Helicopter School when Bob went through and later when he taught there. It has a reciprocating engine with no hydraulics, like driving a Model-T compared to the Cadillac Huey. "This was a three-place bird, pilot in the center, gunner on his right and observer [FO] on the left. The observer would handle artillery fire if needed. The gunner was armed with a free M-60 machine gun and all the smoke and grenades we could carry.

"In the first year in Vietnam, I was shot down 13 times," his letter continued. "Walked away from all of them without a scratch. Typical mission was up at dawn, mission brief, preflight and out to an operations area. Once there, recon of area with wing man and overhead guns and blues." Translation: He flew slow and low, and if anyone shot at him, the gunships and blues, elite scout troops, pounced. He was the bait. No wonder he was shot down thirteen times. "Hot refuels [putting in fuel without shutting the engine off], back in the air, most days were 8 to 14 hours of flying." Other small helicopters, OH-6's (loaches) and H-13's, the old Bell whirlybird, were used for the same kind of scouting missions.

Medevac helicopters served as air ambulances. Dean K. Phillips put it this way: "Because of advances in medical techniques and the courage of helicopter medevac pilots and crews, Vietnam vets survived crippling wounds that would have been fatal due to shock or loss of blood in previous wars." Amputations and crippling wounds to legs and feet were "300 percent higher than in World War II and 70 percent higher than in Korea." U.S. government statistics say it was fifteen minutes from wound to hospital in Vietnam. Fifteen minutes may have been the average, as determined by skillful government statistics, but in my random sampling of vets, I've met plenty of people who did not get medevaced for hours. The wounded vet who was shot down and trapped in the CH-34 had lain on the ground, firing, for eight hours before rescuers could get to him and drag him to the helicopter, because of enemy fire.

"We got a night call to cover a medevac," Dennis Collett, a gunship pilot, told me about a mission that not only illustrates the waiting some people had to live through, but also some of the non-combat dangers of flying in Vietnam. "Monsoon season, soaking-wet takeoff. Head south. Normally within five to ten minutes we'd see the lights of Tan Son Nhut or Saigon. Fifteen minutes, no lights. I'm scared because of the weather. My wing man was this gung-ho first lieutenant flying first ship. I call him to turn back. He says no. Five to ten minutes more, still no lights. We're covering a medevac seventy miles south of Saigon for a guy wounded that day. They've been trying to find someone to cover it all day because of the weather. [Medevacs had to have gunship cover to protect them.] Finally, totally lost, we turned and went back to base . . . We lost our lights [going in to land] and we went in dark in the rain. For some reason I saw something blacker than black where it shouldn't have been, a tree, pulled the pitch [making the helicopter rise] and went down in the ville of Cu Chi, hit the left skid and rolled on the left side and the engine shut itself down. Even though we had a full load of JP [fuel] and thirty-two rockets, five hundred rounds of forty-millimeter and five thousand rounds in the minigun"—he sighed—"there was no fire. I looked up, said 'You okay?' to the peter pilot [co-pilot]. We released our seatbelts and fell out. We were a half mile outside the perimeter [of the base at Cu Chi] in the middle of Cu Chi village. Heard the tower ask our wing man, 'Where's your wing man?' 'Right behind me,' he answers. 'No, he's not.' So he came out looking for me . . . We're about ten feet from a hooch, walked over and poppa-san pointed us to the highway, fifty to a hundred meters through the huts. We're scared shitless by that time and then have to stand out in the middle of the highway. A ship with a searchlight passed over us three times before they saw us and picked us up. They brought a tank unit up to secure the Cobra. I was bruised up and sore. Next morning I had a flight physical and went back out flying." But the wounded guy waited all day and all night. Wounded often did wait in the monsoon, or in the deep jungle, or when there was too much fire for a medevac.

"I volunteered to go to Swing Wing to be where the action was. I had turned nineteen in Chu Lai," Doc Jack, a navy corpsman with the marines, told me. "I went to Phu Bai. We had a squadron each of Hueys, CH-34's and CH-46's." CH-46's were a short version of the Chinook, with two rotors, a big ramp into the back, and the ability to carry about seventeen troops. "Fifty percent of the time when we went in for casualties, it would be a hot LZ, gunships circling above for cover, firing. I didn't always go on the same type of helicopter. I was wounded on a '46, but I also went in Hueys, and I hated the '34's which were antiques, slow and couldn't carry as much . . . On medevac, it's casualties every time. Some could be walk-in, some could be splattered."

"Tell me about being wounded."

"It was overcast, a low ceiling, misty rain, felt cold. I remember I was late to the flight line. I was up late, hadn't gotten sleep the last week [the first week of the Tet Offensive, in 1968]. We had a lot of missions, in and out all day. Last mission was at four P.M., a call for three emergency medevacs—three wounded—near Hue. We're not going up too high because it's only seven miles, flying low and evasive, back and forth . . . have a cigarette before we get into this. Not too far out of Phu Bai, I heard those first snaps, grabbed my rifle and stuck it out the window, shot two times, turned and looked in the gunner's face. Panic in his eyes. I looked back at the ground. It was dark and overcast. I saw muzzle flashes, lots of muzzle flashes. Then I got hit. The bullet came through the bottom of the helicopter, hit me in the thigh."

"When a bullet hits, what is it like?" I asked.

"Well, I hit the roof of the chopper and fell back down to the floor. The gunner got hit, a grazing wound, but he kept firing the sixty. They were firing. I'm screaming 'I'm hit! I'm hit' . . . The gunner came over and ripped open my pants and saw the blood. I felt shock, surprise, numbness, and then pain like someone had hit me with a baseball bat. I knew it had hit the bone. I told him to give me some dressings and how to put on dressings and splint my leg with my M-14. Fuel was leaking—like a mist in my face. We're still flying. I had a sense of impending doom. They said don't worry about it. Seemed like we were flying for a long time. I remember wondering, how much further back? 'If we put this fucking thing down, we'll never get it back up,' I heard someone say. The gunner asked, 'Doc, how are you?' I said okay. I remember wiping JP fuel off my face. I remember oil draining down the sides of the ship and lots of bullet holes. I remember seeing the back of the pilots' heads. Demko had a scar from a burn. They're fighting the controls. One gunner said, 'Doc, we're gonna have to put it down.' They put me back on the ramp. My head was on the edge of the ramp. 'When we hit the ground, we'll drag you right out. We're gonna get you out and set up a quick perimeter.' I felt the ship toss. I remember looking up and they're unmounting the guns. Then the nose slammed down, the ass-end went up and over, and I flew out the back. I remember flying through the air and hitting water face first. Wham! And I went under. When I came up and looked back, I saw fire rolling toward me and went back under. I pulled myself through the rice plants in the water and up on the dike. I didn't even realize I was burnt. I lost the rifle splint. I remember not wanting to look at the 'copter— forty to fifty yards away. I avoided looking at it. I remember seeing movement in the treeline, and I was afraid I'd be taken prisoner. I decided to spit in their face so they'd kill me. I thought of my mother not handling this. My childhood, girlfriend, father. Little fun things. Baseball with my Dad. Being hit with a pitch in a Little League baseball game, and my Dad hopping the fence to come to me. My stormy senior year. I was headed for big trouble so I went into the military. I'd never get a chance to make it up to my parents for the dumb things I did. I couldn't see anyone else. I thought, 'How the fuck will I get back to Phu Bai?' Maybe I laid there fifteen minutes. It seemed like eternity. I couldn't move too much. I was scared: If they don't find me before dark— I heard choppers. Under the fatigue shirt I had a University of Illinois sweatshirt. I took off the jungle fatigues and pulled off the sweatshirt and waved it. They came over, guns blazing, banked. One of them came and landed twenty yards away, shouting for me to come on. I'm trying to yell my leg's broke, but I had a dislocated jaw. A big black guy ran to me, snatched me up and threw me over his shoulder. As he runs, I'm looking at my bird, my head bouncing. I heard it burn, but I wouldn't look at it, not wanting to know. He threw me into the Huey and jumped on. They're firing. I'm covered with gunk and shit. Rice-paddy water in my open wound. I'd given myself a shot of morphine back on the ship when I was shot. They gave me a cigarette. 'Where's my crew?' I asked. 'Forget it.' They talked to me: 'Hang in there. Stay with us.' Then I remember being on a stretcher and four guys ran me into the hospital. I remember sitting up and they were cutting the clothes off me. I felt something was wrong with my face. I was slammed with another morphine. I read later in my chart that I was resuscitated so I died there for a few minutes. When I woke up I was in the 106th Army Hospital in Yokohama, Japan."

Medevac wasn't supposed to be combat, but it often was.

Helicopter gunships supported the guys on the ground by trying to blow away whoever was attacking them. "We used B-models as gunships," Bob told me. B-models were an early version of the Huey, and as the D- and H-models came out, the less-powerful B's were used as gunships, armed with machine guns and rocket pods. Matt Brennan (three tours) said the B's flew lower and slower and gave really good support.

Dennis Collett flew Cobra gunships for the 25th Aviation Battalion, 25th Infantry, out of Cu Chi in 1969. Pilots preferred Cobras, which look like a shark, full of power, and are armed to the teeth. The Cobra became the common gunship in 1968. At the winglets, it was five feet wide. Inside, where the pilots sat, it measured thirty-six inches. The peter pilot, sometimes called the gunner, sat in front and did most of the firing because the front-seat controls were hard to fly with. The aircraft commander, who did most of the flying, sat behind and above him. "I flew to the war and I flew back from the war. It wasn't like the grunts." Dennis repeated what everyone else had said. "I was lucky . . . My first Cobra mission was at night flying with a warrant officer who was fourteen months in-country, a pretty sharp guy. He saved my ass. We got into contact firing at the ground—made our run and came back out. All I could see were red lights coming at me. He hit the pedals and the aircraft shifted to the side and they missed us . . . Tracers! I didn't have time to get scared. After, maybe. Aggravated, yes.

"Our mission was to support the infantry. When they got into trouble they called us. We had two ships, four pilots, on three-minute standby on the flight line at all times . . . Half a mile away at our unit, four more were on five-minute standby. If the guys in the ready shack went, they came up . . .

"We did a twelve-hour shift for three days in a row and then had two days off. The next time it was night shift . . . Sometimes we didn't fly at all, sometimes we flew the whole time . . . We had a firebase on the Cambodian border moved three times in two weeks. The third time we put it right in the middle of a route from Cambodia. I spent dawn to dusk flying a slick. We moved six artillery pieces and the whole place was ready to fight that night. I pulled guns [flew a gunship] that night. At 9:30 P.M. we circled the firebase. Twenty miles east we were watching them come over the border so we went back and refueled. Took about fifteen minutes and then we could be on station for an hour and a half. On the radio we told the CO to give us about thirty seconds and pop a flare, and we started our run.

They were on the south side. He popped the flare and we went on from 11:30 until dawn . . . The body count was three hundred and fifty and we lost one LP [listening post] and fifteen Americans. Lots of blood trails went back across the border."

Al DeMailo, a three-tour gunship pilot, sent Bob a T-shirt that said DEATH FROM ABOVE, but gunships were also hope from above, life from above for the grunts. "Ninety percent of the time I couldn't see the target," Dennis continued. "They'd radio 'Receiving fire from the hedgerow' and you'd blow it away . . . We realized they were the ones on the ground. Two times we got a hassle from a REMF [rear-echelon motherfucker] colonel thirty miles away trying to tell us what to do. We told 'im to shut up, we were working for the people in the field . . . One time we caught some enemy going from Cambodia toward Saigon in a rice paddy covered with rice mats which didn't match the color of the paddy . . . sitting ducks . . . sixty-five body count. It was one of the few times I saw people.

"We'd get ready for our runs at fifteen hundred feet, one ship behind the other . . . Aim toward the target at a twenty- to thirty-degree angle, seventy-five degrees if it was real heavy vegetation, firing down into the trees. The team leader would start the run, firing. The second helicopter is ready to run when the first breaks away from the target. That's when you're vulnerable. You're only three feet wide, but you're a big target from the side. The other helicopter covers you, tips his nose and starts firing. He'd climb, and I'd make my run. He'd be back up and cover me by the time I'd finished."

"On my second tour [1971]," Thomas Barnes wrote, "I was in Delta Troop, 1/1 Cav . . . I really loved the Cobra. My last mission: had a heavy Cobra in a standard 6-ship recon team. The target area had lots of bunkers and when we set up a racetrack [a type of attack formation] on this one bunker complex, another one on the side of a hill opened up on us with a .51 cal. Took about 18 hits, several in the ammo bay which cooked off some of the 7.62 ammo [his own bullets]. Several rounds came up through the floor, hit the gunner and me in the legs and jammed the cyclic. We put the bird down in a field. Ended up stateside. [Seriously wounded people were sent stateside.] Never went back. We made friends (perhaps foolishly) the first tour, but not the second. I felt like I spent the whole 6 months alone the second time. I was really discouraged about the war. I knew that as a country we didn't want to win it, just keep making and selling arms. The war had become good for business."

Besides flying the helicopter, pilots were also responsible for checking over their ships before they flew, preflighting them. Failure to do so could be fatal. Two guys Bob saw didn't notice the red X in the helicopter logbook, nor the fact that the control rods were disconnected. When they cranked up the Huey, the blades sliced off their heads. Pilot error.

"Cobra crew chiefs didn't fly," Dennis Collett told me. "They were on standby with us to get us off the ground and meet us . . . They did preventive maintenance . . . When we were coming back, we called ahead and they met us at the ammo depot to help us rearm so we're ready for the next mission."

On Huey slicks, crew chiefs and door gunners had a rough job: Besides providing maintenance, they also went flying around in a target, hanging out the doors shooting the machine guns, their life in the hands of the pilot. "The first few days is just getting familiar with the job, door gunner." Frank Hewitt flew in Bob's old unit, the 48th Aviation Company, in 1970–1971. "Gunners floated unless a crew chief liked you. When we went across the border in '71, I got a permanent AC [aircraft] so I knew what to expect. November to February, I was a gunner. In four months we went from Ninh Hoa to Lane Air Field in An Son supporting the 129th. The week after Thanksgiving took a flight of us to Pleiku and worked out of Camp Holloway for a month with the 170th doing a lot of FOB [flying over the border] to clean up in Cambodia where we were standing down—going in and destroying vehicles. After New Year's, we had a two-week stand-down at Ninh Hoa to bring the ships up to one hundred percent. The major called us in by platoon. 'I can't tell you where we're going but we're moving to Dong Ha.' We were asked to sign voluntary flying slips for across-the-border missions and couldn't write home about it. We went into Laos February twenty-something, 1971. For two days we flew to Khe Sanh and PZ [pickup zone] Kilo, worked with ARVN's. I hated them. When we jumped off, every gun and slick, it was a relay race: seven ARVN with gear per trip, constant ferry . . . On the second sortie I noticed the dinks were stealing from us . . . Going back, we hear the first flight going into

[LZ] Hotel One landed in a base camp bivouac area where an NVA regiment was eating lunch. They lost the first four birds going into the LZ. The second day back into Laos, the shit hit the fan. Almost had the feeling of wetting my pants going out of an LZ, taking fire from everywhere. First ship in wakes 'em up. Second they sight in. Third catches hell. The next two–three months I wasn't coping very well. I remember parts. I was smoking smack. They caught me one night. Sergeant Carter—I missed my preflight—chewed my ass. I'd been shot down twice so they gave me a break—straighten up and get my act together. A crew chief from North Carolina from the top of the mountains gave me my break. Jake said, 'Ah'll fly with him.' Zero-one-six was his bird. Me, him, and Ron Toothman, Aircraft Commander, flew the next month together. I got my act together . . . On one extraction, these ARVN's, I'll never forget, like ants on a sugar pile tryin' to get on the birds, climbed up each other's backs. We watched them pull a 101st ship down into it, but it recovered. We ended up going to a clean LZ . . . One bird ahead got shot down. Someone else went in to get 'em and we gave cover. Went down close to a creek bank and took fire. A Cobra popped up and helped . . . We had plywood on the deck, felt it jump, knew we took a hit but not how bad. We climbed out, heard the idiot beeper: transmission oil pump failure. Smitty [the pilot] called Mayday— According to Bell you can fly one half-hour with no oil pressure. According to the Army, put it on the *ground*. Ning, ning, ning! the idiot light is going . . . Smitty climbs while we have oil pressure. Got up to where we could see the border. The trick to this is to keep a load on it all the way down. We fell through the last twenty feet. Dropped in the middle of a ring of APC's . . . We went back out the next day and worked in Laos till June . . .

"We caught two dinks on a sandbar"—I've asked him how being a door gunner, shooting people, felt—"bothered me a little bit. Felt angry in some ways. Upset for myself. After we got back it turned my stomach. I'd seen people hit, killed, some burnt up. More or less when I done it, I was getting even . . . I seen a ship [Huey] hit: on its side on the side of a mountain. In three seconds, it's on fire. Seen the crew chief get out. He's on fire, and there's *nothin'* we could do." The look on his face was indescribable. "I ended up with something like twenty-two [kills]. Got to the point where if I caught one

in the open it was all over but the burying. It didn't bother me."
His voice was full of pain. "The first time it hurt. I was only eighteen
years old. I had returned fire but never saw anyone shot. We caught
them two on the sandbar that day. Watched the tracers of the sixty
walk right up the sand to 'em. One guy went thump. The second
guy looked like he wanted to throw his hands up. Smitty says, 'Get
him.' I did." He didn't say anything for a while, then continued: "I
was becoming an animal, no washing water, slept in the mud in our
clothes. I felt bad about it, but it got to the point I enjoyed it. We'd
get down low level and fly rivers. Asking for it. I'm here and you
can't get me. I'm invulnerable.

"Sometimes you sleep on the deck. Dark when you get up. Check
the fuel level. Check the forty-two-degree and ninety-degree gear-
boxes, oil levels, transmission oil, engine oil, pop the tailboom covers
open to check the drive-shaft couplings, check slippage marks. The
peter pilot and AC [aircraft commander] are checking the rotor head,
push-pull tubes, stabilizer, the horn. Check the battery and hope
avionics came out that night and re-keyed the frequencies . . . Sometimes we spent half a day waiting for a pass to clear, pick up your
dinks, and go across the border, or sit, bad days, and wait on PZ
Kilo with the NVA putting mortar rounds in. At night or waiting
at Kilo—I carried enough parts so I could build two spare guns—
I'd take care of the guns. Guns come first."

"You were there late in the war. Did you feel the Vietnamese
were good fighters?"

"No. When the shit got hot, they would swap sides in a minute.
After Laos we supported the ROK's and Americans at Marble Mountain. Got a DFC. We went into an LZ. I was short—ninety days.
It was a flight of six. Insert a platoon on top of a hill in Arizona
Territory. The Snakes [Cobras] prepped the LZ, a pinnacle approach, and started a fire. We were the first ship, went in and
dropped six troops. The second ship dropped six. The third, a few
got off, then the whole LZ came apart. We aborted . . . The RTO
[radioman] is hollering they're hit. We're doing a three-sixty [three-
hundred-sixty-degree turn]. It was booby traps in the LZ. The heat
from the prep set them off. Smitty said to me, 'You're short. Should
we go back?' 'Let's go.' I put on my chicken plate [chest protector],
and we went in. It took us three tries to get in. First we hovered

and drew the flames right up. Second trip we found a rock to balance on, sucked flames in through Diaz's door on to the cargo deck. He was singed. Smitty was burnt behind his neck and [on] his whole face. Felt the bird nose out of the LZ. Broke the ammo belt ready to dump the ammo can because I thought we would go in hard [crash]. We lost a lot of rpm, recovered. Smitty made a go-round. We got out eight Americans. Loaded on my side. One guy I remember real well. One piece of skin was holding his arm on. Guys were busted up, no arms, no hands. We pulled fifty-two pounds of torque coming out of the LZ," he said, describing the extra power they needed to take off with such a load. "Army says use only fifty. Had a new L13B [type of more powerful engine]. Couple died on the way in. The peter pilot freaked out, crying and hollering. I had four First Aid kits, trying to patch guys up, keep 'em from bleeding. You don't think about what you're doing. The twenty-minute fuel-warning light came on. Called Marble Mountain Airstrip for a direct cross-field approach to the 95th Evac [hospital]. Coming in hot, low level, with eight wounded. A hundred and twenty knots. We lost one or two on the flight back. Out of fifteen guys we pulled over half out of the LZ. Back to the company we set down and refueled the bird. The *first* thing you do. Pulled in by the big revetments, took a fire hose to wash the blood out, took half an hour to clean it up."

I asked if he was particularly bothered by the memory of any other mission. "One resupply mission, we took hot chow to some APC's, picked up the cans, and left. Get a call for medevac. One of the APC's ran over a five-hundred-pound mine. My whole den would fit in the crater." He gestured toward the big family room off his kitchen. "We had shot the shit with them for a few minutes. One guy—a pair of boots is all that's left. One pair of boots and three body bags." And pain.

Aviation units had people in them besides the pilots, crew chiefs, and gunners. "I went to radio school." Tim Beebe sounded amused over the phone. "Learned to fix the insides of helicopter radios. All my classmates went to An Khe and worked forty-hour weeks in air-conditioned trailers. I was immediately snatched away to the forward area fixing helicopters on the LZ's, living in sandbagged bunkers, flying door-gunner missions. Me and twenty-seven helicopters—all the electronics, navigational stuff, and radios. I was with the First

of the Ninth Cav. One day with B Troop, north of Chu Lai, I remember at first light we had twenty-six operational helicopters and
at noon there were three left. They were shot down, shot up, or had
mechanical failures. We worked all night and went out flying on them
the next day. We went all over. I would fly [door gunner] when
needed, maybe once a week. We filled in if a crew was short, or took
the door for some guy that had been up forty-eight hours straight.
When the outfit was in trouble, everyone pitched in. There were
cooks who took off their aprons to jump in the helicopter and be door
gunners. Not all of them made it back."

Fixed Wing

"FAC's [forward air controllers] flew out to Polei Kleng in Bird
Dogs [small two-place Cessna aircraft], which had four spotting rockets. The rockets were markers: WP, willie-peter, white phosphorous,
which they used for marking where air strikes should go," Dennis
Le Sage told me.

The forward air controller had a very important job. If the FAC
made a mistake, the bombs and napalm would miss the enemy and
could hit our own troops. The FAC was also a target. The enemy
wanted to shoot him down before he could spot them. Some FAC's
flew Mohawks equipped with SLAR [side-looking airborne radar],
which nosed around trying to draw enemy fire so they could mark
targets for air strikes. Neither job is conducive to a long life.

Called in by FAC's and by the ground troops, fixed-wing aircraft
played a major combat role in Vietnam. Close air support of the
infantry involved flying missions to prepare LZ's where the Huey
slicks would drop off the troops for combat assaults, and to bomb,
strafe, or napalm the enemy as required during battles or big operations. When a place was being overrun, "There were air strikes
all around, Navy Phantoms coming down to treetop level and dropping napalm all around the perimeter all day," Jim Shields, a radio
operator who was at Dak To, told me.

According to Anthony Robinson's *Weapons of the Vietnam War*,
800 sorties, average, were flown each day at the height of the war
by various fighter bombers. The F-100 and the F-4 were common.
Navy, air force, and marine jets dropped bombs and napalm and

strafed treelines for the grunts. Propeller-driven planes like A-1E's also bombed and strafed. Their comparative slowness increased accuracy and decreased pilot safety.

Then there were Puff, Spooky, or Snoopy, older C-47s that had been outfitted with Gatling guns and sprayed down a stream of fire that looked like the breath of a dragon. They were used a lot when the VC/NVA tried to overrun places. Mike Geokan described one incident: "Suddenly a brilliant pink cone of fire poured from the side of the plane. The ground to our front turned into a huge dust cloud and a noise like a big piece of canvas being ripped apart was all we could hear . . . They'd put at least one 7.62 round in every square foot of the target area . . . It was obvious the battle was over."

Each plane had to be maintained by mechanics like Steve Goldade, rearmed each time it came back from a mission by guys who handled explosives all the time, gassed up by guys who spent their days around highly explosive aviation fuel, and if the plane was in trouble, a rescue team stood by to douse the plane if it crashed and pull the pilot and crew out. All these guys had dull-sounding jobs, but the opportunity to get blown up on the job was always there. Rockets and mortars were a fact of life.

"I used to work," Jon Anderson told me, "with Air Force pilots quite a bit . . . Coordinate air strikes for the Fourth Infantry Division [in 1970]. And they just loved Vietnam. They just thought that was great." He paused. "Granted, they were removed from it, you know, they weren't so close. They wouldn't see it. But they still took a lot of risks. To be quite honest, I wasn't real comfortable with them 'cause I wasn't gung-ho and they were . . . When I arrived there, everyone knew it was over, like going through some deadly motions. Everyone tried. They tried just as much—but who wants to die in a stupid lost war or wrong war, whatever? . . . I used to pick the targets. This was a free-fire zone—mostly Montagnards out there. Everyone else had been resettled, so the Vietnamese, they didn't like Montagnards—we could kill anyone we wanted to. I thought it was pretty hokey, you know, but we did it anyway . . ."

"Although the airplane [B-57 twin-engine bomber of 1950s vintage] was vulnerable to ground fire," Chuck Yeager wrote in his autobiography, "and you had to be adept at 'jinking'—weaving and twisting to avoid gunfire on the deck—it was damned effective as a light bomber. I flew . . . mostly at night, firing flares and hitting troops and supplies coming down the Ho Chi Minh Trail . . . Strafing was always dangerous because it meant coming in on the deck and drawing ground fire, especially over villages occupied by the VC. A rifle bullet in the right spot could bring down a jet . . ." He continued: "We hit only villages where VC had moved in, slaughtered the local leaders, and taken over the rice fields."

Paul Bicknell, a navigator in the air force, "ended up going into gunships, AC-130—fixed wing. All the guns were pointing out of the left side of the aircraft so you had to do a standard pylon turn [around the target]. It had miniguns, Gatling guns, 20 mike mike [mm, or millimeter], 40 mike mike, and by the time I left, it had a 105 howitzer on board. [A 105 howitzer is an *artillery* piece!] We were painted black. We flew only at night. Our mission was to interdict the Ho Chi Minh Trail. Interrupt the supplies, the flow of ammunition, re-supplying the Cong. Inside the aircraft they had a large room . . . my office for the next year, and it looked like a prototype of the bridge of the Starship *Enterprise*. One guy's job was to protect the aircraft electronically . . . He had screens and all kinds of scopes. Next to him sat a guy who operated an infrared [IR] machine with all kinds of lasers and high-tech tracking instruments, and another guy back there operated another piece of equipment, low-light-level TV, and things like this . . . A great massive array of sensory systems that were extremely high-tech. The thing could see at night."

"Did it work?"

"Oh, dazzling. We flew along at night and with the punch of my finger I could choose who I wanted to look at. If I wanted to look at IR or TV I could chhchhhchhh." He stabbed his finger and made a noise. "And so we would verify targets that way. We would see a convoy of trucks or a bunch of tanks coming down, we would fly into orbit around this convoy and lay down the appropriate fire . . . With infrared we could see them getting out of the truck, trying to park under the trees. We could see them walking around under the trees right through the foliage. The IR could see the heat from them taking a leak on the side of the trail . . . No hiding from the Spectre.

"We had a 105 howitzer and when you fired that thing the whole airplane just went sideways six feet . . . swinging the tail of the aircraft. The irony of it was we had state-of-the-art sensory systems and all World War II type of cannons, a curious match of technology . . . The worst night was a night where we got two thousand rounds of anti-aircraft fired at us, 57- and 37-mm from the ground and unguided rockets and missiles. Part of my job was insuring the safety of the AC. I operated a lot of very sophisticated electronic equipment which was designed to foil the enemy's attempts to knock us out of the sky. We flew around with the cargo ramp down, and a guy hung out the back of the aircraft on a steel cable. I would call, 'At twelve o'clock we've got a track,' and he would pick it up visually—see the exhaust plume from the rockets or the tracers from the ammunition. If you see the tail of it, it's all right, but if you just see the nose of it—what he would do is he would call, 'Break left, hold the heading, okay, hold it, freeze,' and let the rounds slide through past the AC and then break back in and put the guns back on the target and start firing again. We'd do that all night. Many nights you could just look through the AC. It looked like a sieve from all the shrapnel holes.

"We staggered Spectres into the field . . . If we found a lucrative target, a big convoy, and we expended all our ammunition and we still had more [targets] left [another Spectre was already in the air] . . . When various people got trapped in bad situations, like Special Forces camps, we'd go bail them out. We all wore black flying suits, black hats, and flew black aircraft."

"Did you carry your dog tags?" I asked.

"Ah, we sanitized ourself completely." I wanted to know if that made him angry, and he said that he didn't really like it. What it meant was plausible deniability. The government could say they're not our men, and with no identification, their status as U.S. armed forces personnel could not be proven. He went on to say that he has five DFC's and fourteen Air Medals, six of which have no explanation of where they were earned and for what—which I take to mean he got them for things we didn't do in areas we weren't in (Laos and Cambodia). "We got DFC's, when we would do massive interdictions. When we were extremely successful and took a lot of hostile fire we would get DFC's for it . . . all, about fifteen crew members because it was absolutely a crew effort."

A lot of bombs fell on North and South Vietnam during the war, more than were dropped in the whole of World War II. B-52 raids, called arc-lights, are always described the same way. The earth shook, there was a low rumbling off on the horizon, and flashes of light. Afterward, the land looked like the moon. Still, Ric Hill told me, "They B-52ed the mountain [Dong Ha] every night, and later each night, they'd rocket us, just so's we'd know they were still there."

A lot of pilots carried the war to the North. Try reading a fascinating book, *Phantom over Vietnam*, by John Trotti. He flew a two-man jet that dropped bombs in both North and South Vietnam. His first mission puts the reader in the head of the pilot flying to bomb North Vietnam. He spells out all the decisions the pilot has to make and the often-fatal alternatives if he chooses wrong.

Mechanized Combat

When tanks and tracks (armored personnel carriers—APC's) were used to protect convoys, running in front of and behind them, they often engaged the enemy during ambushes. Everyone knows what a tank looks like. A track is sort of like an armored box on wheels.

In the book *Seven Firefights in Vietnam*, we get what I consider almost a metaphor for that whole war. A convoy is ambushed. We learn the full name, initials, rank, and position of every officer from the colonel back at base to the LT in command of the convoy, the name of the forward air controller flying overhead, the master sergeant, the intelligence officer back at HQ and the executive officer's full name, the squadron commander back at Long Binh: first name, middle initial, last name, unit, rank, but "the driver of the burning C-18 [one of the tracks] finally got it started again and drove it down the road in a hail of small-arms and antitank rocket fire, hoping to distract the enemy's attention and allow the other crewmen to make good their escape. He succeeded, but four hundred meters down the road met his death when one of the thousands of small-arms rounds fired . . . found its mark." The officer who researched and wrote up the fight couldn't even bother to find out the name of the man who did that, so I can't be bothered to mention his. A man in a tank or APC is riding around in a large, conspicuous, militarily important *target*.

"The thing I was most afraid of the whole time I was there was hitting a mine," Larry Heinemann wrote me. He served a year in an APC, a track, first as a driver. "The left-side tread hit the ground right under your foot . . . The drivers were always ripped to shreds . . . The gunners were blown off the back; the TC [track commander] would be shot up out of the hatch . . . If you got in a firefight, everybody else could get busy, but the driver had to sit there in front and drive . . . You had to use both hands . . . I was absolutely terrified of burning to death. All the VC had to do was hit the gas tank and POOF, you and it and everything for a stone's throw around went up in a fireball that melted the armor plate and reduced your body to a corpse, then a carcass, then a wee cinder, then a skeleton in nothing flat. Some drivers were just never found, some looked like a charred turkey carcass . . . The corpse I discovered in the wreckage of the seven-six, that day of the big firefight, that corpse was about the size of a burned turkey. The tracks had something like a 90-gallon gas tank, which topped off would make a fireball you could see for miles. I don't know whose bright fucking idea it was to send gas-powered tracks overseas, but I hope I never meet the son of a bitch (him and the guy who thought up the M-16 rifle). The tracks are made of welded panels of 1¼" aluminum alloy armor plate and when you hit a track with an RPG (rocket-propelled grenade), the round went through the armor like spit through a screen, and when the gas tank blew, the whole contraption went up like the head of a kitchen match, and everyone inside was incinerated." Later on, diesel tracks were introduced and the danger of fire was somewhat lessened, but with all the ammo they carried, most tank and track personnel feared burning to death.

The TC (tank/track commander), who wore a CVC (combat vehicle communication) helmet so he could receive and send over the radio, controlled the vehicle. The whole crew also wore CVC's so they could hear directions from the TC. Talking was not an effective means of communication because of the noise level inside the vehicle. The driver couldn't see very well, especially when buttoned up in combat. The third and fourth members of a tank crew were the gunner and a loader. When their unit was shorthanded, the gunner loaded and the TC fired the big 90-millimeter main gun. The TC also handled the 50-caliber machine gun. "I moved to tank commander when Sgt. Colister left," Mike Geokan of Company C, 2nd Battalion, 34th

Armor, wrote, "mostly because Wallass didn't want the hassle with the radio, and Avias said he'd just as soon drive."

On a track, there's "a .50 cal mounted on the front turret," Larry Heinemann wrote me, "and 2 M-60's mounted toward the back on either side. There were four troops on a track: driver, TC (the NCO), and two observer gunners. First, I worked as a driver (who were exempt from ambush patrols) . . . If you did not drive you were a machine gunner. When I became a TC and NCO, I saw to it that my driver took care of the track, the g/o's kept their guns cleaned. I cleaned and mounted the .50-caliber machine gun—which is both the oldest and most reliable weapon in a line company. It never jammed, never heated up, never misfired, you could just about knock the pecker off a fly at 1,000 yards. It had an effective range of a solid mile and could blow your head off with one round." Larry wrote an incredible book, *Close Quarters*. If you want to feel fear, feel the dirt from the roads, feel what it was *like*, read it.

Tanks and APC's guarded bridges, where they made nice big targets for VC attacks. Tanks could be used to clear the roads when minesweepers weren't available. They'd just thunder-run the road, figuring that they'd set off any mines, and the armor would protect them. Most of the time. Remember the 500-pound bomb mine John Dexter found in Chapter 2?

Tanks and APC's were often sent to reinforce firebases or LZ's in danger of being overrun. Tanks or tracks would pull up beside the bunkers for added firepower. Mike Geokan, in a book he's writing called *Aces of Iron*, describes one attack:

An RPG roared overhead, its thunder filling my ears. Small arms on both sides started firing again. Our five-ton ammo truck exploded with a bang behind us, its fire lighting up the whole area . . . Wallass threw a half dozen 90 casings out of the loader's hatch clearing the floor of the turret. A second rocket tore through the perimeter. It glanced off something behind us and arched up into the night . . . I heard the crack of rifle bullets above my head. I ducked lower in the TC hatch as more rounds slapped against the turret . . .

The rocket came in low.

The fire roared out of both hatches of 3-3 [one of the tanks]. Somebody, a human torch, clawed his way out of the flames and leaped from the turret, running into the darkness. He fell and rolled as the medics got to him. They bent over the still-smouldering, glowing body . . .

[After it was over] I walked back towards the mess tent, or what there was of it . . . The stoves and cooking gear were laying here and there, but I couldn't see any of the cooks. I walked closer. Something moved . . . the cooks and KP's all huddled in the hole . . . in their helmets and flak jackets, rifles in their hands.

"Where's the coffee?" I asked.

They just looked up at me, blank looks on their faces.

"No coffee, huh?"

"Coffee? I don't even got a fuckin' stove anymore!" one of the cooks answered. His voice sounded high . . .

"They ain't got any coffee," I said disgustedly as I climbed back on the tank . . .

The conversation died as we watched the medics take Styes and Sgt. Hall out of 3-3. They were having trouble getting them out of the smouldering tank and into the body bags. The charred corpses were burned into strange grotesque shapes. Sgt. Hall's skull was gone, leaving only his lower jaw; the row of exposed white teeth contrasted with the blackened flesh.

I didn't want to see any more . . .

"They are gonna take Sergeant Hall's tank back in, and they want us to keep the ammo that didn't burn, so go over and pick up a few rounds."

We . . . picked up a few main gun rounds and carried them back to the tank.

I poured diesel over a rag and began to wipe the huge shells down, cleaning the ash and charred flesh from the metal surface.

I thought about Sgt. Hall.

Tanks and APC's went out with the infantry and were sent on sweeps by themselves. "Busting jungle went like this," Heinemann continued. "All the tracks got in line, and the lead track would pick a tree . . . The driver would punch it, the treads would dig in, and the front of the track would climb up the tree . . . and just push the tree over, pulling down vines and shit and the track would simply fall with the tree, drive over it and drive on to the next . . . making our own trail. Those red pissants, large red ants that would cover a man from head to toe in no time and pinched and bit like crazy, the radio antenna would knock a nest out of the tree and it would smack some guy and in an instant they'd be all over him . . . You ended the day covered with shit and bugs, and the tracks got all banged up . . . We never surprised anyone."

"In the spring of 1969," Richard Gilpin wrote me, "I was moved to the executive officer's track and commenced a more active operational role as a radio relay and command co-ordination track right with the forward beating-the-bush troops. Life was more dangerous but less boring. We carried infantry troops now and then . . . I spent a lot of time into and out of small firebases . . . The squadron executive officer . . . never rode on the track the entire time I served on it . . ."

Tanks and tracks also carried troops into battle and went into battle themselves, charging through all kinds of terrain to reinforce and rescue the grunts or wipe out some enemy force.

"Antenna valley, the whole company went." Dave S., a medic with the armored cav, continued his story. "We knew it was something bad if they send the whole company. There was one road in, the only way in. A cliff on each side, one up, one down. Heavy jungle so thick we couldn't see. There were three NVA regiments in the area, a battalion of ARVN's and a battalion of infantry in the hills to catch stragglers . . . I weighed a hundred and twenty-three pounds so I went into a lot of tunnels . . . As a medic I felt I was doing something worthwhile. They needed me. It was the *last* time I felt I was doing something worthwhile . . . The ARVN and infantry took eighty percent casualties. We took forty percent. One thing sticks the most: At the end of two weeks, the others helicoptered out. We on the APC's had to drive out on a heavily mined road. Took us fifteen minutes to get out but every three to four minutes we lost a track. Only nine of fifteen engineers were left. They were running a big huge dozer. They were the first to go. Blew the tracks off it. Blew it two feet off the ground. One guy lost an eye. They were dusted off. We pushed the dozer off and then an APC hits one. Driver dead. Always dead. Two wounded dusted off. Another APC hit one. This time the driver was wounded pretty bad but survived. The APC teetered on the edge, and we barely got him out. The gunner on the track behind flipped out, a close friend of the wounded driver. We tied him up and threw him on the dustoff. Never saw him again either. Everyone walked except the drivers. We walked about a hundred more yards and then got on the tracks and got out of there. That was my next-to-last mission."

On his last mission: "I got halfway out in a rice paddy and guns open up . . . The first round hit me in the foot. All I know, suddenly I was flying through the air and then I was lying on the ground and hearing guns going off. I got scared. It was the first time in a long time I felt anything. I was getting a lot of sand and dirt from the bullets hitting so close and I lay there and the tracks came in. Almost ran over me. I heard rumbling coming up behind me. I only had one phosphorus round and I fired it toward the track so they'd see me, went within six inches of the TC's head and the track was two-and-a-half feet from my head when it stopped. They called in a dustoff, but the company commander said he'd pick me up, but he wouldn't land till all fire was suppressed. For two and a half hours I lay there. Then they landed twenty meters away and hollered, 'Run over here!' I shot 'em a bird, and the gunner ran over and got me. I flew to the aid station and was bandaged, flew to Da Nang to the 95th Evac, then to Japan and the States, an amputee ward, but I refused. Finally they discharged me. My foot stopped oozing seven years ago."

"When were you wounded, and what was it oozing?"

"It was oozing green," he says, "a staph infection, stopped in 1980. I was wounded in 1968."

Mike Geokan saw this after another tank was hit by a rocket:

> Stanger . . . was burned a little. Romero looked the worst. It was hard to tell the difference between his blackened flesh and his tattered fatigue shirt. He was holding his arms out from his sides as he rocked slowly back and forth . . . Stanger shook his head. "Romero wouldn't get out. He just sat there in the fire. Had to drag him out," he said quietly. "He's burned real bad." I looked at Romero again. The thought of him sitting in the flames was too heavy.

"The first of our own KIA I saw," another veteran wrote, "was a track driver whose vehicle hit a mine. His nickname had been 'Dirt Snuffer.' He was being sent back down an unsecure road from a village cordon and search operation in order to recieve an Article 15 for drug possession. My track and an engineer track were sent back to secure the vehicle and survivors . . . I had to help lift him out of his seat. We wrapped him in my poncho and placed him on the floor in the back of our track until we got back to Phu Loi . . . One of the confusing things over there [Vietnam] was how priorities were set. We had a lot of mandatory safety procedures (flak jackets, malaria pills, etc.) but it only took a single thoughtless order to negate all of them . . . In 1982 I looked Dirt Snuffer's name up on the Wall, Dedication Day morning. The emotional impact was intense . . ."

"Some days we were dog tired," Richard Gilpin wrote, "layered with caked dirt from the road, and stopped only long enough to be ordered on . . . We had logged well over a hundred miles on the track that day, stopped in a traffic jam as an ambush was taking place up ahead . . . We sat watching the Cobras work over the tree line, then passed by a burned-out truck when traffic resumed. The next day . . . the tank whose tracks we were following hit a mine. No one was hurt . . . Needless to say our much lighter aluminum track would have been the worse for wear. Normal procedure was to follow in the tracks of the vehicle ahead of you . . . but a track could only match one side, being narrower. As the saying goes, I was 'too short for that shit' . . . The engineers had located a mine in the road, and we all started backing up when there was a big explosion with shrapnel flying everywhere. The ground crew had set off a booby-trapped homemade claymore . . . A couple of engineers [were] wounded on the road, one fellow probably lost his leg from the knee down, but the KIA was on the back of the track right ahead of ours. He took shrapnel right between his unzipped flak jacket. He just slowly slumped over. It took a minute or so for me to associate why. There was also shrapnel in the trim vane of our track about a foot to the right of my driver's head."

Tanks and tracks were not comfortable or easy to maintain. Larry Heinemann went on to tell me: "The 4/23d [had] virtually brand-new diesels. At the 2/22nd . . . the equipment was junk. The tracks were gas-powered . . . with a 283 cubic-inch Chevy V-8 engine with a 4-barrel carburetor and forced air induction (what dragsters call a blower) . . . A track weighed something like 13 tons, and the Chevy V-8 was just too small. Thirty MPH was positively top end . . . The RPM's would be just winding in your ear. I always had a ringing in my ear . . . The road noise and the engine noise were deadening. The driver sat on a high stool in front on the left with just his head sticking out. I piled sandbags on the floor . . . drove by working the treads—long handles that came up from the floor. Pull the right-tread brake (slowing down the right-side tread) and the track pulled right; pull the left brake handle and the track went left . . . You worked with your arms and back all the time standing on the gas pedal, which was the size of the top of a shoe box . . . The heat was exacerbated by the engine heat . . . The driver's seat was right next to the engine compartment; I'd guess it got to be a hundred and twenty degrees . . . I was dusted off for heat exhaustion three times despite the fact that there was never a shortage of water, though often we didn't drink it (couldn't on the move) and I was religious about taking salt pills . . . At night we were supposed to pull maintenance . . . We did the sort of work a Sunday shade-tree mechanic would pull, cleaned the air filter (very important), which was about the size of a waste basket so you had to beat the dust out of it. That took half an hour. You borrowed the socket wrench and went around and tightened up the lug nuts on the two drive sprockets, the ten road wheels (the wheels that rode on the inside of the tread), and the two idler wheels—altogether 70 lugs which were tightened a quarter turn at a time. Then you switch wrench sizes and tightened the nuts on the pins that held the segments of tread together . . . cast iron, about the size of a toaster and each weighing 20–30 pounds . . . hinged together with pins about three-quarters of an inch thick, threaded at each end. The nuts that go on the pins . . . tread nuts, have to be tightened every night—both treads, about 180 nuts, a quarter turn at a time depending on how hard you drove that day. Not to tighten these up was serious because the next day you could throw a tread on the move and really hurt people and probably kill yourself. The last thing you did was pump up the tread tension—the other way to throw a tread. First of all there was not a complete set of tools in the whole fucking platoon; so we kind of swapped around. Many nights we were too exhausted to do the work, but if the Deltas didn't do it, it didn't get done so you just went ahead and did it . . . If you fucked up people died, and I felt a responsibility to do it right. Sloppy driving cost people their lives;

sloppy drivers cost people their lives . . . You had to pull the maintenance rain or shine, day or night, good, bad, or indifferent."

Mike Geokan's unit moved so much that none of their spare parts could catch up with them:

> "What is this?" [the major from maintenance] said pointing to the half-butterfly handle I'd made . . .
> "We couldn't get the right parts so I used what I could get. A tree dropped across the barrel and destroyed the elevation mechanism, so I just use the butterfly handle to raise and lower the barrel and I use the TC override to traverse the turret . . ."
> The major just shook his head as he ran a fingernail down the crack in the .50 barrel. Aside from fire coming out the side it didn't seem to matter much . . .

There was always the danger of getting bogged down in a rice paddy or on some godforsaken road. Or losing a track in VC territory, which meant you had to stop and work on the tank while someone kept watch. Not an easy life.

Brown-Water Navy

The riverine war was another world. In the creeks, the canals, the slow byways, and the wide reaches of the Mekong Delta, it was a war of night ambushes and speeding boats.

Mike Morris, who sent me a cassette tape of answers to my questions, was in Vietnam from June 1969 to June 1970 on a patrol boat. "Since I was a gunner's mate, the main job was taking care of the weapons on the boat . . . We had two fifty-caliber machine guns on a single mount forward and a single fifty aft with numerous other small arms such as M-60's, M-79 grenade launchers, and M-16's . . . [We] patrolled in a twelve-hour increment . . . We never really stayed on the same patrol schedule, meaning we never went out all the time at nine in the morning or nine at night. You never tried to get in a routine on your patrols . . . That could cause trouble. Sleep at times was nonexistent, especially if you went on an all-night patrol. Sometimes we would anchor out in a large river and half the crew could sleep or rest. You never went out with less than two boats. We had a patrol officer in charge of the whole patrol . . . [The crew included] the boat captain, who was in charge of knowing where we were and driving the boat, the gunner's mate, an engine man who took care of the propulsion pumps and two V-6 diesels we had for our main drive. Then we had a regular seaman who took care of the aft fifty. Sometimes, like I say, we would anchor out, part of the crew would stay up, use our starlight scope, or binoculars watching for any river traffic. As soon as the sun went down the locals were informed—no river traffic whatsoever—so anything moving on the river from sundown to sunup, pardon the expression, was fair game.

"We patrolled small canals where we had tree branches scraping each side of the boat. The boat was eleven feet wide, so you can get an idea of the width of some of these canals that we had to patrol. It was rather unnerving when you had a total foliage canopy cover over the boat where anything could drop down on you . . ."

Mike's boat often was at "advanced staging area bases. One area I'm referring to was in a man-made canal that paralleled the Cambodian border. It was straight as an arrow and we would go out at night to a prearranged ambush spot trying to interdict . . . the bad guys coming over from Cambodia into what the locals called the seven mountains. It was a VC/NVA stronghold. We also . . . had Chinese mercenaries that rode in air boats and these were gentlemen that you did not want to trifle with."

"Describe a really bad day," I said.

"Well . . . sitting down in your gun tub, no ventilation, patrolling a river, just floating with the current on a hot day, flak jacket, helmet, that was kind of a hard day. *My job with the river division there was a lot easier, a hell of a lot easier, than the fellows that had to pound the bush.*" Mike's voice grew intense as he said this. "I thank my lucky stars that I'm sitting here today, that I was in the Navy, and if I had to be over there, I was glad I was on a river boat.

"I hadn't been with the division very long, couple of months I think . . . We were out on a four-boat patrol on a good-sized river . . . As we came back out into the maintream of the main river there was a very large explosion, probably a quarter of a mile downriver on the right-hand bank. Well, I'm up in the forward fifties, and my first thought was, well, one of the other boats shot off a LAW [a light antitank weapon], but then the explosion was much too great for the size of the explosive head in a LAW. So we turned around and went over there . . . The explosion occurred right in front of a popular forces outpost . . . There was a log bridge that spanned the creek. As we got closer, we saw a lot of people milling about and one lady screaming, jumping up and down, and falling on the ground. As we got closer we could see a person lying on the ground. Sometime in the night, the VC had placed a large charge underneath the bridge and the first person to walk over the bridge happened to be two seventeen-year-old girls. One girl was laying in the path, and it wasn't a very nice sight. The woman . . . was the girl's mother. As we pulled up, the boat captain—who had been there, this was his second tour—said to be very careful, watch the water . . . there might be other booby traps on the bank. He looked at me and he says, 'Wait until you see one of our guys look like that.' And I thought to myself, 'Hey, that's not going to happen.' Well, I don't like to admit it but it did happen, November 29th to be exact. We were holding an ambush. Well, it backfired. We took three rockets in the boat plus automatic weapons, and one of the rockets detonated off the patrol officer. The hardest thing for me was that the patrol officer had bled to death. Well, on a situation like that you would hope that the original explosion would kill somebody outright and be easy on him. I really felt bad about that. He was a very nice man. Everybody enjoyed him.

"Well, up till five years ago, I thought that's what happened . . . [Then I learned] that wasn't what had happened with the patrol officer. He was very much aware of what had happened, he pleaded with the corpsman— From what I remember the patrol officer had no arms, had no legs. The man would have been very much disabled had he lived. He didn't want to live that way, so he asked the corpsman and the corpsman took care of it. The corpsman, if you want to call it, played God or whatever. I would have done the same thing if I were the patrol officer. I wouldn't have wanted to have lived that way.

"I think that was the worst thing that I experienced over there: Wait till you see one of our people like that, and saying that's not going to happen and find out how it finally ended up . . ."

While guys like Mike were speeding up and down the rivers, other men served aboard the Riverine Assault Force, which had four squadrons of monitors and armored troop carriers with helicopter landing pads. They took infantry battalions on assaults all around the Delta.

Exercises

Think not only about the pilots and the crew chiefs and door gunners, but also the grunts they flew in. If flying makes you sick, think about being flown into an LZ by some hot pilot and jumping off sick as a dog in the middle of a firefight.

How would you feel picking up a pair of boots and three body bags, all that was left of some people you'd brought food to a few minutes before? Could you deal with being shot down thirteen times? Would you go back up? What motivates someone to risk his life to go into an exploding LZ when he was ninety days short? Think about seeing another ship crash and the crew chief leap out on fire and be unable to do anything. Think about seeing your own allies so undisciplined that they almost destroy one of the ships trying to save them. How would you feel? What would be the long-term effects of experiences like that on you? Think about serving in so many different areas and operations that you can't remember the details.

The amount of maintenance involved in flying deserves thought: All the details of pre- and post-flighting the machine, the guys who had to do the repairs, refuel, rearm, were often the same guys who flew as gunners. If the pilots didn't check the aircraft before they took off, they could die. The responsibility to remember details was tremendous and came on top of the stress of combat flying.

How would you handle being in a big target? After you saw someone burn to death in another tank or track, what would you feel? How would you keep on doing your job?

How would you feel about doing maintenance without the right tools or equipment or replacement parts? Would you need the extra aggravation?

Think about the dust and dirt from the roads. The only good position from this point of view was leading the columns, and then you were the most likely to get the mines. Think about the bugs, ants, snakes, and shit falling out of the trees onto you when busting jungle. Think of the VC concealed right over there in that bush with a rocket aimed at you.

Most of us don't associate mortars and ambushes with boat trips. Think about what Mike Morris saw and how it affected him. How would you feel in the same circumstances?

Mike Morris's story about the patrol officer who was hit by a rocket was filled with pauses in which he struggled for words. How difficult it still is, eighteen years later, to talk about it. Notice that he didn't even mention that he was also wounded badly enough to keep him in the hospital for three weeks. What do you think that means? Why would he discount it?

5

In the Field

From the Delta in the south to the DMZ (demilitarized zone) in the north, Americans humped the hills and fanned out along the paddy dikes, waded streams in the deep jungles. Long-Range Reconnaissance Patrols (LRRP's) slid through the jungle shadows. Search-and-destroy missions went out, some looking to protect people, some looking for trouble—burning and blowing up everything in their path.

Each corps (from mountainous I Corps in the north to the swamps of IV Corps in the south), each city, town, ville, hamlet, and AO (area of operations) was different. Units were moved constantly from AO to AO. When they finally knew the ins and outs of an area, either they DEROSed (date of expected return overseas) or they were moved to another AO.

This lack of continuity was one of the things that made the war so difficult for the grunts. If they knew an area, knew what to look for, knew who was friendly, they could keep alive. If they were new to an area and couldn't trust anyone, the tension level was a lot higher. When the Americans got some area pacified and moved out, they often signed the death warrants of Vietnamese people who had been friendly. The next group of Americans wasn't trusted after the last group had let the local Vietnamese down.

The grunts saw it all. Babies barbecued by napalm. What artillery does to a grass hut and the people hiding in it. What an M-16 does to the human body. What the sun does to the human body after a few days.

124

"We flew to this big field about the size of a football field, right in the middle. They're telling us it's a hot LZ so we have to *jump* off. The helicopter doesn't land. I jump. Bullets are whizzing by. '*Run for cover*,' they yell. Hell, the closest cover is a hundred and fifty feet away. I didn't know whether to shit or go blind!" The way this big black 1st Cav trooper is telling me about his introduction to his job, we're both laughing, but his story gives new meaning to the phrase.

"What did you do?" I asked after I stopped cracking up.

"I *ran*."

"My first CA [combat assault]," Bill Hutchinson remembered, "I got all my gear, bombs, bullets, grenades, got in the aircraft and looked across: One of the guys, a real wise ass, was *praying* with his helmet off. I thought. 'Oh, no!' The LZ was wet. We had to jump. I hit and fell to my knees and could not stand up. I had seventy-five pounds on my back. I was sucked into the mud. Everyone was running away, so I used the butt of my M-79 to push myself up."

Some guys had a less-exciting introduction to grunthood. They arrived by truck or helicopter at a cold LZ (no shooting going on), or a forward base with an actual physical perimeter of concertina wire and bunkers. "I went by helicopter up into the Dong Ha Mountains to a place called Camp Carroll." Ric Hill gave me an ironic look. "Monsoon season. It was dismal. Muddy. Red clay oozing everywhere. Looked like the tent city in *M*A*S*H* . . . We report to the HQ tent, standing in the mud . . ."

"A brand-new pair of jump boots lasted two weeks, then started falling off my feet [rotted away]." Ossie Burton was with the 101st Airborne Division in Vietnam in 1965 to 1966, one of those rare times that a unit went over together. "We walked up that mountain, almost straight up, pulling each other up, got to a clearing on top, stayed overnight and fell down the other side. I was an assistant machine gunner. I carried either the gun, twenty-three pounds, or the tripod, nineteen pounds. I carried the tripod over my shoulder so you could flip it out and open it up, and three hundred rounds of ammunition, nine C-ration meals and three canteens of water."

Most likely your vet was a replacement FNG and spent a few days getting to know the guys in his unit before they went out on patrol, on search-and-destroy, on a sweep, on listening post (LP), or night ambush. Maybe someone took him under his wing and showed him the ropes. "I met an Italian guy at that time," one veteran told me. "He was a point man. I learned with him. After he went home, I replaced him. Spanish people are told since childhood, be proud, be a warrior. All the time you like to go in front to show you are macho. Most of the time I was a point man."

"Everyone in the field was gentle and generous with me," Bill Hutchinson remembered. "Troop strength was low and they were glad to have me. There were about eighty guys left out of a hundred and twenty."

"I had a case of beer strapped to my back when I jumped off the chopper in the middle of a firefight," Joe Haldeman said. "They were glad to see me. I couldn't see them, just arms waving me over so I ran over. For all I knew they could have been VC waving me in." He shrugged. "The guys really jerked me around. There was constant fire." He laughed quietly. " 'Is it always like this?' I asked. 'Whaddaya mean?' this guy called Killer answered. 'This is easy.' It was the worst firefight they'd been in in months."

Tony DiCarlo, a tough-looking, lean guy who was in the 173d Airborne Brigade, remembered his first sight of his outfit. "My company came in off Junction City I [an operation] looking like wild men, filthy, bandaged, cut, smelly, grenades hanging all over them . . . A few days later we flew on a C-123 up near Tay Ninh, marched out into the bush, hot as hell, a long dirt road, heat waves just dancing over the road like a furnace, an endless tunnel through a rubber-tree plantation. Halfway down the road I was wondering if I had what it takes to get down this road."

Each individual's war was different. Because of the one-year tour, almost no one had the comfort of a unit of men he had trained with and then served with, a situation unique to Vietnam. Some men were in two or three different units in one year. Some grunts spent months in the bush. Some grunts went on three-day patrols. Some grunts climbed up and down mountains and some slogged knee-deep through Delta swamps.

Some years were quieter than others. Some months were quieter than others. Tet (January 30) was always a bad time. In 1968 the holiday ceasefire was broken by surprise attacks, and each year thereafter. Some days were really bad. "You're always waiting for HE [high explosives]. The silence is always charged with an impending explosion," said Bill Hutchinson.

Each unit was different. Tony DiCarlo was disgusted after seeing *Platoon*. "It wasn't like that in the 173d [Airborne Brigade]. We all pulled together. Those guys were so slack they are lucky to be alive at all." Two days earlier in a phone interview a marine had told me to see *Platoon* because it was "very realistic, not a false note." Keep this variation in experience in mind.

In the bush, racism was less of a problem. When lives were at stake, it often disappeared completely. Bill Hutchinson recalled a *Time* correspondent's asking if there was a lot of racism in the field. One of the black guys yelled, "Hell, no, man. We're all niggers out here."

In a sense, this was literally true. In 1965, 24 percent of all army combat deaths in Vietnam were blacks. In later years the government made a concerted effort to bring this down to the percentage of blacks in the population. Phillips reported that "blacks averaged about 9.3 percent of total active duty personnel in 1965–1970, they suffered 7,241 or 12.6 percent of the deaths—35.5 percent in excess of their percentage of the U.S. armed forces and 30 percent in excess of their presence in Indochina." You will still read deliberately evasive statistics meant to prove that there were no racial inequities in the entire war. There were.

When he got out in the bush, maybe no one spoke an unnecessary word to your vet until he'd proven himself in a firefight. Maybe the LZ was just a bare spot, and the grunts who had been in-country awhile looked through your vet with that thousand-meter stare men have when they've seen too much (the one he's gonna grow into if he lives that long) and told him he'd better scramble to dig a hole if he wanted to live through the night.

On one of his first ambush patrols, one vet I interviewed walked into a wait-a-minute vine, so called because the thorns seemed to grab onto you and made you stop. When the vine grabbed him and held him, he screamed. The ambush froze because his scream had revealed its position. The men waited, sick with fear. Luckily Charlie was not nearby and nothing happened, but when they got back he was told that if he ever yelled again, they would kill him. "And they would have," he told me quietly. They couldn't afford to die for him.

Due to the tour system, the guys in a man's unit were constantly changing as people DEROSed (date of expected return overseas) and new guys replaced them. All the men went through recognizable stages during their tour. First they were called newbies, recruits, boots, pogues, cherries, and FNGs (for *fucking new guys*), a term that reveals a major disadvantage of the one-year tour rotation system. New guys don't know what is going on or how to stay alive. In World War II, they all learned this stuff together. When replacements came they were going to be there as long as you were, for the rest of the war, so you helped them get good. In Vietnam, an FNG could do something stupid and get your vet killed the day before his DEROS date. Short-timers hated and feared and avoided them. Or they hated and feared them and still tried to teach them the ropes, risking their lives in doing so.

"Boots were dumb." A marine leaned toward me across the table in his apartment. "Classic example: We were pulling across a ridge on patrol. You don't talk, joke, smoke. You use hand signals. There was a dud 155 round on the ridge. The guy in front points it out to you, and you point it out to the guy behind you so he sees it. This new guy went over and *kicked* it." His voice held amazement and pain. After a pause he went on: "It blew. He was lucid, just had no arms or legs . . . He died in the chopper on the way to Da Nang."

One vet I know spent his third night in-country at an LZ/FB (landing zone/firebase), fighting for his life as human-wave attacks tried to overrun the place. He spent his fourth morning in Vietnam dragging VC bodies and pieces of bodies off the wire, and then, because he was the FNG, he had to ride in the back of the truck with the bodies to some ditch where they threw them away. Did something similar happen to your vet? Can you picture yourself if it happened to you?

Later on in his tour your vet became experienced, and with experience came various changes. He may have learned a lot of ugly things about human nature, including his own: how to stay alive;

how to kill; how to be good at killing. Not to make friends. He may have learned to like killing, which will make his readjustment to the world a lot harder.

At the book signing for *Chickenhawk*, a tall, rough-looking man said to me with a kind of bravado, "I was a grunt." His face hardened, ready for some kind of attack, and it didn't soften until I said, "That must have been rough." What is a grunt? Infantryman. Rifleman. Marine. Foot soldier. Vets will test your knowledge of Vietnam by using grunt, 0311 (the marine designation), 11B (the army designation), or 11Booze, 11Bravo, 11Bush, boonie-rat—a litany of names for the guys with the rifles who are gonna be walking for the whole year. *Humping the boonies*, they called it; *in the bush, in the field, out.*

"I don't say much when these guys talk about being out for two or three whole weeks. We were out for over a hundred days once," Marty Rodgers, a 1st Cav trooper, said quietly.

What does being "out" mean? Have you ever walked all day? How about with 75 pounds on your back? Doesn't make any difference how short or tall, fat or thin, you are. The military doesn't care. If you don't carry it, you won't have it. This means water, food, ammo, personal supplies.

"Life was such a drag," John Chambers told me. "We carried everything. Other units only had to carry food and ammo because they had plenty of chopper support. In the 199th, we even carried a chainsaw and a five-gallon can of gasoline to cut an LZ. Spent weeks and months humpin' the boonies—went on sweeps looking for anything. On a sweep, you were a traget. You were looking for a fight."

"What exactly did you carry?"

John listed the things for me. "I had an M-16, web gear [those belts over the shoulders and around the waist to which all the other stuff is hooked], a steel pot, a combat pack, a protective mask, four fragmentation grenades, two smoke grenades, a claymore, two pop flares (aluminum tubes, you take the cap off the top and put it on the bottom and smack the bottom and it goes off). Three hundred fifty rounds of M-16 ammo. Since I was the FNG, they gave me a Fiberglas packboard with straps and I carried three ninety-millimeter rounds, which weighed four or five pounds each. I carried a fifty-foot coil of rope for crossing rivers. We were supposed to carry three days' C-rations, but you can't. Nine meals come in a box a foot and a half square so you just take the major things out and put them in your combat pack. I had an entrenching tool, too, and two canteens of water. Our unit carried two M-60 machine guns, two M-79 grenade launchers, and two 90-mm recoilless rifles to provide extra firepower. They're like a bazooka but have a better sight and are more accurate. Much heavier too, and the safety is only on when it's straight up. We carried it loaded with a beehive round—had *seven thousand* darts in it. Shit grabs it all day long in the jungle. The guy behind's job is to watch the safety and make sure it's on so the thing doesn't go off by accident. He's a nervous guy. [A recoilless rifle's back blast disintegrates whatever's behind it.] The guy who walked in front of the 90-mm was nervous too." I laughed nervously myself, imagining how he felt with 7,000 steel darts aimed at his back.

The simple physical weight of his load, combined with the heat, humidity, and the fact that most of the time he won't have any spare water to wash in, is immediately going to cause the grunt's skin to start breaking down. Soon he will have jungle rot, open sores on his legs, on his feet and ankles, between his toes, on his groin, under his arms and the straps to his pack. These sores will scab up at night and break open every morning.

"I got rot under my arms, between my legs, behind my ears, and my skin peeled right off with my socks," Jerry Gilbreath told me. "We'd go to Doc. He gave us a salve that looked like something you pack wheelbearings in. We'd rub it in and roll our pants up and be on light duty for three or four days till it scabs up. Then you go out again. It's sore to the touch. The scabs come off over and over till the sores are real deep like bedsores. Where I was at, there was a lot of dirt and mud . . ."

"I got jungle rot in my knee so bad that they sent me to Plei Djerang for a week," Joe Haldeman said. "We called it the Oasis. [Bob called it "the asshole of the world" in *Chickenhawk*. Different perspectives.] I burned shit and read all day and worked details replacing barbed wire. Cut up my hands pretty bad even with gloves." Joe, who carried an axe in the field as a combat engineer, was laughing.

"Didn't that make you mad, having to work when your leg was messed up in the field?" I asked.

"I didn't mind." Joe laughed again. "It was better than the bush. I had to fall out for inspection the first day in fatigues I'd been wearing for six weeks, filthy, unshaven, my weapon slung on a loop pointing forward, boots falling apart. The captain took one look and laughed. I laughed back. He could have given me an Article 15. The way I felt, please give me an Article 15. Send me to jail. They gave me new fatigues instead."

Tony DiCarlo said, "We spent almost a solid nine months in the bush, maybe two weeks off altogether. We were overjoyed if we would pull castle guard, perimeter security on a firebase. Day patrols, no rucksack—loved 'em . . . The bush was endless rainy nights sleeping in the rain, red clay dust or mud, leeches, mosquitoes. Leeches look like little black tornadoes, rising up, feeling towards you—really disgusting. I hated seeing them sensing. Red ants folded leaves together to make a baseball-sized thing. If they got on you, you got naked real quick. Everyone beat them off you. I believe they could kill a person. Drive you out of your mind first. Sleeping on the ground was cold in the highlands. Cold as hell when it rains. Clouds come in. Zero visibility, damp cold, no choppers. We had to carry the wounded out."

"We spent a month at a time in the bush," Bill Hutchinson remembered, "without showers, without real relaxation or any amenities and then came in and filled sandbags . . . We weren't allowed to sit down during duty hours." Bill served in the Americal Division, "the division that couldn't do wrong right," as he put it, referring to the My Lai massacre. "You'd be out in the field, fighting for your life, get back with a dirty uniform, and the garrison troops'd say, 'Haven't you any pride?' "

"You spend all day thinking, don't drink yet—concentrate on not drinking water till noon," John Chambers said. "After doing that for a year, where the most pleasing thing you can think of is to sit down and drink half a can of hot water, or in the wet season, to go for a day and night with no rain and actually dry out, or find a nice place [on the ground] one night and actually get some sleep because you lucked out and pulled either first or last guard, that becomes the utmost thing. You learn to create things in your mind that help you make it. Rain is pouring on you and you think of a dry place. You create the ability to survive emotionally and physically. Then all of a sudden it's over. You can't uncreate those things, and they seem so much more important than things here because they meant life and death. Here people worry about what to wear to work. It creates a difference between you and everyone else."

The lieutenant, LT, ell-tee, was often the greenest man in the platoon. If he thought he knew it all, he could get a lot of men killed. "It was easier for an RTO [radioman] to tell if an officer knew what he was doing. If they asked questions of experienced NCO's and grunts, they lasted longer and lost less men. If they knew it all, they lost men and got themsevles killed, too," Larry Raskin told me.

Sergeants led each squad. Several rifle squads made up a platoon, which also included a weapons squad (the guys with the mortars or the 90-mm) and a platoon headquarters, which hopefully included an experienced senior NCO, the platoon sergeant. Experienced sergeants could be either priceless or worthless. "Lifers in the field were fucking pissed. They'd been in the Army for seventeen years and what gratitude does the Army show them? Sent 'em to combat. We'd laugh," Bill Hutchinson said.

Grunts didn't just flow through the country like a flock of chickens. Each squad of eleven men was organized into two fire teams so they could cover each other. In Vietnam, a squad of grunts often consisted of only seven or eight men, which made it harder to cover one another. Never any shortage of clerks, though.

Grunts covered one another, but they didn't bunch up. The enemy went for the bigger target. If they had a choice between one guy or two, they'd shoot the two, or set off the booby trap on the two. If some scared FNG was keeping close to an experienced grunt, he was likely to be told at gunpoint to back off. When one of his squads crowded around a claymore they'd found in a tree and radioed Matt Brennan, "I knew they were dead." As Matt tried to warn them, the enemy set off the claymore and blew them all away.

Riflemen were the backbone of the grunts. During the advisor years (1959–1965), Americans carried M-14 rifles. The army had M-16's in 1965. The marines got them later. A controversial rifle, the M-16's advantages were supposed to be that it was lightweight (7.6 pounds), it had enormous firepower compared to the M-14s, and it never jammed. Even the bullets weighed less and were smaller, so a soldier could carry more ammo. The M-16 rifle could fire almost 600 bullets a minute on full automatic, full rock and roll. "I just split him right up the middle" or "I cut him in half" are descriptions I often heard. "Three NVA came around a curve in the trail, and they were wasted," Ric Hill told me, "they were *gone* . . ." The 5.56-mm bullet was also designed to do maximum damage. One bullet could blow an arm off.

Ric Hill, walking point in 1968: "That first time, we were walking down the trail when three NVA regulars come around the curve with no weapons. I pulled the trigger on my M-16 and the son-of-a-bitch jammed. They took off across the field. Ninety guys turned on line and fired, and the last thing I saw was them beat feet to the horizon. I threw my rifle away, but they made me go get it." He still looked disgusted. He wasn't the only guy to tell me his M-16 jammed, either. In *The Vietnam War Almanac*, Colonel Harry Summers stated: "Because they were rushed into mass production, early models were plagued by stoppages that caused some units to request reissue of the M-14. Technical investigation revealed a variety of causes in both weapon and ammunition design and in care and cleaning in the field."

Anthony Robinson said in *Weapons of the Vietnam War:* "The weapons were issued with the notification that it was unnecessary to be too particular about cleaning them, since they were immune to fouling from powder smoke. Experience showed this not to be true . . . Investigation showed that the fault lay in an unannounced change in the composition of the powder in the cartridges: The new composition produced fouling, which, when it cooled, set rock-hard inside the rifle's mechanism and prevented it from being operated." A lot of people died because of that.

In 1967 the Hill Fights signaled the start of the siege of Khe Sanh. "We left with close to 1,400 men in our battalion and came back with half," a wounded marine wrote to his parents. "We left with 250 men in our company and came back with 107. Practically every one of our dead was found with his rifle torn down next to him [meaning it had jammed and he was trying to clean it when killed] . . ." Robert Pisor reported in *The End of the Line: The Siege of Khe Sanh* that this letter was read on the floor of Congress by New Jersey Congressman James J. Howard and prompted a congressional investigation.

Tony DiCarlo added, "The M-16 jammed in the beginning. It had a three-pronged flash suppressor which caught on the vines in the jungle real nice and jammed. The new one had a ring around it and never jammed."

"My M-16 was serial number 911349," Jerry Gilbreath said. "We had a newer version, never jammed, but every now and then it wouldn't fire, the bolt wouldn't go forward all the way. You had to hand-eject it . . . No serious problem other than getting too damn hot. It ejects shells on the right. Sometimes the shells would fall on your neck or arm—extremely hot. If you were left-handed they hit you in the face." The M-16 was one of those double binds: If it jammed it was the vet's fault, even if the powder was changed in the States. And he was certainly the one who died.

John Chambers told me of another peculiarity of the M-16. "I loaded my magazines, twenty rounds each. My squad leader came over and told me, 'Only put in eighteen.' The spring in the magazine was too strong and if you put in all twenty bullets, two bullets will jam into the chamber and jam the weapon." Lucky the guy told him. Why didn't they learn that in basic training?

When the infantry was moving, the point man led the way, constantly alert for booby traps, ambushes, danger. Matt Brennan, of the Blue Platoon (scouts) of the 1st of the 9th Cavalry, wrote to me: "Always at least 10 meters between you and the back-up with the machine gun. You know that your rifle may jam, but the machine guns rarely do. Walk slow, the careful heel-to-toe walk to test the ground and gradually put down the full weight of the body. Use sense of smell to detect Vietnamese body odor and cooking. Both are quite distinct . . . [Bob Hawley of the Special Forces also wrote: "There was a peculiar smell that seemed to pervade where they had lived, and once you knew it you could recognize it again."] Use peripheral vision to detect slightest movement, from ant moving on bark of tree to movement of leaves. I still have this sense. Use hearing to detect startled animals, talking, rustling leaves or trees . . . Walk with weapon set on full-auto. Communicate only with hand signals . . . Watch trail for signs of enemy movement such as fresh footprints, bent grass, loose rounds, secondary paths to campsites or rest areas . . . Wait for the moment of contact that may never come . . . We patrolled almost exclusively on the same trails the enemy used every day. We did not have to worry about booby traps or stay-behind farmer snipers. In that very significant way, we were raised above the tedium of life in a line company."

"They wanted me to go on point with an M-79 grenade launcher when I first got there. I said I wouldn't. It's stupid, and I'm not stupid." Bill Hutchinson held up a finger. "*One* round! I said I *will* walk point with an M-16—and I was a good shot with an M-79, too . . . I got an M-79 grenade launcher, no 16. My sidearm, a .45 automatic, had been redirected to the black market in Saigon. They issued me shotgun rounds with lead pellets outlawed by the Geneva conventions."

Mike Costello laughed about walking point with an M-79 grenade launcher, thinking he was cool. FNG days. When he ran into trouble, he shot the round. Then he realized he was walking point with a one-shot weapon. He fell down. The other guys shot over him. "After that I carried an M-16."

"I liked point," Ric Hill said. "My theory was an ambush would hit the main body. Most people hated it because of the booby traps . . . It wasn't like *Platoon*. When I walked point, I was fifty to a hundred yards ahead of everybody."

Behind the point was called walking slack. Sometimes the guy with the M-79 grenade launcher, the bloop man, walked slack, sometimes the machine gunner or another rifleman. Then came the rest of the column.

The M-79 grenade launcher, a lighter weapon (6.2 pounds) with a bigger boom, broke open like a shotgun to be loaded with grenades. A good guy could fire five to seven grenades a minute, and they could go as far as 375 yards. When they blew up, the casualty radius was five yards unless you were in the thick jungle. "M-79's went off sometimes—broken safeties. Lucky the round has to go ten feet before it arms, so they never exploded, but I saw some guys get broken ribs when they got hit by it," John Chambers said. Bob had one go off in his helicopter, too, but it didn't go far enough to arm itself.

Machine gunners carried an M-60 that weighed 23 pounds and could shoot 600 rounds a minute. "I also carried fourteen pounds of machine-gun ammo," Tony DiCarlo told me, "four belts, grenades, smoke [grenades], a claymore mine, food, a poncho and liner." The other thing about carrying a machine gun: bigger firepower, bigger target. Every fifth round was a tracer, marking its position nicely at night. Tracers also made it possible for the machine gunner to see if he was hitting his target. Some guys carried the M-60 cradled so they could shoot from the hip. Some had it over their shoulder. "I could flip it off and have it pointed at the enemy by the time I hit the ground," Tony added. "We were attached to a rifle squad. They bitched when we loaded them down with ammo, but were glad when we used it." The machine gun always had a starter belt in it. The assistant gunner was next in line, with two cans of ammo containing two hundred rounds each. *Hamburger Hill* is one of the few movies that shows the importance of keeping the weapons supplied with ammunition. Instead of firing off fifteen thousand rounds of ammo without reloading, guys were actually yelling for more ammo, as in real life.

The rifle company had RTO's (radio telephone operators) and medics (navy corpsmen with the marines). With each squad, an RTO carried a prick-25 (PRC-25 radio), which "weighed fourteen pounds plus a two-and-a-half-pound battery," Jerry Gilbreath said. "I carried a spare. I had a frequency book for the radio because from time to time they changed the frequency and you had to have a code book to get the new ones. We had different antennas depending on how far you were going and what frequencies. You could grab it and bend it over or it stuck straight up. Range was about five miles on a good clear day with a proper antenna and a new battery. [If a unit was farther out than antenna range, someone had to do radio relay for them.] To I.D. [identify] yourself you break squelch—mash the button on the handset in code. The handset is attached to your shoulder with a metal hook. To talk you had to mash the button. You listened all the time. During a firefight you had it on wide open; walking or at night you keep it real low. You couldn't talk during the monsoon, the rain was too loud. 'We need three RTO's, you, you, and you.' "

Jerry Gilbreath's finger jabbed the air. "That's how I got picked. I was an 11B and they just handed me the radio."

"Yeah, we were kind of a target," Larry Raskin, who served with the 4th Marines in 1965–1966, told me. "My job? Trying to hold back feelings of frustration and emotions and stay calm and collected so I could give a quick, clear transmission for medevac, supporting fire, air support."

A forward observation team from the artillery usually went with the grunts to call in artillery. "The FO calls in, 'Fire mission; VC patrol in open,' and gives the grid: eight numbers for the coordinates," Scott Camil explained. Some forward observation teams were used as relays, walking out or dropped off somewhere between the grunts and the firebase to keep them in radio contact.

"Our forward observation teams were three men, the FO who was an LT, the recon sergeant, and the RTO—me," Ron Livingston told me. (Remember Ron? He enlisted to be a field wireman, but wound up crewing a 102 howitzer, busted the racist LT in the mouth, and his services were needed with the forward observers.) "My second mission my FO got killed, a second lieutenant." At the very edge of radio range, he said, "We ventured out an extra hundred yards. The FO told the recon sergeant to come with him and told me to stay. The recon went twenty yards. The FO went forty. Most of the time I could see him and definitely hear him. He called, 'Stay where you're at. I see something.' I've got this radio strapped to my back, and I'm scared to death. The CP [command post] wants to know what's going on, so I go forward to the recon sergeant, and we went about a hundred and fifty yards." Silence. "The LT had been decapitated," he finally went on. "I'm standing there in the middle of the jungle. I'm eighteen. The recon sergeant is nineteen. I want to sit down and cry. Scared to *death*. What's next? I'm sitting with the headset in my hand, a cold sweat, I'm so scared. I call in and report, and they say get back fast and quiet. We started to move and lost our bearings. Got out the compass and tried to read it. We were fired at. The recon sergeant got grazed. By the time we got back, I can't talk. I'm mad. I'm scared. I'm trying to talk, but it won't come out. 'Where's the LT?' I feel like they blame me. I'm afraid, and I want to crawl in a hole . . . I still have dreams . . . When you walk up and see the man laying there, his body here"—he pointed down—

"his head there"—he pointed about five feet away—"and you see the *fear* in his eyes, on his face—" He shook his head and turned his face away.

Another FO said, "I was an FO attached to M Company. I went back in to the battery every three months, but I never knew a soul there."

"I extended to become an FO," Scott Camil told me. "My technical job was to be a map reader so the artillery wouldn't fall on us. The infantry LT is supposed to know where he is, but LT's got lost all the time—'Hey, Arty, where do you think we are?'—so I'd make him look good. It was my neck too . . . It was exciting, calling in artillery. When we got hit it was 'Corpsman up! Arty up!' When we got fire from a village, we called in artillery fire on that village . . . It was easy to do it because I never thought of them [the Vietnamese] as people. I lost every RTO I had as an FO. I was bad luck. I came back, but not the RTO."

"I was a line corpsman in Khe Sanh Valley with the grunts," Marty Comer said quietly. "I volunteered so my brother wouldn't have to go back. Right after I got there, I was on a truck convoy that was rocketed on the way to LZ Stud, and I got to practice my craft. A guy who I'd seen on the ship—off to himself with the thousand-yard stare—caught the rocket. I ran over to him and turned him. Only the top half of him turned over, and his intestines spilled out on the ground." His voice stopped, then continued, without inflection: "Welcome to Vietnam.

"I carried a .45 pistol, morphine and the med kit, three C-ration meals, a poncho liner, poncho and rubber bitch (an air mattress). A mortar barrage blew her apart after five months. I carried ten morphine syrettes in my pocket, fifteen to twenty battle dressings of various sizes, a large bottle of various pills—I knew which were for what: malaria pills (Sunday pills), aspirin, penicillin, tetracycline, Librium, thorazine [for anxiety and depression, two common problems in the field], an assortment of salves, Neosporin, bacitracin, povidine, adhesive tape in assorted widths, twelve Ace bandages, various sizes. Three canisters of serum albumin, IV volume replacements the size of a sixteen-ounce beer can: self-contained with the needle and the tubing in the can, two to three dozen tongue depressors to splint fingers, etc., a minor surgery kit: suture materials, scalpel blades and scalpel blade holder, needle driver, retractor to pull the wound open and look in so you can clean it out—dirt, leaves, fragments of clothing or weapons or flesh and bone. A lot of things are flying around in a firefight. Hemostats. Forceps. You hold one side of the wound with these when you sew. You drive the needle from the other side and it pulls together. I didn't do that much. Usually they were medevaced and this stuff was done at the hospital. Dull/sharp scissors to cut clothing away—"

Imagine this scenario: Somewhere in the woods, there is a sudden eruption of fire, and a wounded guy is lying there with dirt and stuff in his wound, bleeding. The medic, perhaps still under fire, has to cut his clothes away to get to the wound. He has to do it fast so the wounded man won't bleed to death. It's not like the movies, where blood seeps politely and makes a small stain. It pumps out. It runs. The whole thing is a race to get the dressing on before the lifeblood runs out. Before he dies.

"I passed the battle dressings out among the Marines. I would have liked to have carried more IV's, but practically speaking a mortar round was more important. You know, the malaria pills were non-FDA-approved, experimental." Marty laughed. "I carried water-purification tablets, too, and a thermometer. FUO was a big problem—fever of unknown origin. We lost a lot of kids over there to that, if you didn't catch it early. Leave it just one day and they died anyway, despite IV's and sophisticated antibiotics . . . Most of my work was dermatological and foot problems, jungle rot; cuts from elephant grass got infected. Hygiene was nonexistent in the field. It was fifty-eight days from the time I left Dong Ha till I saw enough water to bathe in—same uniform, no underwear. We had jungle rot, impetigo, skin diseases. Feet crack and bleed between toes. In the monsoon season your feet stay wet for weeks. Poor hygiene wasn't anyone's fault. We had no clean water. That's one of the things wrong with the government study of Operation Ranch Hand. They said the guys who sprayed [Agent Orange] got the biggest exposure. That's wrong. If we went through an area browned out with Agent Orange, say in the monsoon, it washed into the hole you slept in and your clothes and boots were impregnated with it and you *wore* it. We didn't get to change our clothes or wash it off like those guys did when they got back from their spraying missions."

"I suffer from selective amnesia," said Chuck Emerson, who was a combat medic in the 173d Airborne Brigade. "I remember working on wounded, what it was like to work on 'em. It as a—a *mechanical* thing. You had to do it. That's your *job*. I couldn't look at the guy's face and work on the body as a body . . . Booby traps were incredible. You have to disassociate yourself . . . An AK-47 destroys everything between the in and out. An M-16 round tumbles— Frag wounds always smelled like copper, metallic. With booby traps they lost either their legs or testicles, depending on the timing device. They always asked me if their testicles were still there. It didn't matter if a leg was laying five feet away . . . It's incredible that medicine could put them back together. They were just meat, shredded muscle, bones sticking out.

"I have bitterness and regrets about how Vietnam went down," he continued, "because I knew what we were capable of. Nobody ever died on me. There were dead people there, a lot of people calling for mama, a lot of people so damn mad they felt no pain. Initially the body protects itself with shock. Pain comes later . . . I'll always feel that's the most important thing I did in my life. I'll never equal it. One time we spent almost a week without food, taking bean pods off trees and boiling them. Couldn't be resupplied because of the monsoon . . . They called me Doc Dirty. Every time the crap hit the fan I burrowed my way through the dirt to the wounded, looked like Pig Pen in 'Peanuts.' I felt guilty because I never got hurt.

"One friend of mine had to carry a dead friend of ours off a mountain, put his body on the helicopter, sat down, ate a can of peaches, and then he cried . . . The only goal was to stay alive. There was nothing you're fighting for . . . About the Vietnamese, for the most part I despise them. Everything comes home to you, y'know. People who didn't want us there, want to be here."

Combat engineers went out with the grunts. Their job was to clear landing zones in the thick jungle for resupply and medevac and DX (destroy) anything suspicious-looking the enemy might have left. "We carried C-4, twenty pounds," a marine, Mitchell Young, told me. "The team leader carried the blasting caps. Throw them on the ground and they could go off. They were somewhat delicate. If they go off in your hand, you lose your hand. They were carried in a wooden box with holes drilled in it, dropped in it like cigarettes. If the box got hit—shrapnel or a bullet—it goes off . . . Our function was to blow up caves, tunnels, houses, dud rounds. We also fought. We did a lot of checking for mines . . . On one occasion we found six to ten booby traps. The captain told us to dismantle them. We usually blow them up. We weren't trained to defuse them. Night was coming and he didn't want to give our position away. He gave us a bunch of shit and finally we defused them. I was scared, but you have to get over that. Can't be scared and do it well. I rationalized that if it blew up, I would never know it. We were never out of the field, but after six–seven months they sent us to land-mine warfare school in Da Nang. Had a shower, PX, etc. New guys were telling *us* what we would find, had *fat* on them, *pale*. Told us they would appreciate mines to use as examples. One guy tried to get them one when we were back in the field, and it blew him up. Pissed us off."

Joe Haldeman, also a combat engineer, told me more. "I carried my weapon, an M-16 with a broken stock where it had been used as a club. It had 'this machine does not work' scratched on it. It was true, too. It jammed when I tried to use it. I had an axe to bring down cover or to clear an LZ. We didn't have chainsaws. I carried the demolition bag, C-4, det cord, and the blasting caps." (*ten kilograms of fragile/most instant/death*, he called it in his poem "DX.") "I was twenty-five, so I was often in charge of details, getting kids, eighteen–nineteen-year-old, black, urban kids, to be careful with explosives . . .

"We got a new LT. On my birthday, his first combat mission, he put us into a clearing. We told him it was dumb. I went to the edge to drop some cover, took one swing with my axe, and they open up with fifty calibers, a box ambush, three sides. We finally got Snoopy [C-47 with flares and miniguns] at three A.M. Pulled away from the clearing into the woods with four dead. I had to drop this big rubber tree to make an LZ. I'd stand up and take a whack. They'd aim at the noise, I'd hit the dirt. Me and the Arty LT [the FO] did that all night long, and then I dropped it on the dead men and I had to dig them out. I got hit in the canteen. We got lost and ran out of water . . . One time we laid low while a bunch of NVA walked by, not enough ammo to fight. Down to about sixty guys. No mortars. One light machine gun. I had dysentery, no water, shitting blood and couldn't pee. We were under total sound discipline. We were lost. We couldn't even *hear* the marker rounds they called in. When they found us, I had to blow a big tree to make an LZ. I put twenty-five pounds of C-4 on it and a fuse and it didn't go off. SOP [standard operating procedure] then was to grenade it, but the new captain says no [risking Joe's life] so I had to crawl back and re-fuse it. It blew off the mountain like a huge toothpick. Half an hour later helicopters are bringing in cases of beer and laying down fire for us. We got beer. We got food. At eleven A.M. we took off to walk till sundown and dug in. The next day they send a chaplain to do a service for the guys who died a week ago on my birthday and we have a twenty-one-gun salute for them with no bullets. Then two shithooks come and pick us up and take us back to Firebase Brillo Pad . . .

"Another time, we came to a clearing. Charlie was gone. There was a big DX pile [a pile of stuff to be blown up] in the middle. SOP was to blow it in case it was booby-trapped, but the major wanted his men to have lunch first. So the combat engineers stood around it to guard it. One guy was looking at something when it blew. You don't remember the noise. The medic came over to me, took one look, and went on to the next guy. I knew I was dead. But the other guys were dead so he came back and worked on me. I lay there in the sun till someone remembered to call a medevac."

Marty Rodgers, who served in the 1st Cav, trained to be a mortarman in a heavy-weapons platoon. "I started out as a rifle-man for five months. When I got in the mortar platoon, I carried the base plate. It weighed forty-seven pounds and came apart in two pieces. I saw the new one-piece alloy one that only weighed twenty-five-and-a-half pounds over there, too. Later I became assistant gunner and carried the mortar tube; weighed maybe thirty pounds. Then I became gunner, carried the bipods which weighed about forty pounds. The sight only weighed a few pounds, but had to be carried in a metal box with a handle, not so much because it was delicate as because it was a precison instrument. The aiming stakes were metal and came in a canvas cover. Had to put red and green lights on them at night so we could see them to aim. Got shot at while we did it too. When we got where we were going for that day, we had to dig a gun pit—if we could—and set out the aiming stakes before we took a break." Marty explained to me how to aim a mortar, then

laughed at my blank incomprehension. "It was better than having
to pull guard and secure the area," he continued, amused. "Another
advantage of the mortar platoon, you never had to walk point or go
on patrols except the security squad sometimes. We alternated by
month; one squad did security and one squad carried the mortar.
The security squad filled a hole in the line at night or manned the
radios or dug in. We each carried a mortar round, too, and an M-
16, and water, all the usual stuff. We'd get anyone we could to carry
extra rounds. Usually had ten–twelve rounds with us. The FDC [fire
direction controller] was with us, too. He carried a plotting board
and charts and maps to compute where we should fire . . . We tried
to be nice to them guys, because it was hard to do, and you did not
trust everyone to do it." Marty's face grew serious. "A bad one
wouldn't even get close with the rounds."

From each night encampment, from each base camp, firebase, and
LZ, LP's (listening posts) were sent out each night. An LP was two
guys with a radio out beyond the circle of foxholes listening for the
enemy crawling up. They make a sit rep (situation report) over the
radio every hour.

Ambushes went out every night, too. "I dismounted the machine
gun every other night and went on night ambush. I did ambushes
for three months . . ." Larry Heinemann wrote. "I have to say that
night ambush patrol was the only humping I did, but it was certainly
enough for me . . . I was so fucking glad to become a driver, I almost
can't tell you . . . Nothing was worse on night ambush than sitting
in the pouring fucking rain, but my most vivid memory of the rain
was seeing it come down in sheer roaring sheets so that you could
barely see your hand in front of your face."

Every night for seven years all over Vietnam, eighteen-year-olds
were sweating in the dark or shivering in the monsoon rain, in a
circle facing out, waiting, straining their eyes and ears for the first
sign of the enemy, afraid. Mosquitoes feed on them. Can't slap. Can't
smoke. Charlie will smell it. Waiting for the bullet in the dark that
will end it forever. And what if, instead of getting it, your vet heard
or saw something and opened fire? What, then? Wait till morning.
Go see. What if it's a pig or a water buffalo? Some guys were bothered
more by killing an animal than an enemy. What if it's a man, another
human being? If he's lucky it's a VC or a uniformed NVA regular.

What if it's an old man in black pajamas? Can he ever be sure he was VC? There aren't any weapons. The other grunts tell him there never are. Maybe they just find a blood trail. But how does he feel if it's a woman, or two kids, or a whole family? Or a five-year-old, naked, with a bullet through his head? How would you feel?

All the training in the world doesn't prepare you for that.

In conventional warfare, the rifle company advances against the enemy, drives them from their positions, and takes and holds the ground from which the enemy is driven. In Vietnam it wasn't like that. In Vietnam, your son or brother or husband or sweetheart wasn't supposed to take ground. He was supposed to kill VC and NVA, prevent them from going where they wanted to go or from resupplying themselves when they got there, and protect civilian lives and property from the enemy. The war of attrition came about because our country did not declare war and commit all our troops. The Westmorelands of the world thought the best way to use their limited resources was in search-and-destroy missions, later given more cosmetic names like Cordon and Search. "We go into villages and burn them down. And we shoot the people as they run out," a returned marine vet told Mike Costello in 1966, putting to rest in my mind the distinction so many people try to draw between the *good pre-1968 war* and later.

That was the plan. The war of attrition, another big double bind. Win their hearts and minds by burning down their houses.

"It was not like I expected it to be," another marine recalled. "We assaulted the beaches south of Chu Lai [in 1965] to be met by half a dozen mama-sans selling popsicles . . . We'd stretch out in a long line across the rice paddies. The first time, I saw three black-pajama-clad Vietnamese standing at the edge of a clearing. We motioned them over. One turned and ran, and they shot him. He was unarmed. Two days later, two kids were killed, a brother and sister, unarmed. We threw a hand grenade in a tunnel because they wouldn't come out, and it turned out to be kids. Two days after that we destroyed a tiny ville, a family compound with a house made of concrete. The couple who lived there were ancient. We were wiring the place with C-4 to blow it up. They were hitting us, trying to stop us. Then they went back inside and we blew it up. I felt very confused . . . It was not my idea of John Wayne and the Marine Corps . . . I couldn't think about it. I wanted to try and stop it, but didn't. I was a *nineteen-year-old private* [*italics* mine]. I was pacing back and forth, thinking, 'They better not blow them up,' and they did, so I couldn't think about it. It was too overwhelming."

"Did you ever see Vietnamese civilians killed?" I asked Bill Hutchinson. He laughed. "I guess no one ever filled you in on the number-one rule of this war," he said kindly. "If they're dead, they're VC."

"We had VC, suspected VC—those were the civilians or ARVN's—but all the dead people we killed were confirmed VC," Scott Camil said.

If they're dead, they're VC. What could ever make Americans act like that? Just another double bind, courtesy of the U.S. government. In Vietnam the only measure of our success was the dead bodies of our enemies, the body count. If you're old enough, you remember it every night on TV. Americans: 10; VC: 100. Americans: 16; VC: 160. Bob pointed out to me that we always killed ten times as many of them as they did of us. Proof we were winning, right?

"If we didn't get a body count, they punished us." Jerry Gilbreath flushed at the memory.

"Punished? How?" I asked.

"We'd been out three times in two weeks [six-man hunter-killer teams on three-day patrols in the swampy jungles of the Mekong Delta in water up to their knees, sleeping in trees] and hadn't made contact. The battalion colonel came down and told us we hadn't done anything, so from now on it's four days. He expected some results or we'd be staying out a week. If we got a good body count, like five, we got rewards, an extra day in, free beer, a cookout with steaks." He described a kind of unspoken command, too. "If they gave us a LAW [light antitank weapon] when we went out, that meant we'd be using it."

The eighteen- or nineteen-year-olds in a rifle company couldn't take land in Vietnam. They searched and destroyed the enemy, they swept him out of the way, they enveloped him and wiped him out. There was only one problem with this strategy, this war of attrition in which we planned to wear out the enemy. Who was he?

Big problem.

How did the kid in the field feel about this problem? Scott Camil wrote to his mother on 13 Jan 1967: "When we are on patrol, the only way to tell if the people are VC is if they shoot at you or not . . . When we get ambushed out there, there are no civilians as far as I am concerned . . . When you get shot at you don't sit around and try to figure out if the villagers are good or bad, you shoot back first and talk later . . . I have killed people that could be innocent bystanders, but I am not going to wait around and get killed so a Vietnamese won't get hurt. When I get shot at, anything that moves is a VC as far as I am concerned. Now if my country won't stand behind me, then send us back to the States."

In places where the Americans went on regular patrols to protect the South Vietnamese from the VC, where the Americans walked among villagers who never stepped on booby traps, the Americans stepped on booby traps every day, it was a real problem. "Every day people would blow up stepping on mines and you'd never know who it would be. That was real hard, much harder than I could ever explain." Scott's face was bleak. "It wasn't my idea of what war was . . . We were coming toward a village, getting fire, and the LT kicked open the gate and a Bouncing Betty bounced up and got eight of us. The LT lost both hands. Things were in slow motion. You see the ground coming up and you're going down."

John Chambers was carrying three 90-mm rounds on a packboard (among other things) when he came across a little stream into some tall grass. Bullets started zinging around him and he dove for the dirt, driving a punji stake into his thigh. He couldn't get down. "Ready to catch one [bullet] in the top of my head and come out my ass," as he put it. He finally broke the stick and rolled onto his side. The medic pulled the punji out and gave him morphine. Then he walked back to the LZ.

"Walked?!"

"Loaded up on morphine." He was airlifted back to the hospital, where they told him to *go on down the hall* and turn in his helmet and rifle and come back. Then a doctor cut a big slice in his leg and shoved his gloved finger in the hole to get all the shit out. John said it felt weird. They packed the wound with cotton and let it drain a few days.

"They loaded me up with some drug," John continued, "and put me on the operating table and put a tube in my hand and went off.

The doctor came in, pulled back the dressing and pulled the cotton out . . . I came off the table a foot, hit, and just vibrated. He said, 'Oh, sorry.' The nurse came running back over and gave me whatever I was supposed to have had and had me count back from a hundred. I remember hitting ninety-eight. When I said ninety-seven, another nurse was there and it was four hours later. Stainless-steel wires were holding my leg together. The wires kept poking my balls." A few weeks later he was back with his unit in the field with the wires still in his leg, still poking.

If you walked the paddy dikes or the trails, you were gonna get nailed sooner or later. So you waded through the rice paddies and got covered with leeches and slid through the jungle avoiding trails. Or you walked the trails scanning, always scanning for the trip wire, for the disturbed earth that meant a mine, for the punji pit with the shit-smeared stick that would drive up through your boot into your foot. Trip-wired booby traps got the clumsy and the unlucky. Command-detonated ones, like the one that blew away Matt Brennan's squad, got everyone, particularly those who bunched up or looked different. For instance, if your vet carried a .45 instead of an M-16, Charlie figured this guy was an officer, a medic, someone important. Charlie strung grenades in the trees, a daisy chain, to shower death on those unlucky enough to trip them, made bangalore torpedoes out of bamboo tubes filled with explosives and shrapnel.

"VC can start a fire with a one-inch piece of paper and cook enough rice on it for six people," Jerry Gilbreath told me. "Charlie is *slick*."

"Gooks would come during the day," George Hill said, "aim an RPG [rocket-propelled grenade] round on a forked stick during the daylight. They come back at night, it's laying on the fork, all they do is pull the trigger."

"Coke-can grenades killed some guys," Bill Hutchinson explained. "Charlie took the HE out of dud bombs and packed it in Coke cans with screws and other scrap metal. Bend it a bit in the middle, pull a stick back and flip it into the camp. We had all the firepower in the world and they were killing us with Coke cans."

The Killing Zone, by Frederick Downs, tells "the way it was for us, the platoon of Delta One-six." No heroic remarks. No political points. You can't help liking LT Downs as he tells how it was to be hot and sweaty and tired and dirty and smelly day after day, to do your best to keep alive and, more important, keep your men alive, to see your men hurt or dead. Imagine seeing this:

I passed through the gate. My right hand grasped my M-16. My left held my cigarette. I was humming "The Blue-Tail Fly" as I mentally ticked off the positions around the saddle where I would set my men. I noticed the time—0745 hours.

My foot slipped backward a fraction of an inch, hitting the trigger mechanism of a mine.

I never heard the explosion. Black powder and dirt flew by me. My eardrums were ripped. My body was flying through the air. I threw my arms in front of me in a reflex motion to balance myself. My eyes registered the horror of a brilliantly white jagged bone sticking out of the stump of an arm above where my left elbow had been. Ragged, bloody flesh surrounded the splintered bone. My mind cursed as utter helplessness and despair overwhelmed me.

Another part of my body coolly calculated what had caused the explosion—it had been a land mine. But what kind would blow off my arm instead of my legs? Of course! It had to be a "Bouncing Betty," a mine that flies up out of the ground after being tripped and explodes waist-high. That would do it!

My M-16 had been in my right hand. The rifle was shattered; my hand was mangled. I stared in horror at what remained of my right arm. The flesh had been ripped away, exposing two bones in my forearm from the wrist to the elbow. The bones looked like two white glistening narrow rods buried in the raw bloody meat. Thinking *My God! My God!* I felt the total defeat of my life as I landed on my feet five yards from where the mine had exploded.

After landing, I staggered forward two or three steps and then collapsed. My legs wouldn't work. The mine had gone off about six inches from my left hip. From the waist down my body was mutilated and torn where large chunks of flesh, muscles, blood vessels, and nerves had been ripped away by the hot exploding shrapnel. My buttocks were blown away. The backs of my legs were ripped to the bone down to my heels.

I rolled over on my back, being careful to keep my stump and right arm out of the dirt and sand. My body was sending so many pain signals to my brain that it was overloaded like an electrical circuit. It caused me to feel a racing humming numbness.

I lifted my head to view a scene from hell.

My pack had absorbed the majority of shrapnel that would have entered my back and spinal cord. It had been blasted to splintereens. My belongings were scattered in a wide area around me. Ammo, C-rations, poncho and poncho liner, my precious hoard of almost three hundred heating tabs, extra canteens of water, my Green Cat songbook, my grandmother's gift book of *Reader's Digest Condensed Stories*, and various odds and ends were lying among the pieces of flesh and fragments of my uniform spread around the ground.

Rueto, my RTO, who was close behind me, was sitting on the ground, astonishment on his face, screaming in a terror-filled voice that he had been hit. From the waist down he had been shredded; blood covered him like a sheet. The man behind him, Robbins, had caught shrapnel in the guts and was screaming. Two men behind him and one of the point men had also been hit with shrapnel. They were quiet. Altogether six of us were hit.

"The first GI I saw killed had been shot in the face. There was a dime hole in his cheek. From his nose over was gone. It hurt. It could be me," Jerry Gilbreath remembered. Later in the interview I asked if it hurt to kill people. "Not till years later. After a certain point I had an anger, hatred, a real powerful emotion which allowed me to justify my behavior. When we do a body count and search, I could justify it: This is their reward for killing my buddies. Even rifle-carrying women—we only saw one or two—I felt relieved, better her than me." He expanded on this: "The colonel used to humiliate and dehumanize us and we took the anger we felt for him and expressed it toward the enemy. Okay, motherfucker, here's your body count."

A lot of vets say that combat shows you what people are capable of. Another vet told me his company had to hump all day to get to an LZ that was being overrun. When they got there, the survivors had been evacuated, but pieces of Americans lay in the sun, fly-covered, swelling, stinking. Heads cut off. Arms and legs here and there. I don't know if tears ran down their faces as the grunts picked up the pieces of other boys they had known and put them in the body bags for the long trip home. I don't know if they tried to match up the parts, some burnt beyond recognition. I don't know how dead flesh feels, if blind eyes hurt you when they look at you. I didn't ask. *"After that, it was different,"* was all *he* would say about the rest of his tour.

"We had a boy kneecapped—" Ric looked to see if I understood. "Shot in the legs. People'd go up the mountain to try and get him and they'd get popped. He was moaning and groaning. Next day, he's strapped up a tree with his nuts in his mouth. That bothered me."

The grunt who finds half a baby napalmed to the barbed wire eventually reaches the point where human life means nothing. "We dug up this dead gook and cut off his head. I boiled his head in my steel pot for days, whenever we stopped long enough. Then I put the skull on a staff for a guidon for our outfit. It seemed normal at the time." This grunt shrugged. I try to imagine it feeling normal, everyday. He noted my puzzlement. "Look, we ate among dead, rotting VC bodies for days after one big operation. Flies buzzing, bodies black and stinking. We just brushed the flies off our C's and ate."

"Hill 186," Bill Hutchinson remembered. "We were having dinner, ham and limas. We had hot A's flown out. All of a sudden there was a whump and some guys were screaming, 'Medic! Medic!,' 'My eyes, my eyes!,' 'My hands, my hands!' Some guy with no training at all with demolitions was carrying a box full of blasting caps. Repacking the bag, he punched it and it blew up. He lost his hands. I looked down at my plate and there was a piece of flesh there and I just flicked it away."

"I didn't instigate stuff," another guy said, "but by the end of my time, they [killings] were taken for granted. I didn't instigate but do them. Not so much participate as stand and wait, have a cigarette while they do their thing. One thing that bothers me is people who weren't in Vietnam thinking they wouldn't have done it. Vets are aware of evil, of the capacity to kill rather lightly. To learn that at eighteen or nineteen in a questionable conflict generates the problems." This vet either didn't feel safe telling me he'd participated in the killings, or felt as though he were equally guilty of them for not trying to stop them, or he didn't know whether he had participated or not (traumatic amnesia). I didn't push it. "I had twenty-four ears on a necklace when I came back to the States," another vet told me, "and they took them away from me, said I couldn't have them here. Hey, those were my *ears*, my proof that I was *good*. We got a three-day pass out of the field for each set. How could they take them away?" He looked up from the table. "I must have been crazy." Other vets told me that anyone who did stuff like that would have been shot by the men in their own outfit.

What about a firefight? What was that like? "One time up in the Parrot's Beak we were supposed to be looking for enemy tanks. We had extra ammo for the 90 [millimeter rocket launcher]. We all said, 'Shit, I'm not looking for them. Ground troops against tanks. Shit.' " John Chambers spat out the words.

"It doesn't seem like they had much respect for your lives," I pointed out.

"No, but they took care of their own," he replied. "We were pinned down in a rice paddy—small-arms fire, mortars. For four hours in this dry paddy in the baking sun. A mortar lands behind me, in front, between me and the next guy. My nose is bleeding. It feels like someone hit me in the face with a shovel. My ears rang. You know you've been unconscious for seconds. My mouth was full of dirt. The guy next to me had shrapnel in his ass so I crawled over to him and put a bandage on him. A convoy of APC's [armored personnel carriers] came roaring down the road to support us. One of them got an RPG [rocket-propelled grenade] in the gas tank and blew up. The rest of them threw it in reverse and got the fuck out of there. It turned into a long three days—air strikes and gunships and artillery and then we'd assault and they'd repel all day and all night for three days. But what pissed me off was that first day, the platoon sergeant lay in the rice paddy crying and shaking, useless [clear dereliction of duty, for which he should have been demoted or kicked out of the army]. They gave him three Purple Hearts [which meant he went home a hero, a thrice-wounded vet], rather than ruining his career or leaving him in the field to be killed by the people he was supposed to lead. That was it for me with the army.

"By the end of the second day," John continued, "I was exhausted. I just didn't care anymore. I wished they'd go ahead and do me because I didn't give a shit. I lost fear, didn't care anymore. I just did whatever I had to do. No one else liked LAWs (light antitank weapons) but I did. Most guys were afraid of them. Makes a weird sound when you snap it open. Then you put it on your shoulder and push a button and the rocket fires. I fired twenty of them the second day, till I got a bunker that had us pinned down. Some guy directed me, I couldn't see it. After that big firefight, most of the company was new guys. New guys were trouble. They made mistakes."

Spencer J. Campbell wrote in *Reflections of a a Vietnam Veteran*, a pamphlet published by the New Jersey Agent Orange Commission: "During the first days of combat, after the body counts, there was nausea, vomiting, and confusion within. When this passed, so did many values, feelings, and dreams of the future."

He went on to say:

> Power in combat is a feeling that can never be equaled . . . someone you can't see is shooting at you, trying to rob you of life. The anger and frustration build . . . With the most powerful hand weapon of that time, an M-60 machine gun, you leap up and assault . . . Your weapon stops firing, you are out of ammo, and still yelling your lungs out. Then it grows quiet, you hear the sound of your heart beating, you smell the black powder from the ammo, you don't know what you are doing standing alone, you grow numb, your squad yells to see if you're okay. You move into the village, not sure of what you will find and not really caring. Then you see a body in black pajamas, about your age, with a single-shot weapon beside him. Somehow this does not seem tragic anymore.
>
> Someone smiles and calls you a hero, you look at him with death in your eyes, his smile fades. Today you discovered what heroes are made of. Men who are afraid, cold, wet, tired and don't care anymore. Heroes are those who experience the point of no return, action without thought.

Jerry Gilbreath said, "After four months in-country, I'd gone on several operations into the same area, same enemy. We hadn't gained anything. We're always losing something. I *never* remembered feeling we'd accomplished anything or gained anything. It was neutral or we lost, and unfortunately what we lost was lives. Having to come back in and take the personal effects of guys who were dusted-off [medevaced], photos, wedding bands, pictures of mom and dad and kids, or motorcycle, car, girlfriend, etc., to send home. That was painful.

"Monsoon season in the Mekong Delta was three months," Jerry continued, "two times a year. It rains *hard*, and then it rains *harder*. It may be a hundred degrees. The humidity is just unbearable. The rain slacks off, and it's so hot it looks like fog. Steam rises off the land. You take salt tablets like candy, one for one, salt and a drink, or you'll go into shock and die. Guys turn white, cold and clammy, from heat exhaustion and go unconscious. That's serious trouble— the body doesn't have enough fluid to function . . . Where we were— the rise and fall of the tide—we'd start out on mud and be up to our ankles in water by afternoon. In the rainy season, it's all wet, stays covered in water and we were just wading till you get to higher ground, sometimes all day, then climb trees and set up to spend the night at a certain location."

In the deep mountainous jungles, a big problem was heat of 110 to 120 degrees. Put yourself in your vet's place. Only two or three canteens of water. Water discipline. One sip. Sweating like a pig. If you drink it all now, you'll suffer worse. Just one sip and then move out. Follow the man in front. Not close. Don't give the enemy an inviting target. Put your feet where he put his feet. Christ, up we go. With 70 pounds on your back you start up another steep slope, pulling yourself up by the trees and rocks and vines. Your arms ache. Thirst maddens you. The jungle tries to drag you down and trip you up. If you stop, you'll never start again. Heave and pull. Heave and pull. Heave and pull. Almost there. Don't stop now. Heave and pull. Heave and pull. Your arms are like lead. Your back aches. Your legs hurt more than you thought possible. But you can't stop. There are guys behind you depending on you, guys in front of you depending on you. There is no way out except up and over this ridge. The skin rot on your shoulders and arms and legs and feet is a dull burning. The scabs fell off when you started out this morning. The sores on your hands fester but you hardly feel them because you've promised yourself another sip of water at the top. Heave and pull. You're there, but you have to move out, over to that outcropping of rock, and watch while the rest of them struggle up beside you before you get that sip. Maybe you get to sit and eat a can of C-rations before you saddle up again and start down the other side. Maybe not. Maybe you're humping it in a rush to cut off the NVA. Maybe your colonel is trying to earn a Silver Star by moving his men around faster than anyone else. Who knows? *It don't mean nothin'.* All you know is that now you have to slide down this fucking mountain into the ravine, and then you'll have to climb that one on the other side. At least when you're down in the sunless damp ravine, if there's water you'll be able to fill your canteen and put in the halzone tablets and the Kool-Aid, if you have it, to kill the taste, but while you're frozen in the deep forest, waiting for the point to check something out, you're gonna see that forest floor start to move as all the leeches sense your warmth and rear up, waving their mouths in the air, and begin the slow crawl toward you, toward food. If you have to stay there long, you're gonna be covered with leeches with no chance to get them off until you stop at night. And then you're gonna have to dig a fighting hole, cut a field of fire so Charlie can't sneak up on you through the bush, and set up a perimeter before you get to relax and take off your ragged smelly clothes and burn the leeches off, or spray them with bug spray so they die and fall off.

"I had these rotten old fatigues," Joe Haldeman told me. "The fly was gone. I was cutting my field of fire when I felt a leech fall down my leg. You can't feel them when they attach, you know, so I stop and open my pants and there are *forty* of them on me." He still looked sick at the thought.

At night the jungle resounds with frogs, and maybe if you're new, you're scared shitless when someone starts to whisper near your foxhole, "Fuck you. Fuck you." You freeze, too scared to speak.

The sergeant comes over to your hole and sees your terror or feels you shaking in the dark. "It's just a fuck-you lizard, not a VC," he whispers. He calms you down and then suddenly goes rigid. Silence has hit the jungle. Dead silence. Your heart thuds and thuds because the sergeant's scared. "Keep your eyes open," he breathes, and glides away over the rough ground. A muffled WHUMP sounds close by and you smash your nose hitting the bottom of your hole, cursing that it isn't deeper. WHUMP again and then someone's screaming "Medic! Jesus! Oh, God. I'm hit. I'm hit." There's a noise down the hill from your foxhole. Don't fire, you remember, and pull the pin and toss a grenade so you won't give your position away with a muzzle flash. The machine gun begins to rattle on the other side of the ridge. An M-16 opens up from the next hole aimed at the muzzle flash and characteristic sound of an AK-47. "GI, you die!" someone screams. Then silence. All night, terror cradles you as you listen to Menendez slowly dying and strain your ears for the slightest sound of the enemy, but all you hear is the tree frogs calling lovesongs in the rain. In the morning a chopper comes and takes Menendez away on the first leg of his journey home to El Paso. He only had a month left in-country. If I'm gonna be killed, you think, let it be now. Don't let it be after eleven months of this shit. You get out your P-38 and lever open a can of green scrambled eggs and choke them down. Then you saddle up and begin all over again. The scabs break off your rot as you flex. A sip of water. Start down the mountain. The weight is pushing you downhill even more this morning, because the chopper brought more supplies and you've got two belts of machine-gun ammo draped over all the other gear and you're loaded up on C's and managed to scrounge an extra canteen and some water.

"First you're scared you die. Then you're sure you're gonna die, you see so much of it. Then you start thinking, 'Damn, I might live through this. I better start taking care of myself.' " Marty Comer laughed. "You dig a hole six feet deeper than your body: FNG's didn't dig deep, too tired. Mid-tour you didn't give a shit so you dug shallow. Short-timer might live to get home so he digs a cavern."

"The first time I saw a guy got really shot up," Tony DiCarlo said, "thirty or forty bullet holes, I remember walking back behind a litter, through the jungle, the body dangling over the end of the litter with the tag on it. I realized it was serious. You couldn't live through a year of it."

"At four months, you know what's happening, and you've got *nine* more," said the wounded marine in Chapter 4 who *gave up* in the CH-34. "After a while you know: I'm getting short and I'm gonna get shot soon . . . When I got it, my patrol of twelve guys walked into a swinging box ambush. There were thirty-some rounds in the point man. Everyone was hit except for three of us. We're trying to get the bodies back in a pile. The rule is no movement without fire and no fire without movement. I picked up Strange. He had two sucking chest wounds and his gut—I put him on a poncho and took off, but I crossed in front of Jones, crossed our cover. The rounds came in from the right, three of them, smashed through my femur.

A chunk of my bone and the bullets hit Jones and opened his skull, broke his cheek and flipped it back and opened his jugular. It was eight hours till they got to us."

Some units started the day with a mad minute just at dawn. People were quietly roused, except the guys who'd had the last watch and were already up. Imagine it. Roll over, out from under your poncho or shelter half if you had one, out of the little hole you dug. Stretch quietly and feel the scabs break off your rot, the pains in your back and arms and legs as you first move in the gray dawn. On the LT's word, spray the area around the encampment with automatic weapons fire in case Charlie has set up an ambush during the night. Disarm and pack up your claymore, if you have one. Heat a little water for coffee with C-4, plastic explosive that burns if you light it. Open a can of C's with your P-38 can opener. Then pack up your shit, check your weapon, your ammo supplies, your grenades. Saddle up. Walk all day, sun, rain, hills, mountains, rice paddies, swamps, villages where they smile, villages where they don't, and you get real careful. Maybe you get resupplied, mail, more ammo and food. Walk till you reach your objective. Put down your pack, but keep your web gear and weapon, and cut a field of fire, dig a hole, plan what you'll do if you're hit in the night, eat, go to sleep because you have second watch and need every second. "You can't imagine what an environment of such intense deprivation is like," Bill Hutchison said. "The high points are things like mail or a can of peaches in your C-rats . . . You go a month at a time in the bush, without showers, in the same clothes, without any real relaxation in a-hundred-and-ten- to a-hundred-and-fourteen-degree heat with seventy-five pounds on your back walking up and down hills waiting for that explosion. It wasn't an act of volition."

Heroes never have to move their bowels in the movies, but people did in Vietnam. Howard Anderson, a grunt in the 1st Cav, wrote: "Ingredients: entrenching tool, at least one pack of C-ration toilet paper (2 if you can splurge really helps on the loose wormy outings), and an M-16. Let your friends know you are taking a little walk to the front so they don't welcome you back with a bullet—dig hole, drop pants, take gook squat position, get good aim (comes with practice), one strong silent grunt and bingo—it's in the hole—a direct hit offers a real sense of accomplishment . . . Have your paper ready prior to launch so all paperwork is completed ASAP. This way you can lift your fatigues quickly and thereby keep the flies on the outside where they belong. Oftentimes they're on it before *it* hits the ground. Congratulations are in order. You will probably feel better about this movement than any other you will make as a foot soldier." Howard was describing the ideal: enough toilet paper and good aim.

"I could never get the hang of the squatting business good enough to clear my trousers or the heels of my boots—" another guy wrote. "I was always shitting on my clothes—so I would dig my little one-by, then stick the shovel into the ground in front of it, shuck down, and hang onto the shovel handle. It was like leaning out a window."

A number of other guys have told me how embarrassing it was to have disgusting diarrhea while someone stood guard for you, as they did in most units, to have cramps and have to stop every five minutes in the deep jungle, holding up your buddies, maybe getting them killed. To have worms. On top of that, toilet paper disintegrated in the dampness of Vietnam. There was never enough either because of the constant diarrhea or the worms suffered by men who'd been out for weeks or months.

One other aspect of combat was related to me by several guys. "I jumped out of a chopper into hip-deep mud and the NVA were shooting at me. I shit."

What about food?
"C-rations," Larry Heinemann wrote, "there were no favorites. The beefsteak was always topped with a chunk of grease as thick as the wax over the top of homemade preserves. The ham and eggs was this disgusting scrambled-egg thing with bits of diced ham folded into it. The beans and franks made you shit. But positively the absolute worst was the ham and lima beans which everyone called ham and motherfuckers. In the can it looked like puke and was just not edible. The white bread was impossible to get out of the can, a biscuit about the size of a bathtub plug. It was so dry it made you more thirsty than the pork. The other little tidbits that came with each unit were okay—the crackers and desserts and canned fruit . . .

When you opened a C-ration can with one of those P-38 can openers, some of the green paint got in the food. Lead-based, no doubt." Other guys sent me favorite recipes.

When they weren't out, grunts spent time on bases. "We'd stay out three weeks at a time on patrol, come in for a shower, hot meal and a beer and in two hours be back out in the hills," Ossie Burton of the 101st Airborne told me.

A veteran of the 4th Infantry said, "I went back to base camp when I went on R&R, when I got malaria, when I was wounded, and when I got out of Vietnam. The rest of the time I was in the field or at a fire-support base. We did search-and-destroy missions for two or three weeks, then went back to the FSB to resupply overnight or two–three days at most. We pulled guard, cleaned weapons, had some fun."

John Chambers "spent two or three weeks on the firebase out of the whole year. Brigade firebase was like a hotel and they took VIP's there to show them the front. There was big-time prejudice about grunts, but we took pride in shoving it up their noses that we were grunts, reinforcing the stereotype. 'Fuck em. What are they gonna do? Send me to Vietnam?' The rear had new equipment, and we had old. Couldn't get anything from our supply room. My cammo cover for my helmet was ripped down the middle and looked like Mickey Mouse ears. Couldn't get another."

Scouts had a different mission than grunts. Instead of looking for and engaging in fights, these guys were supposed to sneak around looking for trouble and call it in. The marines sent out recon units. In the army they were called LRRP's. "I was a LRRP, Patience," Mike Costello explained, "but I was in a LRRP *platoon* for the 199th. We went out." He gestured. "There were *companies* of LRRP's over there who went *out*." He gestured much more widely. "When the platoons from a LRRP company went out they carried a lot of stuff. They were gonna be out for a *long* time."

Costello continued: "We were lost sixty percent of the time. We climbed trees to find out where we were. We didn't dig holes at night. We weren't supposed to, so no one would know we were there. No fires either, just burrow into the woods. If gooks walked by us, we didn't shoot. When we were lost, we made a group decision not

to call in and say so. We'd send people out till we found a road or a
village. Sometimes we had LRRP rations, dehydrated stuff, but you
needed water for them. One time we were out of food and water.
Drank that liquid shit inside the bamboo. The Southern boys would
hunt, and we'd eat that: some scrawny fuckin' rodent, so you wouldn't
get much. Wasn't food you wanted to eat either."

On November 11, 1984, in Washington, D.C., the 1st Cav had a
reunion at the dedication of the statues near the Wall. Two big Sioux
Indians came up to a pilot I was talking with and said, "How come
you fucking pilots never came back and got us? Huh? You always
took the fucking LRRP's out and dropped us off, but you never came
back and got us. Fucking Indians could walk back, you said." They
swayed, turned, walked up to another pilot, and asked the same
thing, and another, and another. I watched till they were out of
sight.

Costello was left to die, too. His LRRP unit was dropped off at
the wrong coordinates, in the middle of an NVA unit, and the helicopter pilot refused to come back for them. They dropped their
quick-release backpacks and ran and ran, calling frantically for help
on the radio. When they were surrounded in a field that the NVA
were burning around them, some guy flying a slick came up on the
radio, took a vote with his crew, came in, and got them. He was
killed about a week later. "When we got back in the air everyone
was screaming"—Costello paused—"or not screaming, including the
gunners. One had his legs shot to shit, and one was killed. I'd never
been in anything like that before. By the time we landed, me and
one guy were the only ones alive, and he died later from his wounds.
It took hours to calm down . . . I told 'em, 'Fuck this! I'm not gonna
do this and I'm not signing up for more time,' and I still had my gun
when I'm saying this. I had to go to Echo Company and see the
commanding officer, who we never saw"—his voice was knifelike
with sarcasm—"and then out to the firebase to see the rest of the
platoon and tell them I wasn't gonna be in recon. I'm gonna be in
the CRIP. The lieutenant was disgusted with me like I'd quit the
football team, never spoke to me again. I felt guilty, like I was
punking out, thinking it's a fat job I'm gettin in the CRIP. It was
oddly hard to stick to the decision of not going back out with them.
I shouldn't have been leaving them but I did."

Exercises

If your vet saw a lot of combat, the effect of his experiences on him may be deeper and more profound than you have ever realized.

Becoming aware of what it is like to face the realization, every day, that *these people are trying to kill me* is almost impossible, but sometimes some little thing helps us comprehend the enormity of what our veterans have been through; some detail strikes us and gives us that feeling: *He went through hell,* or *This must have been hard on him,* or *Could I have done that?*

Details of everyday life were a drag. I keep bringing them up because I know that I didn't really have a feel for what it was like to be in Vietnam until I loaded up about thirty-five pounds of canned goods into a military pack one day to see what it felt like. I was trying to put myself in the veteran's place. It's so hard for me to conceive of fear and violent death that I felt if I understood the hassles of just living over there it would become more real to me. I put in only thirty-five pounds because it was all I could lift, and the idea of carrying twice that all day was inconceivable. I couldn't have. Try it yourself. Then I took the pack outside and sat on the ground. It wasn't comfortable, but I'm doing an experiment, right? So I lay down. That wasn't comfortable either, and I kept thinking that sand or ants were getting down my collar, and it was hot as hell. I lasted about two minutes. Then I went inside to the air conditioning and thought about doing it for a year.

Try on a helmet. I wore John Chambers's helmet for a while. It was like being a turtle. Those things are made of heavy steel. My head sank slowly into my shoulders. My neck ached. The helmet cut off a lot of peripheral vision, too.

Perhaps the idea of going to the bathroom—we can't even describe the act without referring to a *room*—in the jungle is the one that will enable you to get a feeling of how different and difficult Vietnam was. Have you ever used the squat-and-shovel method? If you can find a place where you won't be arrested for trying it, it might bring some enlightenment.

Walk in the woods. When I take my morning walk here in the woods of north-central Florida, sometimes the air is so oppressive that sweat runs off me and my clothes stick to me. I walk into my first spider web, pick up a stick to hold in front of me so I won't walk into any more, and compare this to Vietnam. My adrenaline is pumping from the spider web. I'm hot. A summer's walk in the woods with or without a pack is a good way to try to get into the experience. Look around for disturbed earth, suspicious piles of brush, trip wires. Try to walk quietly. Duck down. Do some crawling. Try this in the rain and at night. Try it without bathing afterward. Drink some hot water while you're doing it.

Try sleeping on the ground.

This is gross, but the next time you see a run-over dog or cat, one of those really awful ripped-in-half ones, notice your reaction. How fast do you look away? Now look back at it and take in the ruination, torn meat, shredded bone. What are your feelings? This is how your vet felt, but he was seeing his buddies like that, guys his own age. If it is hard to think about and picture such things, think how much harder it must be to remember them in full living color with sound effects, and the fear that you're next. When I asked him about seeing wounded and dead, Bob once said to me, "You're seeing an example of what you could be soon. It's not like it's a veiled threat." I think about that a lot.

I can't think of a way to replicate some of the hard decisions that have to be made instantly in combat except to imagine yourself in such a situation. Black night. People are coming down a path near a ville where booby traps have gotten three of your squad in the last week. No villagers are supposed to be out after dark. Do you shoot? You're under fire from one of the other huts in a village and you hear a noise behind you. Do you turn and fire? In combat you do not have time to think it out and evaluate all the factors, weigh the merits of shooting or not. Your reactions have to be instant, not just to save your life but everyone's life. Think about if you had had to shoot someone. Suppose it turned out to be a kid with a rifle or grenade? Think about how you'd feel for the rest of your life. Think about how you'd feel if the person were unarmed.

While you're imagining combat, also face the knowledge that the cavalry, or U.S. government, is not going to rescue you, that you might very well not only be expendable but *be expended*, and that the only people who would care are your squad and your family. On average, twenty-two people died per day in Vietnam. How can you keep from being one of them? The stress is incredible. Can you feel it? How would you deal with it?

Maybe eating some C-rations would help your perspective.

One final story: A vet was telling me about his tour, while sitting under the bright lights in a fast-food place. I was probing for every-day detail. Where-did-you-walk, how-did-you-sit detail: "You always made sure you knew what you're doing. Going out at night, we'd go sit in a HP [holding point, so that Charlie won't see where they set up the ambush] till it was good and dark, an hour or so, then move to another NL [night location pre-picked so that artillery can come to the rescue in case of trouble and so that the patrols don't run into one another in the dark] and set up a perimeter. Sometimes we slept in trees because a hole would fill up with water. Or we'd squat against a tree, knees up, radio on chest, the handset on shoulder, M-16 beside me, and my poncho over all that. Take straps and buckles off the M-16, tape 'em or pry them off, lace your dog tags, one in each boot—" He started to shake.

"What is it?"

"Nothing," he said.

"But you're shaking. Are you all right?" I was ready to cry. I didn't want to embarrass him.

"I was just remembering what it was like to be afraid," he replied, his eyes indescribable.

Like the others, this vet has volunteered to be interviewed, to remember in the hope that my book will help other vets. What these guys still go through when memory ambushes them makes me want to weep. I had interviewed quite a number of vets by this time, had seen tears, seen people look away, had guys refuse to really tell me what it was like, but this drove it home to me. I didn't know what fear was, never mind what controlling that fear for a year was like. Nor remembering the things each vet has to remember for the rest of his life.

6

Back in the World

Although some guys liked it in Vietnam, *the world* was what most of them dreamed of. They thought constantly of how it would be, what they would eat, where they would go, what kind of car they'd get with the money they'd sent home. Back home. Back to their girlfriend, parents, friends, to where everything was safe and sane and American, where people didn't sell their sisters, where there were no trip wires, no sappers, no lifers.

For the grunt right out of the field, coming home also began a series of losses. He left his squad, his buddies, his friends, behind, in danger. He surrendered his weapons, the things that kept him alive, to some REMF (rear-echelon motherfucker) who proceeded *to tell him what to do*. He gave up the power of life and death with those weapons. He gave up the freedom of action he'd earned in the field, to stand instead in long lines while rear-echelon fat cats loaded him with the military paperwork necessary for getting out of Vietnam. He had to put his life in someone else's hands, someone who'd never been in combat and didn't know shit. All to get home.

In their book *Vietnam Veterans: The Road to Recovery*, Drs. Joel Osler Brende, M.D., and Erwin Randolph Parson, Ph.D., mention other losses: the loss of one's youth and the loss of innocence and the loss of a sense of excitement, because whatever else Vietnam was, it certainly got your adrenaline going at times. To these I add one more loss that was expressed to me most clearly by medics Dave S. and Chuck Emerson: the feeling that what you'd been doing was really important.

Guys who had been in the rear may not have felt quite such a sudden shift to powerlessness, but they did have to put up with the lines and the bull about the haircuts and the clean Class-A uniforms. (Don't want the American public to see what our boys look like when they come in out of the field, do we? Rotten fatigues on bodies covered with sores. Nah. Bad public relations.)

No matter how cynical or burned out the short-timer had become, some part of him still felt that when he got home he would receive the respect and honor that come with fighting for his country, the other half of the bargain society makes with a person who goes off to do the dirty work of war.

Some grunts had a decompression period of being a REMF for a few months before they came home. Others came straight from the field to the airport to the United States, in forty-eight hours or less. Stinking of death and shit, with blood and mud still on them, they were plunged into the rules-and-regulations military life, a complete contrast to the get-the-job-done attitude in the field.

"One week before I left," Bobby Smith told me, "a guy got bumped off the plane for a haircut and was killed by a mortar. I was bumped because my shot record was not up to date, so my sergeant forged it and I got by. The night I left," Bobby added, "that's the night I was scared the most, because I didn't have a rifle."

Tension was at an all-time high in those last days. A mortar could hit a short-timer hooch and kill the men in it the night before they left Vietnam. The VC could be rocketing the field as the airplane came in and then took off again. *Don't let me die on my last day!*

The veteran got on an airplane, the freedom bird, a civilian passenger plane. A stewardess welcomed him. This may have been the moment when he realized how much he'd changed. He didn't know how to relate to her. One belief most veterans shared was that once they got back to the States, their problems would be over. Coming home was a fantasy they'd dreamed of for a year, coming home as the same person to the same America. But they had been through experiences that had transformed their view of the world and of themselves, and America had been changing, too.

Maybe a couple hundred other guys, some grunts, some fat cats, cheered as the plane took off. Until the plane was over the South China Sea, the vet couldn't relax, and probably not then either. He figured with his luck it'd run out of gas over the Pacific. He was still trying to believe he made it out alive. He'd survived!

A painful joy. Free at last, but aware that even as he sat in the plane, taxied down the runway, flew over those long sunlit waters toward home, someone could be dying because he wasn't there. A FNG replacement could be revealing the squad's position. The track could be hitting a mine at that moment. A rocket could be killing all the guys in the bunker that second. Ric Hill went home on emergency leave. "I left the bush, had been out eight days in the rain, arms covered with jungle rot. In two days I'm home on an airplane in the same clothes I'd worn in the field. I went in the bathroom on the plane and scrubbed my arms and wrapped them with Kotex and Ace bandages." He laughed. "That was all I could find. Got back. No one was home. The next morning I went to the Marine Corps Reserve— 'Who are you with? 2/9? Oh, we have a body here from Deerfield.' I knew him. He'd been killed the day after I left while I was in Quang Tri, and his body beat me home."

The flight home was a period of solitude for the veteran. The people on the plane didn't discuss their experiences. Perhaps the mixture of combat vets and rear-echelon men prevented communication. Perhaps it was because no one knew anyone else. Each guy remained a stranger wrapped in his own world and worries. Some people talked incessantly. Some never said a word. Some smoked. Some smoked dope. Some sat stunned, unable to take it in that it was over. A plane ride was too short to process the changes that had overtaken your vet in Vietnam.

Catapulted from one life into another with no time to make any adjustments, the combat vet who told me he came home with twenty-some ears just couldn't understand why the army wouldn't let him keep them. Remember what he said? "They were my *ears*. My proof that I was *good*—I must have been crazy." But in combat in Vietnam, it was eminently sane to be good at killing, to have a way to let others know so they wouldn't fuck with you, and to do whatever it took to get the three-day pass the men in that unit got for each set of ears, because those might be the last three days of your *life*.

John Ketwig, a mechanic, felt so defiled, so changed by what he'd seen, that he signed up for a year's tour in Thailand because he knew he wouldn't fit in at home.

Some guys mentioned that the wire-covered bus windows in Vietnam were replaced by blacked-out bus windows at home so the protestors couldn't see who was on the bus. "They had to protect us from our own people."

The depth of alienation some of these guys felt can be ilustrated by a quote from Clark Smith's article on oral histories of the war in Charles Figley and Seymour Leventman's 1980 book, *Strangers at Home:*

> We walked in this door . . . and there's this great big American Flag . . . Most of the guys are ready to spit on it, if not kick it. They had lost people who really didn't die because of any kind of belief. It wasn't like they had walked across the street and got killed. It was because somebody else had pushed them out in the street. The flag represented the people who were pushing . . .

The bum's rush out of the service didn't help either: "Half the stuff on my DD-214 [discharge paper] was wrong. The line for getting out of the Army was ten hours long. The line for getting changes in your 214 was thirty-six. Think I gave a shit? I got in the ten-hour line." Mike Costello laughed bitterly. "I said to myself this is the last line I'm ever going to stand in."

The message to the returning vet? *All your efforts are nothing to us. Your heroism, the desperate fighting on the big operation, didn't mean anything to us, man. We forgot to write it down. But you can spend sixteen extra hours in the army in a line here in this hall and try to get it straightened out. We don't care.* Naturally, most of them said *Fuck it* and got in the short line. The military provided the first elements of what the psychologists call *disreception.* Returnees got a steak dinner, a new uniform, and hassles from bored clerks. No parades. No welcome home.

Some of them felt as if they were thrown away. "Arrived at 2 A.M.," Archie wrote, "1 July, and could have been discharged with the rest of the group by 7 A.M. . . . I didn't feel like leaving the security of the Marine family so I missed musters until the 8th, when they discharged me while I was still in my rack."

Many vets were so angry at the military that they threw away their uniforms in the airport rest rooms and spent the extra money for the flight home. (To get a serviceman's discount a vet had to wear a uniform.) John Ketwig wore his uniform and the stewardess wouldn't even talk to him until he said he'd been in Thailand. He didn't mention he'd been in Vietnam, too. Vietnam vets were untouchable.

Disreception continued beyond the military bases, at which point life took on a surreal quality for the eighteen-year-old who signed up to do what he could for his country and then lived through a year of hell. Coming back to the world was all he dreamed of that whole year. He knew there were protestors, but just as he didn't realize the depths of his own vulnerability till the bullets were whizzing by in Vietnam, he hadn't expected to be personally attacked when he got home. Some guys were not, but I met many with stories like these:

"My arrival at El Toro was like my departure. No bands, family, or welcome committee. One plane of Marines leaving for Nam, one plane returning. I guess it happened like this every day. The only thing different was today was my day . . ." Spencer W. Campbell remembered his return in *Recollections of a Vietnam Veteran*. He was met by demonstrators. "One young girl got up in my face and screamed, 'How could you kill innocent women and children?' I remember calmly looking back at them with my heart pounding and my palms sweaty . . . squared my shoulders and looked her directly in the eye with the same hate I had come to know so well in Vietnam, and replied, 'You don't aim quite as high, or lead them quite as far'. . . ."

"I never thought much of those protestors." Clant Clayton's voice was, as always, calm and reasonable, only his eyes showing the pain. "When I came back, I was walkin' through the Chicago airport in my uniform and three or four of them jumped me. We had a scuffle. I don't much care for 'em."

Another vet, who was pulled out of a pile of dead bodies at Khe Sanh and came home critically wounded, remembered being spat upon by protestors as he lay on his litter.

Those who were attacked received a psychic wound, which, however carefully covered over with rage or indifference, has *never* healed. It can't heal. At the meeting of the Society for Traumatic Stress Studies in Baltimore in 1987, I saw a video produced by the

FBI to train people who are going to debrief agents who have been involved in traumatic situations. The speaker was Agent Gordon McNeill, who was wounded in a shootout in Miami in which several agents died. His words, which I've paraphrased here, engraved themselves in my heart: *The way you ask about the incident will remain with the person forever. Be careful how you ask. You can inflict scars that will last forever.*

John Wilson, president of the Society for Traumatic Stress Studies, said in his paper, "Predicting Post-Traumatic Stress Syndrome Among Vietnam Veterans," that "the vast majority of combatants were ordinary, naive, decent, youthful, innocent, and well-intentioned Americans doing what they thought they were supposed to do."

Many of these vets were in effect debriefed by those protestors who spat on them rather than taking risks and protesting the war in an effective way: voting, going to Washington and protesting day and night to the people who were *running* the war till it was over, or filling up every jail in the country.

What were those protestors getting out of it? The same sadistic pleasure they had decided the veteran felt in Vietnam pulling that trigger. It's easier to call someone a murderer than it is to kill a fellow human being. You don't have to live with the same pain afterward, remembering that person's face, wondering why or if it was worth it. The protestor will never see the festering rage or pain, the prolonged agony of the postwar years, or the quick suicide: the vet with the gun in his mouth, the protestor's face in his memory, shadowing the faces of all the friends who died in Vietnam and all the people he blew away there. There's no consequence for the protestor.

Veterans were not scapegoated by protestors alone. The military abandoned them by labeling those with problems as defective, rather than as suffering a normal reaction to a mismanaged war. Most politicians were willing to agree to this: It wasn't their fault the war was going badly, it was the soldiers' fault. World War II vets found this convenient, too. It enabled them to sit around and talk about "the big one" and how tough they'd been, without having to pay attention to the double-bind, no-win situation the younger soldiers were struggling with in Vietnam.

Some disreceptions were worse than others: "Coming back with my medals, et cetera, my dad laughed and called me a drug-addict baby-killer and told me to get out of the house," one former soldier told me.

Several guys told me their parents had spent every dime they'd sent home. "We figured you'd be killed," one guy's dad said.

Your vet may have faced a wall of silence about Vietnam. "It's over now, son (or hon). Let's not talk about it." People were afraid to *hear* about what their veteran had just *lived* through. Maybe he'd tell them things they didn't want to know, there in the comfort of home, about fear and death and hardship. How could they keep on thinking it wasn't a real war if he did? Everyone protects himself from other people's pain by refusing to know about it, but if it's your own son in your own living room telling you of pain and agony and death, it will be hard to deny. Better focus on the four-letter words he's using in front of his mother. It's safer than the fucked-up war he's talking about. If he revealed to them how crazy the war was, they often wouldn't believe his stories but instead be convinced that *he* was crazy. Not talking about it was safer. Maybe he'd tell them about atrocities. Maybe he'd get upset. Maybe he'd *cry!*

Many families also labored under the common misapprehension that the best way to get over anything is not to talk about it. This idea is deeply engraved in our society. It is also wrong. John Wilson said, "Psychological isolation means the veteran feels trapped in the trauma and unable to talk about it with significant others," and that "if conditions are favorable, especially if there is a supportive recovery environment, the individual may gradually assimilate and 'work through' the trauma to a successful outcome. On the other hand, if conditions are not favorable, the survivor may need help in the working-through process."

Part of this silence was self-protection, because most people think they have to judge everything they hear, and if they heard what they were afraid they'd hear, they'd have to *do* something. Turn off the TV and make waves. The TV never let the veteran forget Vietnam. As he sat there in his living room, other guys were dying in Vietnam. He knew what that meant, but those around him didn't seem to care. In . . . *and a hard rain fell*, John Ketwig expresses a feeling a lot of vets had:

Playboy shows pubic hair now, and people think that's perverted, but they sit in the living room and watch some grunt in a green body bag, and that's respectable. What the fuck is wrong around here? Do you realize that is somebody's kid, and they're gonna unzip that bag and find just an arm, or just a leg, and the rest of him is part of the Vietnamese terrain now? You didn't mean to upset me? You didn't upset me! The war upset me! You're fine; it's the casual way you all look at hell and sip your coffee that fucks my head up. Oops! Sorry. That's a pretty acceptable word over there. Yeah, I realize I'm not over there anymore and that I can't say that here. (But I can fucking well think it!)

The TV coverage of the war made it an everyday event and therefore okay, acceptable, and, finally, boring.

TV did the veteran one more disservice. As Paul Camacho said in *Strangers at Home*, the stereotype of the Vietnam vet on drugs, the random madman who goes berserk and kills a bunch of people, the no-good loser-bum was a creation of prime-time TV series. Remember "Kojak" telling his men, "Round up all the recently discharged Vietnam vets" for every major crime? Remember *First Blood?* The movies were not slow to follow. Many vets may have felt like doing what Rambo did, but most of them didn't, and they still resent the stereotype.

The veteran himself had changed. His ideas about life had been radically altered by what he saw in Vietnam. He didn't fit in anymore.

"When I came home I felt lost in many ways," Mike Kinkennon wrote me. "I couldn't talk to my friends. They were just getting out of high school, talking of girlfriends, football games, and the high-school stuff. Then they wanted to know how many enemy I killed. They talked as if it was a game, and this was bad on me. My girlfriend, the lady I'd lived for, rejected me. I was a baby-killer. This tore me up. I felt like I was betrayed for no reason. Then I watched TV and saw my flag burned, people protesting me and my brothers dying for the country. I felt a hatred building and no way to relieve it. Then I and Mom would get into fights for nothing and Dad would too. I hated to be home. I felt lost. I wanted to die. I know Mom

and Dad cared about me but they couldn't understand my feelings.
I felt empty . . . I remembered sitting out in the snow wondering if
I could lead a normal life . . . I never told anyone how I felt . . . I
thought of Joe [his friend who was killed the day Mike was wounded]
a lot and how I felt when I saw him the last time. I wanted to die
the rest of the way. I was already dead inside."

John Ketwig put it this way:

> People in The World . . . what would they say when they
> looked into my eyes and saw a hollow ball filled with blood and
> gore? . . . "What happened to your eyes?" Well, I was watch-
> ing this whore one day, and she took a douche with a fire hose,
> and just kinda exploded into a pink mist, and the old eyes ain't
> been the same since . . . must've caught some of the spray.
> "I'm sorry, sir, the position's been filled by a person who
> doesn't utter obscenities in every sentence." Fuck ya! "What
> a beautiful day!" Easy for you to say, sitting in your rocking
> chair admiring your roses! What you fail to realize is, in a few
> hours that very same sun is gonna be looking down on a bunch
> of guys in a hole, and they'll see the dead Charleys hanging
> on the barbed wire, and they'll smell shit and piss and death
> and gunpowder; and they'll cross off another day on a calendar,
> and a lot of them are gonna die. They'll scream and twitch and
> cry and beg, and grab their intestines with both hands and try
> to cram them back into the hole where their belly-button used
> to collect lint, and they'll choke to death on the blood in their
> throat, or look down and discover their legs aren't there any-
> more. Nice day.

Your vet was trying to cope with two realities, one filled with life-
and-death decisions, and the other with what flavor ice cream to have
for dessert and whether the Wilsons really got that raise. People
were dying in Vietnam, yet his mother or wife or girl was more
upset because he kept saying *fuck*. People who had never been hungry or thirsty or seen what a mine does to the human body felt free
to correct the veteran's language as if it were more offensive than
death. They also felt entitled to judge something they could not
understand and, what is more, often *refused* to understand.

One of the vets interviewed by Smith in *Strangers at Home* put
it this way:

For umpteen years the American public went along with the war with the attitude, "No artillery shells are landing in my backyard with the kids playing in the swings, so I don't give a damn."

"That skull I had as a guidon," that vet told me, "that wasn't being tough. I just did it. Seemed like the right thing to do. Kind of looney tunes—let's dig this guy up and cut his head off—yeah, that's a good idea— That's the kind of mentality you wind up with in a war. You come back. People think you're fucked, crazy, bizarre. *There's no defense you can offer.* You weren't doing it in the name of good. It was so hard, so different over there, that it's impossible to explain what it was like. There isn't any possible way. But if they understand, they can help carry the burden a little bit and that helps."

Going home to his family sometimes presented another problem for the returned veteran. In her article "Some of My Best Friends Are Dead," Sarah Haley, a social worker who was one of the first mental-health professionals to work successfully with Vietnam vets, mentioned a vet who never went home because he was afraid his mother would "see the change in me, in my eyes—my mother didn't raise me to be a killer." Archie didn't go home for two months. Other vets I've talked to didn't go home for days or weeks or years. A lot of combat and non-combat veterans knew they'd changed and didn't want to dismay their families. They knew that they weren't going to fit into civilian life.

Physical reactions embarrassed your veteran. Sudden sounds would find the combat veteran on the deck, yelling *"Incoming!,"* his astonished family or friends embarrassed or laughing. Who likes to make a fool of himself? Yet these were the same reflex actions that kept him alive in Vietnam.

"I had lots of nightmares," Jerry Gilbreath said. "When I came back—I've talked to my Mom about this—I thought that if you looked at me I appeared cool, calm, and collected. She says I looked ready to explode. If the phone rang, I jumped a foot. I could not sit still at night. I was prowling the house and around outside. I could only sleep two to three hours at a time. I couldn't rest, slept restless, banging around, getting up. I drank a lot. Although I was home, my psyche was still in Vietnam. Seeing it on the six-o'clock news in a chair with a cold beer in my hand. I couldn't get away from it. It was like a car horn"—he made a shoving motion with his hand— "honk, honk, honk. Even now my ears perk up at 'Vietnam.' "

"When I got back to the States," Bobby Smith told me, "when the sun's going down, I'd get this strange feeling inside. And I never did understand, and then I remembered, and I said, *You know, this is the feeling I used to get in Vietnam when darkness started comin' on.* You get on automatic then . . . When I got out, I started drinking . . . and I could never, ever sleep at night. I would just stay up all night and I'd party and I'd come home and I'd just sit up. I had a few buddies from the Marines, who had been to Vietnam, and we'd just sit up all night in the car drinking and talking and as soon as dawn came I could go home and sleep . . ."

Larry Heinemann told me he heard recently from a Vietnam buddy. Why did it take so long for the guy to get in touch? Larry asked. "I've been drunk for the last nineteen years," he told Larry.

Families did not have any idea how to cope with these types of behavior. Sons who couldn't sleep, who screamed in nightmares, who acted as if they were still in Vietnam, who dug bunkers under the house, who went into rages or stayed drunk day after day, who had no feelings anymore, or who just seemed to have no interest in anything—they were all suffering from Post-Traumatic Stress Disorder. But no one had even invented the term yet. There was no help or advice from the military. No one said to get your vet to talk. Listen, and don't judge what he says. The military was too deep into denying that what was happening in Vietnam was a mess and was messing up our men and women. The military line was that the only men who had problems after Vietnam had taken them to Vietnam with them.

I can describe the changes that occurred in one Vietnam veteran.

When he went to Vietnam, Bob was an optimistic, idealistic person who could do anything, work any job. At seventeen he'd gotten a private pilot's license, working five jobs to pay for the lessons while he was in high school. He joined the army in 1964 to learn how to fly helicopters. Three months after he graduated from flight school, the 1st Cav sailed for Vietnam and he sailed with it. I still have a picture of him I took the day he left, with one-year-old Jack tucked underneath his arm, both of them smiling. His face is young and enthusiastic. He's skinny but handsome, carried about 140 pounds on his five-foot-eleven frame.

In August 1966, I ran across the parking lot of the Greyhound bus station into his arms. I couldn't believe it was over. He'd *lived*. I had him *back*. Incredible joy swept through me and tears poured down my face. As I hugged him, I could feel every bone in his body.

When he got back, Bob weighed 119 pounds. As a combat helicopter pilot flying almost every day, toward the end of his tour he had been given tranquilizers, quite illegally, to help him sleep. He flew combat assaults up to the last day. He had lost *15 percent* of his body weight. He'd always been thin, but now he looked as if he'd been in a death camp. His wrists looked enormous. His eyes glittered. He was honed down.

"See, Jack, this is *Daddy!*" We'd been kissing that picture goodnight every night for a year. Bob's mother and sister and future brother-in-law were there, but all I remember is driving home, sitting in the backseat of my father-in-law's Lincoln, watching Bob make friends with Jack. He talked to his two-year-old son and drew him out with an intensity and interest most people spend only on adults. It was the same way he treated me, as if I was human instead of just a girl—a rare quality, believe me, when we met in 1962— and perhaps what I loved most about him. Having him back was actual painful ecstasy. Bob. My own true love.

That night a loud *smack!* woke me. I swear I could see between Bob and the bed, he was so far above it. The smack was the sound of his snapping awake. He didn't make anywhere near as much noise when he landed. This was to be his pattern of sleep for the next ten years. It became a family joke: "Oh, Daddy's levitating again."

Not only could he not sleep, but he was also very restless and smoked like a chimney. For about a month he flicked ashes and butts on the floor. It surprised us both every time he did it. "Sorry." He'd grin. "You have to realize I spent a year living in a tent." I thought it was pretty funny. I was so glad to have him back. But I really had no idea what he'd been through.

I was deathly afraid of palmetto bugs, those big cockroaches we have in Florida, and I'd scream when I saw one and want him to kill it. He'd spent a year carrying guys with their legs blown off and their brains blown out, body bags, grunts who didn't even make it to the edge of the LZ, and now he had to deal with someone who screamed when she saw a *bug*. He would get up, catch the cockroach, and put it outside. "I've seen enough things killed," he finally explained.

I asked him about what it was like and he told me a lot of funny things and some horrible ones. The one that surprised me the most was that *Catch-22* was *realistic*.

Huh?

My view of war had always been the John Wayne view—heroic battles and right triumphant. I didn't know that the military could be stupid, petty, cowardly, and full of double binds. I didn't know that low-ranking pilots would get to fly too many hours, while higher-ranking ones who got more flight pay would not. I didn't know a commissioned officer could get a DFC for something a warrant did, because the military assumed that his higher rank made him braver. Bob didn't care. He didn't want the medal. He told me about the operations officers in his unit giving themselves medals for heroism when they'd never flown any combat hours, and his unit breaking ranks and walking away in the middle of the awards ceremony. He told me about the pilots fighting among themselves, about not being allowed to sleep in the daytime even if they'd flown all night, about not being allowed to wear flight suits (which are treated with fire retardant) in the Cav because everyone in the Cav was a grunt so they all had to wear fatigues, about government-sponsored whorehouses, about the bunch of women and kids who stood around a VC machine gun and let themselves be mowed down, even though he had his gunners walk the bullets up to them so they could run. He told me about being warned to keep the ARVN soldiers he carried covered with a weapon at all times, and having to force them to get off the helicopter and fight. He told me about the one successful operation he was on and how the guy who planned it was sent home and they went back to the bullshit land-in-a-clearing-so-everyone-knows-where-you-are-and-try-for-a-big-body-count operations. He said we shouldn't be there. He was so cynical about it all, it just floored me. It also disgusted me with the military and convinced me that the war was a mistake and a waste.

Because Bob was a pilot, he didn't have the physical reaction to being touched in his sleep that guys who spent night after night in the bush have. He never struck out. As a matter of fact, when he started jerking in his sleep, sometimes he could sleep if I just held him. That helped me a lot over the next years, so it makes me sad to think of all the men and women who were, and still are, denied that comfort.

One final note: Bob, who never fired a gun in Vietnam, who flew too many hours and too many hot missions, who saved hundreds of lives by going in for wounded when it was too hot for the medevacs, just like most of the other pilots in his unit, got off the plane to buy some magazines in Hawaii. The clerk smiled at him and asked if he was coming back from Vietnam. He smiled back and nodded. "Murderer!" she said. August 1966.

Sometimes the wall of silence around veterans was breached with a question better left unasked: "How many people did you kill?"

Another lethal phrase met them down at the VFW or the American Legion hall if they made the mistake of going there: "How come you guys are losing?"

"How come you motherfuckers are sending us off to die without declaring war?" would have been a good answer, but your vet was in no shape to think of that.

In Vietnam, grunts had to get permission to fire at the people who were shooting at them. Would the World War II vets have put up with that for a second, much less bombing halts, while we negotiated with Hitler and Tojo? Why did they send their sons to face such conditions? Why didn't they get involved? Perhaps the combat veterans had done all they could do, fighting in World War II. But most of the World War II veterans didn't see combat so what was their excuse? Decisions about the war were left in the hands of people who were willing to let the soldiers make any sacrifice as long as big money rolled into corporate coffers and the politicians didn't have to tell the American voters the truth about that place.

For the guys who came back wounded, life was pain. Wounds don't heal correctly unless they are debrided every day when the bandages are changed. This means they rip off the old bandages, which are stuck to the wound by pus and scabs, and scrub and rub the open wound while you scream, or don't scream, *twice a day*. Physical therapy is required so the injured muscles don't shrink and shrivel.

PT hurts, too. *For Self and Country*, by Rick Eilert, is a moving book, which starts on the day Rick was wounded and describes life in a military hospital and after release from it. Rick quietly portrays an intensity of suffering that most of us have never dreamed of, but as he shows in the book, he wasn't alone. *Aftermath*, by Frederick Downs, covers a similar period in his life.

"Getting wounded was the tip of the iceberg, to say the least," Doc Jack told me. He was in intensive care for two months and in the hospital for a year, debrided and put in the whirlpool twice a day, in traction the rest of the time for his broken leg. Twenty-six percent of his body had been burned. "I look back on it now, and I don't know how I did it, how I survived it. When I got out of the hospital, I weighed ninety pounds." Seeing the shock on my face, he grinned. "One-seventy. I weigh one-seventy now and did in Vietnam." He described his condition upon getting out of the hospital. "I was crippled, walked with a cane, all these ferocious scars."

Mike Kinkennon remembered being given ice cream in the hospital in Da Nang and apologizing to the nurse for bleeding on her sheets. Back in America, he called his parents with a borrowed dime, and then his grandmother with his one free Red Cross call. "When I called, she was crying but I told her I was okay . . . She asked what happened. I only told her part of it [a firefight in which he lost his best friend, Joe]. After, the Red Cross lady said if I was her son, she'd slap me. I asked why, and she said telling my grandmother what happened."

Hero worship by the lifers hurt, too. Mike had a further operation. "The doctor was an asshole. He said since I am a war hero, he'd let me have a fifteen-day leave. I wanted to belt him. He knew nothing of that war . . . Most of the things in the hospital I blocked out . . . I remember a nurse, Miss Michaells. She was good to me . . . always had a smile on her face. She was an ensign when I last seen her in May '68. She was a woman first, an officer second. Great lady, and if you put this in the book, I hope she reads it." I do, too, Miss Michaells, and all the rest of you nurses. Thanks.

Another part of the veteran's problem when he got home was the loss of authority. He had been powerful in Vietnam, especially if he was in combat. He could cut people in half with his M-16 if they pissed him off.

One helicopter pilot told me, "At nineteen I led a heavy gunship team, four gunships. If my aim was off by a few feet, I could kill a hundred Americans in less than a minute. When I got home I couldn't buy a beer, and my fucking father had to come down and co-sign for me so I could buy a car."

When he got back, your vet found that his friends had pulled ahead of him while he served his country. In terms of hourly wages, Andrew I. Kohen and Patricia M. Shields said, in *Strangers at Home*, a year's experience in a civilian job was worth eleven cents an hour, and a year of military experience about two cents. Guys who had finished college or had been working had an economic advantage.

By the time the war began to wind down the economy was beginning to go bad, too. Vets had a hard time getting jobs despite a number of highly touted employment programs. Fred Milano reported in his paper "The Politicization of the 'Deer Hunters' " that "the rate of unemployment of Vietnam-era veterans throughout the early 1970s remained at twice that of non-veterans in the same age group."

Lawrence M. Baskir and William A. Strauss reported in "The Vietnam Generation" that one of the reasons for this was a system developed by the Department of Defense called Spin numbers (Separation Program Numbers), a confidential code developed to show why someone left the military. Out of the 446 Spin codes, more than two hundred of them were "derogatory to damning," but there was no precise system for assigning them, and they were not subject to review. If the company clerk didn't like your vet, he could put 382 at the beginning of the discharge number on an honorable discharge, and since the numbers were soon leaked to large employers as well as the VA, they would assume your vet had been discharged because he "demonstrates behavior, participates in activities, or belongs to associations which tend to show that the individual is not reliable or trustworthy." Did this mean he belonged to a black-culture group, wore his hair long, wore a peace sign, or was he a member of the KKK or a black-market ring stealing medical supplies? The number 461 meant "inadequate personality"; 288 was "habits and traits of character manifested by antisocial or amoral trend"; 362 was homosexual tendencies; and 512, 513, and 514 were Homosexual, Class I, II, and III. No one reviewed these numbers when they were assigned. None of them was assigned by qualified psychiatrists or psychologists. If the officer didn't want to be bothered, the clerk picked them. Most vets had no idea that they even existed. One vet found out when the VA refused to treat him for serious leg wounds for which he was discharged from Vietnam. His Spin number on his honorable discharge was 384, "unfitness—drug addiction or the unauthorized use or possession of habit-forming narcotic drugs or marijuana."

When the black veteran came home to the land of the free and the home of the brave, he was *still a nigger*. That's not a word I was brought up to use, but as the black veterans I talked to put it, "Why not? It was true."

In 1969, one of the guys I interviewed was sitting in a restaurant near Fort Benning, in Columbus, Georgia. "Everyone around the table, white and black, was a vet," he said. "Someone at another table said out loud, 'Why are they with them niggers?'" Meeting his eyes, I asked if there were other incidents. Slow to answer, he finally sighed and said, "When I got off the Trailways bus back from Nam, three whites standing on the corner said, 'Man, you think we need to whip this nigger?'"

The same principle applied to all minorities. No matter how hard the black, Hispanic, or Native American veteran fought, how well he did his job, there was no change in his position in society. As a matter of fact, it was worse. Not only was he a minority, he was one of those crazy, fucked-up Vietnam vets.

Some guys still had time to serve, and stateside duty was full of bull. They'd been through the reality of war and were now required to play at it. "I went back to Pendleton," George Hill said, "and this was worse, man—stateside duty—terrible. I hated it." Some, like George Hill (two tours) and Matthew Brennan, who served three, went back to the only place they understood: Vietnam. They were more comfortable in the war zone than back here with the protestors, and the hippies, and free love, and even the patriots who supported them by swilling beer in front of the TV every night as they watched the day's body count, swelled by rules about where you could shoot.

Other guys served out their time in the States, but many had trouble conforming to stateside military conditions. "I was assigned to guard duty on a walking guard post," one combat veteran told me. "I'm not supposed to be on a walking guard post due to physical injuries. My mind was not adjusted either. What the fuck am I doing here, freezing cold in the middle of the night, guarding what? So I climbed into a dumpster and built a fire and slept through my watch and two others guys' [watches]. They can't find me in the A.M. so I'm AWOL. A young LT—I'm back two months from Nam—gets all in my face and yells at me about a *firing squad*—so I physically attacked him and knocked him around pretty good. The MP's came and handcuffed me and took me to the company area, sat me by the first sergeant's desk. The first sergeant starts yelling. I cleared his desk." He made a sweeping gesture with his hands together, as if handcuffed. "He called the MP's back. They took me to the stockade, stripped me down naked, and put me in a holding cell. I was full-goose-bozo. I didn't know shit from Shinola, yelling, screaming, totally incoherent, foaming at the mouth. I never saw a doctor, no meds. I only saw guards: ten days in solitary, ten days in the stockade, ten days as a parolee in the barracks."

Clant Clayton was assigned to play a VC in war games until he tied up two instructors and left them hidden for two days. After that he didn't have to play anymore.

Other returnees were hassled and ridiculed by the stateside lifers who called men who had earned their stripes in Vietnam "rice-paddy NCO's." "One senior Pentagon official," it says in *Chance and Circumstance*, "described the military's treatment of the returning Vietnam veteran as 'our most shameful episode of the war.'"

Girls were another problem for returning veterans. They couldn't get dates—at least not until their hair had grown out and they'd given up telling people they'd been to Vietnam.

A lot of eighteen- or nineteen-year-old vets had never really dealt with any girls, except whores in Vietnam. They didn't understand American women. Some of them had girlfriends who'd stopped writing, or wrote the whole year but then dropped them. Some of them felt betrayed by the changes in women, the new sexual freedom. Girls weren't ladylike and nice anymore. In the movie *The Stuntman*, the fatherly screenwriter asks the Vietnam veteran if he expected the girl to be a virgin. *Yes* is the passionate answer.

Married veterans or guys who married when they got back had difficulties, too. Waking up with your hands around your wife's throat is frightening to the vet and to the wife. Is he crazy? Does he hate me? What the hell's going on? There were no answers to that, nor to short tempers, deep depressions, drug and alcohol use. A lot of it ended up in divorce.

Some returning combat veterans experienced a complete lack of physical desire. One guy I talked to got in touch with his girlfriend after a week or so. They got into bed. He did not make love to her, just got up and left. Closeness, love, sharing just weren't possibilities anymore. Many combat veterans simply turned off that aspect of life. One rough, tough marine told me that sex was simply not a consideration, it was so far out of his mind and life when he got back. For the first year or two he was back, if a woman tried to pick him up at a party, what she wanted was inconceivable to him.

Vets who went back to school often became outcasts if they admitted to being vets. "When I got back to the States," Bobby Smith said, "I was sticking my chest out. I felt really good about myself. I went up on campus—Bethune-Cookman College—and I was dating this girl, and I said, 'Hey, how you doing?' And I had my patches on and everything and she said, 'Hey—' These people are looking at me real strange. I thought people were gonna say, 'Hey, where you been? What was it like over there?' She didn't want nothin' to do with me. Nobody wanted anything to do with me. I went home and pulled off my uniform. Not gonna put it on again . . . There were some little kids, my brothers and some little kids, they made me feel better than anybody . . . I got on at the hospital as an orderly. They said, 'You're really good. We'll give you a scholarship to go to nursing school.' I wanted to work with mentally disturbed people so I took my GI Bill and went to school . . . That first year in school was when the My Lai incident came out. I had met this guy. He befriended me . . . I just could not believe people were saying what they were saying about Vietnam—we were baby-killers—and this guy who had befriended me, he said, 'Bobby, I didn't know you were a Vietnam veteran. I just can't be your friend. I just can't support what you guys did over there,' and that just tore me up inside." The pain of that moment was all over his face. "I said, 'Hey, you just don't understand, man, what happen to a guy when he got over there.' I almost walked away from campus, but I just held it together . . ."

The Ivy League was no better. Matt Brennan wrote: "I have a ten-year period when I functioned on one level, school or work, and that was it. I am still trying to figure out what I did from 1970 to 1981. School for seven years and work for four years. I tried to study hard to forget—that was seven days a week, all waking hours. Never allow myself time to think about anything else. I went from a poor high-school record and no college credits to a Harvard Ph.D. in less than 7 years. They thought I was smart. The 1975 fall of Vietnam set me back by a couple of years. I was a silent vet who told no one I had been to Vietnam. That gave me little in common with everyone else. When I did carefully open up and confide, I usually lost the friend I had told."

Veterans with obvious physical scars of war were openly insulted by antiwar activists on college campuses.

Frederick Downs wrote in *The Killing Zone:*

> In the fall of 1968, as I stopped at a traffic light on my walk to class across the campus of the University of Denver, a man stepped up to me and said, "Hi."
> Without waiting for my reply to his greeting, he pointed to the hook sticking out of my left sleeve. "Get that in Vietnam?"
> I said, "Yeah, up near Tam Ky in I Corps."
> "Serves you right."

Another aspect of the disreception was the GI Bill, the establishment's reward system for veterans. Under the new bill, veterans got a monthly stipend if they went to school full-time. It wasn't enough to live on, and it didn't pay for books or tuition, as it had after World War II. Charles Moskos reported in *Strangers at Home* that the new GI Bill "contained—in constant dollars—less than half the benefits of the GI Bill of World War II . . . Yet the federal government found the wherewithal in the 1970s to expand grants and loans to college students who had not served in the military."

Disreception at the Veterans Administration hospitals and clinics was an added burden. The common attitude among the older employees—"They ought to have to have a haircut to get help here"— was reported in a study published by the VA in May 1972, *The Vietnam Veteran in Contemporary Society*. Vietnam vets were called whiners, treated like dirt, ignored. Ronald Bitzer reported in *Strangers at Home* that within six years after World War II, 10.8 percent of veterans of that conflict were receiving compensation from the VA. In 1976 only 5.7 percent of Vietnam-era vets were getting VA compensation, although Dean Phillips reported in the same book there were 300 percent more traumatic amputations or severe wounds to the lower legs in Vietnam than in World War II. Part of this was due to the hostile attitude of the VA. Part was due to simple self-protection on the part of Vietnam vets. Bitzer says VA hospitals were well known for the excessive drugging of patients. Thorazine was their answer to Vietnam.

For the wounded veterans who had to live in VA hospitals, the years of the war were pure hell. Robert Muller was a marine who came home permanently paralyzed from the chest down. "I go to the veteran's hospital and get this GS-5 shucking and jivin' and giving me a ration of shit because I need a pitcher of water, because I can't get out of bed . . . 1972: Fucking Richard Nixon vetoed the Veterans Medical Care Expansion Act the week before the election as inflationary. 'It's fiscally irresponsible,' to quote his veto message. I called in $100,000 a day [in bombs and artillery shells] destroying fucking villages and killing people. And now to get me in that shithole VA hospital where I was put in bed with fucking drunks and derelicts and degenerates and old fucking has-beens, to call it 'fiscally irresponsible' and inflationary to give us two sets of parallel bars instead of one? A set of graduated steps? Some sense of privacy in the fucking enema rooms?"

Nixon purred "peace with honor," while amputees and spinal-cord-injured guys lived in roach- and rat-infested wards. The U.S. government found the money to invade Laos and Cambodia, but the money for hospital attendants for people who lost legs and arms and faces in service to this country just wasn't there.

While the detective shows on TV portrayed the Vietnam vets as drug dealers and hostage takers, headlines blared "Vietnam Vet Hits Man," while on the next page a mass murder by someone who was never in Vietnam was reported in a two-inch column. Reading *Back Home*, by Bill Mauldin, I found out that this also happened after World War II. Remember the postal clerk who killed many of the people he worked with a few years ago out in the Midwest? The story broke as "Vietnam Vet Kills Thirteen," and he had never been to Vietnam.

One of the results of all this scapegoating has been that a lot of veterans become angry at the implication that all Vietnam vets have problems. Some even become angry at the idea that any Vietnam vets have problems. "I'm not one of those whiners," they say, buying into the denial that Vietnam caused problems and the official military line and scapegoating of vets with problems—that the only vets with problems had them before they went. The final element of disreception was the splintering of Vietnam veterans into many separate groups or individuals, unable to support one another or work together to prevent what happened to them from happening again.

Why do I keep emphasizing support? Because according to John Wilson, Ph.D., "During this time what is important in terms of predicting PTSD is the relative degree of support from significant others and a meaningful community, the opportunity to talk freely about the traumatic experiences of the war, and the social and institutional mechanisms that facilitate a rapid return to normal psychosocial functioning." None of these was present for most Vietnam vets.

Exercises

Think about the implications of leaving behind in the bush the people you are closest to in the world: still in danger, the war unresolved, their future unknown. Think how that would bother you for the rest of your life. Did your buddies live? Many veterans don't know. They were afraid to find out. However unjustifiably, they felt they had abandoned their comrades in hell.

Think about being in the field, being a good soldier, wary, skillful, alert, strong, lean, smelly, tough, hard, good at what you do, the ultimate fighting machine, as one marine laughingly told me, and then going to the rear, giving up your rifle, your boonie hat, beads, long hair and drooping moustache, beard, Afro, peace symbol—*whatever* gave you outward identity—for clean Class A's, a haircut, and a lot of bullshit. How would it make you feel to go from being an important member of a tight group of jungle fighters to being just another number, treated just like the rest of the returnees? The fact that you now have no importance is rubbed in by the fact that your DD-214 (discharge paper) is wrong.

Think about coming home to jeers and insults or assaults. Think about the wall of silence and its implications:

We don't care what you've been through.

We don't want to hear something that will upset us.

You've done something so dreadful it can't be talked about.

Don't bother me with your problems.

When men go off to war there is a pact made between them and the society for whom they are doing the dirty work. They risk their lives and in exchange they are promised respect and honor. Think how you'd feel if you'd done your half and came back to what our vets came back to.

How would you feel if every time a car backfired you hit the floor? How would you feel if you woke up strangling or hitting the person you loved most in the world? Would you feel nuts? If crowds made you feel uncomfortable, how would you hide it? What if everything around you seemed flat and pale and dull? These are some of the common reactions of people who have been under prolonged stress in a combat zone.

Think about how angry you'd be if you served eighteen months in the bush, lost a lot of friends, and some World War II vet said it wasn't a real war or asked why you guys are losing.

Think how hard it would be to be stereotyped as fucked-up on top of feeling angry. It's sort of like when a woman is legitimately upset about something and some man asks if it's her period.

Think about never being able to talk about the most important year in your life, about friends you would have died for, who died for you.

Think of the experiences that would make men write the answers I got when I asked how they felt when they got back:

"Like I wasted my time . . ."

"I felt a deep sense of loss."

"Disrespected, abandoned, afraid, humiliated and criticized."

"I lost a wife and my feelings for others."

"I will never forgive the American people for what they did to us . . ."

"My, had times changed!!! Short skirts, more pot and pills than you could shake a stick at, and an attitude that set me back a ways."

When I first joined Nam Vets, our local organization, we provided coffee breaks at a rest area out on the interstate to raise money. I remember one guy who bought coffee. He said to one of the vets that he was one, too.

"Oh, really," I said, in this bright cheerleader voice that makes me cringe when I think of it now. "What unit were you with?"

He looked at me for a long moment. "I don't talk about it," he said, and left.

Left me with a lot to think about, too.

Part Two

The Aftereffects

7

So What's So Different About Vietnam?

"My husband was in combat for five years in World War II, and he doesn't have any problems." The woman's shrill voice came over the earphones. I was on a radio talk show in San Francisco on tour for *Chickenhawk. I bet he doesn't,* I thought. She continued to scream. "Vietnam vets are just whiners." *I sure wouldn't tell you my problems, lady,* I thought. *Your husband probably gets a word in once a year.* Still, it's a common attitude, and I suspect most of my readers don't know what to say when the topic comes up. What *is* so different about Vietnam? What do you say when people hit you with that question?

Age

The average age of the men who served in World War II was twenty-six. In Vietnam a twenty-six-year-old was an old man. The average age of those who saw service in Vietnam was nineteen. That means that for every forty-year-old colonel or master sergeant in Vietnam, there were twenty-one eighteen-year-olds. Guess who was most likely to see combat in Vietnam? The one whose nineteenth birthday was likely to be the day a buddy got his legs blown off. In World War II, you had to be nineteen before you could go overseas.

Shared Burden

The shared burden is another major difference. People from all social and economic classes served in World War II. William Man-

189

chester mentioned in *Goodbye, Darkness* that ". . . the sons of both Harry Hopkins, FDR's closest adviser, and Leverett Saltonstall, one of the most powerful Republicans in the Senate, served in the Marine Corps as enlisted men and were killed in action." It was the thing to do. Men who didn't serve will still *explain* why.

Ross S. Carter said in the preface to *Those Devils in Baggy Pants*, his memoir of the 82nd Airborne in World War II:

> Every level of society had its representation among us. Senators' sons rubbed shoulders with ex-cowboys. Steel workers chummed up with tough guys from city slums. Farm boys, millionaires' spoiled brats, white-collar men, factory workers, ex-convicts, jailbirds, and hoboes joined for the thrill and adventure . . .

Most of Carter's buddies were volunteers. In World War II, the U.S. government drafted men from seventeen all the way up to forty-six. There was no signing up for three years to get a guaranteed non-combat job. Contrast that with the information in Chapter 1. Vietnam was just the opposite; people with money dodged the draft, and you had to explain why you *did* serve.

Tour of Duty

When you read *Those Devils in Baggy Pants*, it's obvious that being in the war for the duration was too much. In a combat unit, it could be a death sentence:

> Through luck or fate or whatever you choose to call it, I find myself again a civilian after three years . . . My friends call me a refugee from the law of averages. My regiment still exists as a name, but the regiment in which I trained, fought, and almost died now lies buried in obscure Army cemeteries in ten countries.

On December 19, 1944, Carter's unit was thrown into battle to help stop the Germans at the Battle of the Bulge. At that point only twelve original members of his company were still fighting. Four of them survived the Bulge. Carter's unit had a 200 percent casualty rate by the time he was wounded that December. Between the spring of 1943, when he sailed for North Africa, and the time he was wounded, I counted up more than 265 days in combat. He was wounded the night of December 20, 1944, and rejoined his outfit on February 26, 1945. His brother said in the epilogue that his final campaign was "a picnic," whatever that means. The European war ended in May.

The average combat veteran of the Pacific theater saw six weeks of combat spread out over the duration. William Manchester, whose unusually honest book about World War II, *Goodbye, Darkness,* came out in 1979, saw two months of combat on Okinawa.

During the Korean War, the government developed a point system that was used "to some extent . . . After accumulating so many points, an individual was rotated home, regardless of the progress of the war." This was partly in response to the high psychological casualty rates in World War II.

The combat credit system was converted to a one-year tour of duty in Vietnam in the combat zone, whether or not the vet ever saw combat. This system resulted in having guys who saw up to 395 days of combat, and others, "guys over there who even brag about how well they had it in Saigon, the officers livin' in Saigon, y'know, eating hot meals every day," as Bobby Smith said. In defiance of all former military practice and knowledge about the morale of combat units, men were treated as interchangeable parts of a machine, not as living, breathing people who wanted to keep on living. Under this system, the officer's personal responsibility for the welfare of his men almost ceased to exist.

The original one-year tour plan had men serving half a tour in the field and half in the rear, like the officers, and then going home. It didn't work out that way. Experienced combat men were too valuable to their units to be sent to the rear and often too angry to go back and take any rear-echelon shit for six months. The option wasn't even offered to many grunts. Since the LT was usually newer than the short-timers, he needed them. He didn't know what his experienced men had been through, nor did he have the kind of concern for them that a man who had trained with them and been through many campaigns with them would have had. This insulated him from awareness of the damage being done to these men by the conditions in Vietnam, so he kept them out in the field. Officers rotated from field to rear after a few months, if they lived—being an LT was often lethal—so everyone could get "combat experience," which looked good at promotion time. The next FNG lieutenant had the same needs and the same blind spots.

The intention of the rotation system during Vietnam was further subverted by multiple tours and tour extensions. Experienced combat troops were induced to gamble. They were in no shape to be making any decisions, but the military offered them an early discharge out of the service if they extended their tour for an extra three or six months. A lot of them felt that they'd never be able to put up with a year of stateside duty, so they took the chance.

For many lifers, especially sergeants, Vietnam became something they did every other year. They wound up in the position of the rare World War II vet who had fought through all the campaigns, having seen too much.

The government turned a blind eye.

Unit Solidarity

"The military art is deeply concerned with the performance of the human group under stress," said General Sir John Hackett, who served in combat in World War II and was later commander of all NATO forces, in his book, *The Profession of Arms*. The human group is the main difference between Vietnam and every other war fought in recorded history. The one-year rotation system—which made the World War II veterans see red because they were overseas for years—guaranteed that the Vietnam War was not fought by cohesive groups of men who had trained together and thus could rely on each other.

World War II vets trained together and went overseas together, fought together, had officers they knew, learned how to stay alive together. The military was structured around units which had long traditions. National Guard and reserve units were called up and sent overseas. Some of them had served in the Civil War. The officers and men usually came from the same part of the country.

Herbert Spiegel, M.D., wrote in "Psychiatry with an Infantry Battalion in North Africa:"

These men did not feel like romantic heroes who had charged forth in the face of danger to rid the world of evil forces. Nor were they, as many thought, tough characters who loved to fight. By and large they were sober, realistic, peace-loving citizens who much preferred a baseball field to a battlefield. Most of them served in our Army as the result of selection. It should be noted that they expressed very little real hate for the enemy . . .

If abstract ideas, hate, and the desire to kill did not motivate the men, what did? What enabled them to attack and attack and attack, week after week in mud, rain, dust, and heat? It seemed to me that the answer lay not in any negative drive but in a positive one. It was love more than hate that propelled these men. This love was manifested in a number of ways: in regard for their comrades who shared the same dangers; in respect for their platoon leader or company commander who led them well and supported them with everything he had; in concern for their reputation with their leaders; and in the urge to contribute to the success of their group . . . Morale seemed to be predicated on a positive principle. The men were fighting for somebody rather than against somebody.

They were fighting for their buddies.

The fact that unit solidarity had been proved to be at the heart of troop morale in World War II was well known. No one else in the world has followed our lead in interchangeable assembly-line structure of the modern army, because unit solidarity is one of the main things that protects a soldier from the stresses of combat. It is a tremendous psychological advantage.

In World War II, no one removed the experienced men just when they were needed. The officer didn't rotate out after three months to give some new gung-ho second lieutenant a chance to punch his ticket with combat time at the men's expense. Everyone in the unit was equally at risk. Carter described World War II replacements:

. . . scared, bewildered, shy, eager youngsters who acted awestruck around us old boys. We felt sad when it became our duty to lead them into battle because a large percentage of them got killed before they learned how to woo the narrow percentage or safety accorded by lady luck to discerning and sagacious warriors. They would die in the damnedest ways:

One would trip over a mine and get a leg blown off; another would shoot himself or get shot accidentally, a third would let his foxhole cave in and smother him. And in the first battle they usually died in heaps.

Periods of Retraining

Even in units like the 82nd Airborne, combat vets of World War II were not *in combat* for the entire war. They had long periods between fights. Carter spoke of long months doing nothing in Africa before the drop on Sicily. Between his other combat periods were times of living in everything from a sheep barn complete with five kinds of lice to an apartment house in Italy and barracks in England. After being in combat for days or weeks or even months, World War II combat troops were replaced, pulled out, rested, refitted, resupplied, retrained—which they did not appreciate one bit, as Farley Mowat related in his moving memoir, *And No Birds Sang*—and brought back up to strength. Compare that to what you've learned about some of the combat units in Vietnam; to Ossie Burton, John Chambers, and others, coming in and filling sandbags for a few days and then going out in the field for another two weeks or a month, humping.

Safety in the Rear

Rear areas in World War II were relatively safe. By the time Americans arrived overseas, the blitz was over. Although there might be bombs or V-2 rockets, World War II veterans did not spend time worrying that the British and French were setting booby traps. Most Italians, rather than setting punji stakes, helped the Allies rid their country of the Germans. On the Pacific islands, we were welcomed with open arms as liberators.

In Vietnam there was no rear. Satchel charges and grenades were thrown at passing Americans even in Saigon. Sappers would come through the wire on supposedly safe bases and blow up people at night. Sometimes with no warning human-wave attacks would overrun secure American positions. Rockets and mortars hit rear areas every night. There was no safe place.

Support of the Population

In World War II, your hooch maid didn't turn out to be one of the bodies on the wire carrying an AK-47 with a kid strapped to her back. World War II GI's weren't subject to partisan attacks. The British didn't mine their roads to kill Americans. The French wept with joy when we liberated them. The Italians, supposedly our enemies, went out of their way to welcome Americans. Undergrounds in most of the occupied territories helped our men. In Vietnam, the underground was on the other side, and it never gave up.

The U.S. government poured money into a corrupt and a poverty-stricken country and corrupted it more. We supported a Europeanized elite that oppressed a peasant majority. We destroyed the villages of Vietnam in an effort to save them, and we didn't know what this meant to the Vietnamese, whose lives were centered on the village of their ancestors. We will never know how many enemies our methods made us. We turned their women into whores and their men into ARVN, pimps, black marketeers, or VC.

Put it down to Oriental inscrutability if you want, but if some of the incredible sacrifices the VC were willing to make had happened in the American Revolution, we'd still be talking about their patriotism. While the VC, including old men, women, and kids, were dying for what I have to assume they believed in, we had to force the ARVN's to fight. They ran, and ran often, leaving Americans unsupported. Whether this was because they were only in it for the money they earned, or draftees who didn't care, or a bunch of poorly trained and armed panic-stricken amateurs, or chickenshit cowards didn't matter. The guy who was there couldn't tell what the ARVN problem was and he probably didn't give a damn. He just knew he couldn't rely on the people in ARVN uniforms.

What about South Vietnamese civilians? Most vets who had any contact with them thought they just wanted to be left alone, but they were not left alone. If they put their trust in the Americans, our policy of not taking land left them to be killed by the VC when the Americans moved on. If the VC used a village to get Americans, we burnt it down. As one guy put it, "When whole families were moved from the rice paddies to cities . . . they're not going down to a GM plant and get a job making cars. So the women would turn into whores . . ." We were, he continued, ". . . not only destroying the country with bombs, but destroying the lives of families."

Support at Home

Everyone was behind the war effort in World War II. Well, most everyone. There were strikes by war workers and letters from home about "the horrors of sugar rationing," as Farley Mowat put it in *And No Birds Sang*, but no one visited the Germans and Japanese to show solidarity, no one sent them food, there were no pro-Hitler demonstrations in the streets.

In Vietnam, the combatant knew the Vietnamese couldn't be trusted, and the officers were out to get him killed so they could get promoted. What about the American people? Half of them were out screaming in the streets against the war. The other half were making money and watching with indifference while young Americans died every night on TV.

The government never asked for a declaration of war. Taxes were not raised to support the Vietnam non-war, and the government could not send enough troops to take land. Most vets will tell you, "We could have won, but our hands were tied."

"We didn't lose a war," George Hill said, the bitterness in his voice echoing the feelings of all Vietnam vets. "We just quit a war. [The people] didn't support us . . . When they had a bombing halt, we knew every time. That's when we got hit strong, after the bombing halts. We said them people don't care about us. We cared about each other . . ."

As John Wilson put it, "The controversy over the war as well as their experiences in it led many veterans to feel stigmatized for their actions in Vietnam and cynical about the honesty, integrity, and trustworthiness of authority and political leaders."

Declaration of War

The big double bind of being asked to fight a non-war is very different from the experiences of World War II veterans.

When war is declared in this country, it means that the free expression of opinion is at an end. Plenty of people opposed World War I and World War II before war was declared, but they shut up and did their part or went to jail while we were at war. Without a declaration of war in Vietnam, people had a legal right to protest, visit North Vietnam, whatever. This hurt the fighting men in several ways. Emotionally, they were stabbed in the back at home as they risked their lives in Vietnam. Physical damage was done when bombing halts were declared. American lives were lost because the enemy was able to reinforce and resupply his troops.

In *Phantom over Vietnam*, John Trotti said:

> Then, for no apparent reason, we would cease our strikes for weeks at a time. The official word was that it was to show our desire to achieve a negotiated settlement rather than a military victory . . . As we would increase our level of activity, our losses would mount for a period of time, level out and then drop off. Just about the time that we seemed to be able to strike targets with virtual impunity, our raids would be curtailed for several weeks. When the strikes resumed, the enemy's air defenses were back in business, showing ready improvement as the conflict wore on . . .

Ever hear of a bombing halt in World War II? "You think of the lives which would have been lost in an invasion of Japan's home islands . . . And you thank God for the atomic bomb," William Manchester wrote in *Goodbye, Darkness*. That is how important the lives of Americans were to the men who ran World War II. They dropped the atomic bomb to save them because American soldiers did not *and do not* deserve to die if we can prevent it. The fact that they are willing to die for this country does not mean that we should be willing to waste them. *We're gonna take that hill and I expect you men to do your duty (and afterward we won't leave any of your bodies behind when we leave it to the enemy).*

In World War II, after a formal declaration of war, we conquered the territory of our enemy and forced surrender on our terms. At the start of the Vietnam *conflict* (a word, which expresses the feelings at home as well as in the war zone), there was a gray, hazy area of lies. We sent men over to make important decisions who *could not speak the language.* Our *intelligence* officers could not speak the language and received their information from hired agents. No wonder it so often matched their preconceptions. Back in World War II, the OSS used agents who spoke the languages fluently. What in the world happened between World War II and Vietnam?

In the early 1960s, rather than exposing the government's position, the press voluntarily suppressed stories at the request of the U.S. government, stories about VC strength, South Vietnamese corruption, our refusal to allow free elections, the American covert operations in Vietnam before Congress voted the Gulf of Tonkin resolution in August 1964. This granted the president permission to take necessary actions to repel armed attacks in Southeast Asia.

Why didn't President Johnson ask for a declaration of war if, as he claimed on August 4, 1964, the North Vietnamese PT boats carried out "unprovoked attacks"?

Perhaps because on February 1, 1964, he had agreed to the use of Plan No. 34-A, which called for covert actions against North Vietnam. Raids were carried out by U.S. fighter-bombers disguised as Laotian Air Force planes. Sabotage raids on the coast of North Vietnam by U.S.-led South Vietnamese commandos just happened to occur on the nights of the "unprovoked attacks" by the PT boats, of which we sank three. This information didn't come out till several years and many lives later. No torpedoes fired by the PT boats ever hit the U.S. destroyers.

Our Constitution requires a declaration of war by both houses of Congress because it was written *by people who had been through a war on their own territory.* After what they'd been through, they did not feel that war should be entered into lightly. It was the worst thing human beings could do to each other, the last, not the first, resort. And the very idea that we should be promoting American interests overseas would have been both ludicrous and criminal to them. *Keep out of foreign entanglements* was their policy. *No Vietnams* was their intention.

What does the fact that we did not declare war mean to those who died?

Nothing. They are still dead, whether or not it was a declared war.

What difference did it make at home?

Plenty! Plenty of jobs, plenty of consumer goods, plenty of student deferments and loans to keep your kid out of Vietnam, no reason for the burden to be shared. No hurry to end the fighting so everyone can get back to normal life. Life *was* normal, except in Vietnam.

By not declaring war, the president and Congress put American servicemen in double jeopardy. If there is no war, who is this guy we just captured? In *Hanoi Hilton*, an excellent and distressing film, the problem for the POWs is clearly shown. Because of the lack of a declaration of war, they had no protection under international law. As a result they were murdered, tortured and beaten, starved, kept in isolation for years. We still don't know what happened to many of them.

The very conditions of combat in Vietnam, the rules about where to fire, and getting permission to shoot back, and not taking land, were also a direct result of the official lack of commitment.

Fighting for Freedom

People declare war when they are fighting for their own freedom. In World War II, the goal was to conquer the Axis lands and force the unconditional surrender of the Axis powers before they conquered us.

What was the goal in Vietnam? Democracy? We didn't allow free elections in 1956 because Ho Chi Minh would have won even in the South. Freedom? Under a military dictatorship? Capitalism? Colonialism? Exploitation? A chance to try out new weapons? Test the traumatic impact of an M-16 round on a live human subject? A chance for officers to punch their tickets with combat experience? Stop the spread of communism in Southeast Asia? Is that why we consider Pol Pot and the Khmer Rouge, who murdered millions of their own people, the legitimate rulers of Cambodia? Whatever it was, it wasn't a militarily obtainable goal. It was political.

Seymour Leventman and Paul Camacho said: "The purposelessness and meaninglessness of avowed goals, the mixture of bureaucratized fantasy and absurd actuality . . ." were some of the biggest differences between Vietnam and other wars.

Many vets share this opinion. Jim Goodwin, Vietnam combat veteran and psychologist, said in *Readjustment Problems Among Viet-*

nam Veterans, an important pamphlet published by the DAV (Disabled American Veterans), "The ideological basis for the war was difficult to grasp . . . It appeared the whole country was hostile to American forces . . . The only observable outcome was an interminable production of maimed, crippled bodies and countless corpses . . . Rather than a war with a just ideological basis, Vietnam became a private war of survival for every American individual involved."

Vietnam veteran Chaplain William P. Mahedy put it more succinctly in his book, *Out of the Night:* "Body counts, the military careers of their leaders, and big bucks for the folks back home—this was what the war was all about."

One guy put it this way to Clark Smith: "I knew the regular military was fucked up and that you were very lucky if anything got done right . . . I thought it was just the way we were doing it that was wrong. And then I switched over; if we were doing it wrong, then we shouldn't be doing it . . ."

In Vietnam we were destroying villages to save them. Fighting for democracy by propping up a corrupt military dictatorship. Expecting grunts to give their lives while "the embezzlement of massive funds from the PX system by Army officers" was ongoing, but smoking marijuana was a major crime.

Double binds were the Vietnam War's middle name: *Go out and waste those gooks, but don't kill any innocent civilians. Remember when you do the body count, if she's dead she's VC. We're fighting for freedom and democracy, but keep your guns trained on the ARVN at all times when they're in the chopper with you. We had to burn that village to save it.*

Double binds like this have a tremendous effect on the person who has to live under them and even more so on the person who has to fight, kill, and possibly die under them. If you went to Vietnam to fight for democracy and freedom and America and saw innocent civilians killed, how would you react? You can decide they weren't innocent (blaming the victim), you can decide that you were lied to about the war, or you can decide to stop thinking. Any one of these decisions is not going to make you easy to live with.

Consistent, Experienced Officers

World War II officers were aware that combat was hard labor in more ways than one. They participated in it. They were in for the duration. They moved up, but even colonels and majors went out with the troops and fought and died with their men.

In Vietnam, one officer could give three-day passes for a set of ears, and another would have you up on court-martial charges. An officer could tell his men he didn't care if they lived or died, and not be relieved of his command as long as he maintained a high body count and a low VD rate. Matt Brennan was told by one officer not to report wounds unless the soldier had to leave the field, because it made the officer's record look bad. From the point of view of the guy who was trying to serve his tour and get out alive, officers and lifers were just trying to get him killed for their own self-aggrandizement. My perception is that the high-ranking officers and lifer NCO's were mostly "go-ons," and that this had a great moral effect on the war. Who wants to die for some guy in an air-conditioned trailer?

The rear echelon could start at the captain and the lifer sergeant, in the combat units, who could stay back in the base camp and run the war over the radio. Drop by an LZ when it was secure to look at the bodies and try to get the men to give them souvenirs, as one officer mentioned in *Brennan's War*. Or receive a Silver Star for directing the defense of Dak To from high above, as is mentioned in John Ketwig's *. . . and a hard rain fell*. Not all officers and lifers were like that, but there were enough to make a big impression on the literature of the Vietnam War.

Many officers risked their lives right along with their men. Matt Brennan had a CO who was shot down thirteen times in the 1st of the 9th Cav. "Second lieutenants had a life expectancy of seventeen seconds in combat," John Anderson had read in *Time* just before he went to Vietnam.

It was a rare LT who chose to serve out his year in the field, although a good, experienced LT made everyone's life safer and better. This meant that the "experienced" colonel who was running your vet's life could have absolutely no idea what it was like to be in the boonies for months on end. Yet he made decisions that affected people's lives.

No officer who knows his men, has trained and worked with them, and knows their wives and kids is going to throw those men away in search-and-destroy operations or take a hill with loss of life and then just abandon it. In order to participate in a war like Vietnam, where men were *wasted* every day, the military had to be structured the way ours is now, like a corporation in which slots are filled with anonymous grunts whose value is the same—nothing—and with officers who need a few months of combat time to punch their tickets for promotion. (Two years with a unit is considered barely sufficient for promotion in the British army.)

Of course, one of the true ironies of Vietnam was that there was no front line, and so there was no real rear. Safe in his bunker, the colonel could still be blown away by a well-placed rocket attack or a sapper with a satchel charge, or by his own men.

Clear Combat Zones and Visible Progress on the Ground

Every time Vietnam vets went into an LZ and took a place, they abandoned it at the end of the operation. Every time they patrolled an area, they pulled out afterward. Every man who was shot or stepped on a mine or whatever did it for nothing in the way of territory. Afterward the enemy bodies had to be found, searched, counted—*Does this leg go with that one, or is this two guys?*—and then buried or left in conspicuous places to rot, often by the same men who killed them. In World War II campaigns *conquered territory* and, in the end, we won. In Vietnam, operations *lost men*. Then we counted dead bodies and left.

In classic warfare, campaigns start at one physical point and end when an area of land has been conquered and cleared of enemy troops. Names like North Africa, Sicily, Italy, Normandy, Guadalcanal, Tarawa, Iwo Jima, and Okinawa resound from World War II, names of places we conquered. In doing this, World War II combat vets did not have it easy. Far from it. Often they faced a kind of concentrated battle that was rare in Vietnam.

Farley Mowat wrote:

> What followed was the kind of night men dream about in after-years, waking in a cold sweat to a surge of gratitude that it is but a dream. It was a delirium of sustained violence . . .
>
> During the next thirty-six hours eleven separate counter-attacks were flung against us . . .
>
> . . . When the firing died down on our sector, stretcher and burial parties scouring the slimy slopes and the tangles of shell-torn debris found one hundred and seventy German corpses. Our own dead and wounded amounted to a third of the four hundred or so Hasty Pees who had gone into the valley . . .

The battle Mowat described was just a diversion, not even the main battle, a side action to distract the Germans, while the real battle took place elsewhere. Yet in those battles it was clear to every combat soldier who and where the enemy was. They never had to get permission to defend themselves or to attack the enemy. They were at war.

Since World War II we have fought two police actions, Korea and Vietnam. In the Korean police action we took territory up to the 37th parallel and then had an armistice. We neither won nor lost, but we never left. The armistice is still in effect, and our troops are still there.

The Vietnam War was fought on an entirely different basis from any other war. We didn't take land.

Why? The government line: It was going to take only a few guns, a few bullets, a few helicopters to win. In a few months it would be over. Lots of wars since the beginning of time have started with both sides talking this same silly line, as exemplified by the slogans *On to Richmond* in the Civil War, and *Berlin by Christmas* in World War I. Eventually people realize they are in for a long haul and settle into pounding the enemy until he gives up territory and then gives up.

Instead we have the spectacle of Westmoreland's telling Congress late in 1967 that the VC were weak and unable to mount a serious effort a few short months before they hit us with the 1968 Tet Offensive. All through the Vietnam War, victory was just around the corner, things got better and better, we won more and more, until finally we had to leave.

All I know is, I wouldn't have wanted to be the last man to die in Vietnam, and neither did anyone else. World War II vets didn't want to be the last ones to die in that war either. No one wants to die for nothing.

Our troops were trained for classic conventional warfare against uniformed troops. As John Wilson put it, "The typical soldier was not ideologically or emotionally prepared to face the complex and often surreal nature of jungle combat against a resilient, tenacious, resourceful, and determined enemy . . . To engage in battle necessitated combat assaults in the enemy's lair, which was always ephemeral, hidden and paradoxically ubiquitous."

So how do you fight a successful counterinsurgency? Not the way we did! We inserted troops at selected places, all of which were cleared with the Vietnamese beforehand, so it was never a surprise. Those troops were flown there in large, noisy targets (helicopters). We usually managed to drive away the enemy, sometimes at large cost in American lives, in which case the statistics would be fudged, *not by the news media*, but by the public-information officers who provided the statistics. Real reporters would have been out in the field finding out for themselves, but a lot of them were corrupted, too, by the posh life-style available in Saigon. Remember the bulldozer driver in Chapter 2: *Casualties light to moderate, and they're taking them out, taking them out—half the battalion?*

If we killed lots of the enemy, we reported that. If no bodies were found, statistics were made up from the kill radius of the weapons used or other such constructs. In casual conversation at Fort Wolters, Texas, in 1966, one helicopter pilot told me disgustedly about being credited with killing thirteen VC when he'd gotten one man in the middle of a field with a rocket—but the kill radius of the rocket meant that if there had been other men near the one he hit he would have been able to kill up to thirteen. That kind of bullshit permeated the war. Say it's true and it is. As Mike Geokan said, "We didn't win or lose. We left."

Mike was speaking about the whole war, but, I repeat, it was true in the day-by-day running of the war, too. It was also true in the most basic sense for each man who fought in Vietnam. When your vet left, we hadn't won or lost. He left, but his buddies were still there. He left, but men were still dying. He left, but he could see the war going on every day on TV. It wasn't like coming home at the end of World War I or II, with the war over and won.

There were rules about where you could shoot and when. In Vietnam while people were dying, you had to check with the company or divisional command, who had to check with the ARVN—often VC—to get clearance to shoot back. You weren't supposed to shoot up "friendly" villages. It looked bad in the papers back home. The level of casualties this policy caused looked acceptable from the air-conditioned bunker on the big base, and even better from Saigon and Washington. The only comparable situation I could find was the 7,000 casualties a day that the British High Command considered normal "wastage" in World War I.

Since you had to get clearance to defend yourself from friendly fire, it was to the advantage of the field commanders to have more and more places declared *not* friendly, free-fire zones. In a free-fire zone, you could shoot anyone who moved. The Vietnamese were supposed to know that, so it was their own fault if they died, right? Of course the Vietnamese didn't speak English and may not have known what a map was, but that's their fault too, right? But if too many places were made free-fire zones, the public would think we weren't winning. A public-relations war was fought alongside the real one, and the loser was always the vet and the Vietnamese population.

Since we couldn't take land in Vietnam, the only measure of our success was the level of enemy corpses. Leventman and Camacho called it "technical criteria for measuring success . . . in a war otherwise difficult to assess." We didn't have to count bodies to measure success against Germany in World War II. We just took Berlin.

In Vietnam, you could go in expecting a big fight and find no one. Leave and they'd mortar the LZ just to let you know they were still there. Or you could go into a cold LZ and have it erupt into a three-sided ambush that killed everyone. You could be sweeping the same village where you had "friends" among the villagers and lose half your squad to a booby trap. Ambushes erupted in the deepest jungle and in friendly villages or on secure roads. When every step can bring a Bouncing Betty up to blow your balls off, or a daisy chain of grenades in the trees to blow the heads off your squad, or an ambush, when you can't trust anyone, when staying alive is a matter of blind luck day after day for a year, the stress on a human being is incredible. If that same human being comes back and is told he wasn't in a real war, he is going to be embittered.

Clear-Cut Enemy

World War II troops faced uniformed enemies.

In Vietnam, friends and enemies all looked alike. The grunts did not have VC detectors so they learned not to trust anyone. The VC farmed by day and fought by night. Or they worked as barbers on the base by day and fought at night. The women who washed your clothes could be shooting at you at night and you wouldn't know unless one of them was hit.

Remember the sad-eyed little Italian and French waifs in Bill Mauldin's cartoons, the ones to whom Willie and Joe gave candy and food? Well, in Vietnam there were waifs, too. Sometimes they wanted candy and sometimes they wanted to give you a grenade. The thing was, you couldn't tell.

The whore you went to one night might present your head to your friends the next day, as John Ketwig reported in . . . *and a hard rain fell*. Of course, she'd die for that, but she did it anyhow. Why? Was it insanity or patriotism?

The NVA wore uniforms, but they engaged mainly in battles they thought they could win. If they didn't want to be found, they shucked their uniforms and became farmers or hid out in their tunnels and bunkers while the Americans walked right over them. In Vietnam, sometimes you fought uniformed NVA, sometimes VC in the black pajamas of every other Vietnamese farmer. Sometimes you were fighting women and kids. Sometimes you never saw anyone you could shoot at. Men died every day fighting booby traps that the women and kids never tripped. And sometimes when enough of your friends had died, you killed everyone. Sometimes it was rage, sometimes it was unthinking automatic response, and sometimes it was orders.

Even in a conventional war, atrocities occur. In a guerrilla war, they are inevitable.

World War II veterans feel their war was clean and they would never have done what was done in Vietnam. Yet William Manchester reported that, on Okinawa, "More than seventy-seven thousand civilians died here during the battle, and no one comes out of a fight like that with clean hands."

He also mentioned that:

> Bob Fowler, F Company's popular, towheaded commander, had bled to death after being hit in the spleen. His orderly, who adored him, snatched up a submachine gun and unforgivably massacred a line of unarmed Japanese prisoners who had just surrendered. Even worse was the tragic loss of eighty-five student nurses . . . Flamethrowers, moving in, killed them all.

Words like this have rarely been written about World War II, but there is no reason to doubt Manchester. Most World War II memoirs speak so subtly of the horrors of war that it's easy to miss what the author is trying to convey. Ross Carter said in *Those Devils in Baggy Pants:*

> Jokers who began to fight during and after D-day may doubt that the medics [German and American] helped each other out . . . The Italian campaigns were fought more according to the Geneva Convention than the later stages of the war. The killing of prisoners on both sides didn't occur very often until the Normandy campaign began.

Carter went a long way in mentioning this in a book written in the forties, at which time it was practically illegal to discuss the realities of war.

Farley Mowat reported that a lieutenant from another unit in the Italian campaign told him:

> "Jerry took everything the people had in the way of food and livestock, then turfed them out, burned what would burn and blew everything else to hell. In one village the bastards

blew down the church with women and kids sheltering inside . . .

"Keep it under your hats, but our boys are so fucking well
brassed off about it, they aren't taking any prisoners. Not
those First Para bastards anyhow!"

In Vietnam, our men faced people who were willing to cut off their
cocks and balls and stuff them in their mouths if they had the chance,
who skinned people alive, cut out their eyes, and made "Christmas
trees" out of them by slitting open their bellies and pulling out their
intestines and draping them all over the place, leaving them to die
slowly. On our side the South Vietnamese did the same thing, given
the chance. All a guy can do for someone in that state is kill him as
quickly as possible, but how does a guy feel then? How does he live
with what people are capable of? If his allies did it, how does he
feel? If it was the VC, how does he tell who did it out of the sur-
rounding population? And what does he think of himself if he does
it *back?*

Mahedy said:

> Unfortunately, many people are unable to listen to these sto-
> ries with any degree of understanding. Some, on the political
> and religious right, can accept the notion that the "other side"
> committed atrocities but "not our boys." Others, of a leftist
> ideological persuasion, have been able to see our troops as
> baby-killers but are unwilling to accept the truth that the
> Vietcong and North Vietnamese committed unbelievable
> atrocities themselves . . .

Mahedy went on to say, "The man who returns from combat and
says 'I'm an animal' knows a certain truth about himself. The person
who taunts him or cannot bear to hear his story is simply hiding
from the same truth."

Casualties

According to Harry Summers's *Vietnam War Almanac*, 30,000
soldiers were killed or wounded in action in Vietnam in the 1st
Cavalry Division; that's a third more than the unit lost in World War

II and Korea combined. The 1st Infantry Division had 20,770 casualties in Vietnam, compared to 20,659 in World War II, and 22,320 in World War I. The 4th Infantry Division lost 16,844 in Vietnam, 22,660 in World War II. The 3rd Marine Amphibious Force had more casualties in Vietnam than the entire marine corps lost in all of World War II. The 25th Infantry Division had 34,484 casualties in Vietnam, 5,432 in World War II, and 13,685 in Korea. Three brigades of the Americal Division suffered 17,565 casualties in Vietnam, compared to 4,209 for the entire division in World War II. The 101st Airborne Division lost twice the men in Vietnam that it did in World War II.

According to "Soldiers," a PBS documentary, in World War I, two-thirds of the casualties were from artillery, reflecting the nature of static trench warfare. In World War II and Korea, Summers reported that 53 and 59 percent of deaths, respectively, were from fragments. In conventional conflicts, both sides have plenty of artillery and tanks. In Vietnam 51 percent of deaths were from small-arms fire, reflecting the guerrilla nature of the war and the new, improved small arms, the AK-47 and the M-16 when it worked. Fragments accounted for only 36 percent of our dead. Booby traps and mines accounted for 11 percent of deaths—again reflecting the guerrilla war—as opposed to 3 and 4 percent in World War II and Korea, respectively.

Harry Summers said, "In almost all cases at the fighting level, casualties in Vietnam exceeded those in World War II." There were 300 percent more traumatic amputations and serious injuries to the lower limbs in Vietnam than in World War II. It may not have been a world war, but it was bloody.

Psychological Casualties

Twenty-three percent of the battle evacuations of casualties in World War II were psychological. According to the pamphlet *Readjustment Problems Among Vietnam Veterans*, in Vietnam it was 1.2 percent. Does that mean Vietnam vets were braver? Does it mean that knowing they had to endure it only for a year helped? Or was it because the military used administrative discharges to get rid of people who were having psychological problems?

During World War II, every man who broke down in the North

African campaign was listed as having combat exhaustion and was treated for it. In further campaigns, this tradition was followed so as not to shame the soldier. Of course, it didn't really work like that from the point of view of the soldier. Bud Register, a scout with the 28th Infantry wounded during the Battle of the Bulge, told me that in World War II all combat soldiers went before a shrink in groups. "They told us that with what we'd been through, we'd never be the same, and did we have any questions? If you were stupid enough to ask a question, they put you in a group and labeled you a nut." I had to laugh when he told me that.

The one-year tour in Vietnam was designed to prevent the psychological breakdowns men have developed in every war when they saw too much combat. Having a known DEROS [date of expected return overseas] was supposed to relieve the pressure. At first, it appeared to be successful. For most people the one-year tour masked the problems we now know human beings experience when faced with trauma outside the normal range of human experience.

Unfortunately, while psychiatrists were writing wildly optimistic papers about conquering the psychological problems of war, never having faced a bullet themselves and sure that it wouldn't affect them if they did, the lifers were throwing other people out of the military right and left, using a system of administrative discharges that could not be appealed. These *discipline problems* were suffering from acute combat stress reactions, but since *everyone knew combat couldn't affect a person unless he had some kind of defect when he came into the military*, they were thrown away like so much garbage.

"In fiscal year 1971, 72% of the Army's general discharges were for character and behavior disorders," Ronald Bitzer reported in *Strangers at Home*. He also quoted other sources, which mentioned an "increase in character disorder codes . . . from 8.6% in World War II veterans to 16.6% in Vietnam veterans . . ." and "diagnosis of personality disorder . . . from less than 7% of the World War II era to 36% today." Most of this represents scapegoating. If a man had a character disorder or a personality disorder, the government did not have to treat him. By definition, character disorders developed pre-enlistment. Misdiagnosis saved the government a lot of money.

John Keegan quoted a U.S. government report from World War II, *Combat Exhaustion,* in *The Face of Battle:*

> There is no such thing as "getting used to combat" . . . Each moment of combat imposes a strain so great that men will break down in direct relation to the intensity and duration of their exposure . . . psychiatric casualties are as inevitable as gunshot and shrapnel wounds in warfare . . . Most men were ineffective after 180 or even 140 days. The general consensus was that a man reached his peak of effectiveness in the first 90 days of combat, that after that his efficiency began to fall off, and that he became steadily less valuable thereafter until he was completely useless . . . The number of men on duty after 200 to 240 days of combat was small and their value to their units negligible.

In 1968, the year of the Tet Offensive, the psychiatric community in an excess of denial dropped the only category that acknowledged combat reactions from their *Diagnostic and Statistical Manual.* Men with severe psychological problems brought about by combat stress were told they were too weak to take it or innately defective, with pre-existing psychotic, schizophrenic, borderline, or manic depressive personalities that had somehow gone unnoticed when they joined the military. Even though the symptoms that Vietnam combat vets exhibited did not conform to these convenient diagnoses, "when diagnostic criteria for a particular mental disorder are accepted— phenomena which do not fit the definitions or the paradigm tend to be discounted or ignored . . . until the unaccepted-though-still-occurring phenomena can no longer be ignored or accommodated," Steven Silver, Ph.D., explained in a paper entitled "Post-Traumatic Stress and the Death Imprint."

Psychological stress symptoms were very different in Vietnam. World War II guys shook and cried or became paralyzed or blind or deaf. Vietnam vets rarely reacted like that. Although they medicated themselves with drugs and alcohol, and/or became hostile to authority, most of them managed to hang on through their tour.

By being antisocial and, toward the end of the war, fragging or refusing to go on useless operations, they tried desperately to break through the massive denial of the upper echelons in Vietnam and the people back home to make them see that they couldn't waste people. They were screaming into the void: *You can either have a war or not have a war, but not a half war.*

The results of hanging on for that year became clear only later.

Morale

Combat all by itself can get you down. Morale was a problem all through World War II, but at least those soldiers had a clear sense of purpose, were fighting for a close-knit group, and were allowed to win if they could.

Psychiatrist Herbert Spiegel wrote about his experience with an infantry battalion in North Africa:

> [The X factor] was greatly influenced by a a man's devotion to his group, by his regard for his leader, and by his conviction that his cause was right. It seemed to explain why a tired, disgruntled soldier who had the clinical appearance of an anxiety state could keep on going, and why some units could outdo others. Apparently it helped a man to control the ever-present fear and to resist fatigue.
>
> . . . For the majority who were average soldiers, this factor played an enormous part. Here was the critical component that often determined whether or not a man would be overwhelmed by his fear, anxiety, and fatigue. Here was something that often decided whether or not a man became a psychiatric casualty. Here was the Achilles' heel that was vulnerable to news of strikes and profiteering back home and to disregard for the men at the front . . .
>
> Good morale . . . required constant attention. In combat the company commander or platoon leader could not satisfactorily answer such abstract questions as, "Why are we fighting?" "Why the profiteering and strikes?" But at a more concrete level, he was in a position to manipulate morale. He arranged for his men to get the best food under the circumstances. He sent blankets up to them at night if at all possible. He made every effort to keep them well supplied with water and ammunition. He saw that promotions were fair. He made certain that good work and gallantry received recognition. He got mail, news, and information to the men whenever possible;

and he made sure that violations of the rules were dealt with justly and quickly.

By these actions, the leader made his men feel that they were not alone, that he was doing everything humanly possible to support them . . .

The tampering with C-rations in the rear echelons illustrates . . . the impact [small things] could have on the men. "Is that what they think of us! They steal from us and then send us what they don't want."

Cigarettes furnished another example . . . the essential point was the implication of sending cigarettes all across the ocean, across the Continent to the frontline, with a brand name that was considered to be second-rate. To the combat soldier, the message was: "You got what was left. Be glad with what you got." In contrast, he wanted to feel that the people back of him would exert themselves to send him the best available supplies . . .

These nonverbal messages hit hard. They exemplify definite morale issues whose impact is due to the immediacy and the stress of the combat atmosphere. Just as nonverbal messages can be encouraging if they imply, "We're with you completely," so they can be disturbing if they say, "We're with you halfheartedly."

As time went on, the Vietnam experience, the half war, began to destroy the morale of our troops in Vietnam. It became obvious they were caught in a no-win situation. No matter how hard they fought, how many LZ's they took, sweeps they made, villages they searched and destroyed, there was no way to win under the rules they had to follow.

Stuff like that can get you down. So can other things.

Faithful Women

In World War II, there was a stigma to dumping a fighting man. The entire society was a support system for women with men overseas. When I told people that Bob was in Vietnam, they just said, "Huh?" In 1965 they didn't even know where that was. Later on this changed. Women were encouraged to dump their boyfriends on the grounds that if they were low enough to serve in Vietnam, they didn't deserve anyone's love. There arose a stigma to sticking by a combat soldier. I've even spoken to wives of Vietnam vets who said that while their husbands were in Vietnam, they kept it a secret, afraid the neighbors would find out and harass them.

Consistent Values

American values remained pretty consistent throughout World War II, but not while your vet was in Vietnam: The older generation would say that as skirts went up morals went down; language degenerated; standards fell. For a lot of men this was an added source of stress. Women swore and had jobs and didn't want to be taken care of anymore. The rules changed behind vets' backs, and it pissed them off.

For other veterans it seemed that while young people were trying to be more honest and open, the standards of the older generation transmuted themselves from valuing human life, especially those of American fighting men, to bland indifference to death and suffering as it was shown on TV every night. The value placed on heroic veterans after World War II slipped away, replaced by a don't-make-waves attitude and the lure of prosperity. The value placed on honesty and integrity in government disappeared. These changes pissed vets off, too.

Drugs

Drugs were very prevalent in Vietnam, especially during the later years of the war. With a lot of vets trying to clean up their acts, most of the ones I interviewed didn't volunteer much about drugs, but one surprised and moved me with this comment: "Heroin. You don't do heroin for a rush, like they say. You do it because it *fixes anything*. You're not *afraid* anymore, not *hungry*, not thirsty, nothing hurts. You're *fine*, that's all, fine." Self-medication has always been a part of combat. Those bottles of cognac in Bill Mauldin's World War II Willie and Joe cartoons are self-medication.

In Vietnam, the available drugs went far beyond stolen cognac and government-supplied cigarettes, to government-supplied speed and tranquilizers and heavy black-market drugs. Some people used them and some didn't. One guy told me he never smoked pot the whole time he was in Vietnam, even though he'd used it regularly in college, because, "I didn't want any *heightened awareness* of where I was!" I had to laugh.

Other guys got stoned a lot. Smoking pot in Vietnam was "a time-honored response . . . [that] had local precedents," John Keegan said. Sometimes it was easier for guys to get pot in the bush than beer because the rear-echelon fat cats were selling their beer on the black market. Some vets smoked opium and shot up heroin. If some guy said to you, "No, we didn't smoke dope," believe him, but *don't* assume everyone else didn't, either. Some excellent units were stoned a lot of the time. It helped them deal with the stress. Speed, which the government supplied, was used in combat situations to keep awake and alert. Of course black-market speed was preferred because it was better than government-issue: good old government, can't even get the drugs right.

Most combat soldiers used whatever drugs were at hand to deal with stress. I wasn't there so I can't judge, though I can just see smoke coming out of the ears of the World War II guys as they read this. Yet World War II vets took two of the most dangerous and addictive drugs there are, alcohol and tobacco, every chance they got. "Drinking . . . seems an inseparable part both of preparation for battle and of combat itself," John Keegan said in his history of the battlefield experiences of soldiers, *The Face of Battle*. What is more, World War II vets are still using the same two drugs to deal with their pain. Every VFW post or American Legion hall I've ever been to has a bar.

Trip Home

World War II vets came home together on a long, slow boat ride where they got to process their experiences to some extent, or at least be with people who had been through the same things, people who *understood*. This long period of decompression on the boat is now considered to have been one of their greatest advantages over the Vietnam vet. Even if the long, slow boat ride meant they missed the parades, it also meant an opportunity to process trauma. A

Vietnam vet could be in a firefight one day and back on the streets of Chicago forty-eight hours later, too young to buy a drink, and with spit on his uniform. Alone.

Supportive Re-entry into Society

After the long boat trip home from World War II, the military set up a system of hotels where couples could be reunited without the pressures of everyday life. Movies were made to illustrate the problems of homecoming. People were understanding if a guy was a little jumpy or strange. People wanted to hear our heroes talk about their experiences. The VA was a friendly place for veterans. Older vets treated World War II vets well. Many of them had a woman to come back to. After World War II there were plenty of jobs and an excellent GI Bill, which enabled any veteran to go to any school he wanted to without mortgaging his future. It paid a living allowance, with money for books and tuition at any school. Men were helped back into the mainstream.

As discussed in Chapter 6, the Vietnam vet's experience was different.

"The single best predictor [of PTSD] is the factor 'psychological isolation' at homecoming," Dr. John Wilson and Gustave Krause said. Even in World War II, the soldiers were bitter. Willard Walker wrote in 1944:

> The soldier's bitterness is justified . . . He has given everything and recieved very little in return, nothing in fact except a highly perishable kind of glory . . . A notice of induction is for most young men a sentence to hard labor, and for some a sentence of death . . . The concepts of honor and duty have been invented to make such sacrifices acceptable. What, then, if the honor that is the soldier's due in the bargain be withheld?

What, indeed?

> There is a brief period of glory in which those who have done least and come home first play the greater part. The soldier receives the grateful thanks of the nation and that is

all. He finds himself left behind and permanently disadvantaged in competition.

John Chambers said, "They sold me a bill, a line, men do this [going to war], but the people who sold me the line backed out on the deal."

Time Bombs

"To those Americans who survived mines, ambushes, booby traps, and firefights, the supreme irony is to discover . . . that your own Government may have killed you," Fred Wilcox wrote in *Waiting for an Army to Die*. According to the VA, the federal government, and the chemical companies, there is no scientific proof that Agent Orange has caused any problems for anyone. Remember what Marty Comer said about it? There is no scientific proof that it hasn't, either. The government did a convenient study of Operation Ranch Hand. The air force men on Operation Ranch Hand, who sprayed the stuff, went back, took showers, and changed their clothes—don't have a high incidence of cancers. Grunts who walked through the browned-out areas and slept in foxholes in the rain in Agent Orange-saturated water and got to change their clothes every two weeks if they were lucky don't figure in the study.

The psychological effects of the Agent Orange problem were described by Erwin Parson, Ph.D., who served as a medic in Vietnam:

> Whether the pains in one's side, the numbness in one's hands, liver disease, the small cyst in one's back, severe skin rash, ulcers, neuromuscular difficulties and gastrointestinal pathology, are symptoms of a powerful carcinogen . . . To be assaulted by the pangs of anxiety over the possibility of one's most precious possessions—the bodily self—deteriorating and being eaten alive from within . . . The uncertainty over whether the lumps in one's testicles, violent headaches, collapsed lung, chloracne, amnesia, birth defects of one's offspring, numbness of one's joints, dizziness, or mental collapse . . . is extraordinarily overtaxing to the veteran's . . . emotions.

Until people have been exposed to a chemical for generations, how can the government or the chemical companies say it won't be harmful? Remember DES, the fertility drug of the forties and fifties and the cases of vaginal and testicular cancer that resulted from its use? Agent Orange killed the vegetation it touched, yet claims are made that it couldn't possibly have harmed people.

More information on Agent Orange is available in *The Viet Vet Survival Guide* and from the veterans' organizations listed in the back of *Waiting for an Army to Die*.

The Whiners

With all these differences, with all their support systems, World War II vets suffered, and continue to suffer, psychological changes from combat. (Remember the 26 percent of battle evacuations during World War II for psychological reasons?) A veteran with enough of these changes can be diagnosed as having PTSD. Right now, delayed PTSD is striking many more World War II veterans, who adjusted well right after the war, as they retire, or lose their wives. Others of them are revealing that they have felt numb, or couldn't sleep, or had combat nightmares since they got back from the war but never told anyone. And, despite this, most people whom you tell exactly what was so different about Vietnam will come back with the question, "Yeah, but why do they whine about it? Why do they complain so much?"

The answer is: They don't. And they didn't.

The answer is: "What makes you think telling the truth is whining?"

Fact is, people don't want to hear the truth about any war, never mind one like Vietnam. During and after World War II, veterans had to clean up their accounts of warfare to get them published. That's why so many of the Vietnam generation grew up thinking war was glorious. We read *Battle Cry*, but we couldn't read between the lines to feel the rage and the bloodlust. Rather than revealing the truth about warfare, World War II veterans lied by commission (chest-pounding war stories) and omission, and sent their sons off to die.

We didn't know "of John Wayne being booed in a Hawaiian hospital by wounded marines from Iwo Jima and Okinawa, men who had had macho acts, in a phrase of the day, up their asses to their armpits," as William Manchester revealed in 1979.

We didn't know that

> . . .the published photographs [of the dead on Tarawa] touched off an uproar . . . The men on Tarawa were puzzled. The photographs had been discreet. No dismembered corpses were shown, no faces with chunks missing, no flies crawling on eyeballs; virtually all of the pictures were of bodies in Marine uniforms face down on the beach. Except for those who had known the dead, the pictures were quite ordinary to men who had scraped the remains of buddies off bunker walls or who, while digging foxholes, found their entrenching tools caught in the mouths of dead friends who had been buried in sand by exploding shells.

—until William Manchester revealed that, too.

We also didn't know World War II guys were pissed off and embittered when they got back. Bill Mauldin's *Back Home* was published in 1947 with the following jacket copy: "Mauldin feels strongly, although he claims no special knowledge of men's affairs except the obvious fact that millions are recently dead because of selfishness, greed, and lust for power . . . His observations on the privileged strata of our civilization . . . are often humorous and often downright angry." One of the cartoons is labeled "The Unknown Soldier, 1946," and shows a statue of a man in civilian clothes asleep on a park bench on top of a marble tomb with *Semper Sans Cot* carved in it.

Back from Vietnam, one of my friends went to protest the war in Washington. He was bashed on the head with a nightstick and spent the night in jail. That was the end of his trying to tell what it was like over there. That was considered whining, trying to tell the truth.

Bunch o' whiners. I served all the way through the Big One, and I never whine. World War II vets have an attitude problem: No one else has ever been through it. They did go through it. You'll never see a Vietnam vet discounting the experiences of other combat veterans the way World War II men have done to them. War sucks. Read authentic accounts of any war and you realize that.

Some World War II men have been able to see that Vietnam was no picnic. Carolynn Ketwig told me, "My father, who served in the South Pacific, took John to see *The Deer Hunter*. John had to leave two times during the movie. Dad said, 'Is that what Vietnam was like?' 'Yes. Is that what World War II was like?' 'No.' It made them closer."

Bob had a similar experience while he was in prison. A tough fellow prisoner, a veteran of Anzio, came up to him after reading *Chickenhawk* and told him he'd had no idea what guys went through in Vietnam. "You guys have my respect," he said. A more famous American veteran of World War I wrote in 1936 to his wife, Bess Truman: "War heroes are no longer that. They are now looked upon as a sort of nuisance and are considered fools to have gone."

Telling the Truth

The Vietnam vet who says *Hey, you sent me into a no-win situation* is not whining. He is telling the truth, one that society had better heed unless we want to do it again.

When a Vietnam vet says *Vietnam was fucked up and combat there fucked me up*, he is also telling the truth. He's not interested in the euphemisms of earlier wars, in using nice words to describe the blood and shit and bones of his friends flying through the air, hitting him in the face. He talks about Vietnam using the most technically accurate vocabulary, *fucked up*. Combat didn't make him nervous, a little angry, liable to depressive reactions or autonomic nervous arousal. *Combat fucked him up*. It fucks everyone up to one extent or another. Vietnam burned something away in the Vietnam veteran—and that something is the bullshit. He's telling it like it is.

Despite that, he probably still loves this country more than you do.

8

Post-Traumatic Stress Disorder

"It seems so dramatic to say I will never get over this."
"Does it? To me it seems like saying that what people
do is important."

—Jane Smiley
"Long Distance," *The Atlantic Monthly,* January 1987

War changes men's natures. The barbarities of war are
seldom committed by abnormal men. The tragedy of war
is that these horrors are committed by normal men in
situations in which the ebb and flow of everyday life have
departed and been replaced by a constant round of fear
and anger and blood and death. Soldiers at war are not
to be judged by civilian rules.

—*Breaker Morant* (1979)

We've seen in Part One how traumatic service in Vietnam could be,
combat or otherwise. We've seen the poor reception for veterans
back home, and discussed the differences between Vietnam and other
wars, one of which is that in all other wars people broke down at a
greater rate than they did in Vietnam. Instead of breaking down
during combat as often as the soldiers did in other wars, months or
years later, Vietnam veterans began to have problems, once labeled
Post-Vietnam Syndrome but now referred to officially as Post-
Traumatic Stress Disorder. Many people develop some of the characteristics of PTSD without ever having the diagnosable disorder,
or being diagnosed when they do have it. The effects of war can be

seen on a broad continuum of possibilities, including diagnosable PTSD.

Traumatic events have serious, long-term effects on all people who survive them. Those range from moderate to severe, depending on a number of factors: the actual traumatic incidents, the severity and duration of the stress factors, how the person sees the events in relation to himself or herself, the ability of the survivor to find someone to talk to about the events, the reaction of other people to what the survivor tells them, and luck. When the actual traumatic incidents involve mutilation and death, when they lasted for a year's tour, when the person feels angry or used or betrayed or helpless or as though he's become an animal, when he can't find anyone to talk to about what happened, when he's ridiculed, insulted, or ignored by society, and when his luck—in finding or holding on to a job, another person to love, a safe place in society—fails, he may develop a cluster of symptoms that we now call PTSD. It is a normal reaction. Normal! Remember that. A vet may also develop only a few of these symptoms, never have official PTSD, and yet be hard to live with.

So what is this mysterious thing called PTSD? And why did Vietnam vets have to struggle so hard to get it recognized?

Before there was even a name for what happens to combat veterans, there were descriptions of PTSD. Michael Trimble pointed out in "Post-Traumatic Stress Disorder: History of a Concept" that Shakespeare wrote about it in *Henry IV, Part I*. I've put the modern names of these symptoms in a column beside Lady Percy's speech:

Oh, my good lord, why are you thus alone?	*emotional isolation*
For what offense have I this fortnight been	
A banished woman from my Harry's bed?	*sexual dysfunction*
Tell me, sweet lord, what is't that takes from thee	*emotional numbing*
Thy stomach, pleasure, and thy golden sleep?	*sleep disturbance*
Why does thou bend thine eyes upon the earth	*intrusive thoughts*

And start so often when thou sitt'st alone . . .	*anxiety, and startle reaction*
. . . thick-ey'd musing and curs'd melancholy?	*inability to concentrate and depression*
In thy faint slumbers I by thee have watch'd,	
And heard thee murmur tales of iron wars . . .	*nightmares*
Cry *Courage—to the field* . . . And thou hast talk'd	
Of sallies and retires, of trenches, tents . . .	*intrusive memories*
Of prisoners' ransom and of soldiers slain . . .	*survivor guilt*
Thy spirit within thee hath been so at war,	
And thus hath so bestirred thee in thy sleep	
That beads of sweat have stood upon thy brow . . .	*night sweats*
And in thy face strange motions have appeared . . .	

Lady Percy was having a hard time with her husband. Maybe you've noticed a few of these things in your own vet.

The first medical reference I found to acute PTSD reactions was quoted in John Russell Smith's paper, "A Review of One Hundred and Twenty Years of the Psychological Literature on Reactions to Combat," from the U.S. Army Surgeon General's Report of 1888:

> A temporary feeling of *depression* frequently pervaded our camps on account of *discomfort, hardships* and *exposures, especially when these were recognized or assumed by our volunteer soldiers to be of a preventable or uncalled-for nature* . . . While it lasted it was dangerous to their efficiency . . . Occasionally . . . the home feeling became developed to a *morbid degree* and was reported as *nostalgia* . . . [*italics* mine]

The idea of *nostalgia* rather than cowardice influencing behavior of soldiers was quite a breakthrough.

Drs. Herbert Hendin and Ann Pollinger Haas, in their book *The Wounds of War*, discussed the case of Confederate Lewis Paine and Union volunteer Ambrose Bierce. Paine joined at sixteen and fought all through the war. He was wounded at Gettysburg, was captured, and escaped, and saw one brother killed and the other disabled by wounds:

> Once considered easygoing, kind and tenderhearted, Paine became obsessed with killing and death, frequently boasting that he never left wounded enemy soldiers alive and using the skull of a Yankee soldier as an ashtray . . . He began displaying an explosive temper . . . [for instance] beating . . . a hotel's female servant who did not respond quickly enough to his requests.

In 1865, Paine tried to assassinate Secretary of State Seward in conjunction with the assassination of Lincoln, stabbing Seward, beating and stabbing two of his sons, and killing a servant, screaming "I am mad! I am mad!" as he fled. His lawyer pleaded that he had developed "homicidal mania" as a result of his "four years as a combat soldier." He was hanged.

Ambrose Bierce enlisted as a private in 1861 (aged nineteen) in the Indiana Volunteers. He fought at Shiloh, Chickamauga, and Chattanooga, twice risked his life to save wounded buddies, and was wounded twice. His postwar life displayed evidence of PTSD. In his stories, "brutal recall of detail, preoccupation with death, and descriptions of blood, maiming, and destruction—suggest that Bierce's postwar life was marked by ongoing, intense images of horror." His nightmares, emotional numbing resulting in a failed marriage, insomia, heavy drinking, rages, and carrying a weapon with him at all times are other characteristics familiar to those who study PTSD.

The first description of any type of chronic PTSD I found was reported in 1871. Dr. Jacob Mendes DaCosta, in the *American Journal of Medical Sciences*, discussed a condition he found in Civil War veterans that he called *irritable heart*. Persistent palpitations, cardiac pain, tachycardia (over 100 heartbeats a minute), headache, dimness of vision, and giddiness were the symptoms. The same symptoms are present in some veterans of Vietnam, including my husband.

In November 1914, at the start of World War I, Dr. Albert Wilson said in the *British Medical Journal*, "I do not think the psychologists will get many cases." He also thought booze would take care of whatever problems there were. By 1915, 9 percent of British casualties were psychological. Although many of them were treated and sent back to the front, by the end of the war, Dennis Winter said in *Death's Men*, 30,000 had been sent back to England for shell shock.

Trench warfare in World War I was a horror beyond imagination. In the constant artillery shelling, which caused among other things the reappearance of long-dead and rotted bodies in smaller and smaller pieces, and with the continuous fear of random death, men were pushed to the edge of human endurance. Remember, two-thirds of the wounds in World War I were due to artillery. Patrols went out into no-man's land at night, through miles of barbed wire and cratered landscape decorated with dead and mutilated bodies. Sometimes men were required to go over the top in futile attempts to overrun German machine guns, using tactics from the Napoleonic Wars.

Shell shock, the common term for acute PTSD in World War I, derived from the fact that men who were under heavy constant artillery bombardment became dazed and disoriented. Doctors theorized that the constant explosions damaged brain tissue and caused conversion reactions, such as going deaf or blind, developing tremors, or having the inability to use one or more limbs.

Two treatment methods were developed for shell shock. Analytical treatment meant uncovering traumatic experiences and resolving them. This was reserved for people who were *judged* to have suffered traumatic-enough experiences to justify their symptoms. If they improved with treatment, identified the trauma, and went back to the front, the diagnosis was confirmed. If they didn't get well, they were malingering cowards.

British, French, and German soldiers who were judged to be hysterical, anxious, of weak character, or malingering cowards got, according to Dr. Pearce W. Bailey in an article published in 1918:

> . . . the brusque application of galvanic [electric] currents,
> strong enough to be extremely painful . . . and the continu-
> ance of the procedure to the point at which the deaf hear, the
> dumb speak, or those who believe themselves incapable of
> moving certain groups of muscles are moving them freely. The
> method . . . requires but little time and practically no person-
> nel . . . One treatment suffices.

This treatment also returned them to the front. Some of them
committed suicide. No records were kept as to how many of these
men survived the war.

By 1922, 50,000 British men had war pensions for mental problems.
By 1929, Winter said, there were "65,000 soldiers in mental hospitals
when pensions were finalized." Notice the rise in the numbers over
time, indicating delayed-onset PTSD. Like any government, the
British government did its best not to award pensions, so we have
to assume that this does not represent all the men who had trouble
coping with their war experience. There is no way of telling about
American shellshocked survivors, because they were put into asy-
lums along with mentally ill civilians.

In 1919, testifying before a German commission, Sigmund Freud
called symptoms of PTSD war neurosis and, according to Drs.
Brende and Parson, in *Vietnam Veterans: The Road to Recovery*,
"advocated recalling and talking about traumatic experiences, a therapy he called 'psychoanalysis'—a therapy he had been using with
patients with other problems." Freud also said it was ". . . *the subjective experience of helplessness*—in other words, the personal explanation of the situation—that determined its becoming traumatic,"
according to Dr. Henry Krystal.

Combat neurosis, combat fatigue, and combat exhaustion were
some of the terms used for acute PTSD in World War II. Reading
papers about PTSD in World War II would be entertaining if it
weren't so tragic and depressing. The proliferation of terms and
discussion of whether it's a neurosis or fatigue or exhaustion all
serve to draw the intellectual powers of the psychiatrists away from
what happened to these guys to various issues of predisposition, guilt,
blame, and discounting of traumatic experiences. Dr. Gihislane Boulanger said:

One might . . . sympathize with the wish of clinicians to spare themselves the task of listening emphatically to the frequently horrifying details of recent traumas by exploring their patients' pasts. Obviously, this behavior—while reducing clinicians' anxieties and enabling them to avoid confronting their own vulnerability and the loopholes in their own theories—has serious ramifications for the treatment of stress disorders.

Men who had been through battle after battle, trauma after trauma, were told that they had problems because as kids they never got along with their mother.

A tragic description of Audie Murphy, who had many symptoms we would now call PTSD, is reported in "The War Hero," by Thomas B. Morgan, in the 50th Anniversary Issue of *Esquire*, December 1983. Read it. Murphy was still not old enough to vote when he came home in the spring of 1945. Here are a few quotes:

He belonged to no veterans' organizations, stayed away from parades . . . [very much like Vietnam vets]

In the far wall, an open door led to another room that should have been the garage. I could see a bed and a desk with another big lamp.

"Garage," Murphy said. "I remodeled the garage to make a room where I could be by myself."

I must have seemed ready to ask why.

"It was necessary," he said cryptically . . .

"But you've got to understand me—" Murphy paused, as though deciding whether to go ahead with his thought, "—with me, it's been a fight for a long, long time to keep from being bored to death. *That's what two years of combat did to me!*" Murphy's voice had risen and he had brought both feet down on the floor. He looked at me wide-eyed and intense.

"Let me tell you something," he said. "Beginning eight years ago—up to last year—I had seven years of insomnia. *Seven years!* Outside of cancer, I don't know anything that can be as bad as that. It was just all of a sudden, I could not sleep. I'd be half dazed. The furniture in my room would take on odd shapes.

"Then there was my nightmare, a recurrent nightmare. A feeling of exasperation. I would dream I am on a hill and all these faceless people are charging up at me. I am holding an M-1 Garand rifle, the kind of rifle I used to take apart blindfolded. And in the dream, every time I shoot one of these people, a piece of the rifle flies off until all I have left is the trigger guard. The trigger guard!

"Then I would wake up. So that's why I began sleeping in the garage with the lights on all night so that when I woke up from the dream, I'd know where I was . . .

"So—there was another thing, too—it was the *noise*. Noise! In combat, you see, your hearing gets so acute you can interpret any noise. But now there were all kinds of noises that I couldn't interpret. Strange noises. I couldn't sleep without a weapon by my bed. A pistol. Because the least little noise bothered me. That's why I had the garage made into a bedroom, to be away from the noise. The least little noise—there was a time when a cannon wouldn't wake me. And now I could barely survive in the garage . . .

"You know," he said, ruefully, "there are only two of us left from the old outfit and we're both half dead."

In 1952, during the Korean War, *The Diagnostic and Statistical Manual* was published to help guide psychiatrists in the direction of standardized diagnoses. It contained a category called *gross stress reaction*, which covered reactions to trauma, including war. This was dropped from the *DSM II*, which came out *during* the Tet Offensive. The psychiatric community had decided that there could be an acute short-term reaction to trauma, *transient situational disturbance*, but persistence beyond six months required diagnosis as a pre-existing condition. Because a lot of the symptoms did persist beyond six months, psychiatrists invented the additional idea of compensation neurosis: People stay sick for the disability compensation. PTSD, they imply, persists not because people *can't* get over the trauma, but because they *won't*.

In the DAV pamphlet *Readjustment Problems Among Vietnam Veterans*, Jim Goodwin pointed out that follow-up studies on World War II combat vets, which found that men who had never gone to the VA or asked for a pension, were still experiencing nightmares, startle reactions, anxiety attacks, etc., *twenty years later*, were ignored. The stage was set for the fiasco of Vietnam.

As more and more Vietnam vets began to have severe stress

problems after being back from combat for months or even years, psychiatrists and psychologists from a number of study areas (survivors of concentration camps, survivors of Hiroshima, survivors of the Cocoanut Grove fire, survivors of Vietnam) began to try to study what people were experiencing rather than what they ought to be experiencing. The observational shrinks saw that no matter how people *ought* to react to having been in a concentration camp or a war or a fire—the theory being that once the trauma ceased, so would the symptoms—they continued to have big problems. Since some of these people with the big problems were doctors, even psychiatrists themselves, and knew they hadn't started out with inadequate personalities, they began to try to figure things out. As they listened to groups of vets process what had happened in Vietnam, they found they could not help the veterans if they maintained the proper pose of *you sick, me well.* They had to be authentic with these patients or the trust necessary to a therapeutic relationship never developed. Talking with these guys about experiences in Vietnam worked, but it was not popular.

A person goes through a numbing phase after any trauma. Even the expected death of a parent, or an everyday loss like that of a job, friend, or lover results in a period of denial. Then the pain, agonizing and intrusive, begins. Since this can be several months after the loss, it can be quite frightening to the person who thought he'd gotten over it. Dreadful, desperate feelings of loss and grief intrude at odd hours, filling up the mind. Meanwhile, everyone assumes that the person has gotten over the loss, so he really has no place to turn. After about two years, most people make it through the normal grief process and are able to go on with their lives.

For a war veteran, the trauma was greater, the losses continuous, and the numbing habitual, both from basic training, from years of Mom and Dad's saying, "Be a man, dear. Don't cry," and from knowing that if he breaks down in the middle of a firefight, he will get killed. Combat vets are experts at numbing when they get home. For some veterans of some wars, the homecoming was welcoming enough, supportive enough, that they could talk about and work out their feelings. Or by jumping into school and marriage and jobs, they were able to hold the pain at bay for years. But we all know World War II veterans who have never talked about their experiences. For other vets, the question "How many babies did you kill?" stopped all attempts to communication forever.

Fear sets in when the intrusive phase starts, whether it's two months or thirty years later. Nightmares come. Long-dead friends die over and over every night. Memories of blood and filth and the smell of flesh burning intrude into the daylight hours. The veterans, including nurses for whom war is a continual procession of mutilated young men, can't stop thinking of their experiences and are humiliated and enraged by this inability. Who the hell is going to go to the VA and say "I keep thinking about my buddy who died and having crying spells. I think I'm nuts"? Not a combat vet. So he medicates himself with two six-packs a day or a quart of whiskey, or wine, or Valium, or pot, or heroin—whatever it takes. His relationships suffer. But at least when he's numb, he isn't nuts. Right?

Sadly, this becomes a cycle, and the vet has to invest more and more energy in keeping himself numb, which means he has less and less to invest in life.

If the vet made the mistake of going to the VA before 1980, his opinion was confirmed by a diagnosis such as "sociopath," "schizophrenic," "paranoid," "borderline personality," "character disorder," or whatever. Bob was diagnosed as "nervous." *Hey, great! Thanks a lot! Now I know I'm just a nervous Nellie, and all along I thought I was nuts.* Such misdiagnoses actually worsened many cases, because these men and women were being treated for something they didn't have, sort of like treating heart disease with radiation therapy.

Finally in 1980, thanks to the work of a dedicated group of people on the Vietnam Veterans Working Group, the criteria for diagnosing PTSD were included in the *DSM III*. At last people with delayed-stress reactions did not have to be diagnosed as schizophrenic if they had flashbacks, or paranoid if they were hypervigilant and angry.

One thing for which the entire world can thank Vietnam veterans is the focus of energy and research on the subject of PTSD. Many other groups—combat veterans of other wars, crime victims, rape victims, incest victims, victims of physical abuse, adult children of alcoholics and other dysfunctional families, torture survivors, concentration camp survivors, flood and other natural-disaster victims, people who've survived terrible wrecks or fires, who have shot someone or been shot in the line of duty—all have benefited from this research, and research done to understand their problems has in turn benefited Vietnam veterans. Research has established a broad range of normalcy, and helped sufferers realize that their problems are not a result of personal failure.

Psychiatrist Harvey Dondershine, M.D., J.D., put the possibility of the development of PTSD more succinctly in the video *The War Within:* "Not only can it happen to any of us, but given the right circumstances, it will."

Informed mental-health professionals no longer think that anyone who can't get over a trauma such as World War II or Vietnam must have been weak or messed up to begin with. Anyone doing therapy with a combat vet who chooses to believe otherwise needs to read Arthur Blank's article, "Irrational Reactions to Post-Traumatic Stress Disorder and Vietnam Veterans," in *The Trauma of War* published by the American Psychiatric Press and do some serious soul-searching. Reading the rest of the book will help provide adequate therapy to combat veterans.

Older psychiatrists who often thought PTSD was an excuse made up for Vietnam veterans now have a much wider body of more scientific research to consult. In the new *DSM III R*—because of research into the existence of PTSD symptoms in many different populations including kids—the diagnostic criteria for PTSD now read:

> A. *The person has experienced an event that is outside the range of usual human experience and that would be markedly distressing to almost anyone, e.g., serious threat to one's life or physical integrity; serious threat or harm to one's children, spouse, or other close relatives and friends; sudden destruction of one's home or community; or seeing another person who has recently been, or is being, seriously injured or killed as the result of an accident or physical violence.*

The criteria say the event *"would be markedly distressing to almost anyone"* for a reason. That reason is found in section C-6 below, restricted affect, which is psychological jargon for appearing to be without feelings. People who have terrible PTSD often seem to have no feelings about the things they've experienced or seen or done. Psychiatrists used to use this as proof that they were sociopaths or psychopaths, instead of recognizing it as a symptom. Now the diagnostician is supposed to look instead at the effect this event would have on most people.

Being ambushed, seeing someone blown to bits, his blood and splinters of bones and guts and brains all over you, is outside the range of usual human experience. Hunting up the rotting pieces of some stranger to put in a body bag, days after his outfit was overrun is, too. That third night in Vietnam when your unit was almost overrun and you manned the machine gun all night and in the morning had to help pick up the bits and pieces of more than forty VC who were hung up on the wire and then had to ride in the back of the truck with them because you were the FNG to some ditch where you threw them away qualifies. So does that moment of terror when Charlie opened up on you for the first time, or seeing the truck in front of you blow up and having a piece of person the size of a steak land on the hood, or waking up as a rocket blows the end off your hooch, or seeing Vietnamese civilians abused and killed, or doing it yourself, or taking pictures of blown-up bodies for a year.

People get PTSD after one terrible car wreck, but for many Vietnam veterans, Vietnam was a car wreck a day—or more. But you can't sit down and cry in a combat zone or you will get killed. People are depending on you. So you bury it until later.

What happens later, often years later—the *post* in PTSD—and what brings many people into contact with the VA or the Vet Center or a private shrink or a vets' group is Section B of the diagnostic criteria:

> B. *The traumatic event is persistently reexperienced in at least one of the following ways:*
> *(1) recurrent and intrusive distressing recollections of the event (in young children, repetitive play in which themes or aspects of the trauma are expressed).*

What this means is that the vet feels as if he's going nuts because he can't stop thinking about the day Jonesy was killed and what he should have done to prevent it. Or whenever he looks at your kids he sees fiery napalm blooming through the palm trees in Phuc Luc and the little children lighting up like torches. Maybe he talks about Vietnam all the time. He's obsessed, and after a while everyone is sick of it.

People get sick of it because they don't realize that he's talking because he can't stop thinking about it. Horrible memories (the fear he felt when he was shot, the bullets hitting him, his blood spraying; someone screaming "Mama, Mama! Oh, God, Help me!" in the dark) intrude.

Intrude. Definition: To put or force in without being wanted or asked. Questions intrude. Why? Why? WHY? *Why did I live? Why did they die? Why were we wasted?*

Terrible thoughts intrude, too. The vet thinks of your head exploding or kids napalmed. He also doesn't want to think of Jonesy stitched with machine-gun fire all the time. He doesn't want to think of death and destruction every time he turns his head, or even once a day, once a week, once a year. He feels crazy, desperate. He doesn't know lots of other guys have this symptom because it's too nuts to mention. Your vet's not going to say anything, but he will be sick with fear, with worry that he's crazy, and that he'll do something crazy and that will probably make him withdrawn or irritable.

So many people think the solution is "just don't think about it." Believe me, he doesn't want to think about it, to remember. He'd rather trade places with someone whose big worry is the bills, or deciding whether to buy a Ford or a Toyota. He's not welcoming these things. They *come*, unbidden. "Until a traumatic life-event can be assimilated and successfully integrated . . . the psychological elements will remain in active memory storage . . . [and] periodically emerge into consciousness as emotionally upsetting intrusive and uncontrolled images of the event," as psychologist John Wilson wrote. They will emerge for the rest of the war veteran's life.

Intrusive memories are not a new phenomenon, either. In his memoir of the Civil War, *Company Aytch*, published in 1881, Sam Watkins wrote:

> And while my imagination is like the weaver's shuttle, playing backward and forward through these two decades of time, I ask myself, Are these things real? did they happen? are they

being enacted today? or are they the fancies of the imagination
in forgetful reverie? . . . Surely these are just the vagaries of
my own imagination. Surely my fancies are running wild tonight. But, hush! I now hear the approach of battle. That low,
rumbling sound in the west is the roar of cannon in the distance.
That rushing sound is the tread of soldiers. That quick, lurid
glare is the flash that precedes the cannon's roar. And, listen!
that loud report that makes the earth tremble and jar and
sway, is but the bursting of a shell, as it screams through the
dark, tempestuous night. That black, ebon cloud, where the
lurid lightning flickers and flares, that is rolling through the
heavens, is the smoke of battle; beneath is being enacted a
carnage of blood and death. Listen! the soldiers are charging
now. The flashes and roaring now are blended with the shouts
of soldiers and the confusion of battle . . .

Victorian prose aside, that is a description of an intrusive memory.

(2)   recurrent distressing dreams of the event

Your vet's dreaming about it, too. Horrible dreams in which he
thrashes and sweats and wakes up shaking, heart pounding, afraid,
angry because he CAN'T CONTROL IT.

Your vet may be lying next to you, seeing his best friend step on
a land mine every night, see the thing bounce up to waist height,
see it blow, see his friend's middle dissolve into a spray of blood and
flesh, cut in half, flopping in two bloody pieces on the trail, have to
hit the dirt, cover the medic, not even get to say a last whispered
good-bye to his buddy's bloody corpse before they throw it in a plastic
bag and send it out on the chopper. If you think this image is too
gross, think what it must be to dream it over and over. How could
he tell you about it? How could he wake up rested, ready to face the
day? How can he face the night without drinks, drugs, tranquilizers?
To your questions he says what Mike Costello said to Patti: *You
don't want to know what I dream.*

Bob dreamed of dead babies being pitchforked off the back of a
truck, still wiggling. To my questions he replied that he didn't dream
anything, although he was leaping awake many times a night. I guess
he felt this dream was too crazy to tell me. Note that it is symbolic
rather than an actual incident. Both types of dream occur.

One vet I talked to dreams over and over about the day a newbie [another word for FNG] got hit. The vet crawls over and puts the cellophane from a cigarette pack over the newbie's chest wound, and then a battle dressing. The guy looks at him with fear in his eyes and death in his face, but the dreamer has to go shoot the machine gun, and the guy dies, and afterward the dreamer reports it to the medic with *no emotion*—and this seemed to bother him more than anything in the dream—and the medic says, "I'll take care of it."

Another vet keeps dreaming that the VC ambush him while he's squatting in the jungle with his pants down having an agonizing bout of diarrhea.

One of the vets in *The War Within*, an extremely fine video about PTSD, dreams and re-dreams a particular firefight—*"I'm tired of seeing my friends die every night,"* he said.

> *(3) sudden acting or feeling as if the traumatic event were recurring (includes a sense of reliving the experience, illusions, hallucinations, and dissociative [flashback] episodes, even those that occur upon awakening or when intoxicated)*

Think of how clearly you remember the first glimpse of your newborn child, or the day Kennedy was shot, or some other important moment in your life, and think how you'd feel and act if what you remembered *that* distinctly was Jonesy's legs being blown off. Spencer Campbell wrote:

> The shadows of Vietnam are composed of many events that the veteran participated in and observed. Recording the actual event occurred with the same amount of effort it would take to snap a picture . . . of faces, names, places, sounds, and fear of impending death . . . graphically captured by the camera of the mind . . . Some may be visited by shadows of women and children running for cover and not making it. Others may experience again the sound of death as they clutch a dying comrade to their chest, and lean their head forward to catch his last words and feeling the warmth of his blood as it flows through your fingers, while they struggle for life together.

Fourteen years later because it has been captured by the camera of your mind you experience again the emotions of that moment.

Your vet may be having actual flashbacks in which, for terrifying moments, he is back in Vietnam in a firefight, reliving the worst, most terrifying moments of his life. Grant, another friend of mine whom I've never met, heard that I was writing this book and sent me the following:

It's Monday, April 8, 1985. I took Barbara to school. It was an afternoon class from 1 to 2. I didn't see any need to go back home so I waited in the school cafe.

I always sit at a corner table where I can see everybody that comes in.

I was a little bit nervous as always when I'm in a public place.

At the table next to me was some people talking bout Vietnam. I strained my ears like radar, but I couldn't understand what they were saying. I didn't need to understand. I had a lot of The Nam in my head.

As I thought about Vietnam I took a trip back in time. I was there. Back in Vietnam.

I was on patrol and great gushes of wind over my head so loud it crackled. It was artillery.

I look around. I was on my feet. No one was staring at me, so I guess I made no sign. I pick up my coffee and walk outside the school.

I wipe the sweat from my forehead.

I sat at a picnic table outside the door.

Thinking about what had just happened, and looking at myself, I noticed I had no green clothes on. I told myself I was through with the war. I was no longer in the lean, green, mean machine. I was also just about in tears but it didn't happen.

It happened so quickly, uncontrollable. I was on my feet, looking around and confused; picking up my coffee, I was scared; out the door wiping sweat from my forehead. All in the matter of seconds. Like picture slides. (Click) Confused. (Click) Scared. (Click) On the run.

This one was different from the other flashbacks I've been having. The others were like I was in the background seeing myself there. Not this time. I was there. It was me. It was real.

I'm comparing the two types of flashbacks. Seeing yourself there (in a combat zone) is real tough, but being there is like, no nightmare can compare, no horror in your imagination can compare. It's the horror of all horrors that's ever been or the horror to come.

Grant has had two different kinds of reliving experiences. Another kind involves unconscious flashbacks. We all have read of the Vietnam vet who walks into a store to rob it or takes a hostage and gets himself killed. Tragically some of these vets are unconsciously re-enacting an episode from Vietnam for which they deserve punishment in their own minds. For more information, read "The Unconscious Flashback to the War in Vietnam Veterans" by Arthur Blank in *The Trauma of War*.

If you ever have to handle a veteran who is in the midst of a flashback, wait for the flashback to be over. Given time, the vet will come out of it. When he does, he will be very frightened and may need reassurance before he can calm down. Remember the fact that he is having a flashback is an almost certain guarantee that this man has been through hell in the service of his country. Don't pay him back with a bullet. Flashbacks do not mean the veteran is crazy. They are one of many normal delayed reactions to combat stress, and they scare him worse than they do you.

Even if the flashback lasts only a few seconds, this is a real signal to your vet and to you that he is having uncontrollable intrusions of his traumatic experiences from Vietnam and needs help. He is also going to be scared shitless and feel as if he really is nuts. What can you do? Reassure him that this is one *normal* reaction to undigested traumatic war experiences.

It might help to think of PTSD as similar to a boil. The flashback is the boil bursting open. It needs to be cleaned before it can heal. The way to clean out feelings and experiences is the talking cure. Unless the vet goes and gets therapy, the boil will heal over raggedly, leave a scar on both of you (especially if he's grabbed you, hit you, or really scared you), and gradually come back to a head. Getting therapy is like taking antibiotics so the boil won't come back. Actually it's a lot more painful than taking antibiotics, because it hurts to talk about these things. But your vet survived the experiences, and with the help of other veterans in a therapy group, he can survive remembering them. Any vet will need a lot of support from you while he is getting therapy, and he will probably seem to be getting worse at first. Therapy is really going to hurt him. There is no use pretending it won't. You have to decide whether or not you can support him in it, present pain for future gain.

Vets: Don't put off going for help. Chapter 10 talks about available sources of help. Getting help should become one of your priorities. If you are having flashbacks, violent episodes, deep depressions, or enough of the symptoms in this chapter to make life uncomfortable, tracking down a good experienced therapist or educating a good therapist about Vietnam is something you owe yourself and your family. The prisons are full of people who put off getting help. There is almost universal ignorance among psychiatrists and judges about PTSD. A Vietnam veteran with PTSD was *executed* in Florida a few years ago, and another recently in Louisiana.

In a paper, "Vietnam-Era Veteran Contacts with the Criminal Justice System," Erich Vierthaler reported:

> A project by Grutkowski (1981) looked at Delayed Stress Syndrome in twenty first-offender Vietnam combat veteran inmates at Pennsylvania's Western Penitentiary who were compared with a random sample of twenty civilian inmates. While the main part of this research concentrated on stress factors, an appendix did give a Table of Sentence and Offense Distributions for the two grups . . . The Veterans received 15-month-longer mean minimum sentence, and 75-month-longer mean maximum sentence than the group of non-veteran inmates, even though non-veterans had committed eleven homicides and the veterans eight.

"If by chance you get in trouble and you are a Vietnam veteran . . . the first thing the prosecutor tells the judge and jury is 'This man is a trained killer and a danger to society and the people of our state,' " one vet who is in prison wrote me.

Another form of re-experiencing, in my opinion, is automatically reacting in survivor mode, reacting without thinking. Some vets hit the floor when a car backfires. They hit out when you touch them in their sleep. They strike out at any perceived threat with force and violence, behavior that kept them alive in Vietnam. Over time these reactions may become less noticeable, unless the vet feels really threatened, in which case they may come back full-blown. The survivor mode is closely associated with rage, which certainly fuels it but is not necessary. It's simply a reflex, probably straight from the reptile brain that takes over to ensure survival, but it can get the vet into a lot of trouble.

> *(4) intense psychological distress at exposure to events that symbolize or resemble an aspect of the traumatic event, including anniversaries of the trauma*

Noises are often going to bother a vet. When a helicopter flies over, he may not show it, but it brings things back. Feelings. The fear when you're on a slick headed for a hot LZ. The anguish when a medevac comes in to get your wounded buddies or the dead. *Whop, whop, whop* was the sound of help and the sound of death. The sound took you into battle, came for you when you needed help, brought food and water and mail from home, your mother explaining why she wouldn't send you booze (*Drinking is bad for your health, son*) or your girl saying good-bye.

Gunfire, cars backfiring, noises in the night, sudden silences, weeping, babies crying—all may have particular, private meanings for him. Whenever there's a thunderstorm, he may find himself getting ready for the VC to probe his perimeter and wishing he'd built that wall out in front of his house.

It may be real important for him to sit in corners, to have his back to the wall. Not to go to big parties, not to get into crowds. Imagine what a rocket or mortar round can do to a crowd, and you'll understand. He may be very observant. He may get nervous in the woods and want you not to walk too close. He may want to lead. Let him.

Restaurants and movies may be hard for him.

Orientals may bring on a reaction that he can't control.

He may not be able to deal with children. In Vietnam they were often a threat. Babies were booby-trapped with grenades. Children were wired with satchel charges that were blown by radio when they got close to a group of GI's. After you see that, you don't let kids close, and if they don't listen to you, you shoot first and check it out later. When you have kids or are around kids, it haunts you. Or when your kid reaches the terrible twos and turns from angel into aggressive little devil, you think you've ruined him, that somehow what you did in Nam and who you became has rubbed off (as Sarah Haley, a social worker who began working with PTSD in Vietnam vets in the late sixties, reported in one paper).

Maybe your vet felt intense rage at all the fuss made over the return of the Iran hostages, because it reminded him of what his homecoming lacked. Tet comes at the end of January. Many vets find it a very hard time. Christmas and Thanksgiving or New Year's and the Fourth of July may have marked tragedies for him. If you think he's just being a jerk, try to think how much you'd want to celebrate a holiday if you'd spent the day out on a patrol where half your squad got killed, or waiting for a turkey dinner that never came because the REMF's forgot to send it or ate it themselves, or came back from Vietnam in time for Christmas to see that the war hadn't made any difference in anyone's life except yours and those of your friends who died and the guys still fighting over there.

On top of that are the individual anniversaries: the day the LT got killed, the day Pat lost his legs, or Lucky was blinded, or Doc was blown up when he picked up a crying baby. For some guys *every* day is an anniversary of something bad. You can't know about those things. He may not even know himself till he's been in therapy for a while.

If he is able to tell you about his anniversaries, maybe you can start some sort of healing family tradition around them. Plant a tree, give a check to Amnesty International, adopt a foster child in Nicaragua or Vietnam or Afghanistan. Have that day be a retreat for him, a day to himself, a day to mourn what he lost in Vietnam, not just his buddies, but hopes and beliefs and optimism and whatever else he misses: joy, or innocence and hope, or the ability to feel. Depression and hopelessness may have been your vet's reaction to the constant production of dead and wounded without any measurable progress to show for it. Or he may be overwhelmed with guilt. Or he may feel only rage.

Whenever a Vietnam movie or documentary is on TV, and people talk about it, your vet may feel all the old rage and grief and pain recur to such an extent that he doesn't know if he can keep it in. He gets distant from you, and you don't know why.

Well, the "why" of it is described in Section C:

> C. *Persistent avoidance of stimuli associated with the trauma or numbing of general responsiveness (not present before the trauma) as indicated by at least three of the following:*
>
> *(1) efforts to avoid thoughts or feelings associated with the trauma*

One vet doesn't talk about Vietnam. Another talks about it (*Nah, it didn't bother me*) with no feeling because he's so successful at numbing. One refuses to move up to any position where he'd be responsible for other people, because what he was responsible for in Vietnam was lives and he lost some of them. Another never gets angry because he did things he considers terrible when he was enraged in Vietnam. Survivor mode is where you shoot before you think. Rage is where you blow the body to smithereens and stomp on the pieces. Rage grows out of the injustice of the draft, out of the loss of friends, the simplistic black-and-white bullshit taught in basic (*We're here to help these people*) that leads to a sense of betrayal. Rage grows out of the fear of dying, out of the pain of killing someone else. Numberless things can combine to make rage the only safe outlet for the pain that causes it, and unfortunately people do things in rages that haunt them for the rest of their lives, things in Vietnam and things at home.

Maybe your vet acts like a mean macho killer to cover up the fear and helplessness he felt in Vietnam.

Maybe you can't understand why your vet feels nothing when his mother dies. That is normal for someone with PTSD. Many vets have spent years avoiding grief. Men also start out with both arms tied behind their backs when it comes to dealing with grief. The stiff upper lip is bred into them from birth. Our veterans saw things that would make a statue cry, but they *can't* because *men* don't.

Normal grieving progresses through a number of stages. The first stage of grief is "*No!*" Denial. Flat, outright rejection. Even in the midst of a firefight, people went through this one, crying "No! NO! NO!" when someone was hit. Rage comes after. Burning anger. Some people also went through this stage in Vietnam, killing, kicking bodies to pieces, using the butt end when they ran out of bullets, or shooting everything that moved. Natural reactions, but sometimes hard to look back on.

In a book called *Healing Life's Hurts*, there's a diagram, "Five Stages in Healing a Memory," based on Elizabeth Kubler-Ross's Five Stages of Grief:

1. *Denial: I don't admit I was ever hurt:* Yeah, Vietnam didn't bother me, not like those whiners. Total denial.

2. *Anger: I blame others for hurting and destroying me:* The veteran knows Vietnam did something bad to him, but he's stuck in the anger stage and can't get out. Fuck the government, the protestors, Jane Fonda, Richard Nixon, the VC, the NVA, all gooks. Many vets are stuck here, in a constant internal rage that no one else knows about. Others show it all too often.

3. *Bargaining: I set up conditions to be fulfilled before I'm ready to forgive:* The VA treats us right; Jane Fonda goes to jail; all the POW's/MIA's come back. Since most of these conditions are outside the power of the vet to bring about, he stays stuck.

4. *Depression; I blame myself for letting hurt destroy me:* Many guys get stuck here, too. Believing Vietnam should not affect them, they can't seek help even though they are aware that they need it. They feel hopelessly stuck because they can't forgive themselves for what they see as a defective reaction rather than a normal one.

5. *Acceptance: I look forward to growth from hurt:* What happens when a man can face the ambivalence of his experience in Vietnam and use that pain to grow and to make the world a better place.

For some vets, the grief process was never possible. It takes *years* of going through this process, sometimes in one stage, sometimes in another, to get over a death. People never get over a death if they don't grieve. Dr. Chaim Shatan, who did pioneering work with Vietnam vets back in the early seventies, coined the phrase *impacted grief* to describe their inability to grieve.

Why couldn't your vet progress through grief to acceptance and resolution? Because it would have killed him. He did not have time to sit and weep or sit and accept someone else's death. He was too busy trying to stay alive. Grieving is a slow process that takes a long time and has lots of little cycles through the various stages. It is not linear. You can't say, "Well, I've denied it and then been mad and sad so now I'm over it." It's not that easy.

Besides never having the time to mourn, perhaps after several deaths, your vet didn't have the strength to face such huge amounts of pain. If he lost his whole squad, how can he face the pain and still function?

Many young veterans never had any pattern for mourning, never saw another man who didn't reject the pain. John Wayne never sat down and cried for his buddies. John Wayne buried his pain or turned it into rage. That's how real men act, right?

Veterans lost more than people in Vietnam. Grief can also be for lost ideals, for lost belief in leaders, for loss of the innate knowledge that nothing really bad can happen, for learning that one is expendable, for one's self-respect, for that other life each guy lost in Vietnam. Some lost their futures. Some lost hope. Some lost the ability to love or trust or care for anyone. Some are frozen in rage because they feel like such suckers.

According to psychologist Erwin Parson, psychic numbing also has the effect of freezing the veteran in time. In some respects the vet's still nineteen, still believes others are either for him or against him, sees the world in black and white, which is one of the reasons he has such problems. Or being nineteen in the head, there's no room for imperfection in you or your kids. Everyone's supposed to be perfect, to work well, to mind, to keep clean, do homework—whatever—faultlessly, no excuses accepted. No failures, even though we learn the most from our failures. Many veterans became stuck at nineteen in the anger stage of grief, and it has colored their whole lives.

Why is this so important? In her article "The Hidden Injuries of War," in *Strangers at Home*, Norma Winkler referred to "widely accepted theories of developmental psychology," which maintain that people from eighteen to about twenty-four are discovering their own identity among a number of possible roles. If the choice is limited to the role of coward or one of several other roles like killer, avenger, demolitions expert, death-from-above, or ultimate fighting machine, it will be hard later on for your vet to develop the side of himself that can be involved in a close, loving relationship.

"The process of self-discovery is the same," Winkler said, whether during war or peace, but in war "the *concrete experiences . . .* are radically different." In war, Winkler continued, "men are called upon to commit acts that challenge conventional notions of morality and that if committed by civilians would be considered criminal as well as immoral." Younger people don't have the frame of reference that helps them decide *I did and saw terrible things but I'm not terrible.* Youth takes to heart what it does. It sees things in black and white. *I did bad things so I am the baddest motherfucker who ever was.* Or: *Nothing I did could have been bad, so nothing the United States did could have been wrong, and every man, woman, and child who died in Vietnam deserved it.* The younger they were when they went into combat, the harder it was to be immersed in death and come out psychologically unscathed.

Robert Muller spoke about the ambiguity of Vietnam in "A Symposium" published in *The Wounded Generation:*

> Vietnam—the experience and the issues—is too often looked at in terms of black and white and, for me clearly you cannot deal with any of this stuff in a superficial way. It is the gray. It is my roommate from basic school in the Marine Corps who served also as an infantry platoon commander and when I said, "Kevin, why don't you join with me in speaking out against the war?" he said, "Bobby, I agree with you but I wrote to 26 mothers whose sons were killed under my command and I cannot publicly acknowledge that their deaths were for nothing." It's that kind of push-pull that makes any simple reduction . . . wrong . . . "

Stephen Sonnenberg, M.D., in his introduction to *The Trauma of War*, wrote: "The soldier who is a few years older than the average combatant and possesses a more integrated sense of self and purpose has great insulation against trauma than does a late adolescent who is still in the process of more active maturation."

"They told us we'll never be the same again," Bud Register said about his combat experiences in World War II, "and I agree. You can't have that type of experience and come out the same . . . It didn't affect me as much as some of the boys because I was twenty-five and had a job and a wife before I went. I knew who I was."

But the Vietnam War was fought by teen-agers.

(2) efforts to avoid activities or situations that arouse recollections of trauma

Most Vietnam vets avoided anything to do with the war for years. Like Audie Murphy, they didn't join the vet organizations, they didn't have those endless World War II reunions, they didn't look up or call old buddies. You were likely to find out that Red was killed two days after you left because some FNG fucked up. Or that the guy who got your bunker after you left was blown to hell in it. Or that Nick came back changed, and the parents he loved so much haven't seen him for weeks, months, years. Or your vet might have had to tell one buddy that another hadn't made it. Many can't sit through war movies. They don't read books about Vietnam. They find all these parades and monuments upsetting. *Where were these people when we were fighting and dying? Where were they when we came home?*

(3) inability to recall an important aspect of the trauma (psychogenic amnesia)

A lot of veterans *can't* remember much about Vietnam, and you can take that as a sure sign that they saw things no human being should have to see, and maybe did things to stay alive or save other lives that no human being should ever have to do. They have seen death in action and some of them have been death in action.

In a wonderful double bind, typical of the VA and Vietnam, veterans applying for disability are required to be able to remember their traumatic incidents, including names and dates, in order to prove that something happened to them that would justify a finding of PTSD.

(4) markedly diminished interest in significant activities (in young children, loss of recently acquired developmental skills such as toilet training or language skills)

What kind of significant activities can a veteran lose interest in?

Loss of interest in sex, for one, is pretty common. In Vietnam, men unleashed violent impulses, according to Kathrin Brantley, Ph.D., a clinical psychologist who has worked with veterans. When they came home they had to put all that away. "Sexuality is another form of unleashing or letting go of emotions, similar to aggression," she said. "Sometimes it's too threatening to people who have let go of aggression. For others sexual dysfunction arises because they can't make their needs known because they don't know or can't express their feelings. Others find it too threatening to take risks. All they want is to control their lives." Sexual disinterest is one normal response to trauma. Therapy focused on Vietnam, combined, if necessary, with sexual therapy, will help.

Dr. Chaim Shatan said, "Impaired adaptability is the central feature of this new lifestyle. Feeling, thinking and action . . . become tighter, more rigid, hemmed in."

"He's just not the same guy he was." Common comment about a combat veteran. True, too. Perhaps when he got back he was not interested in the things he liked before. Maybe just lately he seems to have suddenly lost interest in things (the *post* in PTSD). He used to be sweet and interested in you and now he's angry or indifferent. He used to have big plans, but now he does nothing. He watches TV like a zombie. Bob did for years. He doesn't hunt. He doesn't read. He no longer enjoys his hobbies. He doesn't like people. He doesn't want them around. He won't go to parties, to restaurants, to the county fair. You think he's a jerk, but he's screaming in his head, *Don't bunch up. You'll be killed.*

(5) feeling of detachment or estrangement from others

You feel as if your vet's love for you has gone. He's cold to you and you don't know why. He doesn't know why, either, so he assigns blame to you—if you were nicer he'd be more loving. Or he denies that he's detached, leaving you feeling nuts. Whether you're both busy making up impractical standards of loving behavior for each other, or both denying that anything is wrong with *you*, you are likely to wind up feeling that you don't know what "normal" is. That is normal when you are living with a survivor of trauma.

Dr. John Wilson said, *"intimacy conflict* is a major dimension of PTSD among Vietnam veterans." Part of this is because the vet is numb and can't feel, and part of it is survivor tactics that worked in Vietnam. *Don't get close to anyone.* He keeps his distance from you to prevent the possibility of pain. If you aren't close, then when you leave him or die on him he won't be hurt. Maybe knowing what he is capable of makes him afraid he'll hurt you. He's afraid to love for fear of hurting you physically, mentally, emotionally. He's afraid he might hit you in his sleep. He doesn't want to scar you up with dark stories of Vietnam. He doesn't want to suddenly go numb on you just when you need him the most, yet he knows that's when he will most likely be numb because stress and pressure bring it out. Not getting close to people impairs his friendships, his family life, even his job.

Other vets don't like people. Vietnam vets never intend to be used again. Many of them, like Bob, have no trust in authority, no trust in the system, no belief in goodness, justice, or fair play. They don't even trust people who want to be their friends because of the way many of their so-called friends acted when they got back from Vietnam.

(6) restricted range of affect, e.g., unable to have loving feelings

Okay, so he's cold and he doesn't like people, but what the heck is "restricted range of affect"? It means that the range and intensity of what he appears to feel are small, hemmed in, constricted—as if he's forgotten the normal range of human feelings and even how to feel the ones he remembers.

Helene Jackson interviewed vets with a diagnosis of PTSD. "I am driven. I can't stop. Underneath there is nothingness, no meaning, just black death. I died back there. I feel nothing," one said.

"A Band-Aid has been placed in my head. I have no feelings about it. As if they stuck Novocain in my brain. I can't put it together," said another.

Their perception of themselves has changed. They feel like spectators, mechanical men, not in control. For some of them, memories of Vietnam seem like a movie they weren't really in. They see it as something separate, not a moral issue, but something they can be proud of, something they were good at. And then it comes, memories of what they were good at. Numb and they're safe again, only it gets harder and harder each time to get numb. It's also pretty impossible to be adaptable and assimilate new experiences when they're struggling with the old. But lack of feeling is one of the best combat adaptations:

> Happy are men who yet before they are killed
> Can let their veins run cold.
> Whom no compassion fleers
> Or makes their feet
> Sore on the alleys cobbled with their brothers . . .
> Dullness best solves
> The tease and doubt of shelling . . .
> Having seen all things red,
> Their eyes are rid
> Of the hurt of the color of blood forever.
> And terror's first constriction over,
> Their hearts remain small-drawn.
> Their senses in some scorching cautery of battle
> Now long since ironed,
> Can laugh among the dying unconcerned . . .

World War I combat veteran Wilfred Owen wrote this in *Insensibility*, shortly before he was killed in action a week before the armistice.

The person with PTSD has so much of his energy tied up in not feeling the pain, not showing any weakness, that he may not even be aware that he's doing it. He's cold and unresponsive because he learned to be that way as a survival tactic in Vietnam. It's more than a habit. It's how he stays alive.

> *(7) sense of a foreshortened future*, e.g., *does not expect to have a career, marriage, or children, or a long life*

A lot of veterans spent years living as if there were no tomorrow. Sensation seeking was one way to feel alive. Many still live that way.

Rather than work for the future, they live in the "now" to an extent that can be pretty rough on their families. A description of these behaviors comes later in this chapter.

> *D. Persistent symptoms of increased arousal (not present before the trauma), as indicated by at least two of the following:*
> *(1) difficulty falling or staying asleep*

In Vietnam, the night belonged to Charlie. It was a time of fear and firefights, ambushes and agony, waiting and watching. Even rear-echelon people learned to fear the night, the rocket and mortar attacks, and the sappers with satchel charges. In the bush, every sound, every leaf, every breath in the blackness held a threat.

Men learned not to sleep, or sleep so lightly that they went to full alert in less than a second. They could tell the difference between incoming and outgoing mortars or rockets or artillery, and sleep through the outgoing. They could hear the difference between American weapons and those of the VC/NVA. A sudden silence in the jungle would snap them awake. Being touched would bring them awake with their hands around the throat of whoever woke them. That's how they stayed alive. The results of this constantly interrupted sleep have persisted to the present day, and many of them still prowl, patrol, drink, or smoke pot to get to sleep. Insomnia is also a temporary solution to the dreams.

Bob used to fall asleep and leap awake, over and over every night. Finally after four years, he spent ten days in a sleep study at the Gainesville VAMC. They wired him up from head to toe. We didn't hear anything from the clinic for a few months, and then we got a letter saying he couldn't sleep.

If the vet has bad dreams or nightmares and wakes up screaming or trying to strangle you or the kids, or running through the house with a gun in his hand, he's not getting the necessary rest from his sleep. If he can't sleep, his behavior will become more and more irrational just because of sleep deprivation. This is natural. Sleep deprivation is a well-known form of torture: *Anyone* will break under it. Lack of sleep makes a person really hard to live with.

(2)   irritability or outbursts of anger

Does your vet blow up constantly? Is he a snarly beast a lot of the time? Many vets can't seem to regulate their reactions to things going wrong. They just blow up, going from calm to roaring fury in a few seconds. It is scary. The intensity and frequency also scare your vet, but he isn't going to let on. He's not going to tell you he's afraid he's nuts, either.

When our home-built shower walls started to swell ominously, Bob got mad and ripped them out. He replaced them with clear plastic for about five years—till he calmed down and could afford psychologically as well as financially to fix them. Mike Costello laughed when he saw it and called it a typical Vietnam veteran shower.

Anger arises partly from being stuck in the grief process. Other things cause it, too. Some veterans have permanent physical reminders of Vietnam, ranging from scars that can be covered by clothes to the loss of half their body. Many wounded veterans wind up in more or less constant physical pain, though most of us would like to think that any wound can be healed good as new through the wonders of modern medicine. Pain leads to irritability.

Writing after World War II, Willard Waller said: "Why is the soldier angry? Because he was the one singled out to fight and die and suffer and see horrors." He also quoted a World War I veteran who said in 1919, "The next war, if they want me, they'll have to burn the woods and sift the ashes."

Something as simple and unjust as the draft can cause terrible anger. The sense of being unfairly singled out is inevitable in a system in which not everyone goes to war. Anger and hostility result from many common occurrences in Vietnam. It's hard to take an injustice with a shrug when it may cost you your life. Psychiatrist Helen DeRosis put it this way:

> Hostile people feel they have been done great and irreparable injustices. In many cases this is true . . . A state of hostility thus evolves from a state of chronic fear in combination with chronic anger.

If your vet seems really numb, sometimes holding his rage in where it can't hurt those around him is all he can do. All he knows how to do. All he can do *for you.* Such courage is the only thing he has left, but even that makes him numb.

(3) difficulty concentrating

It's hard to concentrate when you've got something on your mind. Remember the last time you were preoccupied? "What did you say, dear?" You can't hear what people say without a great effort, and you're preoccupied with the quiche in the oven or the sales figures at the store, not with wasted buddies and dead enemies. A lot of guys came back from Vietnam, went back to school, then dropped out. They simply couldn't concentrate. Too much of their energy was tied up in not remembering.

(4) hypervigilance

Hypervigilance prevails. When a combat vet's startled, he hits the floor. Dr. Chaim Shatan wrote in "Have You Hugged a Vietnam Veteran Today?": "A startle reaction is a reflex tactical response to any sudden change in the surroundings. But it represents a failure of peacetime adaptation . . . " From our point of view, he "overreacts" to every little thing. Many vets are jumpy, "unceasingly watchful against the threat of death . . . " as Dr. Shatan put it. Is your vet still constantly checking for trip wires, disturbed ground where a mine might be buried, snipers, ambushes, how he can get out of the room, escape routes, treelines? How can he tell you this? He knows he's not in Vietnam. Dr. Shatan went on to say: " . . . from the point of view of the other reality [which he is carrying around in his head, never forget], there is no deficit in thinking and no inappropriate behavior . . . The survivor finds more wisdom in his Marine dog tag or in the number on his arm than in all the Geneva and genocide treaties." Still his behavior makes him feel crazy, so he medicates himself with alcohol or drugs to try to control his symptoms.

Can your vet hear things you don't? See things you never notice?

That's hypervigilant. Ready for anything. Ready for the next ambush, the next rocket, the next asshole who pisses him off.

Some of this hypervigilance seems to be physical and permanent, opening up a new field of study. Dr. Lawrence C. Kolb reported that changes in physiology in some men reflect "a persisting potential for abnormal phsysiological arousal to any perceived bodily threat . . . " Dr. Shatan said that Archibald and Tuddenham's study of World War II vets after twenty-five years showed that combat vets still had elevated baseline respiratory, pulse, and EEG rates.

Hyperawareness can be focused inward, so that every change in the body is perceived as a threat and increases tension and anxiety, sometimes bringing on anxiety attacks that are devastating and humiliating. They're scary as hell. Sweating, shaking, hyperventilation, chest pains, dizziness, throwing up, tingling sensations, cold clammy feelings, hot flashes—all are symptoms of an anxiety attack. These may happen at any time, leading to even more hypervigilance. Panic attacks are even more humiliating. The vet has thoughts of impending doom, going crazy, going out of control, dying, your dying. He feels as if he's not real, the world isn't real, he can't think straight, and he knows it. Not all vets have anxiety or panic attacks. It's one possible manifestation, one very debilitating possible reaction, after which he will be anxious for hours, and justifiably so.

(5) *exaggerated startle response*

Does he jump when a car backfires? Whirl around ready for anything if you poke him suddenly? Do you have to wake him up by pulling his toe so he won't attack? Dr. Emanuel Tanay, a psychiatrist who has worked with World War II and Vietnam veterans, wrote: "The ideal wartime soldier has acquired talents which are obsolete in peacetime and . . . handicaps in a peaceful society." One of these is the ability to react in survivor mode, to move and act without thinking because there is no time to think in combat.

(6) *physiologic reactivity upon exposure to events that symbolize or resemble an aspect of the traumatic event (e.g., a woman who was raped in an elevator breaks out in a sweat when entering any elevator)*

Or a Vietnam veteran who starts shaking at the sound of a Huey, or begins to freak out when Orientals come into the room, or whose heart begins to race whenever some lifer at the VA, the post office, the driver's-license bureau, or the kid's school starts to harass him.

> *E. Duration of the disturbance (symptoms in B, C, and D) of at least one month. Specify delayed onset if the onset of the symptoms was at least six months after the trauma.*

What a difference from the past! It used to be said that if problems from combat experiences persisted, they didn't exist; your mommy was the problem, or authority figures. And if symptoms began more than a year after you left the combat zone, it wasn't related to war at all—you were just defective. Thank God for the changes, and what a pity we didn't know to use this available information a long time ago.

That is the current official description of PTSD. PTSD is still an evolving field of study. New knowledge is added every year.

Interestingly, the symptom *"guilt about surviving when others have not"* was dropped from the diagnostic criteria. Maybe it's included under those "feelings associated with the trauma" that vets avoid. Guilt makes some vets very self-destructive, or leads them into self-defeating life-styles to punish themselves. The ultimate form of this is suicide, and more vets have died by their own hand than were killed in Vietnam.

Dr. Emanuel Tanay said, "The absence of guilt awareness should not be mistaken for lack of guilt." In my opinion all veterans of combat feel guilty about surviving, but most of them don't realize it. Guilt is one of those sissy emotions that real men don't feel. So how do you determine if your vet feels it? Ask? It's not likely that he's going to have a sudden flash of insight and agree that that must be the reason he gets into losing fights so often, or does things to drive you away, or drinks himself into oblivion each night, or immerses himself in his successful work and can't understand why you want more from him than money and possessions. He likes to fight; he likes to drink; he doesn't like you. Those are the perfectly rational reasons for his behavior, so stop trying to read something into it, he says.

I agree you should stop trying to read something into it. Nothing is as annoying as other people's insights into why we do what we do. That doesn't mean you can't observe, just don't use your insights as ammunition in a losing battle. If he is denying feelings of guilt, it is because he cannot face them. Erwin Parson mentioned in "The Reparation of the Self: Clinical and Theoretical Dimensions in the Treatment of Vietnam Combat Veterans," "atrocity-related guilt, survivor guilt, accidental death-related guilt, guilt over commission ('I did . . . '), guilt over omission ('I didn't do . . .')": nice phrases, but what do they mean to your vet? Perhaps he thinks you wouldn't love him if you knew what he did. And it's happened.

Perhaps he made some mistake for which he can't forgive himself: shot a kid, shot a fellow American, led his buddies into an ambush. The possibilities are endless and indeed often so painful that numbing is only too understandable.

No matter what happens, we want to prevent bad consequences. We also need to believe that we are not powerless. To empower themselves, people often take responsibility for things over which they have no control: ambushes, deaths, if-onlys. Sometimes men who do this have no idea that they are having a feeling or that it is called *guilt*. Such guilt often manifests itself in intrusive memories, going over and over the incident, trying to make it come out right.

A deed that does not conform to a person's idea of himself can also result in guilt. John Ketwig told his wife how aware he became of "how thin a line there was between being a human being and being an animal." In the moral and psychological climate of Vietnam it was easier to do things that may now horrify the veteran. *How could I have done that? Why did I do it? Am I a decent person?* These are really heavy questions, and telling the person who is asking them that it's okay denies their importance. "Don't tell him it's okay," Bobby Smith advised, "because he knows it isn't."

On the other hand, one time when we were talking about the thin line between civilized behavior and violence, my husband Bob said, "You also have to realize it's human. People have been doing it for years. It's not an aberration. You're not a freak, a monster. You're human. Forgive yourself."

"I have pictures of myself holding heads." This marine's voice shook. Tears filled his eyes. He looked away, throat working, until he gained control. "I went to speak at a college to defend the war after I got back. They asked me about killing women and kids." He stopped again to control himself. "And I said—I said—that women can kill you, and kids can, too, and if you kill the women, they can't have kids that will grow up to kill your kids. And I believed it. I believed it. I was so dumb."

"You can't forgive yourself for being such a fool?" I tried to paraphrase what he was feeling.

"That's right. I can't fit in. I don't feel like there is anywhere I belong. I have no respect for authority. They can't change the past or make it up to me. I was idealistic. I went to boot camp right after high school. I didn't question Vietnam. I wanted everyone to be proud of me. I believed it was right. I knew in my head what happened to the Jews, but I couldn't relate it to what we were doing. I didn't see myself as a Nazi. I saw it as a score. It was easy to do it because I never thought of them as people. They didn't even look like people. American lives were worth more than foreign lives. Better to kill a Vietnamese than risk them being VC and hurting me or my men. If we got a round from a village, I called in artillery fire . . . " His eyes filled again and he looked away. The pain on his face was almost more than I could bear.

Another symptom that should be in the diagnostic criteria but probably never will be is *self-medication*. When an M.D. tries to control someone's symptoms through medication, this is "therapeutic." When an individual tries to control the same intolerable symptoms by using booze, marijuana, or any other illegal drug, he gets moral judgments.

When people have to deal with depression, isolation, rage, avoidance of feelings, emotional numbing, survivor guilt, anxiety, nervousness, distrust of authority, inability to sleep, nightmares, intrusive thoughts, flashbacks, jumpiness, trouble in concentrating, avoidance of anything that reminds them of Vietnam, including Oriental people, chronic physical symptoms such as dizziness, pain, or unexplained weakness, and they are blocked from getting help because none of these persistent symptoms are recognized as being related to war experiences (until 1980), some of them *have* to resort to drugs or alcohol. How else could they stay alive? They deserve respect for making it this far, however imperfectly.

As psychologist Janet Woititz said at a conference I attended recently, "The phrase 'Just say no!' is an insult. What are people supposed to do with their pain?" She was not recommending the use of drugs; she was recommending the funding of therapy to help people deal with pain in a drug-free way. "Just say no" is just denial.

Even though the medical profession now sees PTSD as a treatable disorder, and doctors now know how to help Vietnam vets, justifiable anger and mistrust keep many of them away. Getting them in for treatment is one of the big problems, not to the Veterans Administration (which prefers to think they're all fine now), but to the mental-health professionals who do care. I hope this book will help some of the veterans decide to find someone who can help them.

Not every vet with problems has PTSD. Not every vet needs therapy. How do you tell? Psychologist John Russell Smith said:

> Many veterans and other survivors will deny any problems. "I put that all behind me," "I had to get on with my life," and "It doesn't really bother me now" are common assertions about catastrophic experience. Does one take them at face value? Do we presume that such statements are manifestations of denial and resistance masking underlying pathology?
>
> If a veteran or other survivor of trauma can remember and consider the entire experience without consuming passion or mute withdrawal, then this individual's expression can be taken at face value. [That means the vet can talk about it and talk without going berserk.]
>
> The ability to face pain and grief and to recognize the honor, joy, and even excitement of the catastrophic situation indicates healthy resolution. Trauma victims who can hear and accept different perspectives on the traumatic events without rancor or turmoil [that means he can accept that other vets thought the war was wrong, or right, and that even Jane Fonda had a right to her opinion] demonstrate their strength, adaptability, and resolution of stress. If the client does not have these characteristics, then there is a good indication that the traumatic experience is not yet integrated. Whether or not it needs to be integrated is a decision for the veteran and those close to him or her. Whether it *will be* integrated is up to the veteran.

The last sentence is really important for family members to understand.

A word here for people who are saying to themselves, "Hey, I don't have any of these problems." Comparisons are odious. Assume that you're not tougher, just luckier.

Another point. *Delayed stress.* A lot of people sitting out there saying "I don't have no problem with Vietnam" are going to get a surprise one of these days. Losing a job or a wife or being in a wreck are perfect catalysts to a delayed stress reaction. Like surviving in Vietnam, this, too, is basically a matter of luck. If circumstances don't combine against him, a vet may never get intrusive symptoms. Luckily, again, if he gets them now, doctors know what they are and what to expect, and the vet can get help instead of thinking he's nuts.

Remember: A lot of vets have suffered terribly from thinking they're just not tough enough, and help is now available because their suffering and their deaths—yes, deaths—alerted a few people to the fact that there was a problem. Those few dogged people— psychiatrists Robert Lifton and Chaim Shatan, who helped with the Vietnam Veterans Against the War rap groups in the early 1970s; social worker Sarah Haley, at the Boston VA Outpatient Clinic, who began to work with Vietnam vets in the late 1960s; Dr. William Gault, who wrote "Some Remarks on Slaughter" in 1971; combat vet and psychologist Charles Figley, who edited the 1978 book on *Stress Disorders Among Vietnam Vets;* psychologist John Wilson, whose *Forgotten Warrior Project*, funded by the Disabled American Veterans, was published in 1977; John Russell Smith, who fought the VA's indifference, participated in rap groups, and finally trained as a psychologist and worked on the *DSM III;* Shad Meshad and Ray Scurfield, psychologists in Vietnam who worked with vets under horrible conditions at the VA's of the 1970s and then helped found the Vet Centers; William Mahedy; and many, many others—had to fight the monumental indifference of the VA and the medical profession to get recognition and help for everyone suffering from PTSD.

Readjustment Problems Among Vietnam Veterans, by Jim Goodwin, Psy.D., a free pamphlet available from the Disabled American Veterans, helped me understand what had happened to Bob. As a matter of fact, I cried all the way through it as aspect after aspect of my life with Bob was played in a framework of normal reaction to trauma. All those years I spent trying to understand and cope alone, all those problems I tried to shoulder, often failing miserably, had an explanation. We weren't defective, crazy, fucked up. We were normal. We had struggled for years, without help, almost without hope, bound by love that would not give up despite the pain, but what we had was definable and helpable.

I'm crying now as I write this—self-pity, I admit—at the waste of twenty years of my life struggling with a problem I didn't understand. I'm crying for all my pain, for all those times I felt that if only I were better, thinner, more housewifely, neater, kinder, Bob wouldn't be so depressed all the time. If I were a perfect wife, he wouldn't have any problems. Now I'm laughing, because he used to agree with me. But I'll tell you something else: If I didn't cry over it, I wouldn't be able to laugh over it a moment later. If you have lost years, I urge you to cry over them. It's part of your job in getting over them. It is your duty to cry!

You may think: How come old George the Green Beret down the street or Matt Marine doesn't have any problems? Because he's not going to tell you he has any, that's why. Human nature, people call it. Ever asked someone who just lost his house in a flood, "How are you?" "Fine."

Maybe George doesn't have a problem *yet*. Maybe he never will. Maybe he got his green beret at the PX at McDill Air Force Base in Tampa. And maybe he'll get PTSD in 2005. Who knows? Psychologist Ray Scurfield said, "The vets we've seen so far have the least amount of issues with trust. Vets with regular jobs hide and deny their issues. I call it white-collar PTSD. It can be blue-collar, too."

Even vets who are successful and happy today feel pain when they recall the events of Vietnam. This is normal. Some vets suppress the pain more successfully than others. They believe that real men or women aren't *bothered* by anything. The constellation of problems that develops from being in a war can include the ability to suppress *anything*. It's not hard to suppress everyday feelings after you've practiced suppressing overwhelming physical fear, the devastating, violent loss of friend after friend, and the rage to kill for a year.

As mentioned earlier, some vets buy into the scapegoating begun by the antiwar movement, then happily picked up by the military and political establishments. For example, the Vietnam Veterans Leadership Program sent me a huge packet of papers full of statistics about how well Vietnam veterans were doing just before I went on tour for *Chickenhawk*—because Bob was in prison—so that I could present an "accurate view." Their convenient statistics showed that hardly any vets have problems. Thanks, guys. That only makes the ones who do have problems feel: "Oh, not only am I fucked up, but I'm the only one." That just isn't true.

I was very angry at the VVLP. In a way it was a good, but painful, lesson. Vets don't like being told they have problems. Why should they? They went through a lot and now everyone wants them to be defective on top of that. Still, having problems is not a sign of weakness. It's normal. If anything, I believe that being affected by Vietnam is a sign that a person is not an idiot or a moral degenerate.

As a matter of fact, according to the Research Triangle Institute in the National Vietnam Veterans Readjustment Study, presented to Congress in fall, 1988, *one-third* of the men and women who went through the type of experiences described in this book now have active PTSD. This very careful study was based not only on combat but on exposure to war-zone stress, so the nurses and medics and body-baggers or the truck drivers and mechanics who operated in forward areas weren't left out. The study used many different tests and interviews of each veteran to back up its findings, instead of the usual single interview with a bored bureaucrat that the government has found so convenient for minimizing percentages of people with PTSD.

Many current studies of PTSD still focus on proving predisposition, others on the events that produced the PTSD and whether they should have. A lot of time and energy have been spent on trying to figure out why some people "get" PTSD and some don't. Who cares? The nature of the syndrome is such that *no one can say a particular person who has suffered a trauma didn't get PTSD* until the person is *dead*. The most that can be said *scientifically* is that someone doesn't have symptoms yet, or has a few of the symptoms but not the full-blown syndrome. Psychiatrists worry about why some people get PTSD because, like everyone else, they don't want to acknowledge that random violence can strike each of us without warning, even here at home. Searching for defects in the characters of people who have PTSD gives psychiatrists (and even other veterans) the illusion of control, the illusion that *this couldn't happen to me*.

The psychiatric attitude that having PTSD makes a person look worse than someone who avoided it is also problematic. For instance, black soldiers exposed to abusive violence had a higher rate of PTSD than did white soldiers. People at one conference I attended actually used the words *black soldiers came out looking worse compared to the white vets*. WRONG. How can it "look worse" to be bothered by seeing people abused?

So if your vet has PTSD, be proud of it. It means he gave a shit. And if he doesn't, consider him luckier—not better.

Getting a guy with PTSD to talk is almost impossible. At a lot of VA hospitals the person who does intake isn't *interested* in PTSD, so he takes a military history, three questions: "Were you in Vietnam? What'd you do? See any combat?" So, the history of a truck driver who was almost blown up by a land mine and saw some of his buddies burn to death in the cab of the truck behind him while he frantically tried to get the door open can say he saw no combat. True from one point of view, but from the point of view of a traumatic stressor, sure, he has one! "So," this imaginary examiner might contend, "how was I supposed to know? He didn't tell me." An intake person at a VA hospital should be trained in diagnosing PTSD. The VA is there to treat service-connected disabilities, and PTSD is as service-connected as you can get. The intake person should get a complete history of the veteran's Vietnam experiences. Anything less shows lack of professionalism. If the interviewer knows anything about Vietnam, he'd know that a driver in a convoy is likely to have been attacked, and also that a truck driver isn't going to go around saying he's a combat vet because what he went through isn't anything compared to what some grunts saw. The thing is, the interviewer's job is to be *interested* in the problems of veterans. And it's not just Vietnam he should know about, but also Anzio, Omaha Beach, the Battle of the Bulge, Guadalcanal, Ploesti, Chosin Reservoir, and so on.

I'll never forget one World War II vet I talked to. He'd been shot down, almost lost a leg. One hundred bombers with no fighter cover

over Italy (meaning: *expendable*). Thirty planes came back. He drinks. He takes drugs for pain. He wishes he had died. When he said that, he paused, waiting for me to say *You shouldn't say that.* I said *Yeah.* "You understand?" His voice was full of wonder. Yeah, I understand; he has PTSD. But to a lot of people, even those who work for the VA, he's just an old bore full of war stories.

Being stuck in the anger stage of grief is difficult and also incomprensible to many. Being stuck at nineteen in a thirty-nine-year-old-body is ridiculous. (As I discussed earlier, one of the effects of trauma is to interrupt the stages of life.) Nineteen-year-olds may still be pretty idealistic or they may have gotten a little cynical, more aware that what's good for General Bullmoose may not necessarily be good for the U.S.A., what's good for America may not be good for the whole world, that people (like Jane Fonda) can do things for the best of reasons and still do evil. If your vet hadn't yet found that out when he went to Vietnam, he soon did. Idealism made many vets want to go help the Vietnamese, so they can't afford to remember what actually happened: children napalmed to barbed wire, people driven from their homes, or killed to "save them." If we did it, it must be right. Right? The gap between what they'd like to believe about themselves and their country, and the things that actually went on in Vietnam, yawns like a chasm down to hell. Denial is the only answer: We meant to do good, so we did. Learning to tolerate the ambiguity between aims and actual events is one of the things being stuck at nineteen prevents. Learning to tolerate that ambiguity is pure pain.

I always wondered about these guys who would go back, who would kill every gook again, who still radiated simple my-country-right-or-wrong patriotism, who still felt that the president had to know more than us and wouldn't steer us wrong. Now I understand, because that's how you feel when you're nineteen. The world is a simple place. We're right, and anyone who gets in our way is wrong.

This kind of thinking carries over into everyday life and makes it hard for the vet to see your point of view. He also has high (read: *unrealistic*) standards for everything, rigid standards. A man should be this way. Women should. A wife should— A man should— Living with "shoulds" is tough for everyone.

Broadly speaking, PTSD symptoms cluster around either denial or intrusion, and for many vets they alternate either slowly or rapidly. I'm going to describe two imaginary vets, one in the full-blown intrusive phase, and one completely numbed out in denial. Many vets have some of these symptoms, and there may be some guy out there who has every single one. Some of the symptoms fit the stereotype of the crazy Vietnam vet that many vets and their organizations find so irritating. For their sake, let me say that these very troubled men are a minority of PTSD sufferers—many of whom live lives of quiet, numb desperation—but they need help and they haven't gotten it or they wouldn't still be suffering from these problems. Even some of the pros in the PTSD in-patient programs expect these guys to get well at the rate they require, not at the rate the veterans are comfortable with. Failing to push people through on their terms, some professionals then pronounce, "He likes being screwed up," rather than, "He's comfortable with the known misery. He doesn't know how to be otherwise, and I don't know how to teach him." Or, simply, "He can't go this fast." Sarah Haley wrote that some men need "time in the field" away from therapy before they can come back to get more.

The vet with severe intrusive PTSD can be really hard to live with. He may talk about Vietnam all the time, which means he can't stop thinking about it either. He probably dreams about it, and may have flashbacks. He may not be able to keep from acting as if he's in Vietnam: These actions may range from saying *fuck* every third word, on up to reacting with physical violence when anything goes wrong, or when he's startled. He blows up. He hits the floor, or the wall or you or the kids or his co-workers. He disappears and comes back hours or days or weeks later. He carries a gun. He sleeps on the floor. He won't go into a Chinese restaurant, says he'd like to kill all gooks. He overreacts to everything from our point of view. His behavior may make him feel crazy (not that he says so), and he medicates himself with alcohol or drugs, legal or illegal, to try to control his symptoms.

These vets are drawn to isolation. They live in the woods like Bob and me. They live on a mountain. They isolate themselves in the middle of a city. Many don't have friends, and don't want their wife or kids to, either. Many don't have families.

Pain syndromes (migraines, back pain, stomach pains, etc.) are often indicators of PTSD. Drs. Richard A. Benidilet and Lawrence C. Kolb reported that 10 percent of the patients treated at one VA pain clinic had undiagnosed PTSD. Chronic pain is another way the body has of screaming for help. This applies not only to the existence of pain at the site of former wounds but also to headaches, the chronic chest pains of good ol' *irritable heart*, lower back pain, and gastrointestinal complaints. Some of these are a result of generalized bodily tension states that may result from hypervigilance and the startle reactions. Sometimes you can see the muscle tension.

Erwin Parson says a lot of vets feel a sort of "walking time bomb anxiety (or fear of losing control over one's explosive angry feelings, even though in actuality most veterans are overly defended against affective explosive outbursts)." They feel angry about everything.

Veterans often have an unrelenting cynicism about people and the government and a total inability to deal with authority, whether it be in a job or in trying to get benefits or help from the VA. I've had people tell me that the only way they'll go down to the VA is with an Uzi. That's how angry they are at the way they were used and discarded and blamed by the government. It doesn't help them get help, however.

Working for anyone can be a bitch. It isn't uncommon for a vet to change jobs several times a year. Bob's first job, painting apartments after he graduated from college, lasted eighteen days. I still remember my horror that he just walked off a job because he couldn't stand it. How would we eat? It took me a while to realize that he probably used up his reserves of forcing himself to do things he didn't want to while flying into those hot LZ's in Vietnam. After something like that I guess you draw a line at the bullshit you'll put up with in the rest of your life. Sometimes it makes it hard to pay the bills, but what are bills, anyway?

Veterans' anger at the system that abused them can lead to a you-owe-me attitude. The vet can be very insensitive to others. His own problems fill his world to the exclusion of yours. Erwin Parson described him as very sensitive to slights, demanding undivided attention, that every need be fulfilled to his satisfaction and specifications. The standard is perfection. Since it can't be met, he cycles into rage and disillusionment. He can't compromise or delay, needs instant gratification. Helene Jackson, a social worker who worked with veterans for many years, mentioned that he often has grandiose standards and rules, but no realistic goals. Often he believes you are either with him or against him, exemplifying that most common of cognitive distortions, black-and-white thinking. Other forms of distorted thinking can involve how a veteran regards women.

Guys went into the military at an impressionable age. Some drill instructors tried to teach their recruits never to be so weak as to trust a female. Basic training, right? At an impressionable age they were told that all women were whores, and in Vietnam certainly a lot of such evidence was placed before their eyes, from the Vietnamese prostitutes to the "Dear John" letters. Some of them believe it.

To a vet with this type of thinking, women may not be perceived as people, much less people who can contribute to happiness and fulfillment, which are just bullshit anyhow. In a discussion in the vet group at Union Correctional Institution, one of the guys turned and said to me, "You've got to remember, Patience, most women *couldn't wait a year!*" Men who saw a guy stand up in the middle of a firefight and get his head blown away after he got a "Dear John," may be mistrustful of women, too.

Sensation-seeking—whether through infidelity, drugs, violence (against you or the biggest guy in the bar), driving like a maniac, flying, riding motorcycles, running pot or other drugs, criminal activity—often occurs because if the vet isn't doing something dangerous, he feels dead, as psychologist John Wilson put it. Dealing, maneuvering, making things happen—these represent life. Some veterans say they're hooked on adrenaline. Life has never been as exciting as it was in Vietnam, but they constantly try to replace that excitement with new turmoils, traumas, and catastrophes.

Sometimes the vet even labels himself by wearing fatigues everywhere and getting very indignant when he makes people nervous. He does a lot of mind reading—*What's wrong with her?*—and gets angry over stuff the rest of us take in stride.

This is the Vietnam vet we all know from the newspapers, the movies, the TV shows of the 1960s and 1970s, from Sylvester Stallone's *Rambo*. This guy has no idea how he comes off to other people. His violent attitudes drive them off. He doesn't have much self-awareness so he does things that hurt and piss people off without knowing what he has done.

Depression is something many veterans struggle with. When a person is clinically depressed, certain symptoms appear: sleep disturbances, psychomotor retardation (the person is slower and often clumsier than he was), feelings of worthlessness, difficulty in concentrating, suicidal ideas, feelings of helplessness and hopelessness. Jim Goodwin reported that "many have been continuously depressed since their experiences in Vietnam." This symptom fits into both intrusive and denial phases. When you're having intrusive thoughts or dreams, it can get you really depressed. Numbness is often a sign of severe depression, too.

Harder to spot and much more common is the quiet vet, the vet who isn't feeling anything, who "died" over there (and many of them feel that they did die over there). You probably know this type of guy. So-and-so doesn't have any problems with Vietnam. He has a job, had it for 125 years. This is the guy who has numbed himself to deal with life. Withdrawal, stagnation, and despair are his defenses and responses. The only way he can live at all is not to feel anything. He can't remember much about Vietnam. He may not concentrate very well. Too much of his energy is tied up in not feeling anything. Drug use, often alcoholism, turns his aggression into self-destruction. This well-controlled type may have seen and done more than our macho friend in the last paragraph, and has no desire ever again even to think of it. He's passive because any activity may escalate through initiative to assertion to aggression to murder or violence. He does nothing rather than run that risk.

Feelings of helplessness also arise from the fact that, in Vietnam, no matter what you did, it didn't make any difference. Bodies were literally the only things that counted. Someone had to produce the bodies, but it never changed anything. We didn't win hearts or minds or land. Helplessness to influence the outcome of the war no matter how good the individual soldiers and marines were translates into a profound feeling of despair and depression. A lot of vets feel: "What's the use?" Erwin Parson said this despair often manifests itself in wandering, aimless life-styles. The vet can't keep a job, not because he blows up or hates it, but because it just doesn't seem to matter. He can't care for himself because he can't care. Alternatively, he settles for a dull job and a dull life.

This veteran doesn't participate in your relationship, in life, in institutions. Of course he never tells you that this is the result of profound despair, because he never tells you anything. Jim Goodwin said they are afraid that " . . . if they once again allow themselves to feel, they may never stop crying or may completely lose control of themselves . . . Many of these veterans go through life with an impaired capacity of love and care for others. They have no feeling of direction or purpose in life. They are not sure why they even exist."

Maybe the things this vet's not remembering are so terrible to him that he can't stand to be loved. He may feel he doesn't deserve to be alive, never mind loved.

Some vets give up sex to maintain equilibrium. Some of them equate letting down emotional barriers and sexual release with the release of aggression. It scares them to feel out of control in those moments of ecstasy. They are afraid to lose control for even a few seconds, afraid of what they might do, afraid of some intrusion from the whirlwind of violence and aggression released in Vietnam.

For the veteran suffering from PTSD and for his family, life gets repetitious. He makes the same mistakes, follows the same self-defeating pattern. It is not that he's dumb, not that he won't change. He *can't*. The tremendous investment of energy it takes to stay numb is what blocks him from life and from love. Coming home was one of the causes of this. The vets were old men at nineteen. How strange to come home and see that people still cared about the color of the curtains, were shocked about Gladys's not wearing a bra, or got into a big fight over whether to have chocolate or strawberry ice cream. Didn't these people know? Didn't they care? No. They didn't. Without social support, sanction from society for what they did, the vets isolated themselves, physically or psychologically. Alone, lonely, depressed, often drugs seemed like the only answer, were the only answer.

I look back at the time when Bob had severe PTSD and was drinking a quart of whiskey a day and smoking pot and taking Valium—and was still *wired*. I know he couldn't talk to me. I was too busy telling him what a shit he was and running the family, running out to buy his booze, making dinner while he fixated on the war reports on TV. Somehow I was always busy cooking during the news. So while he slowly died inside watching people die for real, year after year, I made spaghetti, chicken cordon bleu, chicken with almonds. I don't like to remember this. It doesn't fit in with the way I'd like to have been, the way I'd like to be now, but it's the truth.

If your veteran has some or all of these problems, wouldn't it be nice if he could learn how to be a survivor of the trauma instead of a reactor? He can never again be the young idealistic guy who went to Vietnam, but he can learn new ways that will help him, can learn to regulate his reactions, can have good relations with people, especially you. How nice it would be if he could not only bear to look at himself and live more comfortably with the ambiguity of what happened in Vietnam, but could also see the value of his experience for the world and for others. How wonderful if he could once again feel a sense of being a worthwhile part of the world.

To be able to do this, he needs to know that what he is going through is NORMAL. I can't emphasize enough how important it is for the vet to realize that the feelings and thoughts, numbness and withdrawal or nightmares and eruptions of rage or fear or anxiety or physical symptoms are NORMAL. They are also signals to get help: not drugs, but a good PTSD program involving therapy about Vietnam.

Circumstantial evidence is the key each vet can use to determine whether he has a problem. Flashbacks, rages, and suicidal feelings are the strongest signals, because they often wind up involving life and death. Numbness and feelings of alienation are also signals to get help, as are the rest of the symptoms of PTSD listed in this chapter.

Where to get help is discussed in Chapter 11.

Whether or not the vet does get help is up to him.

9

Our Problems

So far I've been talking as though the veteran's the only one with problems. But his problems can become your biggest problem, and it can wear you out. What can you do if you're at the end of your rope? How do you find the strength to go on?

I can tell you how I find it. I think about the year Bob spent in Vietnam. Whatever else he could have done, he endured something I'll never have to. Even if he had shot himself in the foot or turned in his wings, he would have still done something very difficult, something that I've never had to face. I try to understand how small civilian concerns must seem compared to life or death in Vietnam. That gives me perspective. If he could do that, then I can do this: stand by him.

Standing by is not giving and giving and giving. I did that, too, and for as long as I did so, it prevented Bob from changing. Psychologists call giving and giving and giving, *enabling*. By shouldering all the problems, we enable our vets to stay the way they are.

Standing by is being available—but *not responsible*—for what Bob is feeling, or for Bob's problems, or for doing everything. Sometimes this is hard. I get tired of problems. I'd like to bail out to that imaginary life we planned before Vietnam, in which he was an airline pilot and I had a Ph.D. and taught English at a college and we had four kids and a perfect life. It's a natural feeling and one we all have at times, but I don't let it blind me to the fact that I'd have problems in that life, too.

History is a consideration, too. When I was thinking about getting a divorce and finding someone who would love only me and be nice to me, I can remember feeling so clearly: *But then it won't be Bob. I will never have gone out with him in Texas to cut down a cedar tree for Christmas, or been to Spain with him. He will never have spent the whole of his first paycheck on a pair of sandals that I wanted.* I didn't want to throw out the good with what was bad at that time. I decided I'd rather try to work it out. Now our problems are somewhat different from the problems other people have, but they are manageable. They'll end when we die. I suspect that's one sure sign that you're dead—having no problems!

If the vet in your life is a son or brother or father, divorce isn't even an option. You may be suffering terrible feelings of hopelessness. Just understanding some of the reasons why he is the way he is will help your dealings with him. So will the suggestions in Part Three.

Ruth Scott, the wife of a medic, wrote me: "The hardest thing for me to deal with has been people asking 'why I put up with it.' I think the people who were hurt the most by Viet Nam were the ones who were the best, the ones who were the most sensitive and the most caring. That's why I put up with it . . . " Me, too.

I knew Bob before he went to Vietnam, but most vets weren't married when they went. Maybe you met this rough, tough Vietnam vet, or Mr. Cool who's never fazed by anything, or the man with no feelings, or a workaholic who had "no problem with Vietnam, not like all those whiners." If your vet begins to develop problems, or if you begin to see the behavior that attracted you to him as a problem, what can you do? Can you see what's under there, under the armor Vietnam vets have built over the years?

Some vets practiced a "wandering, aimless life-style" or were hooked on adrenaline for years. If one of these vets has gotten into a relationship with you, and you've picked this book up in an attempt to find out why he has problems or what he's been through, getting into a relationship is a good sign. He's trying to heal, to go on with his life. If you've read this book from page one, you know he's lost enough in his life. You may literally be his lifeline. Many vets go for help because it's that or lose their wives or girlfriends, so you do have a measure of influence on him. Use it. How? Small steps, a little bit at a time. More on that in the next chapter.

You may never have heard of PTSD. Marsha Livingston, Ron's wife, said, "When I saw you [speaking on PTSD at Namvets of Marion County, Florida] was the first time I heard it talked about."

If you've lived together for a while, you may be facing some of the same problems as your vet and be having some of the same PTSD symptoms: You may be isolated because you've moved so many times, because you've tried to please him by not wasting time on other friends or activities, because all your friends tell you to leave him and you don't want to hear it so you've stopped seeing them, because you've needed help so many times everyone has dropped you. This isolation is increased by emotional isolation from him.

You may have rages. Your vet may have made you so angry over the years that you'd just like to beat him up with a frying pan. I've felt like that. You've held in all your feelings so long to keep from upsetting him that when you lose it, you go out of control. I used to scream my head off at Bob. I jumped on him in bed once *to kill him*, but my arms went weak. When I went totally insane one day because he was so unfair to me, and screaming with rage threw a wooden box through a window, I got a friend of mine to take me to the infirmary (I was a student at the University of Florida at the time) to see a shrink. It was one of the best moves of my life.

You may also have a deep, burning rage at the military, the government, and the VA for what they have done to your vet. I do. What was my husband's life worth—then or now—to them?

Following a more common pattern, you may have buried your anger at your vet for failing to meet your authentic needs so deeply that you don't even know you're angry. Instead you get headaches, colitis, back and neck pains—whatever. Circumstantial evidence may help you identify this feeling: You may spend a lot of time telling your friends about his problems and what he should do to fix them, like I used to, or you may spend a lot of time correcting his manners and language, in the nicest way, for his own good. You may lecture, nag, or give him the cold shoulder. These are time-honored ways in which women express anger.

Like your vet, you may distrust everything and everyone and not believe that anyone could understand what you've been through.

Many people have been so insensitive over the years to what happened to our men and women in Vietnam, and said so many cruel things to us about Vietnam vets, and this makes going for help really hard. It's also why self-help groups are so great: Meeting others with the same problems can be quite a relief. I'll talk more about groups in Chapters 10 and 12.

You may be hyperalert to everything that may affect your vet's mood "walking on eggshells." You may spend a lot of time and energy trying to head off possible problems or hassles for your vet because you don't want him upset. You may avoid anything that might set him off. You may know his early warning signs. I was always on the lookout to keep things from bothering Bob. I made a lot of work for myself.

You may be depressed. You may be unable to think of one thing you'd LIKE to do (I couldn't), because it's been so long since you allowed yourself to try to be happy. It isn't worth the risk. You may find yourself driving slower and slower as you get closer to home, as I used to, because you just don't want to know what he's upset about this time, but you know he'll be either angry or depressed about something.

You may be so depressed you feel like killing yourself. I often have been. If you do feel suicidal, get help! I did.

You may feel numb all the time. You don't have time to feel anything. There are too many things you have to get done. I was always either numb or angry, and always saying 'No, no. I don't mind'—when I did. I thought that would make things better. It didn't.

You may feel guilty for every mood change in your vet, for not being good enough to make him or her happy. I used to. You may feel guilty for not having known or understood about Vietnam and PTSD. I did. I still do sometimes.

Your self-esteem may be at rock bottom because you feel that if you did things right, your vet wouldn't have these problems. That's what I felt. Maybe you feel you must be a really bad person, or you wouldn't have such bad things happening in your life. Or it may seem that every good thing you try to do for your family backfires, as it did for me. Nothing worked. Or maybe your mom and dad and friends and church have all erroneously told you that more patience, more love, and being a better wife would solve all your problems. Know this: Nothing *you* do will solve his PTSD.

You may be anxious all the time, trying to control everything so nothing will upset your vet or get him down. Me, too. Everything had to be perfect all the time. Of course, it wasn't. As you get more anxious, you lose perspective and it seems just as important that the dishes get washed as it is that you make love. Just another in the endless round of things you have to do.

You may be living in fear because you don't know when your vet is going to go into a rage again and what he might do if he does. I was terrified of Bob's rages, even though they were pretty rare.

You may feel like a rabbit, running here and there, able only to react to what's happening in your life. When Bob was depressed, I would desperately try to cheer him up, all the while feeling responsible. When he wanted isolation, I'd struggle not to become isolated. When he got in a rage, I'd cower, but days later I'd still rage over it and never let him forget what he'd "done to me." When he couldn't be loving, I was always demanding: "Hug me. Kiss me." Everything that happened mired us both in guilt: his for having problems, mine for not being a good enough wife. His anxiety reactions, sleep disturbances, nightmares, and intrusive thoughts fed my panic. All I could do was try to keep things going. For years all I could do was react, never act.

You may be full of self-doubt because your vet keeps saying there's nothing wrong with him, that you should straighten out your own act instead, that if you were a good wife you'd know how he feels without being told, have dinner ready whenever he gets home, even if he's late, manage the kids better—whatever. Bob used to yell about my housekeeping, my sloppy bill paying, and my child rearing, but he could never help me with any of it. The quality and quantity of his criticism and of how upset he got were directly related to Vietnam, but since neither of us knew what was wrong, we tried to blame each other.

You may wonder if your perceptions are crazy or wrong. *Is what I am feeling normal? Is what he's doing normal?*

You may not be able to sleep because of fear, anxiety, anger, or obsessive thinking about your problems. Me, too. Or sleep may come to mean the same thing to you as to your vet. Marsha Livingston remembered years of nightmares: "He was not in our bed. He was back in Vietnam. He'd stand up and holler for people and cradle the bodies of friends. I didn't know what to do or where to turn . . . I didn't want to tell everyone I was failing—not doing something right . . . One night after a funeral, he dreamt he was walking point with a buddy and the guy stepped on a claymore mine and he was picking up body parts"—her voice broke—"and trying to put the guy back together and screaming for the medic." Tears ran down her face. "I never told him any of his dreams. I tried a few times and he changed the subject. Sometimes I'd ask about names he'd mention in dreams—he'd tell funny stories and then, 'Oh, they are dead.' "

You may experience crazy, intrusive thoughts of terrible accidents, horrible results from each little thing. Curtains burning, houses afire, cars crashing, kids run over on their bicycles. I visualized horrendous consequences for every minor act. My worrying wore me out.

You may even abuse substances yourself, to be cool or less anxious and afraid. There have been periods in my life when I drank too much with Bob, and other times when I used pot to relax in the evening. You may abuse food as I did. Other addictions, such as being a workaholic, a compulsive shopper, or addicted to relationships may also affect your life.

You may also be struggling to fulfill every role in your vet's life. You may be the provider, the cook and cleaning lady, the only parent to the kids, the lover, the only person he can talk to, the only person he can show his anger to, his only friend, his rescuer, his persecutor, and even his punching bag. (See Chapter 11 if he hits you. He has no right to hit you.) I was everything to Bob except a punching bag. I used to say I had two kids, Jack and Bob. Managing multiple roles can wear you out.

Families of vets with problems, according to psychologists Tom (a vet) and Candis Williams, often identify the vet as the only one with a problem and the only one who has to change. They report that "family members usually do not understand how their own behavior can perpetuate dysfunctional patterns in family relationships." It took me years to realize that what I was doing was actually making things worse, and then years to figure out how to change my own behavior to be less dysfunctional. And I still have some of the same problems!

Family members may also experience a feeling of helplessness and powerlessness. Your vet may have tried to control his symptoms and failed. You may have tried to make everything perfect for him and failed, as I did. Now you both feel that it just can't be done. Nothing will ever get better. Bob and Jack were mad at me for being so bossy, and all I was trying to do was to handle things for them so they wouldn't have so many problems. I was trying to be *nice*. I even tried to be cool about our problems, not to bring them up, and I wound up eating my heart out with repressed rage. I used to feel helpless and hopeless all the time. It was like bashing my head against a wall.

Learned helplessness develops from living with a chronic condition, especially an undiagnosed one. Hopelessness and resulting despair are big problems for us. We have a hard time trying to do anything because we've had such bad results from what we've tried so far.

If you are the mother or father or sister or brother of a Vietnam vet, you may have seen a great change in him after Vietnam. Or he may have just begun to have problems that you don't understand. You may feel that if his wife or girlfriend was nicer or kept him happy, then he wouldn't have a problem. Maybe you think she should straighten him out. These attitudes are based on the misconception that your vet's woman can control him or fix him. She can't. You may wind up criticizing or fighting with someone who needs your support and who may be feeling pretty inadequate most of the time, and no wonder. Whatever she does is not going to change what your vet experienced in Vietnam, and that is what causes many of his problems. That's what he has to work on. If you have been enabling to him to deny that he has problems by scapegoating his wife or girlfriend, it is absolutely essential to his recovery that you begin to detach yourself lovingly from his problems with this woman and from the crises that may develop in his life. Rescuing him will only keep him stuck. Specific advice on how to do this is available through Al-Anon—just substitute "vets" for "alcoholics" when you read the organization's pamphlets—and in *The Dance of Anger*, by Harriet Lerner, Ph.D.

Families of women involved with Vietnam vets may feel that their daughters are fools for "putting up" with problematical vets. They may feel that getting rid of the vet will solve all their daughter's problems. Or they may feel that their daughter could fix all the problems by being nicer, a better wife, and so forth, or by demanding change and raising hell. None of these is true. Nothing your daughter can do will fix the vet because his problems are his. Your daughter has problems that will not be cured by leaving the vet, either. Support is what she needs while she works out her problems.

Children of Vietnam vets may also feel that their mothers either cause their fathers' problems or are fools for staying with them. Advice and criticism can only further hurt women who are doing their best with a painful reality over which they have no control.

Parents and siblings of vets have often gone through many of the same problems with their vets while the vet has either had no significant relationships or run through a series of women. They may have rescued him time after time with money, a place to stay, someone to complain to about the current girlfriend or wife, or by being the only person the vet can talk to about Vietnam. They may feel torn by the needs of the rest of the family or by disapproval from other family members for "wasting so much time on that jerk."

Children of Vietnam vets may not understand what happened to their fathers in Vietnam. They may feel that they caused the vet's problems. "I thought he sat in the basement, depressed and suicidal, because of *me*," one college student told me, "and I didn't know what I'd done. I would try so hard to cheer him up, to be what was missing in his life. The other kids didn't worry about it, but I thought it was me that had made him like that and I should fix him." Other children just feel that Dad hates them if he's emotionally unavailable or constantly angry.

When one person in a relationship has a chronic problem, a denial system often develops. Vets like to deny that anything is wrong with them or that Vietnam has anything to do with their problems in relationships. If they do recognize a problem, they tend to deny that anything can help them, especially if they ever pursued what thoroughly inadequate help was available in the seventies. Their partner adopts the role of savior, or joins in the behavior to bring it under control, or becomes the martyr, or goes through all three in sequence and then becomes the tough one who is going to force a change. The belief that we can change our loved ones and their natural defiance sets off a game—either a power struggle that no one wins, or protestations that no one really believes: "I'll never do it again"; "I'll do better in the woods in Oregon"; "I'll do better in a new job"; "Next time it will be different." It never is. Then the two of you feel helpless, hopeless, worthless, and mutually resentful, even hostile.

A system of blaming often develops along with denial. Everything is all the other person's fault. "If you were a good wife, we wouldn't have any problems" meets "If you just forgot about all that Vietnam stuff, we wouldn't have any problems," head-on and another fight starts. Assigning blame is a way of avoiding doing anything about our problems. It is also very painful to both partners, and we've had enough pain in our lives.

If you're deep into this painful stage of relating to each other and feel that if your vet would just change, everything would be fine, you are wrong. If he "just changed," you would unconsciously push him back into his old patterns, by sabotage or enabling, so you could be comfortable in your old role. When the wife of an alcoholic goes out and buys him booze so he won't yell at her, that's enabling. When you don't let someone know how what he does is affecting you so he won't be upset, that's enabling. Sometimes screaming at someone enables him to stay a bastard because "you're such a bitch." Remarks like "You're no fun anymore" to a newly sober or clean vet are purest sabotage. Parents, in-laws, and children can enable and sabotage, too, often in the form of criticizing the vet's partner and agreeing with him that she should change.

The kinds of behaviors we develop as a result of enabling are called co-dependence. Co-dependent was my middle name. I focused on Bob. I did everything I could to keep him happy and none of it worked, because I wasn't the problem. He had the problem and I was trying to solve it, control it, make everything perfect. I had to learn what he already knew from Vietnam—life is unmanageable. A lot of vets spend the rest of their lives trying to forget that (it's too scary), and in the process become terrible, controlling co-dependents themselves.

I read studies in the fields of substance abuse and family therapy that showed that families who sought help were depressed, isolated, anxious. One person was identified as the problem, and one person did most of the care-giving. They called these kinds of families *co-dependent*. Everyone in a co-dependent family can use help. The whole family needs information on how the family got this way, and tools to work their way back from hopelessness to health. *Co-dependent No More*, by Melody Beattie, is the book with which to start.

We become co-dependent when we live with PTSD, whether it is denied or overt. Also, sometimes people in pain are attracted to other such people, and what attracts some of us co-dependent types to vets is their problems. If you come from a dysfunctional family— even one that is dysfunctional in the most socially acceptable ways, like being workaholics or very religious—the one thing you know how to live with is problems!

There are three C's to co-dependency: the belief that you *caused* the problems your loved one is having; the belief that if you do things right, you can *control* it; and the belief that you can eventually *cure* it.

The three C's are exactly what I thought and how I acted.

I am a co-dependent.

Some of our problems arose from trying to deal with Bob's undiagnosed, untreated PTSD. Some of them arose from my undiagnosed, untreated co-dependency. Co-dependents can be born or made. Maybe trying to deal with Bob's undiagnosed PTSD had made me co-dependent. Maybe my mother had taught me. Did it matter?

The other important fact I learned about co-dependency is that it is a progressive condition. As we become more focused on the other person's problem, we become increasingly tolerant of inappropriate behavior: We let him drive when he is drunk or stoned to avoid a fight; we let him yell at us; we let him sit home and watch TV while we have a job and do the cooking and housework; we let him work an 80-hour week and never talk to us.

We find ourselves putting up with things we never thought we would. We also begin to take over more and more of the family functions as he does less and less in the family. One adaptation is workaholism. Another can be alcoholism. Either way, any way, the family stuff gets dropped in our laps, or we take it over because if we don't do it, it doesn't get done. We develop a tunnel vision about our lives, a sort of learned helplessness, because nothing has seemed to work.

Ray Scurfield, a Vietnam vet who has a master's and doctorate in social work, has been working with Vietnam vets since the seventies. I asked him what he'd say to the partner of a vet: "First point: You may have been denying or giving secondary consideration to your own needs and wants over the years and may have accumulated stress time and time again because of your love and connection with a troubled war vet. So it is essential that you are clear that you are entitled to, and almost surely need to have, significant positive time and attention paid *to you: who you are, what your needs and wants are as an individual, your identity as a woman and an adult*."

If you are so busy and so tired you can't find a few minutes each day for yourself, that in itself is *circumstantial evidence* of co-dependency. Describe what is going on in your life as if it were happening to someone else. What would you suggest that person do? Would you tell her to give herself a break?

One way I use to detect co-dependence in myself now is to see if the story of my life is still the story of Bob's. When yours is the story of what your vet and your kids have done, and not your own experiences, you may very well be co-dependent. At a conference I attended, psychologist Janet Woititz put it even better: "How do you tell if you're a co-dependent? When you're dying, someone else's life flashes before your eyes."

I expect that eventually someone, somewhere, will do a study like John Wilson's first one for the DAV, *The Forgotten Warrior Project*, and find that just as a healthy person from a normal background could come out of Vietnam with terrible PTSD, the day-to-day grind of living with a person who has PTSD, especially if undiagnosed and untreated, will also lead to a similar result: a dysfunctional family focused on the problem of the identified problem person. How could any *other* result be considered normal? People care about one another! What are you going to do when someone you love has problems? You get involved, try to help, put your own needs aside. Then it's twelve years later and you don't know how to have fun anymore. You're exhausted, pissed off, anxious, profoundly depressed, guilty because you can't fix it. As a matter of fact, overfunctioning to hide your partner's problems from others is defined as normal in this society.

What is "normal"? In *Adult Children of Alcoholics*, by Janet Woititz, she stated: "Adult children of alcoholics guess at what normal is." That struck me as such an important concept for people with PTSD and their partners. All those times Bob and I would disagree and he'd wind up yelling, "Okay, okay, you're right and I'm just crazy!" All those times I'd wind up wondering if I was crazy. Was I too demanding? Did other people hug? Neither of us could really feel certain about what normal was, because although PTSD reactions are normal reactions for the survivor and co-survivor of trauma, in the context of everyday life they make you feel quite nuts.

Other characteristics of co-dependency and dysfunctional families Janet Woititz described were:

- Having difficulty following through on projects from start to finish
- Lying when it would be just as easy to tell the truth
- Judging ourselves without mercy
- Having difficulty having fun
- Taking ourselves very seriously
- Having difficulty with intimate relationships
- Overreacting to changes over which we have no control
- Seeking approval and affirmation all the time
- Feeling different from other people
- Being either super responsible or super irresponsible
- Being extremely loyal even when there's evidence it's not deserved
- Getting locked into our lives and seeing no alternatives

She really hit *me* on the nose with a lot of those. Many of them apply to our veterans as well. If some of them hit home with you, reading about co-dependency and adult children may help you feel a lot better about yourself. These are normal reactions to stressful relationships.

Another factor besides co-dependency also operates in our lives. Our vets have faced death, faced immediate, traumatic, life-threatening situations. They had to react instantly to stay alive. As psychologist Linda Moffat and Vietnam vet James Moffat stated in *Families After Trauma:*

> *The person is powerless to do anything but survive, no matter what it takes* [my *italics*]. Witnesses of traumatic events are also considered survivors, as they develop fears for their own safety as well as the same guilt for surviving and prospering when others did not.

Survivors develop behaviors that keep them alive, but unfortunately when the situation that caused them to develop the behaviors is over, the behaviors do not always go away. They come back whenever a threat is perceived along with the emotions of rage, fear, depression, and anxiety, and:

> . . . are passed on to significant others through the behaviors and feelings exhibited and experienced by the survivor.
> This post-trauma interaction makes us *co-survivors of the original trauma without ever having been there* [my *italics*].

Co-survivors can deal with such effects of the trauma only if they know more about it. Sources of information include books, documentaries and films on Vietnam, books like this one, and conversations with your vet at the vet's own pace, time, and ability to tolerate. We also need to know about PTSD and the long-term effects of trauma so we don't expect our vets to "forget it" or "get over it" because it happened fifteen or twenty years ago.

We need to know how it felt to be in Vietnam and how it affected our vets' beliefs and feelings about life since then. I've devoted a chapter to learning to listen because it's a skill that changed my life.

As the Moffats said, knowing about Vietnam will help you "identify patterns of behavior established in order to survive," and understand that "the survivor lives in a changed world. His/her perception of the world as a safe place has been altered by a personal awareness of death and disability. Innocence has been lost." Seeing myself as a co-survivor helped me, too, because my problems with Bob, and with life itself, seemed more reasonable from that perspective. I wasn't defective. I was a co-survivor. Bob's behavior became more understandable. It wasn't aimed at me—nor were his attitudes. They were both learned in Vietnam.

Learning about co-dependency helped me see my adaptation to co-survivorship as normal but not healthy. Co-dependents get worse. They tolerate more and more inappropriate behavior, and they get sick and die. PTSD is also a normal reaction, but not healthy in the long run. Behaviors used to distance the pain—running the gamut from drug/alcohol/food abuse to workaholism—also shorten the life span.

Co-surviving and developing co-dependency seem to go hand in hand, seeming to be the only answer when we're living it. But they are painful and leave us profoundly depressed and exhausted. What can we do?

Look at it this way: If we take care of everything, how can our vets grow?

If we look at it from a different slant, who are we to say our vets can't handle problems? They handled Vietnam, didn't they? Trying to help out with everything can be a not-so-subtle form of criticism, a vote of no-confidence.

Our vets may not *want* to handle problems, but if I take care of my vet, he stays stuck in the problems. I'm not saying to dump everything in your vet's lap and say, "Here, you handle it." Giving his problems back to him will be a slow process, and scary for both of you. It was for us. Easy does it.

Get help! Be fussy. Hunt around for a group or therapist you can trust. (More about that in Chapter 11.) Get *good* help, but get it! If you get help for yourself, as I did, you'll decrease the problems between you and your vet, perhaps to the point where your vet can do something about his.

You probably feel a lot of resistance to getting help. It's scary to admit to problems. *Suppose I get some crackpot therapist? Suppose things get worse? Can't I just read self-help books?* I highly recommend starting out with self-help books, and there is a list of them in the back of this book. Read books about Vietnam and the effects of PTSD. I even read books about different types of therapy so that when I walk into the office of a Gestalt therapist and she wants me to talk to the chair as if it were my vet, I recognize a Gestalt technique.

Educated clients *engage* in the work of therapy or self-help groups. They get more out of it than people who just go in to be cured or saved or whatever. But at some point, a group or a therapist can speed up your progress or help you stick with the changes you want to make in your life.

Let me say again that the problems that affect us as families do not necessarily show on the outside. I've had friends tell me it was great Bob had conned a disability out of the government, while he couldn't sleep and was prey to rages and intolerable depressions and it took a quart of whiskey, five or six Valium, and constant pot-smoking to keep him calmed down to wired.

Sometimes we deny the problems that affect us so well that we don't even know they're there. I spent years telling myself that Bob was the coolest guy I knew and admiring his ability to frighten other people with a look, or down a quart of whiskey a day without any observable effect. That was not a *problem* to me. I was *wrong*.

I suggest the use of circumstantial evidence in detecting co-dependency or co-survivorship or other problems if your automatic response to this is: *Oh, we don't have any problems.*

What do I mean by circumstantial evidence?

Are you pushed into doing things you don't want to do? Do you wind up doing everything? Does he work so much you never see him? Does he always wind up losing his job while you support the family? Does talking to each other make you angry, desperate, or depressed? Do you have to agree on everything? Are you depressed? Do you stay sick, especially with headaches, back and neck pain, or stomach problems? Do you have a hard time making time to make love? Do you avoid his embraces? Do you have a hard time having fun when you are together? Can you have fun only under the influence of substances, including food? Do you feel uneasy when you are apart? Do you have a hard time having fun by yourself? Does either of you feel that if the other just changed this or that fault, everything would be perfect? Do your needs never seem to get met? Do you have a hard time identifying your own personal needs? Does the day seem too short for meeting the needs of both yourself and your family?

Is life hard for you? Does joy seem to elude you? Are you profoundly exhausted?

If the answers to any of these questions are yes, you do have a problem, and it won't go away by trying to ignore it. I know because that's what I did for years. If you would like to throw this book away, I know how you feel. It's really painful to think that maybe our best efforts have made things worse, that maybe we don't know all the answers, that maybe we can do *nothing* about our problems and that our frantic attempts have been wasted.

What they have *not* been is *wasted*. Misdirected, okay. Look on everything you did up to now as bringing you to this point. Admire yourself. Praise yourself. If you weren't trying to help your vet, you would never have discovered that you need to help yourself.

One night after an ACOA (Adult Children of Alcoholics) meeting I was talking to two other women who wanted to know how I'd gotten to where I was from the time when Bob was a wild man with acute undiagnosed PTSD. When I paused for breath one of them said in a wondering voice, "And all of them were changes you made in *yourself!*" I realized with a shock that she was right. Every single thing that helped our relationship was work I did on me. Even when I was trying to change Bob, the work I did on myself was what helped. It was really pretty funny, for all three of us. We all came to the ACOA group for help in changing our lives. We give lip service to changing ourselves, but we have a tendency still to want to change our loved ones. But unless we do change ourselves in ways that are healthy for ourselves, nothing changes.

Another very important reason to seek help is because of the damage living in a co-dependent, dysfunctional, co-survivor family can cause your kids. To me, a family is any group of people who live together or care deeply for one another, whether or not marriage is involved. A problem is anything that interferes with people's being able to express their love for one another or with each person's development as a unique human being. Having problems is not defective. Having problems is human. Everyone has them.

Kids don't know that, however. As Earnie Larsen, a counselor and writer of excellent self-help books, put it:

> When we felt unloved, we didn't have the sophistication to wonder whether our parents loved themselves. We didn't have any way of knowing that loving has much more to do with the capacity of the giver than it does with the deservedness of the receiver. Children don't reason that way. "If you don't hold me," we assumed, "it must be that I am not holdable. Other kids are loved. The fault must be with me."

Problems that can develop for the family from one member's terrible experiences in Vietnam can range from a commonly admired, easy-to-deny problem like workaholism, which is dysfunctional as far as the family is concerned, to ones as complex and obvious as a person who has full-blown PTSD. If your vet can't talk to the family, the kids don't see a problem with Vietnam. They see a problem within themselves: *I am not lovable.* If your vet habitually calls you stupid or ugly and puts you or the kids down, that emotional abuse will scar them for life.

Sarah Haley and I talked about how wives (myself included) cover up the cost of war to the family. We never talk about unavailability and denial. We pretend Daddy is just fine unless he's foaming at the mouth, and then we deny that his rage has anything to do with combat. We are in on the conspiracy of not telling what the legacy of war really is—the same conspiracy that made possible a half war like Vietnam, that let the psychiatrists pretend war could not possibly affect a healthy psyche, and it's *bullshit*.

If your combat veteran husband throws your son against the wall, it isn't because your kid is bad, or your husband is bad—it is because war taught your husband survivor skills. Because he maintains the war didn't affect him, he hasn't taught himself the skills of peace. But your kid doesn't know that, so he thinks he's a bad person, and your husband doesn't know that, so he thinks he's a bad person, and you don't know it, so you think you're a bad wife and mother, and the cost of war goes up one more notch in human misery.

Does it seem to you like a betrayal to admit our men have problems? Denying it does not change the problems, it just ensures that our vets never get any help for their problems. The costs of war are far beyond the tax money and federal deficits for the bullets and bombs, far beyond the lost lives, beyond the wounds. War already costs society millions of dollars in the health expenses of co-dependents who often develop serious physical illnesses, workaholics and alcoholics and drug addicts who spend the rest of their lives trying to forget combat, and their children who learn that the answer to stress is to get high or become delinquent. War *should* cost society millions, in proper treatment for soldiers and their co-survivors.

In some veteran families, just as in many other dysfunctional families, no one ever talks about the root problems: what happened to Dad in Vietnam and why he and Mom don't get along too well. Instead, the whole family focuses on why Billy isn't doing well in school. This is pretty human. Maybe Billy's problem can be solved, Mom and Dad think. It isn't as hopeless as the one we don't talk about: us. If you have what they call a scapegoat in your family—a kid everyone identifies as bad—it's a pretty good sign that a major problem between Mom and Dad is being denied, and that Billy thinks it's his fault.

"Perfect" kids who never make waves can also develop in dysfunctional families, kids who grow up with no self-esteem and sometimes no self, but are careful always to meet their parents' need to have "perfect kids" with nice manners and good grades. If your kids feel that they have to tiptoe around the house, or if they help you run the family because Daddy blows up when you ask him to help, they are being denied a normal childhood.

Dysfunctional families develop a set of rules that prevent the expression of feeling as well as the discussion of problems. Having learned to numb out feelings and not think about problems in Vietnam, many veterans have established families in which Vietnam has never been discussed; many other important issues are never discussed either for fear of rocking the boat. Often this is a reasonable fear. If the vet has a problem with rage reactions, both of you may be justly afraid. Two problems come with this adaptation of not rocking the boat, however: one, you raise a dysfunctional family; and two, time and fate may, and probably will, rock the boat for you.

Dysfunctional families may seem perfect. "The main task of the children in this family was not to grow and experience their own lives, but to prove that they had a perfect family and that their parents were perfect parents," as Anne Wilson Schaef reported in *Co-Dependence: Misunderstood-Mistreated*. Many children of World War II vets come from families like that. They'll even tell you with pride that their father never talked about World War II. Many of them will go on proudly to give you a picture of the workaholic, perfectionist, numbed-out vet father *as if this were normal*, and they prefer not to "whine" about Vietnam and have *no problems*. Having no problems should make you suspect that denial is at work. Normal people have problems. People who do not know what normal is anymore, due to having survived trauma, will often claim to have no problems.

Dysfunctional families can center around perfection, religion, work, rational-logical-unemotional thinking, as well as the more obviously damaging chemical dependencies (alcohol, pot, cocaine, tranquilizers, speed, or any other drug, including heroin), addictions to food, sex, gambling, etc. Families that center around PTSD can be all mixed up with various addictions that the whole family uses to distance and control the pain they feel that comes from an experience none of them can control—what happened to Dad (or Mom) in Vietnam. One kid may get all A's and be president of his class and on the football team (workaholism), the other may stay stoned, while a third may get into fights acting out the family's pain, while Mom and Dad work so much that they are never at home. Dad weighs 240 pounds and Mom weighs 98, or vice versa. These addictive behaviors are all ways of avoiding and denying pain and grief and guilt.

Don't talk, *don't trust*, and *don't feel* are the three rules psychologists see operating in dysfunctional families. "Don't feel" is probably the most destructive in the long run, but in the short run it can save your life, as it often saved our vets' lives in Vietnam. Drama and turmoil in the family and rage reactions in the vet can teach your kids not to feel. So can the example of a numbed-out, workaholic, successful vet.

We need our emotions. Emotions are signals, information, clues; they let you know what you need to do to take care of yourself. So if you don't get the signals, you won't take care of yourself. Important data for your decision-making process will be lacking—like making a budget without knowing your income. Kids who don't know what they feel or that they have a right to feel often wind up in abusive relationships. Do you want that for your kids?

Most people think that the absence of a substance-abuse problem indicates a healthy family, not realizing that the "don't trust" rule can also be established by something as nice as Mommy's always saying "No dear, I'm not mad at Daddy" when the kid can see Mommy is furious. Then the kid learns not to trust his perceptions, even though he can *feel* the problems. He will soon stop having feelings, too, except maybe nice acceptable ones like *I love you, Mommy.* He won't be able to trust you to accept what he does feel. Normal kids feel anger and fear, and when they do, they need to learn to express them and handle them.

During the research for this book, I read a lot about substance abuse because many vets with PTSD medicate themselves. Many people who abuse substances themselves are the Adult Children of Alcoholics (ACOA's). I was really struck by the strong parallel between the first characteristic mentioned in all the descriptions of ACOA's—adult children of alcoholics do not know what normal is—and the fact that Vietnam vets do not trust their own judgment. They are often not sure if what they say sounds sensible. They check—*Does that make sense? Am I nuts?* They don't trust their own perceptions, preface everything with "apparently" or "seemingly."

Like the children of a very rigid dysfunctional family, other vets may trust their own judgment exclusively, but their judgment is lousy in the everyday world because they are still reacting in a combat-survivor mode. This is normal, considering what they have been through, but it needs to be dealt with so life can be better for the whole family.

Finally, in dysfunctional families, no one ever talks about what is going on. Dad may come home on Christmas Eve drunk, knock over the tree and stomp the presents, and Christmas Day everyone will pretend it didn't happen. (This is parallel to the experience of the young soldier who went to Vietnam and saw us destroying a country to save it and no one said anything.)

Family problems need family therapy. Painful things cry out *in your kids' souls* to be discussed. We all like to pretend that the kids don't know what is going on, but they do. They also think whatever is happening is their fault. They know they're not allowed to talk about these things, so you grown-ups have to, unless you want to leave them thinking, as most kids do, that they, and not traumatic experiences in Vietnam, make Daddy and Mommy hate them.

Linda Reinberg, a psychologist in private practice, studied 56 families in which the father was a combat vet. The families had come for treatment and agreed to be in her study—so they were not denying problems—and Dr. Reinberg excluded alcohol-, drug-, and violence-oriented families from the study, although she still treated them. These families were also affluent enough to have private insurance. Some of the patterns she found were that the mothers were just as, or *more*, depressed than the vets, and the kids were depressed, too. The families felt different from other families and felt a lot of grief over the fact. The dads were overprotective *and* emotionally distant. The kids thought they and their moms had to "take care of Dad." The saddest thing for me was the clusters of symptoms she listed for the kids: aggressiveness, underachieving at school, feeling they had to take care of their parents, impairment in the expression of affect (Remember affect? *Feelings!*), impairment in concentration and attention, impaired feelings of belonging, and a tendency to self-medicate with alcohol and drugs.

One final point. Linda Reinberg found that four out of ten of the wives were ACOA's or incest survivors. Ross Mayberry, Ph.D., reported at the October 1988 meeting of the Society for Traumatic Stress Studies that many wives of vets who come in for treatment of PTSD have survived traumas of their own as ACOA's, or have been survivors of physical, emotional, or sexual abuse. These are called dual-survivor families. If that is the case with you—if you were whipped or slapped or shamed or molested as a child or experienced a life-threatening experience such as a fire or flood or car accident or rape or lost a parent and never grieved sufficiently because as a child you weren't supposed to feel it as much—these issues must be dealt with by you. Or else, like your vet, if he doesn't deal with Vietnam, you will have trouble getting close to anyone. More on that in Chapter 12.

————

We deny that anything is wrong, or that what is wrong could be related to Vietnam, lying to ourselves up to the last minute, but when we finally admit that things have gotten out of hand, we want a quick fix.

If things are bad between you and your vet right now, due to PTSD (or any other problem), and you want him to get help, it will not be quick. Therapy is a long, slow process. During therapy he will learn various skills, like anger management, which will help in your relationship. He will also have to face the deaths of his friends and other traumatic experiences he went through in Vietnam. He'll live through gut-wrenching rage, moments of sheer terror, agonizing losses. Therapy is going to hurt him. He may seem *worse* when he's mourning his losses.

What are you going to do while that is going on?

What can you do for yourself?

You'll have plenty of time to work on yourself, on your co-dependency, and your co-survivor issues. You can stop focusing on what's messed up in him and work on what's *naturally* become messed up in you. That's what I do.

This suggestion may bring up a storm of feelings in you—depression, inadequacy, fear, anger, quick agreement; whatever it is, *examine it*. Write down the feelings you have, and why. See if there is a pattern. Have you felt this way before?

If you are not really interested in working on your own issues, think of this: When you stop focusing on your veteran's problems, it will help him.

I remember the look on Bob's face when I first said to him that I thought I had probably (notice the hedging) been hard to live with, too, and that he'd had a lot to put up with, too. And yet every time I repeat that statement, I realize more deeply how true it is. How hard it must have been to live with someone who screamed at roaches when he was seeing bloody corpses in his mind. How hard to live with someone who possessed and clung to tons of things when he knew that their value compared to that of human life was *nothing*. How hard to live with someone who was always right, who let everyone know in subtle and unsubtle ways *what she had to put up with*. Someone who was always pointing out what was wrong with him and how to fix it. Now I see the tremendous double bind Perfect Patience (who was far from perfect), the earnest, helpful know-it-all, put my family in when I was doing that stuff, and how hard life was for all of us.

Working on myself has made it a lot easier on Bob because it's lifted the burden of being the defective one off his shoulders and put it where we can share it—as partners should.

If you feel you have no problems, you could try going for help *as if* you did. This technique is suggested in some of my ACOA literature: Act as if you are confident, and eventually you will feel confident. If you decide to act as if you have problems, too, even if you don't yet see them as problems, if and when that insight finally comes, you'll feel less foolish and better prepared.

If you want to get help and your vet thinks you don't need it, Ray Scurfield said, "This may be difficult for the veteran to understand and accept, especially since he may be very self-centered at least partly due to his war-related difficulties. *Both* you and the vet must understand your rights and needs as an individual." You can say in a loving way that you don't feel very good about yourself right now and that going for help will help you, and stick to that like a broken record.

Here are a couple of things to practice while you think about working on yourself.

If you can, don't take his problems personally. This is a hard one. When someone is screaming in your face, or has let you down again, or is just not there when you need him physically or emotionally, or is screwing around again, it is hard not to take it personally. It's hard not to feel you caused this somehow, even though you didn't. Still, he is not having these problems to hurt you, although they *do* hurt you. Whatever he is doing is not part of a private vendetta against you, although it feels that way. Bad feelings overwhelm him and his pain comes out splattered all over you because you're closest to him and the easiest target, but it's shrapnel from the war. After a horrendous fight in which I'd screamed, "How am I supposed to think you love me when you treat me like this?" Bob said to me: "But you know I love you. You're my *wife*." He sounded really surprised, too. I realized that in some dumb way he did expect me to know that he did love me, no matter what rotten things he said.

You can try to see the things your vet is able to do for you with new eyes. It's hard on a person if he can never be right. When I was able to accept what Bob had to give, rather than stay mad over whatever it was I thought he should have known I wanted him to do, we got along better.

I'm not a religious person, but I think the parable of the widow's mite in the Bible is a good example to us. The widow gave a penny but she gave more than the rich man because it was everything she had. Our guys don't have much to give when they are wrapped up in the pain of Vietnam, but what they do give is worth more than the easy generosity of a man who has everything and has never had to go without or had to kick someone in the face in order to live. You just have to be aware, to be *able* to see what they are giving. When Bob used to come up behind me once a year and hug me and say in my ear that he loved me, I used to weep with joy. It meant so much because it was so rare. Our vets may not be able to give us what we were brought up to expect or want, but sometimes what they *can* give is better.

We, too, may not have much to give because we are wrapped up in so much pain from living with all these problems, but every step we take to help ourselves will help us have more to give.

In line with being able to see with new eyes what your vet has to give, perceiving what he *hasn't* got to give can help, too. If your vet's yelling at you, it's because he feels badly about himself. How can you help him? What does he need? Attention and respect? How do you give them? Listen. Don't give advice. This is called loving detachment. It is hard not to take it personally, I know. I always used to take everything personally.

Finally, stop blaming yourself for your vet's problems. Your vet would still have problems related to Vietnam *even if* you were the perfect wife. No deficiency in you is the cause of those problems. No perfection in you can cure them. Of course he isn't going to tell you that. Being human, he may say, and perhaps honestly believe, as Bob did, that if you were thinner or a better housewife or whatever, he wouldn't have any problems. Don't *you* believe it.

Reframing my thinking in these ways helped me get rid of a lot of guilt (if only I were a better housewife, he wouldn't get mad), and a lot of anger (damn him, why is he doing this to me?) and let me see how much he was hurting. Unfortunately, realizing this won't let him see how much *he* is hurting because he may not be able to recognize his feelings at all. If he can't see it that way, *don't keep telling him he's hurting*. It never pays to tell a person how he feels. All you can tell him is how you feel. If you say, "I feel pretty bad, and I'm going to go for help," this is also setting a good, life-affirming, healing example.

Where can you turn? We'll talk about that in the next chapter. Meanwhile, if you've been down and feeling pretty hopeless for a while, think about the following quote from Jesse Jackson, which my friend Wallis sent me:

> You may not be responsible for being down,
> but you are responsible for getting up.

So let's get up.

Part Three

Help Yourself

10

First Aid

So here we are.

I've given you an idea of how rough it was in Vietnam and how it feels to be a vet, because I don't think you can deal with anyone successfully, much less have a warm, loving, intimate relationship, without understanding where he is coming from.

One of the ways to get up and begin healing is to change your perspective. All of a sudden, you see reasons for behavior that before was inexplicable and therefore hopeless. Facing the reality and significance of each other's experiences enables you to respect the pain of your vet's existence as a survivor, and will eventually enable him to respect yours as a co-survivor. Then you'll be helping instead of hurting each other.

Every couple has problems. If you're on the verge of bailing out, remember that any new relationship you establish will eventually have problems when it gets beyond the honeymoon stage. You may even bring the same problems *with you* to a new relationship.

If you stay and work through your current problems, you and your relationship get stronger. Beyond that, you've showed your partner something very basic: He or she is worth the pain. This can be very moving to a person who wasn't worth a shit to this country.

Sharon Wegscheider-Cruse, counselor and a founding member of the National Association for Children of Alcoholics, suggested that a way to find the strength to go on is to commit yourself. In *Choicemaking*, she quoted a friend: "Very simple—either you commit yourself to staying, and one by one work through the problems that are present. Or you commit yourself to leaving, and one by one work through the problems that result from that decision . . . The pain and anxiety are from the wavering. If the relationship has enough value, stay. If it's taking away too much of you, leave." The decision is up to you, not your mother, your sister, your best friend, or your vet. Love does not have to be reasonable or justifiable or logical. It does not have to be painful, either.

"You and Bob have such a wonderful relationship," my friend Nancy said to me one day. "Of course," she went on, "most of the women I know wouldn't have put up with what you put up with." I had to laugh. It's the putting-up-with (on both sides) that has made our relationship so good, the working through things that were painful. Not giving up. Commitment to each other. Still working things out. Always will be.

The problems of those of us who love Vietnam vets are different from other people's. Our men have faced death. They have been changed by war, by blood and death and pointless agony. Their problems reside in them, are buried in them. Some of them may *never* uncover and face those memories. They have a right not to. Many of them cannot face these buried memories at this point, can't even face that they have them. There's no point in saying "Well, I know you do." On the other hand, they do not have the right to blame us, to hurt us, to destroy us with their pain.

We have the right to be treated respectfully and to live decent, honorable lives.

Everyone has that right.

He does, too.

If you think your vet has PTSD, you need to find a source of good help. Maybe your vet can see that he's got a problem: He has nightmares or he can't stop talking about Vietnam, and if he tells one more war story, you're getting a divorce. But because of the way the VA treated Vietnam vets during and after the war, the only way he'd go to the VA is in an ambulance, unconscious. You might want to research available help in your community and provide him with a number of options because that kind of stuff is easy for codependents to do (helping), and really hard for people with PTSD to do. The hard part for you will be not to push any of the options!

Find out from other veterans what has helped them. Is there a rap group sponsored through the VA, the Vet Centers, or a veterans' organization such as the Vietnam Veterans of America? The community mental-health center or the crisis center may have suggestions. Look in the phone book for therapists. Write or call the nearest VA hospital and see if it has a contract with a local therapist or clinic to provide care for local veterans. Educate yourself. I talked to one woman whose husband suddenly began to have PTSD problems after years of marriage. He was a good provider, seemingly one of those guys Vietnam didn't affect. Her reaction? "I decided to educate myself," she said, "but there was nothing, no information."

She finally found *Vietnam Veterans: The Road to Recovery*, by Drs. Brende and Parson, and that helped. "I was just ignorant," she continued. The experience of her strong, silent husband suddenly coming apart was terrifying. After one nightmare he told her, "I'm still there. I just want to come home. I've never come home." Another time when she tried to roll him back into bed he cried out, "No! No! Don't! My guts will fall out!" He would be crying, curled up in a corner, and all she could do was sit with him. The whole family slept on mattresses on the floor in one room for a while because he felt safer.

When I talked to her, her husband was going through an in-patient PTSD program. She said, "It hurts me to think what he went through, and that he's down there suffering."

If you've been telling your vet to forget Vietnam, or avoided letting him talk to you about it, perhaps, as psychologist Charles Figley pointed out, this strategy is an unconscious effort on your part to deal with the unbearable pain it causes you to acknowledge his pain, and your inability to help him. *Tell him how much it hurts to be unable to help*, whether he's your son or brother or husband or lover. If you can't deal with the pain of his experiences, there is a good counselor somewhere who can. Help him find one. Even psychiatrists never treat their own families. You are not required to be your vet's shrink. Getting counseling yourself will help you learn to listen without feeling responsible for the pain or for curing it, either.

Vietnam vet James Moffat and his wife, psychologist Linda Moffat, wrote in *Families After Trauma:*

Often the survivor has tried to talk about the experience, only to be told that it wasn't really as bad as he/she remembers it; or that their concerns are not "normal." Often listeners diminish the importance of the event by denying its impact.

Alienation is one of the inevitable results of having traumatic experience discounted. The Moffats continued:

Survivors often feel like they are on the outside of life looking in at oblivious, well-adjusted people who cannot share their reality, much less the secret of how they survived. These events and thoughts isolate survivor families.

"One of the most destructive things you can do to another person is to deny the reality of what's troubling them," John H. Riskind, Ph.D., was quoted as saying in Judith Jobin's "Lifting Someone out of the Dumps" in the February 1986 issue of *Self*. Are we so self-centered that we can't perceive that someone else has been through something worse than we can imagine?

Some of us have had our experiences as family members discounted, too. Has your vet ever said that you don't have any problems? Or has your husband ever told you not to worry about your Vietnam-vet son? Have any of your friends ever said that the solutions to your problems were simple—dump your vet? Remember how that hurt? If discounting your experience has hurt you, too, you can use that pain to help you learn not to discount your vet's experiences.

Suppose you feel that your vet uses Vietnam as an excuse for everything? Well, therapy will help him see that if it's true. Remember, if you really want true intimacy, you have to accept *him*, not an edited version of him.

Recently several wonderful books written by prominent women— Betty Ford, Carol Burnett, Suzanne Somers, Elizabeth Taylor, counselor Sharon Wegscheider-Cruse, evangelist Carolyn Koons— have revealed the problems alcohol has caused in their lives. A strong movement has developed of adult children of alcoholics who are able to deal with and to reveal to others what has gone on in their lives, and how it has hurt them, and that the problems they are struggling with are natural. Denial and shame kept people like them silent for generations, but when I read about their struggles and pain, all I feel is admiration and respect. I also feel sorrow that they had to go through such rough times. But the freedom they now feel to tell the truth frees the rest of us to seek help if we have problems.

I'd like to see something similar happen with the families of veterans. We love our men, but every time we deny the effect war had on them, we enable the whole society to pretend that war is one of a number of equally acceptable political options. Men who faced single-shot muzzle loaders and cannon in the Revolutionary War knew this was not true, and for that reason they set in place mechanisms in our Constitution to prevent things like Vietnam from happening.

In *Out of the Night*, William Mahedy said: "The impact of Vietnam for the veterans who actually fought—psychic stress, moral confusion, and the dark night of the spirit—are the true costs of war." War destroys men. It doesn't just destroy the men who die.

We can stop blaming and belittling men who are being slowly destroyed by their normal reactions to war and reach out to help them.

Coping with Signals for Help

• FLASHBACKS: As I said in the PTSD chapter, these are strong signals for help. A person having a flashback does not know where he is or who you are. He is dangerous. If you are caught in the middle of a flashback you can try to reorient the person: "You are safe. You are home in Ohio." Shut up if he tells you to. Be as non-threatening as you can. Flashbacks *do* end, so waiting it out may be the best option. Then go directly to therapy. The longer you wait the easier it will be to believe that it wasn't as dangerous as it was, and that it will never happen again.

• RAGES: If your vet has frequent rages, this is a signal to get help. Rages, like the flashbacks in the PTSD chapter, are like boils, a physical symptom that shows something is going on beneath the skin.

When your vet goes into a rage should you yell back? Well, it's never helped me for Bob to yell when I'm acting a juvenile. What has helped is when he listens, doesn't tell me to calm down, and lets me vent my feelings. This is discussed further in Chapter 11, "Listening."

You can both talk after this natural process is over and things are calmer. A good point to make then is that he can use his anger to work for him instead of against him, and that this is one of the things he will learn in a good PTSD program through assertiveness training. Another point to make *very quietly and lovingly* is that you and the rest of the family are afraid of him when he is in a rage. He needs to know how what he does affects his family.

In a good PTSD program, your vet will also learn to slow down his automatic reactions. It takes time. Meanwhile, if you are the object of your vet's anger it might be wise for one of you to leave the house for a while. If he says he has to leave, let him. He is protecting you in the only way he can. Take it as a sign of love.

• PHYSICAL VIOLENCE: If your vet hits you, *leave*. Not necessarily forever, but *nobody* has the right to hit you. If you don't leave, you are giving him a message that it's okay to hit you.

As a combat veteran, your vet knows firsthand the devastation that physical terror brings to the human spirit. He has no right to inflict that on you. There is also evidence that family violence is transmitted between generations. When he hits you, he is teaching his sons to be batterers and his daughters to be battered. Most Vietnam vets care deeply for kids, so perhaps the idea of his son's growing up to have the same ugly, shameful, painful rage reactions he has, or his daughter's letting someone she loves beat and humiliate her, will get him into therapy.

If your vet remains persistently violent, having him arrested will show him hitting you is simply not acceptable. If he learns that from other sources—the police, lawyers, the courts—the lesson is more likely to stick. If you feel badly about getting him arrested, think about his spending *the rest of his life in a maximum-security prison*. If he kills you, he probably will. The first thing the prosecutor will say is, "This man is a trained killer and a danger to society."

If the two of you think *you make* him hit you, remember that he has to lift that arm to do it. Your behavior does not control the muscles in his arm. You can't make him move that arm in the set of coordinated movements that winds up with his fist in your face. Try it with his arm limp.

Some people may feel that the wives of batterers provoke what happens to them. This may appear to be true to an outsider because just as sights and sounds that remind your vet of Vietnam can send him into a spin and even into self-destructive behaviors, signs and sounds of family violence are going to provoke PTSD in you if he has hurt or scared you in the past. The only way you may be able to feel any control of the situation is to put him in a rage and get it over with. Your actions may be as self-destructive as his. He needs to see that when he scares you, he is putting you in the same position, through the same pain and fear and helplessness and anger as he feels when he is reminded of Vietnam or has a flashback or nightmare. This may make you quite unreasonable sometimes, too, just as it does him.

Although there have not been studies on Vietnam-vet battering, many Vet Center people seem to feel that the precipitating factor in many vets' coming in for help has been actually losing it and hitting someone they love. Left untreated, battering commonly becomes a cycle. The batterer will be apologetic and loving for a while afterward, and women often buy into this magical change and take him back. If your father hit your mother, you are very likely to fall into this cycle yourself. Don't!

Get your vet into therapy while he's willing to do a lot to get you back. Don't settle for roses and a pat on the head. Therapy will help him control his anger. A self-help group for batterers will help him work through the batterer's issues of helplessness and lack of self-esteem. That is what batterers feel: powerless and like shit. Witnessing and participating in abusive violence is one of the experiences that can cause Vietnam vets to develop PTSD symptoms. How can a batterer help but have it, too? Total denial and the inability to feel anything but rage can be characteristic of both problems. PTSD is responsive to appropriate treatment. Why not battering?

If you get therapy, too, your chances of a good relationship will go way up. Families that have been violent often need to stay in therapy and self-help groups for a long time. As for any kind of dysfunction, there is no quick cure, only slow, small steps. Reducing family violence takes time. Change is slow and both partners need to have realistic expectations. Second Step, in Pittsburgh, Pennsylvania, is an eight-month program and offers a continuing support group for batterers after the eight months. The founder, once abusive himself, feels that as long as they stay in the support group they don't batter.

Every day new information is published on family violence and its treatment. Check the library, the bookstores, and the self-help publishers. If you are in crisis or need a referral, you can also contact the National Coalition Against Domestic Violence, P.O. Box 15127, Washington, D.C. 20003-0127, at 1-800-333-7233. You may have to hold.

If this is the first incident of violence in your family, it may result from PTSD. PTSD is treatable. If your vet has never hit you before, enrolling in a PTSD program may be enough for him. If battering has gone on for a while, you might want to make it a condition of his coming back that he *finish* a PTSD program somewhere. Despite the current rash of *"Men who hate . . ."* books, men, given help, are as capable of changing and growing as women.

• SUICIDE: Another big signal for help is suicidal talk or actual attempts. Vets who get drugs rather than therapy often stockpile and take them all. On March 6, 1986, the *New England Journal of Medicine* reported that vets were 65 percent more likely to die from suicide and 49 percent more likely to die in a motor-vehicle accident than non-vets of the same age. The National Council of Churches reported in 1971 that 49,000 Vietnam vets had *died* since returning from Vietnam. The war was still going on! The number of those deaths, which included suicides, accidents, drug overdoses, and other violent deaths, was one of the things that started concerned professionals on the track of PTSD.

Do not ignore your vet if he says suicidal things. A lot of people say, "Oh, he just wants attention." WRONG. He's letting you know that if he doesn't get some attention, he's going to stop the pain in a way he's very familiar with: death. If your vet talks of suicide, or he starts giving his belongings away, saying he won't be around, get worried and get help. When people are suicidal, they're asking for attention because they NEED it. Give it. Why wouldn't you? If you're afraid you'll spoil him, a bullet through the brain will spoil him a lot faster. And if you think people don't need or deserve attention, what are you doing in a relationship?

If you're ready to leave and he says he can't live without you, that is a bargaining chip to get him into therapy. And the fact that he would try that kind of emotional blackmail means he needs therapy. So give him all your attention and take him directly to therapy. Do you want him to die for something he did or didn't do in Vietnam when he was nineteen?

One very important point: Suicidal people who suddenly seem happy and unworried may have made a decision to die.

At the crisis center where I was a phone volunteer, we let suicidal people talk and we listened actively and acceptingly, paraphrasing what they said to focus our attention on them and be sure we understood how they felt (a technique I'll go over in depth in the next chapter, not because I think you should try to handle his suicidal feelings yourself—you should not—but because it's a technique that will help any relationship). We didn't judge and we didn't give advice. One of the reasons for this is that a suicidal person is so overwhelmed by things that everything has the same value; someone's death and a spilled cup of coffee are equally horrendous crises. Suicides have no sense of proportion because they are in crisis. They need to talk and feel and cry and rave and weep. They don't need advice. They need professional crisis intervention.

Help

What kind of help is available? "PTSD is responsive to appropriate treatment," said Ray Scurfield, a Vietnam vet and doctor of social work who has worked with PTSD for years, "and PTSD symptoms may well continue for years or decades and get worse if not treated properly, so you are not helping yourself or the vet by continuing to avoid getting the right kind of counseling help. This will be difficult since many vets have had prior negative counseling experiences, but the effort to find a good professional or peer-counseling resource— for the vet, for the partner, for the family, if needed—must be a top priority."

Richard Gilpin, a vet who drove and then commanded a track, wrote me:

Molly and I have been married 14 years as of the 25th of May. We tend to think of our marriage as only about half that long because it wasn't much to speak of until we both started counseling about seven years ago. Prior to that there was a lot of anger in our marriage, and tho' it didn't go away instantly (we are each still learning) we are communicating better, supporting each other, and not using our faults against one another.

I started drinking while in the service and I let circumstances lead me into drinking a whole lot after getting back. I sought to deny my problems and drinking fit right into that system. Emotional denial was trained into me. Vietnam and the drinking intensified that internal denial. I have since realized that denial keeps me operating as a victim. It used to be I would not allow myself to have any emotions unless I got drunk and then all the bitterness and anger stored up inside would surge out, sometimes in a manner destructive to myself or my relationship with Molly. I quit drinking in August 1984 and have no desire to resume.

Our counseling started out focused a lot on day-to-day problems where we were each dissatisfied. With patience and increased understanding, thru group and individual therapy sessions, the focus has shifted to the major areas of stress and a whole lot onto the cause of that stress. It seems as tho' when we communicate on a regular basis that it's easier to sort out the day-to-day stuff and be honest about what we each want and don't want.

We were fortunate in finding therapists we liked and who were helpful and compassionate, yet still able to maintain objectivity, impartiality, and restraint. I view therapy sessions as help with finding out who I am, what I want, and how I can learn to communicate with others. The basis of it all is learning to allow myself to have and accept my emotions.

Our therapy started out as marriage counseling. It quickly shifted to individual groups. Mine is a personal growth group led by a Vietnam veteran and Molly's is a women's support group. We have each spent considerable time in individual therapy with D., Molly's group leader. For a period of three to four years I went every two to three weeks for an individual therapy appointment as well as attending my two-hour group once a week. Therapy seems expensive just looking at the money outlay, but the money seemed a smaller issue as we both started feeling better almost from the start. We currently are working in joint sessions again with D., and attending our groups . . .

A lot of things used to make me angry and many things still do, but I think realizing I have choices helps a lot. Sometimes the choices may seem insignificant, but nothing is ever accomplished without taking small steps, at least in the beginning . . .

Molly added:

If Rich and I had not been willing to go to therapy, and not for just 3 visits, we would not be together now. Rich would be an angry drunk and I would be an angry everything.

I view therapy as classes in how to control—run as much of my life as possible the way I want it run. Because of my childhood, I knew nothing about . . . healthy adult relationships. I didn't even know how to love or be loved. Because our counselor is the kind who helps us learn about our emotional selves and not the kind who sits mute or has us look at funny pictures we are free to discover ourselves. She teaches or has taught us the art of compromise, of the use of options, the necessity of knowing and sharing with each other our emotional beings . . .

Rich and I don't fight anywhere near as often as we used to and, most of the time, we are able to keep the anger directed to the issue. I guess we have learned to argue . . .

My advice to other women is to seek counseling if you think it might help even a little. Go even if the old man won't. Go if you were abused as a child or if you feel you deserve to be abused in your present life . . .

Continue to go even after life gets easier. As it turned out the pattern has been easy, hard, easier, harder, and so on . . . I feel my counselor deals in real life stuff . . . She doesn't let me get away with not being truthful to myself . . . So for the women who are looking for a counselor, don't be afraid to shop around. You have to trust the counselor for the therapy to work. If you don't like their methods or their body language, try elsewhere. And for heaven's sake if you get some weirdo who wants to do touchy-feeling, get out now and report them. . . .

Most, if not all states, have county programs where you can

pay what you can afford. You can choose if you want a man
or woman counselor. A more expensive psychiatrist is not
necessarily better than a less expensive social worker. Being
in therapy is not a disgrace. Your family and friends may think
so and will probably tell you. To me being in therapy is a
strong healthy place to be. The woman's group I belong to and
attend once a week gives me a safe place to talk about anything
I want, any way I want. No matter what happens during the
week, I know Thursday at 6:00 there will be support and encouragement.

I feel very fortunate that Rich wants to straighten his life
out also. More women seek counselors than men and I know
women who come while their man stays home, and these wom-
en's lives have gotten better. It isn't necessary for both partners—easier but not necessary.

Where do you get good help? Where does he get good help?

The VA Hospital

The Veterans Administration is a federal agency that is supposed
to care primarily for those veterans with service-connected disabilities, those received as a direct result of military service. Veterans
can also receive services there on a space-available basis if they are
too poor to get care elsewhere. The VA runs the largest hospital
system in the United States.

Proving to the VA that any vet's problems are service-connected
has always been difficult. After World War II, survivors of the Ba-
taan Death March were asked to prove that years of starvation and
beatings by Japanese were responsible for their physical and psychological ills, because there were no "official Japanese records" of
the beatings and tortures.

The current form of VA obstructionism is that your vet has to
remember details of his traumatic stressors including names and
dates, although one of the symptoms of PTSD is psychogenic amnesia. Another kind of VA obstructionism is the eternal paperwork.
A third is the farming-out of psychological reviews to psychiatrists
who are paid a flat fee—which does not encourage quality work. The
five-minute psychological evaluation interview that sometimes results is totally inadequate to detect PTSD (or any other psychological
condition). The final form of obstructionism is the idea that if a vet

has any knowledge of PTSD, he's faking the condition. Patients are not supposed to think.

Getting help from the VA takes dedication and effort. I wouldn't send any veteran down to the local VA hospital alone. The VA hospitals have an unspoken motto: help *with* hassles. Part of this is not their fault. Budgets and federal regulations make it very difficult for them to do their job. Paperwork abounds. Waiting is inevitable and eternal, and it pisses off most vets. Your vet'll spend hours in the evaluation clinic and come home in a homicidal rage.

If you have a local VA, find someone over the phone who is interested in PTSD and get some advice about how to slide into the system with minimum discomfort. If your vet's going to have to sit for a day in the evaluation clinic, either go with him or get a volunteer to go with him.

Although your local VA may be a warm and friendly place, I would take a very visible pad and document how long you have to wait and how your vet is treated by each person he sees. Write down the names and occupations of each person he sees. Also write down any remarks made about getting "free care" or people "always dying in war." Nothing makes bureaucrats treat you right like writing down what they say. The VA is actually trying to be more sensitive to the needs of Vietnam veterans, now that more of them are in Congress and the Senate and the World War II vets are beginning to die off. So get names, which you should do anytime when you see any medical person, and take notes. Give them your coldest stare along with a freezing "I beg your pardon" if they are rude. Waiting is the only thing you should have to put up with.

Bob asked one doctor at the Gainesville VA if he treated his private patients the way he was treating Bob. The guy got real indignant and said, "It's free, isn't it?" No. Bob spent a year in combat and three more in the military to earn the privilege of being insulted at the VA. Most of the doctors and other personnel are no longer like that even in Gainesville, however. All the more reason to make waves if you run into a jerk. You'll be helping the VA improve itself. Noble work!

Many vets have a hard time with the bureaucratic bull. Perhaps your vet can think of going to the VA as an ambush. If your vet breaks cover first, gives up on his legitimate claim, the VA wins.

Your vet learned a lot of patience in Vietnam when he was on ambush, waiting for Charlie. Let him use some of that here against the VA. Wait them out. Winning the case is the best revenge. Voice of experience.

Applying for service connection for PTSD is hemmed around by red tape. If your vet decides to go for it, send for the booklet "Self-Help Guide on Stress Disorder," published by the Veterans Education Project (address in Some Further Sources of Help), and read the excellent book, *The Viet Vet Survival Guide,* and follow their advice. The book has good information on all kinds of other help for veterans.

Get a service officer to help you, too. Many veterans' organizations have service officers right in the VA hospitals. Find one who is knowledgeable about PTSD. The Disabled American Veterans, Paralyzed Veterans of America, Vietnam Veterans of America, American Legion, Veterans of Foreign Wars, and other organizations all have service officers. We have used the DAV and the PVA and were pleased with both.

Be aware that the Veterans Administration does not want your vet to become service-connected for PTSD. It puts new regulations and demands in the way every day. If you don't supply the VA with the evidence it wants within 60 days—evidence you may have to write away for and that may have been destroyed by the military— the VA may deny your claim administratively. This is illegal but earns the VA bonuses for having a high rate of settling claims. The VA is currently being sued over this. The November 1986 issue of the Vietnam Veterans of America's newspaper, *The Veteran,* reported which regional offices have been accused of improperly processing claims.

Although the VA considers drugs and alcohol use "willful misconduct," more beds are assigned to alcohol-treatment programs than to PTSD programs (though by their rules alcoholism cannot be a service-connected disability).

After applying for a service connection for adjustment problems, eventually your vet will go in for an interview. This interview is very important. Dr. Arthur L. Arnold, in *The Trauma of War,* in the chapter called "Diagnosis of Post-Traumatic Stress Disorder in Vietnam Veterans," stated:

Specific information is needed to make the diagnosis of PTSD, and the inclusion criteria in the *Diagnostic and Statistical Manual of Mental Disorders*, Third Edition, are a clearly stated description of that information. *Some clinicians who are fully aware of these criteria, however, report the mental status examination as within normal limits and do not diagnose PTSD even in individuals who have the disorder in severe form* [my *italics*].

If this has to be clearly stated in a medical text, you can bet it's a big problem. I recommend taking a written statement with you and putting it in the file.

According to Dr. Arnold, the interviewer should spend at least an hour with your vet going over his experiences in Vietnam, including—but not exclusively—traumatic incidents.

In "The Reparation of the Self," psychologist Erwin Parson said, "Without allowing the veteran to share Vietnam, a broad range of issues essential to diagnosis would be unavailable to the clinician." The interviewer should ask about the vet's life prior to Vietnam because he is trying to get a picture of how Vietnam changed him. He should ask what it has been like for your vet since Vietnam, including whatever it was that brought the vet in for help. The vet should be asked about thoughts, feelings, dreams, flashbacks, and a range of avoidance behaviors.

Bring to the exam a description—in the vet's own words and handwriting—of the symptoms he is suffering. *Keep a copy of it!* Ask that it be attached to the file. This is helpful, because your vet may be so upset by the interview that he may not be able to express himself. It could read something like: *I can't sleep. I have nightmares. I feel numb. I can't help my wife or kids when they are upset. I have to leave, instead. I can't work for people. When my boss talks to me I get so upset I have to leave. I get so mad I'm afraid I'll hit him.* You and your vet can go through the diagnostic criteria in Chapter 9 and write down each one that affects him and how it makes life hard.

If your vet's interview is over in five or ten minutes, the examiner has not done his job on two levels, both the general psychological exam and the PTSD exam. The examiner is required by the standards of the medical profession to give every patient he sees professional treatment. The psychological exam required by professional standards to evaluate whether your vet has any problem (never mind the hour the examiner should spend on the PTSD evaluation) cannot be completed in five or ten minutes. If this happens to your vet, insist on the examiner's reading the statement of problems you brought with you and attaching it to the file. I would then make an immediate objection to the clerk right there in the hospital. This will be hard to do, even embarrassing, but you are being *fucked*. Make the clerk mark down in her book and on your appointment slip the time the appointment ended. Then tell the clerk you want to see the head of the department or the administrator of the hospital right away. Even if you don't get to see them, you've made a big wave. From my experience, if you allow an exam like that to pass, your claim of a service-connected disability will be denied. It may take you years of appeals to reverse the harm this one interview might do to your case. It did us.

If you have cause, when you get home, write a letter describing the exam and why it was deficient. Keep one copy and send copies of it along with copies of your vet's statement, *return receipt requested* (because otherwise it will get lost in the mail), to the head of the Veterans Administration. Send it to the president, too, to your congressman, both your senators, the heads of the Veterans Affairs committees in Congress, and *especially* to your county and state medical associations and the American Psychiatric Association. Get all their addresses from the reference librarian at your local public library. This is a lot of work, but the VA gets away with this kind of thing because vets don't stand up for themselves.

The VA's own standards for psychological disability are as follows, and if your vet fits any higher level of disability you should appeal the decision:

> A 100% evaluation will be assigned for a nervous disorder when the attitudes of all contacts except the most intimate are so adversely affected as to result in virtual isolation in the community. Totally incapacitating nervous symptoms border on gross repudiation of reality with disturbed thought or behavioral processes, such as phantasy, confusion, panic and explosions of aggressive energy resulting in profound retreat from mature behavior, associated with almost all daily activities.

There is demonstrable inability to obtain or retain employment. A 70% evaluation will be assigned when the ability to establish and maintain effective or favorable relationships with people is seriously impaired. The nervous symptoms are of such severity and persistence that there is pronounced impairment in the ability to obtain or retain employment. A 50% evaluation will be assigned when the ability to establish or maintain effective or favorable relationships with people is substantially impaired. By reason of nervous symptoms, the reliability, flexibility and efficiency levels are so reduced as to result in severe industrial impairment. A 30% evaluation will be assigned when there is definite impairment in the ability to establish or maintain effective or wholesome relationships with people. The nervous symptoms result in such a reduction in initiative, flexibility, efficiency and reliability levels as to produce considerable industrial impairment. A 10% evaluation will be assigned when the impairment is less than above, but with emotional tension or other evidence of nervousness productive of moderate social and industrial impairment. A zero percent evaluation will be assigned where there are nervous symptoms which may somewhat adversely affect relationships with others but which do not cause impairment of working ability. [38 CFR 4.132 DC 9400]

A 10 percent rating means he gets about sixty bucks a month and all the free pills he can eat.

If your vet's claim is denied, or you feel the rating is too low, appeal. Get a service officer to help. Shop for one you trust and who is experienced in PTSD cases. The appeals process is slow and absolutely enraging. Voice of experience. We have been through some pretty funny experiences at the Gainesville VA, but the time Bob's disability was cut from 50 percent to 30 percent was not one of them.

On July 19, 1985, Bob had a five-minute reevaluation exam. On August 15, 1985, his VA disability rating was illegally cut to 30 percent despite no change in his symptoms. VA regulations state: "Examinations less full and complete than those on which payments were authorized or continued will not be used as a basis of reduction. Ratings . . . of diseases subject to temporary or episodic improvement such as psychoneurotic reaction will not be reduced on any one examination . . . [38 CFR 3344]."

Bob appealed. On January 23, 1986, the VA turned down the appeal, which it referred to as *asking for a raise in his disability*, a phrase *designed* to be so insulting that most vets would quit fighting for their rights right there. Bob filed another statement of disagreement, objecting strenuously to the VA's suggestion, so on June 6, 1986, the VA sent him back for another exam with—guess who?— the same doctor. Meanwhile, Bob's eighteen years of medical records disappeared from the Gainesville VAMC and have never been found. Finally, after seeing the VA traveling appeals board, Bob's 50 percent disability for nervousness was reinstated in June 1987, since his condition had not changed. It only took two years.

Treatment

VA hospitals have both Psychiatry and Psychology departments. There may be either a DAV or PVA service officer in the hospital who can steer you to someone in either department who knows about Vietnam. Your local veterans' group may also be familiar with the VA staff. You can also try the vocational rehabilitation section for advice on whom to see, or even for counseling.

Group therapy is the recommended treatment for Vietnam vets because it breaks through the isolation so many of them have lived in since coming home, and helps them reestablish ties with other people who understand what they've been through. Sometimes a wife or girlfriend who has been "everything" to the vet, and been pretty burned out by it, too, will suddenly find herself jealous of the group's influence and importance to the vet. This is a natural feeling. Getting in a group yourself will help you work it out, and create a community of friends for you, too.

Don't ask your vet what goes on in his group. That is strictly confidential. Don't tell him what is said in your group, either. The combat group is not going to be discussing you, and your group should be focusing on yourselves.

If your vet cannot be persuaded to go to group, individual counseling is also available, but this is a chancier proposition. Most VA psychiatry departments are understaffed, and most of the doctors have to spend all their time prescribing drugs and have very little time for therapy. The VA pays so badly compared to private practice that it often hires foreign doctors who barely speak English. It ain't exactly conducive to good therapy.

Some VA's are training grounds for medical schools in the area. Your vet may start to see someone who is on a three-month rotation through Psychiatry before Obstetrics and after Gastroenterology who may still be called Dr. so-and-so. Find out who this person is, where he or she trained, and what experience he or she has had with PTSD. No matter how well intentioned a medical student or intern is, the treatment of PTSD is not a short-term process and should not be left to students. In group therapy, having one of the group leaders be a student who rotates is acceptable, but the primary leaders of the group should be well trained in PTSD theory and practice. Starting individual therapy with a student and then being transferred to another student may ruin any chance your vet has of establishing the necessary trust in his therapist.

From my experience, the psychology department at your VA is more likely to be into actually doing therapy. Ask what types of programs and groups are available. Social workers, counselors, and psychologists have less of an investment in being top dog than a lot of doctors do, so they are simply more able to do the kind of nontraditional work that has to be done with PTSD people.

Remember, *treatment at the VA is not free*, not some kind of welfare. It is a contractual obligation of the United States government. When your vet went to Vietnam, he risked his life for his country. His country agreed to take care of any damage he sustained there for the rest of his life. His war-related, combat-related problems *should* be the first concern of the VA.

If your vet is lucky, he may find a program that emphasizes therapy rather than pills. Because of staffing problems and budget cuts, many VA's provide pills rather than therapy. Pills help the VA a lot because it can schedule thirty patients an hour instead of one. Bob's record psychiatric visit at our VA was one minute and forty-five seconds. Powerful drugs prescribed in large quantities can also help your vet maintain his denial and numbness—which doesn't help your relationship. Pills help the psychiatrists avoid talking about Vietnam, too.

"Prudent and careful utilization of medications along with psycho-social counseling may be justified, but to do medication only is a travesty," one expert told me. Still, pills *can* help—if your vet can take the occasional pill instead of taking it out on you, the kids, his boss, his friends, or himself.

For example, Bob recently snapped awake in the middle of the night with a pulse of 120 (resting, it's usually about 50) and a feeling of panic and impending doom. He knows this is probably a result of being mortared when he was sleeping twenty-some years ago in Vietnam, but that doesn't bring down his pulse or take away the feelings. It helps a lot that he can go downstairs and take a Valium and sit for about fifteen minutes till the feelings subside.

Up until recently our Gainesville VAMC had what the vets, laughing bitterly, called *bus therapy*. It went like this: *Well, we don't really have much here in the way of treatment for you, but you could take a bus to Jacksonville or Tallahassee to the Vet Centers or you could take a bus to Bay Pines or Augusta. They have in-patient PTSD programs there.* Recently, the psychology department hired a PTSD specialist who has developed a good program, but how can one person deal with an epidemic of PTSD?

Remember that a good therapy program is going to hurt. It is going to be upsetting to the vet. He is not just going to coast to a cure. He'll have to work at it. He will relive all those moments of fear, the mistakes he made, his friends' deaths, perhaps his own wounds, and it will hurt. But it should involve group therapy and stress management and understanding and competence. If we all work together, we can make the VA what it should be, what it ought to have been in 1966 when the first Vietnam vets, including my husband, came back. We can prevent this sort of waste of human lives in the future. For veterans of future wars, quick, competent treatment of acute PTSD may prevent its becoming chronic.

Fee Providers

If there is no chance that your vet will be able to tolerate the VA hospital, there is also a little-known fee-provider program which enables your vet to be seen in private therapy away from the hospital. This program was designed for the Vietnam vet who simply won't go near a VA but has a service-connected disability. Ask about it.

Vet Centers

If you live near a Vet Center, go there. After being annually proposed for ten years by Senator Alan Cranston, and being opposed by the VA, the VFW, other major traditional veterans organizations, and the House of Representatives, federally funded Vet Centers were finally established during the Carter administration to fill a need for readjustment counseling that was not being met because Vietnam vets would not go the VA hospitals.

The Vet Centers abide by a different motto: help *without* hassles. Any Vietnam-era vet can just walk in and get help. Some Vet Centers are better than others. A busy Vet Center may not pick up on your vet's needs right away unless he does something dramatic. Speak up for him if he can't. Vet Centers offer group and individual counseling to both the vet and his family.

Vet Centers do outreach, too. Call them and tell them about your husband if you think he is at risk or needs help. You're a good judge. Someone from the Center should come see him. Recently one Vet Center counselor I know said he was met at the door by a man with a shotgun and told to get out. "You can't give me that shit. I've been there," said the counselor. He came away with a suicide pact, a .357 magnum, another pistol, a rifle, and a shotgun. The guy still hasn't been in to the Vet Center, but the counselor goes out and checks on him and calls him and eventually expects to wear him down till he comes in.

The fact that Vet Centers provide job counseling and a lot of other services besides therapy may make the step of going down there easier for your vet. Your vet could even start going down there just to volunteer to help out other vets by answering the phones a couple of hours a week. You could volunteer there yourself. Vet Centers have libraries of books on Vietnam. They have tapes. If he's in a stage where he can't get enough information about Vietnam, use this as an opening. On the other hand, don't in your enthusiasm urge your vet to read or watch Vietnam-related movies if he doesn't want to. Avoidance behavior signals *go slow*.

Vet Rap Groups

If you're not near a Vet Center or a VA, perhaps there is a veterans' rap group in the area run by a local veterans' organization.

Rap groups can provide education about PTSD and a focus for healing. Peer counseling can be very helpful. These guys were so isolated when they got back that just being with a bunch of other guys who understand what they've been through can really help. Joel Brende, M.D., developed guidelines for a group called Combat Veterans Anonymous while he was running an in-patient PTSD group at the Bay Pines VAMC. His Twelve Steps and Twelve Themes can be used to organize and guide rap-group discussions in a therapeutic direction. Information is available from: Joel Brende, M.D., The Bradley Center, 2000 Sixteenth Ave., Columbus, Ga. 31993.

Other Sources

Crisis centers can also be sources of help if they are accredited and available. Information and referral services can often point you to such resources as mental-health clinics. Clinics offer a variety of services, including family therapy and individual and group counseling. Sometimes choosing a therapist at a clinic is done for you, but you can often get really good help. If your vet finds he can't work with one therapist, he may be able to ask for another.

Therapy doesn't have to be done through government agencies, either. Lots of vets prefer to go for private therapy because they don't like putting up with the hassles or what they perceive as the stigma of getting help through the VA or Vet Centers. Some excellent PTSD counselors have left the VA and Vet Centers, partly because of the bureaucratic hassles.

Searching for good counseling is like anything else. You can start with friends who have dealt with similar problems. Sometimes they can be helpful sources of information about who and what helped them.

Look in the phone book. Some of the headings counselors are listed under are: Clinics, Counselors, Hospitals, Hypnotherapists, Information & Referral, Marriage & Family, Child & Individual Counselors, Mental Health, Physicians & Surgeons—M.D.—Psychiatrists, Psychologists, Psychotherapists, Social Workers, Pastoral Counselors, and Social Service Organizations. Look for counselors with professional qualifications. *Ph.D.* means the person has a doctorate, but it may or may not be in psychology. Ask. *Ed.D.* means a doctorate in education, but it may or may not be in counselor

education. Master's degrees include M.S.W. (master's degree in social work), M.Ed. in education, and M.A. or M.S., which can be in
psychology or any other field. Professional organizations license people whose training and skill levels meet their qualifications. Books
at the library can fill you in on different professional organizations.

The next step is to call the prospective counselor and ask what he
or she knows about PTSD. Does he or she belong to the Society for
Traumatic Stress Studies or any other professional organizations?
Has he worked with veterans in the past? Can she give you refer-
ences? Anyone who gets indignant at being questioned about his
qualifications, knowledge, and experience will not be able to be nonjudgmental, open, or authentic with the veteran, either. Find someone else. Find someone else if the therapist guarantees a cure, too.
What may have worked for Tom and Dick may not for Harry. All
vets are individuals.

For a book that doesn't mention PTSD or co-dependency, *The
Psychotherapy Maze*, by Otto and Miriam Ehrenberg, offers sound
advice on finding therapy. *Hope*, by Emily Marlin, has wonderful
chapters on self-help groups and psychotherapy and self-help. Since
the book is aimed at adult children of alcoholics, you may have to
modify the advice to meet the needs of your situation: Instead of
questioning the therapist about "his or her background in the field
of alcoholism" substitute PTSD, but do find someone who understands "its effect on the whole family," or who is willing to learn.

Your vet needs to find a kind of therapy he is comfortable with.
Gestalt and Transactional Analysis treatment approaches to PTSD
are discussed in the psychological literature along with hypnother-
apy, cognitive therapy, group therapy, and individual therapy. One
of the problems Vietnam vets have is trusting other people. Finding
a therapist who is willing to learn about Vietnam from your veteran
is more important than whether the therapist was in Vietnam or
not. Despite the vet's fears of not being understood, often a woman
makes a very good therapist for a combat vet.

AA can be tremendously valuable. Lots of vets develop drinking
problems through years of self-medication to control PTSD symptoms. Others develop drug dependencies and can find help at Narcotics Anonymous. Stopping substance abuse is vital because you
can't do therapy with someone who is drunk or high.

Veterans can also become addicted to sexual excitement and use constant infidelity as a drug. Sexual addiction is a new field of study, but the Augustine Fellowship and Sex and Love Addicts Anonymous, have been tremendously helpful to many.

Vets who use food as a drug are also at risk of shortening their lives. Overeaters Anonymous can help.

Even if your vet never goes into further therapy, the Anonymous programs are successful in helping people who have survived trauma because of the Twelve Steps . The Twelve Steps help release us from the crippling burden of past experiences which can keep us stuck in present misery. They teach us step by step that we can choose the behavior we exhibit right now, one day at a time, to become the person we'd like to be instead of being stuck in the pain of the past.

Betty Ford said in *Betty: A Glad Awakening*, her latest book, that everyone can benefit from a Twelve Step program. I agree. Millions of World War II vets are members of AA. One of my favorite books, *The Twelve Steps for Everyone*, by Joe Klass, is dedicated to Pappy Boyington the World War II ace. The Moffats' *Families After Trauma* actually gives Twelve Steps for trauma survivors, adapted from the Twelve Steps of AA.

Beyond becoming sober or clean, learning to have a life beyond addiction can become a continuous process for the vet involved in AA or NA or any other Anonymous program. *Stage II Recovery* and *Stage II Relationships*, by Earnie Larsen, are good guides in this process.

Veterans who grew up in families that were dysfunctional in any of the ways mentioned in the "Problems" chapter might be helped by Adult Children of Alcoholics (ACOA) groups. Sometimes getting help for one problem frees a person to go on to find help for others.

I found several helpful books and ideas when I studied the religious response to the problems of Vietnam veterans. *Out of the Night*, by William Mahedy, who was a chaplain in Vietnam, pulls no punches. I have to admit that what he said made more sense to me than anything religious has in a long time. No easy answers and no denial in this book. *Anyone* would profit from reading this book.

After describing the experiences of Vietnam veterans he has counseled, Mahedy said:

Where is the vet to go with his experience of God's absence from a world of evil? He cannot find a place among the religious fundamentalists who retreat from evil, denying its presence in their own souls by projecting it outward onto the communists or the "secular humanists." For these people the "evil empire" is always somewhere external to themselves and their own group. The vets know better, for Vietnam proved that evil resides within the hearts of all of us. Vets also know that authentic religion cannot be identified with American culture, with the endless pursuit of personal fulfillment, or even with feeling good about Jesus. The networks of religious and emotional props that conservatives and fundamentalists construct to insulate themselves from evil are useless after Vietnam. On the other hand, many religious liberals seem to believe that a sense of personhood and human fulfillment are the end product of religion . . . While their efforts on behalf of peace and justice are noble indeed, they seem to overestimate their own power and consistently underestimate the power of evil.

The American Church has evaded the dark night [of the soul] through near-total immersion in a culture that seeks personal and national well-being at the expense of every other value. War has always served as a means to bring about personal glory and national hegemony, both of which "feel good" in our culture. In the life of Jesus, there is certainly a connection between His own suffering and His unwillingness to use violent means against those who persecuted Him . . .

Mahedy goes on to describe a process of coming to terms with Vietnam that might help some veterans. Men who have faced death in battle, or seen women and children die, will not be able to submerge their experiences for long in the kind of shallow, revisionist Christianity that is so common these days. It has no answers for the despair and rage many combat vets feel, yet it accuses veterans of lack of faith if their problems are not miraculously cured by being "saved." Heads I win, tails you lose.

A vet who takes responsibility for what he has done, who recognizes his problems, has and takes responsibility for getting professional help and doing the painful work that will help him *do no more harm* to wife, family, and world is far more Christian than one who denies the evil we did, however unintentionally, in Vietnam.

If you're telling your vet that God loves him and that is all he needs, you may be making a mistake. God may love him, but if he has PTSD he needs a therapy group of other Vietnam vets and a competent therapist to integrate what happened in Vietnam. If you've been trying to convince your vet that your church has the answers (co-dependent solving of his problems), it would be nice if you could see that he is the expert on his own salvation, and he may need a different church to answer the unanswerable questions he faced in Vietnam. Or there may be no religious answer for him at all. Either way, it isn't in your hands.

If you want to find help for your vet, avoid churches that ascribe evil to outside forces, the devil tempting or taking over people. One reason for this is that maintaining an external locus of control ("the devil made me do it") precludes adult responses such as growing and profiting from experience.

If your minister tells veterans to forget the past, or that what they did was wrong but God will forgive them, or that the devil possessed them, he is doing them actual harm and should be stopped.

Why?

Telling them to forget the past keeps them in it forever.

Telling vets what they did was wrong puts all the burden on them and places little guilt where it belongs—on the society that sent them and on the churches that conveniently forgot that while patriotism may be a civic virtue, it is not a religious one. God is not American.

One of my most terrifying moments was when the wife of a vet who had what sounded like a bad case of PTSD told me that her husband was fine except when he was possessed by the devil. Then they prayed over him at church. This kind of theology removes all responsibility for action from the vet and will keep him dysfunctional for as long as he accepts it. Another vet told me of being *saved* by a church that taught that if you really had faith you didn't need medication. Since he was on medication for PTSD and was receiving no therapy, when he gave up his medication for the church, he wound up in the hospital. Needless to say, he's found another church.

One serious problem for families of veterans has been that several fundamentalist religious leaders teach that there is a conflict between psychiatry and religion. The accuracy of this point of view can perhaps best be illustrated by the cases of prominent televangelists whose behavior reveals deep-seated emotional problems that neither compulsive lying, sexual adventuring, shopping, nor praying on street corners have healed.

Healing the hurts of the past through prayer is something else. Ruth Carter Stapleton's *The Gift of Inner Healing* and Carolyn Koons's autobiography, *Beyond Betrayal*, describe healing experiences. *Healing*, by Father Francis MacNutt, and *Healing Life's Hurts*, by the Linn brothers, describe in more detail how to do it.

Most churches feel there is no conflict between psychology and religion, that God gave us brains to use. *Healing* points out the *value* of using available psychological knowledge. "Our experience coincides with the findings of psychologists: that many of the deepest hurts go way back [to early childhood]," he said, pointing out that if a person is unaware of how important very early experiences are, he or she may not probe early memories to find the source of the problem. For anyone attempting to work with Vietnam veterans through prayer, a grounding in modern PTSD theory is crucial.

A visitor's knowledge of the stages of grief enables a sick woman in *Healing Life's Hurts*, by Dennis and Matthew Linn, to pour out her anger (remember getting stuck in the anger stage of grief?) and begin to heal when someone says to her, "You look angry," instead of the usual platitudes. "In the denial stage, anxiety works like pain . . . anxiety warns us of an emotional overload," the Linns pointed out. Their book describes a process of healing inner hurts through prayer that seems very adaptable to the needs of Vietnam veterans.

Father MacNutt suggested: "Since the need to talk about these deepest, earliest memories [substitute "darkest, most painful memories" for a Vietnam vet] is painful—often involving feelings of guilt or shame—the prayer for inner healing is ordinarily something to be done privately . . . The person asking for prayer should have the freedom to select the person or persons he would like to confide in or pray with."

Damage to the veteran will result if an untrained or egotistical religious healer tells the vet that he will be instantly healed of all emotional pain, and he isn't, particularly if this occurs before a crowd. Often this type of healer then blames failure on the vet's lack of faith.

MacNutt gives eleven reasons why healing may not come instantly through the efforts of one particular healer. Further, Father MacNutt said: "If the person is deeply suffering, chances are he will not feel that he has much faith . . . Assume any faith required must come from you."

Even if your vet is not interested in praying for inner healing, a minister or priest or rabbi who is knowledgeable about PTSD and co-dependency, and is nonjudgmental and open, may be of great help to your vet, especially if willing to do some research on the aspects of PTSD and Vietnam with which he or she may not be familiar.

Suppose your vet is one of those guys who think men haven't got any emotional problems. The only problems men have are job-related. The boss is an SOB. No raise. Stuff like that. Or maybe the Red Sox are blowing it again after all he's done for them. The fact that he hasn't kissed you for two weeks is not a problem. Neither is the fact that he's a workaholic, or an alcoholic, or that he's changed jobs three times this year, or wrecked every car you ever owned, or can't sleep for two weeks every year around Tet.

If he thinks he is fine and *you're* the one with problems, how can you get him to get help?

This is hard and maybe you can't. One way is to ask him to get help. I know that sounds ridiculous, but if you're like I was, you're so concerned about not making waves that you simply may never have asked. Don't say, "You are so messed up you better see a shrink, or I'm leaving." Believe me, it won't work. You could say, "I love you a lot and I'm concerned about your pain (or your numbness, or your workaholism—whatever). It would really help me if you would try to find someone professional to talk to who knows about Vietnam."

Asking him to get help may not work, but you can keep asking in a kind and concerned and *non-blaming* way. It may make you wild that he won't go for help right away, but he's got a lot of messages in his head against doing it. Shove angrily against those messages and try to outshout them and you will fail. If you look deep within yourself, beneath *anger* or *being right,* you will find your love and concern for him, a gentle feeling that he needs more than he can ever tell you. Speak from that place in your heart, quietly and lovingly.

Getting him to seek help is a big step for him, but he may be able to take it if you keep asking. Tell him, "I need you to go," rather than, "You need to go to the Vet Center." In some respects it's true. He may be more content than you with the way things are. You're the one who wants changes. Besides, it takes some of the pressure off him. He's just doing it for you, not because he *needs* to. Believe me, it doesn't matter why people get help. A lot of the guys in the vet group at Raiford started coming to get out of work. It has still helped them.

A good PTSD program should include anger management, stress reduction, education on what PTSD is, rational thinking, thought substitution, alternative behaviors, assertiveness training, the whys, wherefores, and elimination of substance abuse, and goal setting.

A PTSD program should *not* be viewed as a place where the vet goes to be cured by the magical actions of some doctor or therapist. No one can make your vet better except himself. The VA or Vet Center should provide the vet with the tools he needs *to cure himself*, and a place to do it, and some guidance. But *he* has to do the work. He has to practice the skills from group therapy in everyday life when he is upset. They may not work the first time he tries them. That's good. It means that when he masters them, they will work. It's a long, slow process working through pain and changing habitual responses. The vet can look on it as basic training, or basic retraining. He couldn't take a rifle apart and put it together the first time he tried, either. He may not be able to relax or use an alternative behavior he's planned the first time a stressful situation comes up, either, but he'll learn. Takes practice. Takes time. Takes guts to keep on trying.

Talking about Vietnam is the most important part of group therapy, but the vet should not start probing into the pain of Vietnam until he has mastered coping skills, such as anger management or alternatives to substance abuse, and until he has known the group for a while (or, the therapist, if he is in individual therapy) and developed bonds of trust. If he jumps in too fast he may get such a rush of painful emotions he'll scare himself right out of therapy. Painful emotions are the ones he needs to identify and deal with, though. The most important thing is to go back when he doesn't want to, because that can be when he makes the most progress.

If he does scare himself out of therapy, remind him that it's okay. Next time he can go slower. Sarah Haley said vets often need time "in the field," away from therapy, before they can go back for more. Dropping out for a while will help him feel as if he can control the process somewhat, and that's important for men who were cogs in an indifferent machine in Vietnam, where nothing they did made any difference.

I repeat: Therapy is not a short process.

Therapy will probably be very, very painful for your vet.

He may get worse before he gets better.

A lot of women see their men getting more and more upset as they go through therapy and want them to drop out. Keep in mind that your vet is feeling and remembering dreadful things, dreadful in the most literal sense of the word, things that he *dreads* remembering. Going through the pain means he is going to get better, but it takes time. He will be very upset, very sad, and very angry as he goes through treatment, and this is *appropriate*.

He wasn't allowed to cry in Vietnam.

He was used.

His dead friends *were* wasted, because of the way the war was fought.

He is going to have to mourn every friend, relive every mistake. He's going to feel that he shouldn't have lived, that he doesn't deserve to be alive or loved. Going back through Vietnam is going to hurt and hurt and keep on hurting.

Let it.

Let him be upset. Here's a perfect chance to work on your own dependency and learn, as they say in Al-Anon, to detach with love. Find a group and get support from other people.

Don't tell your vet it's okay, because to him it's not. You can't keep his therapy from hurting, but you can be there to listen to him or just hold him when it does. The chapter on "Listening" might help with this.

Don't tell him how to get better.

Above all, don't rush him. He lived through more in that year in Vietnam than most people do in a lifetime, and it's going to take more than a couple of hours a week for a year to get over it. While he is going through therapy and things are tough, remind yourself that he won't be this unhappy forever.

Ray Scurfield said: "Please remember that vets with severe PTSD *do not trust themselves*—they fear that if they really get in touch with some memories that they will lose control and not be able to stop crying, or become so angry that they will hurt someone or themselves, or that they will go crazy—so this is not a rejection of you."

If your vet is a pain during therapy, remember when people have cancer, there are nice patients and bad patients. Nice patients never complain, do everything the doctor says, and are always sweet. They also die more. The ones who fight live. So if he isn't exactly an angel while he's going through therapy, he isn't dead yet, either. Thank God for it.

Group therapy is the treatment of choice for our vets because of the disreception they received at homecoming. They need to talk it over with others who shared the same experience, with people who can often point out to them that what they are blaming themselves for was not their fault. You and I can tell them that, but you and I weren't there, and we don't know. Somehow they can hear it when it comes from another vet. Being in a group also helps them form a community and a support system to replace the one they lost due to isolation as a Vietnam vet. This can be a great relief to you if you have been everything to your vet for a long time. It can also be pretty scary if you are used to being everything to him. You may even feel jealous of the group!

Your veteran may never be free of all the pain of Vietnam. "There is always going to be a scar," said one woman whose husband went through a PTSD program. But by going through therapy the vet can decrease the intensity and frequency of his symptoms; he can decrease the pain his feelings and symptoms cause him by finding out that they are normal; and he can change his actions when he feels angry or upset or depressed. All of this takes work and time and the courage to face the pain.

You can look at any veteran's going into therapy as braver than going to Vietnam, when he didn't really know what he was getting into, unless he was already a combat vet. When he goes into therapy, not only does he know what he has to face *again*, but just in admitting he needs help he is doing something magnificently courageous.

If your vet hasn't gotten to the stage where he can admit that he has problems or needs help, don't keep bugging him. Men are brought up to think emotions are for sissies and toughing it out is the only way. A barrage of helpful advice will only entrench your vet in this position. Fact is, *the only person you can change is yourself*.

What can you do for yourself?

Whatever constellation of symptoms your vet may exhibit, they are not aimed at making you feel inadequate, even if that is their result. I always felt inadequate, and I always blamed Bob, because of my unrealistic belief that if I was good enough, he wouldn't have any problems. Sometimes your vet may aim his problems at you and blame you because it makes him feel more rational: He blows up because of your failings and not because of Vietnam. When you realize and accept that your vet's problems are not your fault, it makes this behavior easier to live with. You didn't cause your vet's problems and symptoms, and you can't control them by changing your behavior or trying to change his. Even if one of his symptoms is that he blames his symptoms on you, don't accept that blame. Nothing you do will fix him. Take care of yourself by getting help yourself.

"Getting help" means working on yourself to make sure you don't *enable* him to avoid treatment, or *sabotage* him if he's in treatment. Learn how to make your own ways of relating to others and living in the world—which have been affected by co-survivorship and co-dependency—more healthy. It is a long, slow process that goes on as long as life does.

Enabling will go on as long as life does, too, if you let it. Enabling is when your vet comes home drunk and pukes on the rug and passes out and you clean it up and put him to bed. You've removed the consequences of his action, helped him deny he has a problem, covered up.

Leave him there in the puke. If it happens a lot, go to Al-Anon.

If your daughter-in-law is leaving your son in the puke, and you think she shouldn't, go to Al-Anon with her.

Enabling is also when you sign all the report cards so your vet won't be annoyed by interacting with the kids. When you have *the* job. When you stay with someone who abuses you or the kids. When you don't tell him how his actions affect you.

Enabling is when you agree with your veteran son or brother that his woman is the one with problems. He's fine, and so what if he's got a short fuse? Who wouldn't with her? When you cover up for your son, when you deny his problems, you prolong them. They don't go away by themselves.

Sabotage often becomes a big problem when a veteran finally gets into therapy, and the saboteurs are usually us. We don't like the changes we see. It scares us not to be as important to our vet as we were, when he depended on us for everything, even though that drove us crazy. If you see the problem as a joint one and work on yourself, too, you are much less likely to sabotage your vet.

One vet was on the wagon and getting better, took his wife out to a fancy restaurant, and she urged him to have a scotch because he was "no fun anymore." He did. He wasn't much fun for a while after that.

Parents may do the same thing.

Kids may prefer a father who goes into rages or gets drunk and then repentantly showers them with gifts.

Another woman found herself feeling that the in-patient PTSD program was a country club (except for the therapy, she did admit that) and was furious at her husband for abandoning her. Parents and kids can feel abandoned, too, especially if their rescuing role stops. We all like to rescue people; it makes us feel good. Stuff like that can distract your vet from the business of therapy.

Where can you turn to take care of yourself so you won't enable or sabotage?

You have several options: A Vet Center may be the best place, if it is not staffed by people who think that only the veteran has *real* problems. If there is a Vet Center in your area, your vet doesn't have to go with you. He doesn't have to give permission. They will see you. They'll even see you and your kids. Tell your vet to come along if it bothers him. Tell him you love him and you want to be closer to him and that finding out about Vietnam will help you. Ask him to come with you.

Group therapy works really well for partners of vets, too. Ruth S. wrote me:

> My women's group was very helpful. There were 10 to 12 of us. The leader was a woman who is a partner of a vet with PTSD. She is also a counselor with the Vet Center Outreach Program. Our group had 6 weeks of formal programs and then 6 weeks of informal sessions. During the first six weeks we explored how women and men are conditioned in our society, and how this related to military training, especially boot camp. We saw videotapes of jungle missions and discussed what happened there. One of the vet counselors discussed his experiences and how he felt about them, and we watched video tapes about how PTSD affected families and relationships. During the informal sessions we just discussed our experiences and problems we were having. We received some printed material which I frequently pass on to friends who need it. Attending this group was an extremely valuable experience for me and was instrumental in my learning to accept my husband and his behavior. The work we have done with the Vet Center has really improved our relationship. Although he has gained a lot of insight through his counseling and the more acute symptoms have disappeared, his attitudes toward life are much the same and I doubt he will ever be free from his experiences in Viet Nam. This is why I feel my acceptance of these things is so important.

If your veteran is service-connected for psychological problems, you may be able to get help at your local VA as a collateral of a veteran, either individual therapy or through a women's (wives and significant others) group.

If you don't live near a VA or Vet Center, check out the local vet groups to see if any of them sponsors a women's group. If they don't, maybe you can organize one. In many communities there are concerned mental-health professionals who are experienced in running groups. People who go into the mental-health field often want to help others, and you may be able to find someone who is willing to do a little research on PTSD and Vietnam and co-surviving and co-dependence and to provide this service.

Further resources include Al-Anon if your vet has an alcohol problem, or Narc-Anon if he smokes pot or uses other drugs. You'll be in good company in these groups. They may be of great help to you especially in dealing with the co-dependency you may have developed. Families of vets can find help here, too. I go to an Adult Children of Alcoholics (and Other Dysfunctional Families) women's group because I think we became a very dysfunctional family when Bob was having problems. I also think my own family, which had two previous generations of war vets, was pretty dysfunctional in its handling of feelings.

After reluctantly (I hated the title) reading Robin Norwood's *Women Who Love Too Much*, I think the self-help groups around the country based on that excellent book would also help us out of our co-dependent trap. This is a *long-term* process, as Ms. Norwood warns in her second book, *Letters from Women Who Love Too Much*.

For those of you who have survived trauma yourselves, going to a group focused on your own issues may be the best choice. Such experiences as severe beatings or sexual abuse in childhood, especially at the hands of alcoholic or rigidly religious parents, need to be dealt with through therapy or self-help groups (which can often give you the insight and courage to get therapy). If you are being battered by your vet, a group of women who have been through the same thing will give you the support you need to deal with those issues. Call your local shelter or spouse-abuse hotline. If you were ever raped or were the victim of another violent crime, call the local crisis center or crime-victim organization. Go to AA if your vet's driven you to drink, or NA if you have to stay stoned all the time to live with him. If you've used food to nurture yourself through the rough spots, as I have, go to Overeaters Anonymous.

If your vet gets better and you don't, sabotage or separation often result. Any kind of work that focuses on loving and accepting yourself and changing the parts of yourself you'd prefer to (not should) change will be constructive.

If you prefer private counseling or therapy, shop around for someone with whom you are comfortable. Someone who understands co-dependency and PTSD is ideal; if the counselor knows about only one of these, is she willing to learn? If she doesn't know about either but is willing to learn, that, too, is a good sign.

Aphrodite Matsakis's excellent book, *Vietnam Wives*, discusses how to select a therapist, and she suggests finding a feminist or non-sexist counselor by writing to the Feminist Therapist Roster, Association for Women in Psychology, 1200 17th St., N.W., Washington, D.C. 20036, or by calling local women's centers, rape-crisis centers, the National Organization of Women, or the local mental-health center. Of one client who failed to find good therapy before she came to Matsakis's group, she said, "A feminist view of this particular wife's problems would acknowledge that, to some extent, her low self-esteem, anxiety attacks, and crying spells were the *logical results* [my *italics*] of the strains of being a full-time worker, having three children, and living with a man marred by PTSD . . ." Instead, the woman's therapist had called her a masochist with a pre-borderline personality who was addicted to destructive relationships—which did not help her at all.

What about a male counselor? Okay, if you can find one who knows about PTSD and co-dependence or is willing to learn.

Counselors can be pretty co-dependent themselves. They want their patients to get well in particular ways, which sometimes include taking pills. They may deny basic family problems because they are not familiar with PTSD or family therapy or substance abuse. Your problem may be something the counselor denies in his or her own family and is therefore unlikely to treat in yours. If your counselor drinks a six-pack every night, he won't see that as a problem in your vet. (One psychiatrist told me, "Alcohol abuse is more than the doctor himself drinks, whatever that is.") If your counselor thinks women should be "nice" and support men, he will only encourage co-dependence in you. Some counselors may prefer that you get a divorce. Such a counselor may say "If this man is unavailable to you, get out" without understanding that if you're with one unavailable man, you may go on to another unless you work on yourself.

If you feel the counselor is pushing a solution or an interpretation on you, or not listening, speak up. Most counselors want to help you. If you say, "How do you think it helps me become more aware of myself when you tell me what and why I'm doing things? Is it healthier to go from what my vet tells me to do to what you tell me to do?," this may help the counselor become aware of un-therapeutic habits she's very humanly developed.

Therapy is often painful. The pain arises from openly acknowledging feelings—ones you had to repress or deny so you could keep
on going—that you are now able to express safely. Sometimes your
therapist may gently confront you with something painful you wish
to deny. We all feel a great resistance at times to discussing the
things we need to discuss in therapy. You'll be able to judge, from
how it feels, whether your therapist is doing this in a healthy way
or not. If part of the pain comes from labels your therapist gives
you that leave you feeling hopelessly defective, or from directions
the therapist is trying to force you to follow, find another therapist.

Your church may be able to help you with counseling if your minister or priest is familiar with co-dependency. Many churches sponsor
AA and Al-Anon and ACOA groups. If your church teaches that the
way to deal with problems is to become more and more giving, more
submissive to your husband, it is encouraging your co-dependency.
That may cost you your life. God may not give us any burden we
can't bear, but He also gave us brains so we can help ourselves.

*Grant me the serenity to accept the things I cannot change, the
courage to change the things I can, and the wisdom to know the
difference.*

If professional help or organized self-help groups are not available
in your area, concerned family members of vets can start a group
for themselves. In the back of this book is a format for a 12 Step
group for families of veterans that I have adapted from several
sources. *Guidelines for Support Groups*, by Janet Woititz, contains
ideas about forming a Twelve Step support group that could be
adapted. A group could be formed around the Moffats' *Families After
Trauma*.

Another resource is a series of cassette tapes, *Common Concern*,
from New Harbinger Publishers, which provides a format and information on communication skills. The group provides the information on its own special common concerns. Group work must focus
us on our *own* process to recovery, what works for us, and how we
are working toward health and hope. Instead of saying, "What you
should do is . . . ," we need to be saying, "What works for me is . . ."
or "I'm glad you said that, because I have been having a problem
with it, too." Solutions are not necessary; sharing and support are.

When Dad gets control of his PTSD, and Mom of her co-dependency, family therapy is often necessary to heal the whole family. Family therapists focus "on the functional facts of relationships, on what happens, how it happens, where it happens, insofar as such observations are based on facts," according to a Hazelden pamphlet called *Free to Care*. Finding a family therapist who is familiar with PTSD and co-dependency may be difficult. Someone who is willing to learn is acceptable. "A Five-Phase Treatment of Post-Traumatic Stress Disorder in Families," by Charles R. Figley, published in the January 1988 issue of *The Journal of Traumatic Stress*, provides a framework for therapy.

Family-therapy books have such a hopeful slant. Here's a quote from *Peoplemaking*, by Virginia Satir:

I am convinced that any troubled family can become a nurturing one. Most of the things that cause families to be troubled are learned after birth. Since they are learned, they can be unlearned; and new things can be learned in their place . . .

As you begin to see the troubles in your family more clearly, it will help you to realize that, whatever may have happened in the past, it represented the best you knew how to do at the time. There is no reason for anyone to feel guilty himself or to blame others in the family.

This healthy, non-blaming attitude shows why family therapy is well worth the trouble.

To sum this all up, help is available through the VA, Vet Centers, private therapy, and all kinds of self-help groups, for both you and your vet. If your vet is having acute PTSD symtoms, help may save his life.

Once your vet learns that his symptoms are a normal part of recovery from traumatic events—even twenty years later—he may be able to get himself some help. Meanwhile, whether he gets help or not, you need and deserve it, so that you no longer enable the problems he does have, and will not sabotage whatever recovery he is able to achieve.

Finally, therapy or self-help groups, whether for survivor or co-survivor, do not provide a quick fix, but rather a place to begin and continue a long-term process that can be very painful to both partners, but which will in the end be worthwhile.

11

Listening

There is no way out but through.
——Earnie Larsen and Carol Larsen Hegarty
Days of Healing and Joy, August 14

As the wife or girlfriend, parent, sister, brother, or child of a Vietnam vet, you may feel that you have listened enough. Conversely, your vet may never have talked to you about Vietnam. These are two sides of the same coin—both representing the inability to communicate the experience of Vietnam. The guy who's driving you crazy with war stories is not really communicating what it was like. Neither is the man who never talks.

Research has shown that being able to communicate what has happened to you in a nonjudgmental environment of acceptance and interest is vital to the processing of traumatic events. This applies whether the traumatic event was your tight blue jeans splitting out at a high school basketball game in front of everyone (you told your best friend and she didn't laugh; she sympathized) or your buddy dying in your arms in a Vietnamese rice paddy. Sharing is a form of healing.

Marsha Livingston, who struck me as a very wise woman, said, "I would like to know the whole story. It would help me to be able to say now I understand what he went through. It might hurt a lot, but I still want to know. When he went over there he was joking, laughing, carefree, but since he's come back, no matter how close we get, there is always a secret part walled up. I get the outer fringes of the pain. I feel that if he could open up and let the pain

334

and rage and all that out, there wouldn't be any more rages and flashbacks and stuff. If it helped him to talk to a therapist, that would be okay. I don't know if I could even hear it, but if someone could hear what he's been through and done and seen, it could help him. I can't imagine being transplanted from a small Southern town—to live through that and survive—they had to kill a part of themselves."

In *Post-Traumatic Stress Disorder and the War Veteran Patient*, Robert Marrs's article "Why the Pain Won't Stop and What the Family Can Do to Help" reported that back in the early seventies, a "Communication Outline for Families and Friends of Vietnam Veterans" was developed at Macomb County Community College, in Mt. Clemens, Michigan. They wrote:

> a. Indicate that *you care* and wish to hear if *he desires* to share his experiences and concerns with you. Is it necessaray to know specific war experiences, in order to understand your veteran?
> b. Do not make sharp negative or positive generalizations about Vietnam.
> c. If you find that you cannot hear him talk about his experiences, seek help from those who can.

The rare lucky vet found someone who would listen, but most of them met with utter incomprehension, outright disbelief, or hostile rejection. Listening to the vets now, even twenty years later, is a form of acceptance they really need, a part of the healing process.

Bill Fisk wrote me: "There have been lots of times when I get real hyper and strung out about it all, if my lady would just sit there and let me get it off my chest, after a little while I can calm down. But so often happens, she will say, 'That was twenty years ago. Why don't you just forget it?' Well, all that does is get me pissed all over again." One of the reasons this may be difficult for us is that angry vets can be really frightening, but if you feel safe enough, letting your vet get it out can really help him. You can establish a way to call time out if it gets too intense.

You may never share your vet's entire Vietnam experience, or any of it, but you can learn to share him. Let him tell you how he feels without giving him advice or direction. This will be healing for him, too, if like many survivors he feels that no one can ever understand him. Understanding him is a process, and listening to him

is the tool. Direct communication is the result. For people who have
been functioning in dysfunctional ways—one of which is indirect
communication—this is a good place to start. Start with everyday
stuff, too, if that seems safer. Heavy talks about Vietnam can come
later, if at all.

Your vet can learn to share your interests and concerns, too. He
may start by feeling that your concerns are petty compared to his—
the old "that's nothing compared to what I went through in Vietnam." For people whose normal reactions to trauma have cut them
off from normal human interrelating, learning to share everyday
concerns is a really important process. It can be fun, too. If you are
both in therapy or some kind of group, every insight you get will
help you learn to listen to each other.

How do you learn to communicate and share with another human
being?

Practice! Practice! Practice!

Listening comes first. I learned how to listen over the course of
about eight years. If that sounds silly, remember that I had been
practicing, not listening, giving advice, and knowing what was right,
since birth. In 1970, at twenty-seven, I began to learn how to listen.

Bob and I were into a phase of arguing all the time, long ugly
arguments. I read a book called *The Intimate Enemy: How to Fight
Fair in Love and Marriage* by George R. Bach. The first rule was
to use feedback. The idea was to check the other person's statements
to be sure you were arguing about the same thing. That seemed
really sensible. If Bob wants to know if I've seen the screwdriver
and I take it as an attack on my housekeeping, we're gonna have a
fight. Bob even read the list of rules—not the whole book, but at
least the rules!

About this time, Bob and I got into a fight, and I threw that box
through a window. Then I got a friend to drive me to the infirmary
because I thought I was going to go mad. I started seeing Dr. Yozgat,
a psychiatrist from Turkey, going in talking ratta-tat-tat about what
shitty things Bob had done to me that week. The third or fourth
week, Dr. Yozgat held up his hand to stem the flood, and asked,
"How does Bob feel about this? Is he sorry?"

Dead silence.

I hadn't the faintest idea.

If he had been sorry, I wouldn't have known. Would you?

Bob couldn't have gotten a word in edgewise. Can your vet?

I went home. I listened. Bob was sorry. We're still together.

At that time, through reading *Games People Play*, by Eric Berne, M.D., I began to examine what I got out of the continuing soap opera of our lives. Perhaps you get some of the same "payoffs" in your relationship. Games are a structured series of interactions (transactions) between people that allow them to stay together without ever having to change or grow. Games keep a distance between the couple that both can tolerate. No real intimacy ever develops, and the couple goes through *the same behaviors over and over* (sound familiar?), get rewarded with attention (strokes), and it doesn't seem to matter if they are negative strokes or positive ones.

When I read *Games People Play*, I could see that I played "Ain't It Awful" (all men are shits) with my friends, and "Wooden Leg" with Bob. I took care of Bob so that he never had to change because he had this wooden leg (Vietnam), and then complained to my friends about the way he was. I couldn't figure out how to stop. After all, Bob couldn't help how he acted; *he'd been in a war*. I think that attitude was good, in that it helped me tolerate Bob's real uncontrollable PTSD symptoms, but it also got me protecting him from having to do things he very well could have done, like pick up his own booze. (This is what is meant when they say co-dependency is progressive.)

One payoff was that my friends all thought I was wonderful to put up with so much. The other, which I didn't recognize till much later, was that I got to feel that I was fine and Bob was the cause of all our problems. I was depressed after I read the book, because Dr. Berne said we should stop playing games, but he didn't say *how*. And I couldn't figure out how.

Later on I decided to stop telling my friends what Bob "did to me this week," even though I still thought he was my whole problem. This began to detach me from a circle of friends who were also heavily invested in the "all men are shits" game and supported my martyr role. I felt that if I kept indulging in that game, I'd never grow at all. It was hard to do because I had to stop wearing that comfortable martyr's robe. It took a long time, too.

Berne's Transactional Analysis model of the self shows three circles, one below the other: Parent, Adult, Child. The top circle is called the Parent (P) and is made up of all the things we learned and heard as kids from our parents, teachers, etc., and perhaps, for our vets, in basic training and in Vietnam. The Parent is full of shoulds and oughts. Some of them are essential for survival: *I should nurse the baby. I should bring home the bacon.* Others have less survival value: *We should have a color TV. She shouldn't ask me to help around the house. He shouldn't say "fuck."* Others are just plain destructive: *You shouldn't whine about Vietnam.* (Notice the loaded verb, a very parental word.) *All men are shits. Men don't cry. Don't trust anyone.* These are the ones you have to watch out for.

The power of the Parent came really alive for me when I used to say things to my son Jack that I'd sworn would never come out of my mouth, things my mother had said to me. Maybe that's happened to you, too.

You don't want your Parent to be in control when your vet is in combat therapy. Suppose he comes home and confides some dreadful memory to you and cries and you find your mother's reaction shooting out of your mouth: "Be a man, don't cry!" Unless you've done some work on yourself, you may find it intolerable to see him cry. Or, worse, suppose you tell him he's a monster for what he's done, judge him the way your parents may have judged you. How will that help him? Will he ever be able to trust you again?

Whenever I feel a flood of anger or anxiety, I look for what parental rule is being broken. One usually is. Then I use the middle circle of the TA model, the Adult, to decide if I want to perpetuate that rule in my family now. I used to cram my fist into my mouth when one of my mother's rules with which I disagreed would start to come out of my mouth.

The middle circle (A), the Adult—the part that observes whether our actions are moving us toward our goals, and, if not, puts in a correction without recriminations or guilt—is the part of ourselves we all need to strengthen. The serenity prayer comes from this part of us. You can strengthen this part through education about Vietnam and PTSD, reading self-help books (see Suggested Further Reading in the back of the book), going to many types of therapy (group therapy, cognitive therapy, reality therapy, rational emotive therapy, rational behavior therapy), assertiveness training, relaxation training, self-hypnosis, imagery, visualization, the Twelve Steps programs of AA, NA, Al-Anon, Adult Children of Alcoholics, and so on. All strengthen the Adult part of us.

None of the information I got from books worked consistently for me, however, until I understood co-dependency and began to go to my ACOA group. I learned all kinds of self-help stuff but I could never put it into practice on a regular basis until I read about co-dependency and realized getting me well had to come first, and in any case was the only thing I had any control over.

The bottom circle (C) is the Child. In this part of us, our Child reigns, whether it's a happy Child who allows us to have fun or an adapted fearful Child who is always desperately trying to live up to the standards of a terrifying parent, or, like me, an irresponsible rebellious Child who is constantly getting you in trouble. We can work to strengthen the part of our Child that enables us to play and to enjoy life, especially if we have become a co-dependent co-survivor and forgotten how to have fun.

The other idea from *Games People Play* that really helped me was the crossed transaction, which explained a lot of arguments Bob and I had. Berne lined up two sets of PAC circles. If one person asks an Adult-to-Adult question like *What time is it?*, Dr. Berne drew an arrow straight across from A to A. If the other person answers from rebellious Child (C) to Parent (P)—*Who the hell do you think you are, my mom?*—the arrow for the answer crosses the question arrow, and the *crossed transaction* is going to start a fight. This reinforces the idea of feedback from *The Intimate Enemy*. If I think Bob's trying to be my mom when all he wants to know is the time, we'll get into a lot of fights!

TA helped me realize the source of my problems, right there in the top circle, my Parent. I became able to notice when my reaction was coming from my Parent and react with less anger, which helped. I noticed, too, that much of my behavior was irresponsible, right out of my rebellious Child, but it hardly seemed to matter since our life was so chaotic anyhow.

Reading about TA did start me on the road to recovery. I didn't call it that, though. I still thought that if I did everything right, Bob would be fine. It was my fault he had problems.

Meanwhile, other *Intimate Enemy* principles of fair fighting began to improve our fights. For example, we no longer bring up the past. Unless a time machine comes along, we can't change it, and it takes someone with more grace than I've got to keep saying I'm sorry over something I can't change. Surprisingly, Bob was better at giving up grudges than perfect little me!

Another rule was to bring up *now* what bothers you now. If you do that, you have small disagreements instead of big blowouts. I used to let things build and then blow up about them because I thought Bob should *know* how I felt. If that is one of your strategies, because you don't want to rock the boat and bring on a rage reaction or one of those terrifying emotional absences some of us are familiar with in our vets, talk about it with your vet. Many Vet Centers have a handout on rules of fair fighting. If your vet's read *Chickenhawk*, you could tell him Bob found this useful. Explain that you are going to mention what you don't like when you don't like it so he has the opportunity to know what's bugging you. "I don't mind" is the biggest, most common lie of all. Plain dishonesty. He's probably noticed this. Also explain that you are trying to change your ways so the two of you can get along better. Explain that your mentioning things doesn't mean you guys have to put on boxing gloves right then and duke it out. You'll live if something bothers you. You can make a date to fight later about what bothers you, if it isn't appropriate right now, but at least you're not leading him on to the big whammy. Your vet may come to appreciate this. Please don't say your vet *should* know what bothers you. Mind reading is for magicians. And people who are suppressing traumatic memories often *don't* notice things. They just don't have the capacity. Some of them are very aware of how other people feel, but many are not.

Another rule for fair fighting: Don't call names or hit below the belt by using something that is really painful to the other person. Like baby-killer. Like fat cow or skinny little runt.

Dr. Bach's weirdest and most important rule was *not to fight to win*. If a couple fights to win, that means one wins and one *loses*. Intimacy is not possible between a winner and a loser, only between equals.

This is a very important skill for vets and their families to learn. Vets know how to fight to win. Many of them equate fighting with killing, and when they fight, their intention is to blast us, to annihilate us, and to win. They need to retrain themselves to fight like normal people, which means expressing their ideas, acknowledging the other person's ideas, and coming to a resolution so you both win. It's just like practicing putting that rifle together in basic.

Beating someone down into agreement is not communicating, although many vets feel that it is. Many families, too. Many of us were raised in such homes, too, and learned at our mother's knee to fight, not to listen, because it was the only way we could maintain any sense of ourselves. When we live with someone who has a hard time tolerating differences of opinion, as many vets do *(you're either for me or against me)*, we learn to fight dirty, too, to scream, to twist, to stab with words, never to give up. We do not want to be swallowed up in this other person and become an echo.

Bob and I used to fight to win. Either Bob would drop such a heavy barrage of words that I'd surrender, or I'd fight like a cornered alley cat until he'd say, "Okay, you're right, and I'm crazy." Getting rid of that pattern was really a relief. Bob didn't feel the crushing burden of having to know everything, and I didn't have to fight for my survival anymore. After Bob and I learned to fight pretty fairly we got along a lot better. For one thing we were beginning to listen to each other. Finding solutions was so much easier than the fighting. Circumstances brought a lot of stress into our lives around this time, but we became more able to connect because we tried to listen to each other.

To do feedback, you have to listen to the other person and then say back to him what you think he is saying, paraphrasing what he says. It's self-correcting. Here's an example:

"I hate your hair."

"You wish I were blond!" [a try at feedback, but really mind reading]

"No. I wish you would comb it." [feedback]

Even I couldn't argue with that!

Later, when our son Jack was about fifteen, I simply couldn't get along with him. I knew what he *should* do, but I couldn't get him to do it. Looking around for help, I found the book *Parent Effectiveness Training* by Thomas Gordon. I figured this would tell me how to shape the kid up, so I read it.

Not only did it not tell me how to shape Jack up, it told me I couldn't. It also described a system of actively listening to Jack so that he could tell me how he felt and come up with his own solutions. Dr. Gordon gave lots of reasons why advice-giving, encouragement, warning, and all the old standard parental moves don't work, and I had to admit they hadn't been working for me. *PET* is another way of beginning to take the first of the Twelve Steps, but I didn't know that and wouldn't have welcomed the knowledge anyway. Active listening, as it's called in *PET*, worked, with Jack and with Bob, too. *People* effectiveness training. Bob was having such a hard time being an unemployed writer, feeling so useless. He worried that his book would sell 200 copies and he'd wind up owing the publisher money. He felt like he couldn't write.

The main ingredient of *PET*'s thesis is to listen effectively, paraphrasing what the person was saying back to him to be sure you are getting what he means (feedback, right?). Going through this process tells the person he is important to you. Not telling him what to do tells him you have respect for his judgment and believe he can cope. When we are listened to, we can find our own solutions and they fit us best. So I listened actively and sympathetically while Bob struggled with his book and his pride. It helped him a lot.

Don't misunderstand. I couldn't always do it. Sometimes I caught myself with half a ton of advice sticking out of my mouth like an old army boot. Sometimes I couldn't do it at all. I just *told* them. In trying to incorporate the other half of the *PET* technique, *I-messages*, I also discovered some things I did not admire about myself. I never asked for help unless I *had* to have it. Sound familiar?

I asked only when I was desperate, all the while feeling very noble because I could do it all myself most of the time. But what that means from your family's point of view is that you never *ask* for help. You *order*. If you don't ask for help till you must have it, you're not asking. You're Hitler. It was pretty embarrassing. So I learned to ask early and ask often and really be *asking*, not ordering. It was okay to say no to me (the first crack in my co-dependency). Makes all our lives a lot easier now that I'm not often supermom.

I'll give you an example of the kind of listening I used to do. Perhaps it'll be familiar:

"She's pretty," Bob would comment.

"She's stupid," I'd respond, or some other hostile comment, because I never heard a simple declarative statement, I heard comparisons. I heard, "She's prett*ier*." I heard, "She's pretty *and you're not*." I heard a lot of things, but seldom what he actually said. I heard a lot of what I felt about myself, but I didn't hear him, a common cognitive distortion called mind reading. I thought he was saying he lusted after these girls. Imagine how silly I felt years later after I learned paraphrasing:

"She's pretty," Bob said.

"She's got a nice build," I paraphrased, revealing my own fears and concerns.

"No," Bob said. "She's got a pretty face like you."

I could have saved myself a lot of anguish. As you can see, paraphrasing is inherently self-corrective. If the paraphrase is wrong, the person lets you know.

You can't understand how your vet is feeling unless you listen to him and can express what he is feeling by reflecting what he says back to him in your own words to see if you really do understand. Paraphrasing is a process. Do it effectively enough and you will understand at a gut level what you were understanding intellectually, if at all, before. He will know that you do understand because you have taken the time to listen to him, to follow what he says and feels, to pay attention to him. This can be very important to a vet because it may be the first time since Vietnam that anyone has really closely, acceptingly listened to him.

What if what you learn is painful? What if it scares both of you? "I can't write," Bob would often say when I got home. I used to feel like saying, "You can write. Viking is paying you to write, you dummy. You've got an advance"—all the old fact-marshaling and advice-giving and trying to control. I felt like saying, "Just do it. You can do it, I know you can. I believe in you." Rah-rah encouragement. (What a way to give somebody writer's block.) In another book that teaches paraphrasing, *People Skills*, twelve of these barriers to communication are listed under three categories: judging, sending solutions, and avoiding the other's concerns (denial). I was familiar with them all. Are you?

Bob had feelings about writing he needed to let go of. That's what talking about feelings does for anyone. It releases them. They may come back often, but they're not as strong. The person who is heard—with concern and without advice—becomes aware that one way to let feelings go so they don't keep you stuck is to talk about them.

"It's really hard," I would paraphrase. "You have to produce a book and you want it to be really good."

"Yeah. Everything depends on me. I don't know if I can do it."

"You might fuck it up." [straight paraphrase]

"Yeah, the stuff I wrote today is bad."

"Lousy, huh?" [straight paraphrase]

"Drivel."

"Worries you, doesn't it?" [paraphrasing the feeling rather than the words]

"Yeah, things don't come out right. Besides, no one will ever read it."

"All this effort will be for nothing." [straight paraphrase]

"Right." Long pause. The distress seems to run out of him. "Wanna read what I wrote?"

I listened to him feel that he couldn't do it, that it was too hard, that what he wrote was shit, and that no one would read it. Before I read *PET*, I would have found those feelings totally unacceptable and actually terrifying. At every point in that conversation, most people—*especially* me before I read *PET*—would have forbidden him to feel those feelings through one of a number of methods. Advice: Just do it. Warning: You'd better get going. You owe them a book. Cheering up: You write so well.

Bob would still have written the same great book; but it would have been harder, because he wouldn't have had the strength being listened to gives, and I would have lost many, many chances to become more intimate with him. *I wouldn't have understood what he was going through if I hadn't let him tell me.* Maybe *italics* aren't enough to emphasize how important I think that sentence is. It ought to be in red. That's the essence of intimacy: letting someone tell you how he feels.

I was plenty scared when Bob would say he couldn't write. I didn't want to clean houses all my life. But feelings are ephemeral. Expressing them sends them on their way, not permanently, but long enough to get on with something else. Bob had plenty of legitimate reasons for his feelings. No Vietnam book had ever sold very well.

Usually first books don't sell well, either. He felt badly because I was working as a cleaning woman—even though I had finished college—because that's where I could make the most money.

I feel much differently now about feelings. Whatever they are, we survive them, and we need them. It may seem ridiculous, but I'm going to drag in an idea from *Dune*, Frank Herbert's science-fiction classic, which has always helped me when emotion seems about to overwhelm me. It's called the litany against fear, but I use it for anger and depression and jealousy and self-righteousness and wanting to make Bob or Jack do something:

> I must not fear. Fear is the mind-killer. Fear is the little-death that brings total obliteration. I will face my fear. I will permit it to pass over me and through me. And when it has gone past I will turn the inner eye to see its path. Where the fear has gone there will be nothing. Only I will remain.

Where the need to control has gone, where the anger has gone, where the self-righteousness has gone, there will be nothing. Only I will remain.

Emotions are like winds. They blow into you, powerful and destructive, but then they blow away and you are still there, alive. Feelings can hurt like hell. The only thing that will hurt you more than having them is not having them. Then you're dead, like the 9th Marines in Vietnam, the walking dead. No matter how you deny them, feelings will still pop up and annoy or agonize you whenever they want to. So the pain is worth facing. It's worth knowing you'll live through it.

Later on, while Bob was in prison, I joined a Vietnam vets group that did crisis intervention. We had to take Crisis Training at the County Crisis Center and serve six months as a phone volunteer on the suicide and crisis line. Imagine my surprise when the training was in active listening, which the Crisis Center called paraphrasing. By this time I was pretty good at it. My first real crisis call lasted four hours. The person went from hysterical, unintelligible screaming to feeling as if he were going to be able to live. All paraphrasing. The feeling of being understood. Remember how good it feels? That's all it takes.

Maybe you feel like yelling, "I *do* understand how he feels!" and you're ready to throw this book across the room. I used to think I understood how Bob felt about everything, but when I started to listen and paraphrase instead of mind-read, I found out that I did not. You cannot say "I understand how you feel" to your vet and expect him to believe you. Do you believe him when he says he understands when he hasn't listened to you?

By actively listening and paraphrasing your vet, you will go through the process of understanding together. If *the only way out* for him *is through* therapy about Vietnam, it is equally true of the two of you for reaching intimacy. The only way to get closer is to work through the barriers to communication that exist in most relationships.

Looking back, I would say that paraphrasing helped me so much because (as a typical co-dependent) I really thought that I knew all the answers. Once I started listening to Bob and Jack, though, I had to admit that I didn't. If you've been rescuing and enabling and organizing your family, the feeling of knowing how everything should go is probably very familiar. Learning to paraphrase can help with that, especially if you are desperately tired. It's a lot less work to *listen* to people and let them come up with their own solutions than to *run* to the store for them—or *run* their lives.

Active listening, feedback, or paraphrasing—whichever you call the skill—is a great antidote to being actively co-dependent. Listening to your vet defines the boundaries between the two of you, a problematic area for co-dependents and some Vietnam vets. Listening to him makes you realize that *he is not me, he has different ideas, needs, solutions.* Also, while you are listening to your vet, you can't be mind reading, thinking you know how he feels without asking. He's *telling you* what he feels. While you are listening—if you are really listening—you won't be able to do the usual co-dependent thing of coming up with a solution for him, which helps you realize that *you can't solve his problems.* You will also have to notice that your vet doesn't *want* your advice. He wants to be heard, even though you, as a co-dependent, may look on conversations mainly as opportunities to give advice or pick holes in other people's feelings or opinions. *(Oh, you shouldn't feel like that. Don't feel bad!)*

If you are actively listening and paraphrasing your vet, you will not be able to guide the conversation to your preferred topics, to *control* what is being said or the manner of its expression. If you are actively listening, you will have to hear things you do not want to hear and may have chosen never to hear before, thereby giving up your own denial system. The whole process is a vital learning experience for a co-dependent. Its final benefit is that at the end of the conversation, we do not get to give directions, extract promises, give advice. We have to leave our vet's problem where it really is— *out of our hands*.

If you want to be more intimate with your vet, paraphrasing is good practice because it is acting *as if* you were intimate. Eventually you will be.

Active listening is hard to learn but is worth every bit of effort.

I read somewhere that the signs of a good relationship are also three C's: concern, concentration, and confidence. When you are concerned about someone you love you are willing to listen. Being willing to concentrate on your vet when necessary, to suspend problem-solving and every other thought in simple listening, shows how much you value him. Finally, you show your confidence in your vet when you don't have to provide him or her with a solution.

The average person listens to someone else for twenty seconds before he starts figuring out his reply. Twenty seconds! In other words, we spend most of our time involved with ourselves and our reactions. If you have ever met a good listener, you know what a pleasure it is to be listened to. Heaven, in fact. One of the ways to be sure you have listened to and understood is to paraphrase what the person you're with has said, checking out whether you've heard what he said the way he meant it.

If this sounds like a lot of work, it is. Relationships take work. I don't know if it takes more energy to yell than to paraphrase. I don't know if it is more work to be silently, nobly angry for years. I do know I did both, and that paraphrasing is a lot more fun. What can I say? You can always go back to fighting or fuming!

There's another problem. For years after I learned active listening, every time I'd tell Bob a worry, he'd give me advice. I'd just want to punch him in the nose. It really burned me up that he was not reciprocating. But it was one of the prices I was willing to pay because I love him, and because he pays prices for me, some of which

I'm only vaguely aware of, like the fact that I'm such a know-it-all. In "5 Ways to Get Closer to Your Husband" by Dalma Heyn, in the November 1986 issue of *McCall's*, I discovered an explanation for this behavior that lowered my desire to punch him. Aha! I see! Men are solution-oriented. I just have to make it plainer that I want him to listen to my feelings but I don't need a solution. I learned to say exactly what I need: "Bob, please let me whine and snivel awhile, okay?" (He *likes* my sense of humor.)

Paraphrasing will draw you closer. "Heart-to-heart" conversations, aimed at getting your vet to admit to *whatever* fault, will drive you further apart. We all have been brought up to think that long talks in which one party or the other admits to some hidden feeling or some inadequacy equal intimacy. It doesn't. After a truly intimate conversation you both feel wonderful. No one won. No one lost. After a heart-to-heart, you may feel great and he feels raped. If you find yourself even using the phrase "I finally got him to admit," you are not intimate and you're not trying to achieve intimacy. You are trying to make him do or say or feel what you want, trying to control him. Co-dependent. You may be sugar-coating it, but what you are doing is not sweet. Not only is it self-serving in the most selfish "Aha! Gotcha!" sort of way, it is self-defeating. You are teaching him that intimacy, that just talking to you, is going to leave him feeling like shit. He can't win, so why talk?

Paraphrasing, on the other hand, lets you both win.

If you've been in the habit either of not talking much or of trying to talk him into the things you think he should do, starting to paraphrase is very hard. If you're aware of the three types of questions discussed in the *Common Concern* tapes mentioned in the last chapter, you may be able to start a conversation more easily.

Closed questions such as *Did you have a good day?* require only a yes or no. End of conversation. *How was your day?* is an open question and more likely to result in conversation. The third kind is multiple choice: *Did you have a good day or was the boss in an uproar again?* Multiple-choice questions can be useful, because they begin the process of communication. They show your vet you are aware of some of his concerns. But as you begin to talk to each other more, they can also limit the answers by unconsciously guiding both of you away from uncomfortable topics, which are probably the ones that need exploration.

If your vet simply won't talk, paraphrase his body language.

He slams into the house and throws himself into his chair.

"Looks like you had a rough day."

"Uh-huh." (He's suspicious of your sympathy.)

"Pretty lousy, huh?"

Minimum words. *Long* pause. Just wait. He doesn't believe that you're really interested. Or he may suspect that you are trying for another interminable (to him) heart-to-heart in which all his deficiencies will be exposed in the guise of trying to help or work things out. You can show interest by your position and attitude. Drop in an open question or a multiple choice.

If he still refuses to talk, you have a couple of options. Forcing it is not one of them, not if you want open communication. You can get up and give him a sympathetic pat and go about your business, leaving him amazed. You can get him a cup of coffee or tea or whatever he likes. Rub his shoulders a little. Treat him as if he were a friend in need.

One of the things I found was that I had to watch myself like a hawk. If he says "The boss yelled at me for being late again," don't say "I told you you'd be late," although that thought may rise up in you, full of fury compounded by fear. It's not a paraphrase. Use your knowledge of him to try to come up with how he felt. At first this is difficult. You can't think of any feelings. How about anger, or resentment? "He made you look bad." "You hate being yelled at." Those are all ways of trying to paraphrase what he may have felt. He'll let you know if you got it right. One suggestion is that you don't say the word *feel*. People don't like to be told they feel things.

If he leaps up out of the chair and starts yelling "Yeah, the motherfucker started yelling at me in front of a customer. I'd like to kill the sonofabitch," you've hit it on the nose. You've just completed your first paraphrase, made your first step toward intimacy, understood how he feels. Don't blow it now with those old suggestions: *Don't swear; Don't be angry dear,* etc.

"You'd like to blow him away" or just "Fuck him" is a good paraphrase. If you don't talk like that, paraphrase as strongly as you can: "He's such a jerk!" As you both become more comfortable with the technique, you will learn to try to match the feeling, and match the intensity. If your vet's furious and you paraphrase, "He irritated you," you are going to irritate *him*. When you're both more used to it, you won't worry that he's going to go berserk, because you won't be the object. Letting off steam is just what he needs. He may launch into a half hour of angry statements you can paraphrase. Here's another place where you might lose it if, like me, you were brought up to think loud voices mean we've failed somehow, that no one else ever shouts. Shouting can be good for him and for you—if it's not aimed at each other.

If you feel as if you've heard it all before, try to concentrate on his underlying concern. Maybe it's lack of respect on the job. Maybe it is a personal thing with the boss. If you listen actively enough, and paraphrase, you will find out something. If he starts repeating, he doesn't feel you've understood the feeling or its intensity. Try harder. Match that and he will go on to something else. It can be scary, but it can also be exhilarating.

Saying "I'm sure your boss didn't mean it that way" isn't a paraphrase. You may be right, but it doesn't matter. By listening to his feelings, you are not engraving them in stone, not agreeing with them. You're letting him air them.

At this point don't offer solutions, either. Solutions stop communication. They destroy intimacy. They put you in the position of the problem solver, the expert, which leaves him the fuck-up. Intimacy occurs only between equals. Equals respect each other's ability to solve problems.

As I said, paraphrasing is self-correcting. If you said "He pissed you off" and he said "No. I'm not pissed," don't say "Well, you sound pissed." You're not trying to tell him what he feels, but trying to find out what he's thinking and feeling. You can try another paraphrase, like, "He doesn't treat you with respect." Or you can try the long pause or the "uh-huh," which is often very effective. Hard to do, I grant. But people who are really intimate have long, companionable silences, and if you keep talking you may miss what he might have said. It might be something you really wanted to hear, too.

I've found four books that give the essentials of paraphrasing (see Suggested Further Reading in the back of the book) besides *PET:*

Effectiveness Training for Women; Messages; Straight Talk; and *People Skills.* I recommend them all. Thomas Gordon's *PET* was a book designed for parents dealing with problems with their kids. It might be easier to learn to deal with another adult using *ETW, Messages, Straight Talk,* or *People Skills.* I had to sort of translate *PET,* but I also got the idea about active-listening body language from the section on paraphrasing kids before they can talk. *PET* and *ETW* also teach another important point: You can't solve someone else's problems. Both teach you how to identify who owns the problem and how to ask for your own needs to be met. The only problem with such books is that you expect to be able to apply the skills immediately, consistently, and perfectly, and believe me, you can't. Neither could I.

Slide back. Take your time. Mess it up. Paraphrasing is hard and takes practice. Bob used to get mad at me when I'd come up with a particularly awkward paraphrase, or parrot back what he'd just said. It is okay to make mistakes when you are learning a new skill. Maybe you can laugh about it together. I wouldn't try to paraphrase in every conversation either. If someone just wants information and you're paraphrasing the person's questions, things can get really funny or really frustrating.

A lot of people feel that they sound unnatural when they paraphrase, which may be true. I bet you felt kind of unnatural the first time you got up on your two-wheeler, too, but you got over that. Paraphrasing is certainly not the "I told you so" attitude we grew up with, but remember how you hated that? If no one in your family ever listened to anyone else, though, how could you have learned the skill? In my family conversations were opportunities to correct other people's thinking and pick holes in their enthusiasms. But it becomes the most natural thing in the world to listen to someone else with sympathy.

Giving advice is also natural, but it involves listening patiently until the moment arrives when the person has discharged all those feelings and can listen. I used to think of it as the "burble," like that bubble of air that comes up in a baby after you've patted and patted. I could see a change, hear it in Bob's voice, feel it in the air. The worry and pain would go and if I had something to say, he could hear again.

The other thing I learned from *PET*, and from putting those principles into practice, is that there is more than one solution to a problem. My solutions won't necessarily work for Bob, nor for you, but there are many from which to choose.

Veterans, like everyone else, need to come up with their own solutions. Good practice for living in this world. They often come up with the best ones for themselves. If they don't, it shows they need practice. It is okay to make mistakes!

Ask him, "What ideas do you have for solution?" But remember to listen to his ideas, not to knock holes in them. They aren't engraved in stone. Working out solutions takes time, and he has to start somewhere. Let him find out for himself if they are unrealistic and unworkable.

We can lay out some of the options if we like the sound of our own voices, but if you find yourself telling your vet what to do, you've blown it, which is okay. You'll do better next time.

Paraphrasing is not easy, and it's not something you can do every time you talk to someone. When you can't, don't. We all have our limits. When you have the energy, you will find it incredibly worthwhile to see your vet open up. If you blow it in the middle with some intimacy-destroying piece of advice, apologize and try again another time. I say, "Well, that was an entirely free piece of advice. No charge and sorry about that." Bob laughs, where before he'd have been furious.

Admitting mistakes makes other people trust us. They know we're not perfect anyhow. Admitting it goes a long way toward healing.

"Sometimes I get so mad at myself. I'm trying to learn to paraphrase and there I go, telling you what to do or think again. It kills me. Do you feel like that, too?"

"Yeah. I get real mad at myself when I yell at you after all the times I told myself I wouldn't take my problems out on you."

Boom! There you have it. Real communication, real imperfect people, and real love.

What if your vet attacks? "Yeah, you bitch. You always think you know everything."

Two choices:

Walk away saying "I'm sorry. I can't handle this right now." Make a date to discuss it later.

Detach yourself and paraphrase. Say to yourself, *It has nothing to do with me*. This is a feeling your vet is having right now. Anger is one of the most important feelings to pay attention to, because we all use it to cover up many, many of our other feelings. In *PET*, Dr. Gordon goes so far as to call it a secondary emotion, because in his opinion it is always evoked by another feeling that is suppressed as too painful. For instance, in my first example about myself (remember pretty?), I reacted with anger to cover up the hurt I felt at being compared and found wanting. It doesn't matter that Bob wasn't comparing. I was hurt so I covered up my vulnerability with anger.

What is this anger covering up?

"Yeah, you bitch. You always think you know everything."

Detaching and paraphrasing don't mean you are a bitch. It doesn't mean he always sees you as a bitch, either. By paraphrasing you're not accepting a permanent status as official bitch. But why does he feel that way? Paraphrase. Find out.

"I act like I'm always right."

"Damn right you do. Whenever you make a mistake, you forget it, but just let me get out of line once and I never live it down." At this point your instinct is to fight back, to explain. Try to paraphrase, instead.

"Must be hard for you that I only see your mistakes."

"Hard? *Hard* ain't the word for it. You don't know how it feels to be the ogre, to be always the one with the temper, the drinking problem, the crazy fucked-up Vietnam vet."

"It's tough for you."

"Yeah." But by this point, he's not calling you a bitch anymore and you've learned something important: *how he feels*. You've learned, if you read between the lines, that it hurts him to be in the wrong. (Maybe it's important for you always to be *right?*) You've learned that he cares about you, because why else would he care about letting you down? And he's learned that you do care, that you will listen, that he can get very angry and you'll still be there. You won't die, or leave him. You've been intimate for a few painful moments. They won't always be painful, though. As Bob says, "It's tough work getting things to laugh about later."

Not that the object is to accept a lot of verbal abuse. On the other hand, I used to yell a lot and so did Bob. If Bob called me an asshole in the bad old days, I called him a motherfucking asshole back. It kept up the level of chaos in our marriage, but it also kept me from going under. And it was the best I could do at the time.

I believe that it is better to be angry in the open than to hide it from yourself and others. There are too many sweet people in the world who never raise their voices or say naughty words, yet they're seething with rage that they can't face. It makes them hard to deal with, but you can spot them by their soft voices, sweet manners, physical ills, and complete conviction that they are right. They have different modes of verbal abuse, just as painful and effective, if not as colorful.

"Even someone like you . . ." they say sweetly, twisting the knife. "If you really . . . ," "Why don't you ever . . . ," "Everyone understands why you . . . ," and "Don't you even care . . ." are some of the other phrases "nice" people often use to flay their loved ones. If you use them, give your vet *The Gentle Art of Verbal Self-Defense*, by Suzette Eglin. If your vet never yells, yet you always feel in the wrong and wind up blowing up, get it for yourself. It's priceless.

If you've been in a verbally abusive relationship, it isn't going to end overnight. It takes time and work and practice to change patterns of relating to each other. When someone is yelling at you, you can do what Bob once did when a family member was screaming at him on the phone—he listened. Afterward he turned to me and said, "It's good practice in the realization that words are only sound waves." Now that's detachment.

If you can detach yourself in order to hear the feelings that your veteran can express only abusively ("You hurt me. I'm always wrong" is what the guy above couldn't say in so many words), you will learn a lot. He will get rid of a lot of anger that builds up because it is so unacceptable. Later on you can work on not verbally abusing each other. Or you can work on not being the first to verbally abuse, if that's what your priorities are. Everyone is different.

I found that paraphrasing Bob till the tension seemed to run out of him lowered our stress levels so he could hear me. It was still quite a long time before I could be authentic with him, even when he could have heard me, because, like many other wives—and not just those of Vietnam vets—I had conditioned myself over the years not to say what I wanted, not even to *know* what I wanted.

What can you do if you can't discuss anything with your vet, or you're just too chicken to start where it might turn scary? Practice paraphrasing with a friend or your kids. Believe me, it will help anyone's relationships. It's a skill beyond price. Then you can try it with your vet on little everyday things. Say "Had a bad day?" when he looks grumpy. Or: "He's not fair to you" when he complains about his boss. Even if this relationship fails, paraphrasing will help you with your next one, with your boss, with your kids, with your mom.

What does all this have to do with you if the vet in your family is your son or brother or father? Will listening to him help him or you? You'll have to look back over the history of your relationship. Do you come from a family where nothing important was ever discussed, even before your vet went to Vietnam? If so, learning to listen and paraphrase could be really painful and really enlightening.

You may have other burdens. Did you slam the door on your son or brother's confidences when he got back? Did you jump on him for his language? Call him a murderer or a whiner? If you made that mistake, a quiet apology can help you both. It may not transform your relationship right away, but to tell your vet you are sorry without trying to justify yourself can really mean a lot.

If, on the other hand, you've been enabling and rescuing your son or brother or father, paraphrasing can help you detach by letting him find and implement his own solutions. Because you listen, you still care, but you no longer try to control.

Saying to your vet "I never realized what you had been through" can mean a lot to any vet—brother, son, father, husband or lover. In its way, that's a paraphrase of his entire experiences and an invitation. Willingness to learn from our vets can be very healing for them, too. They are the experts on Vietnam. When they came home they found that this expertise was a handicap. Some buried it. Some lived with it every day. It is still there for all of them, and sharing it can give them a sense of appreciation and respect that was owed when they got back from Vietnam but never paid.

Discussing Vietnam, if it is done at all, should be done at your vet's pace.

The *need* that some of us feel to know our vets' actual experiences in Vietnam can often be a cover for the desire to judge whether they were bad enough to justify our vets' problems. That is a co-dependent trait we need to let go of. Many vets can't and won't talk about actual incidents, and we don't need to know them. Knowing how it felt to be there, and the feelings his memories bring back, may be all either of you can tolerate.

Changes in the world have really made it extra tough on the Vietnam vet. Not only did he face hell in Vietnam, but now at home he's expected to face all this womanly bullshit about feelings. If the woman who wants him to talk about his feelings says things like "Well, I was almost raped and I got over it. Why can't you get over Vietnam?" while he's seeing the pulped faces and shattered bodies of eighty-five people whose names are now on the Wall in Washington, he has to wonder if any woman could stand to hear about it. He has to wonder if he could stand to tell about it. How much pain does one person deserve in this life? And will you respect him in the morning if he cries?

You can't compare experiences and expect another person to trust you enough to reveal painful things about the past. The phrase "comparisons are odious" means they *stink*.

So if you feel that you need to know about Vietnam, remember that you are asking a lot. If what you like in your vet is his toughness and imperturbability, how will you feel if he gets upset? How will you feel if he's upset for a long time, like two or three years, while he goes through combat group therapy? Suppose he's not a "combat" veteran and is brushed off by the therapist or the guys in his group for being upset by one or two deaths when they have ten or twenty or a hundred to mourn. Will you brush him off, too, or can you put yourself in his place and feel the pain?

A friend in my ACOA group said that each person's pain is the worst pain he or she has ever faced. Some people whose stories make yours look painless are often so numbed, so inured to what they endured, that they may not feel any more pain than you do. That may be a helpful thought to some extent, say, if a person feels that the two deaths he saw shouldn't hurt compared to someone else's fifty, but I also think comparing pain stinks.

Many of these guys have never talked about Vietnam. Tom Comiskey wrote me: "I have never talked about Vietnam with any member of my family . . . It hurts, but it still feels good. You are the only person in twenty years to ask me about Vietnam. Thank you, Mrs. Mason." What can I say? Thank you, Mr. Comiskey, for talking to me.

"John *couldn't* talk about it," Carolynn Ketwig told me. "There were bits and pieces—till he started writing—short answers. He didn't want to discuss it . . . When he was writing, those were rocky times. He'd hand me the pages as he wrote. I found out about things. Why couldn't he tell me those things about Vietnam? . . . When he was writing, it was eating away at his insides. He was in pain . . . sweating, irritable, moody. I got scared and called the Vet Center. I was afraid he'd get violent. The guy at the Vet Center said, 'It sounds like he's handling it well. He has you to talk to.' I talked to the Vet Center guy for a half an hour. John wouldn't go."

I had to laugh when she said that. It was so much like Bob.

"On a TV program," Carolynn continued, "a nurse was talking about things like John—about Westy—our government supplies stolen—having to use enema tubing for IV's—I called her and talked with her and she offered to talk to John . . . After a few weeks he called her. He was shaky. Went to meet her. She sat back and listened to what he'd been through. It was the first time he'd actually talked to another person about Vietnam. The most important things in their lives occurred in Vietnam. John finally went to the Vet Center after his manuscript was in New York. Pat and Ed moved to Colorado so he had no other Vietnam vet to talk to. He found good counselors . . . I'm glad he wrote the book. He was holding it inside. I can't imagine having to carry that inside. He *couldn't* talk about it. They couldn't talk about it. It's not our fault. They didn't know how to deal with it."

Carolynn's advice: "Let them know you're willing to listen and wait."

Ray Scurfield said, "The vet's difficulties in sharing about his war experiences are at least partly due to the (mistaken) belief that 'only another vet can really understand what I'm going through.' However, if *you* have experienced profound rage, grief or loss, fear, numbing, horror, shock, violence, tragedy, betrayal, etc., then you *do* have an experience base from which some understanding is possible. The vet has probably had his war experience rejected or avoided by others. Don't let him do the same to you and your valid life experience. Point that out to him if it's happening."

But don't compare. Saying something like "Maybe I can understand some of it. I notice you get so angry, and when my ———— [fill in the blank], I just felt like killing everyone, the police, my roommates, everyone." There's a big difference between this and "I got over being almost raped. Why can't you get over Vietnam?"

Ray Scurfield also advised, "You must ask yourself, do you really want to know some of the dark secrets that trouble this vet so—can you really handle them if they are shared with you?" This is a heavy question and one that must be considered.

If you can't be nonjudgmental, don't ask for details; feelings are enough. Look at some flattened cat on the side of the road and think about hearing about your vet's best friend winding up like that, mangled meat.

If you decide you still do want to hear about Vietnam, and your vet is willing, talk about talking about it first. Warn him that if you cry it is not going to kill you or him. Agree on some kind of signal if one of you needs time out or needs to stop.

Decide if you are going to keep his experiences just between the two of you. Is it okay to share some of them? Be sure you know which ones, and with whom.

Having practiced paraphrasing in a nonjudgmental way for five years, I was able to listen actively to the veterans I interviewed for this book. Some of the stuff they told me was more than painful. For some of them it seemed to be a relief, others went home and had nightmares for weeks afterward. I also felt some of them could talk to me only because I wasn't going to be around after the interview.

The thing that struck me as we talked, and I paraphrased, and we went from the superficial to the fundamental, was their pain. Real anguish. Talking to me hurt and yet they were willing to do it to help their fellow vets. To me and to you as you read, it's all stories. We can visualize Vietnam, but it isn't imprinted in our mind's eye. When I said to a former officer, "You feel responsible," in response to his look of anguish as he told of one of his men losing his legs grading the side of a road to nowhere, I was able to understand what he feels, maybe even to feel it a bit. But I don't see the explosion as he does. I don't hear the screams. I don't wait by the guy for the medevac, blaming myself. I haven't lived with this for sixteen years. It still hurts him, and seeing it hurt, hurts me. If I hurt this much at the abstract knowledge of just a single tragedy, how does it feel to have seen it, done it, been it?

Be careful of your vet.

12

Changing

When we strike out against some old attitude or behavior, we have to realize we're in for the long haul. When the enemy is some aspect of ourselves, we are up against a formidable opponent that won't give up easily. We have to expect that there will be many battles—and not a few defeats. The winner is the one who perseveres longest.

Only continued effort wins the war; we can't lose if we don't quit.

Days of Healing, Days of Joy
August 16

Bob has changed a lot over the years from those worst PTSD days. I could not force changes on him, although I tried sometimes. The times I tried were painful and ugly and they hurt. When I was able to change myself in some small way, he usually followed my changes with ones of his own, after a while, and not always the ones I expected or wanted, but ones that fit him and that he's maintained.

People stop changing when they are dead. Put it another way: People are dead (emotionally) when they stop changing. We all know couples like that, or entire families from grandparents to grandkids, locked in their pain. "That's the way I am and I can't change" is the most hopeless statement in the English language. Bob and I used to say it all the time. "That's the way I am now and I can't change yet" is the first step to a much more life-affirming attitude.

Change is slow and hard for all of us. For people who feel they died in Vietnam and that everything since has just been empty,

360

change will be difficult and painful and slow. But your vet can change. That is the hope I hold out to you.

To you, dear vet, if you're reading over someone's shoulder, change is life, and maybe you can make your life more than bare survival. If you can't do it for yourself yet, nor yet for your partner or family, start to do it for those guys who never got the chance. If you are having PTSD symptoms, your life is probably painful, but treatment is available—even from the VA—if you look for it. Treatment takes time and it will hurt like hell, but you've survived a lot of pain already. Those of us who care about you would give anything to take that pain away, but we can't. You are the only one who can go through it, unfair as that is. To protect your wife and family from the serious problems they can or already have developed as co-survivors, you may want to go through it. Our hearts will be with you.

I know how painful unresolved traumatic issues can be. Bob and I used to live in hell. Both of us. He was in the hell of unrecognized, untreated PTSD and I was in the hell of trying to deal with it. All the problems were normal for someone with PTSD, but I thought they meant Bob was bad and I was worse, because I wasn't a good enough wife to make him good.

We still have problems. When Bob snarls at me at the end of the day, before I snarl back, I now try to examine the quality of the snarl, the quality of the day, what stresses are on him at the moment, and, way in the back of my mind (because it pisses him off if I mention it), what kind of stress he was undergoing in Vietnam at this specific time of year. Understanding what I do, I usually decide it's the PTSD making him snarl and don't take it personally. Sometimes it's a legitimate snarl, and then we argue about it together, using the rules for fighting discussed in Chapter 11, until we solve it. Sometimes we have a juvenile mud-slinging fight, too, but not usually, unless we're both under stress. I now consider this natural.

Relationships are a balance, and every change in one person brings about a change in the other. Whatever your problems may be, looking at them this way may inspire you to try changing yourself rather than your vet. If your vet is stuck, whether in silence or in driving you crazy with war stories or in any other behavior, changing your reaction will eventually change your interaction. It may not come out the way you plan or hope, but it may come out better. This applies whether your vet is husband or boyfriend, or son, brother, or father.

Ruth, a friend who is married to a Vietnam vet, wrote me:

> In learning to deal with PTSD, I found three things that were of great help. The most important was information on PTSD and what it was like to be in Vietnam. Many of Marc's actions and reactions became more understandable and reasonable with this knowledge. Talking to other women who had had similar experiences with their partners was also very helpful. I was amazed at how similar our experiences were. Last, but definitely not least, was Al-Anon. They taught me to accept Marc as he is and how my reactions make a difficult situation worse. They got me to "work on myself" rather than trying to "work on him."

Remember, when you jiggle the scale by making a change in yourself, it scares the other person, so he resists it, whatever it is, either overtly or by sabotage. In *The Dance of Anger*, psychologist Harriet Lerner called this the "change-back reaction." The classic example is the way everyone offers treats to a person who has lost weight. It isn't conscious, but it's sneaky and persistent. *You've changed*, your vet sighs as you head off to your Al-Anon or ACOA or vets' wives group.

My old reaction to this was either anger or irritation. Dr. Lerner's book showed me how to handle it more easily with a "broken record." You, too, can develop a broken record, one that you've thought out and practiced to yourself to see how it sounds. Your broken record should address two things: what needs in yourself you are meeting— how it helps *you* (he may be able to come up with ways it doesn't help him for you to go to your group, but very few men will come out and say I don't want you to do things that will help you feel better about yourself)—and the unexpressed question his behavior poses: *Do you still love me?* Your broken record should have a kind and concerned tone to it even if it's the eight hundredth time he's pulled this, and even if he's screaming, "Your fucking group means more to you than I do!"

"I'm sorry you feel that way, but my group helps me feel better about myself, and whether it's logical or not, it's something I need to do for myself. I'll miss you and I love you, but I have to do this for myself even if it is a mistake. I'll be back."

He may come up with logical arguments: "How can a group of wives of real drunks help you?" Sarcasm: "I'm glad you have time for this." Emotional blackmail: "I miss you so much. Stay home with me. If you go, I'll leave. I'll screw around. I'll go get drunk." He may hit below the belt: "You're a skinny, useless bitch. No wonder your father hated you."

Just keep cranking out the concerned, caring, kind broken record. All of these reactions are circumstantial evidence of how much he needs you and how scared he is of losing you. Although they can often tell you exactly how to take care *of* them, men are rarely able to express how much they need to be loved and wanted and cared *about*, because of the crippling burden of toughness, sexual stereotyping, and emotional numbing that is laid on them from childhood. PTSD reinforces this.

Your veteran will actually find changes in you really hard to understand. *Why do you want to rock the boat?* is what your vet's thinking. He may be voicing the slogans of every dysfunctional family in America: "We can handle this ourselves"; "Don't talk about our problems to strangers"; "We don't have any problems." He may do it more subtly: "I don't know why you go to group or read all those stupid boring books. Come on and watch TV with me"; "Come on, Mom (or sis or child), you're the only one I can talk to. Are you going to let me down, too?"

Keep using the broken-record approach. "I'm sorry you feel that way, dear, but I need to do this so I can feel good about myself. I love you, and I think this will help me." Say this over and over again in a loving, concerned tone, because, I repeat, you are trying to answer the unspoken question we all have when someone we love starts to change: "Will you still love me?" Most men, but especially guys with PTSD, are unlikely to ask that.

Remember that unspoken question when your vet is acting like a jerk: *Is he asking me if I will still love him if I change? Is he scared of losing me?* When you realize the answer to that is usually yes, it should lower your desire to "straighten him out" or "let him have it." You might even feel flattered. Let him be a jerk and love him anyhow. Just don't take it personally.

Back when Bob began having problems—1967 and 1968—I began hunting for ways to change and fix him. The funny thing is that everything that actually improved our relationship was something I changed in myself—not changes I made to please Bob, but things that worked for me. Things I tried to do to please Bob made me sick. I felt like throwing up when I tried to keep house like his mother, and I couldn't do it. Paying the bills made me furious and ill and rebellious. Trying to change ourselves to please someone else is a pointless exercise. Trying to get them to change to please us is, too.

Working on yourself is your best option. Even if your vet is a son whom you hardly ever see, or a brother you worry about from a distance, or a father you don't understand, you can become informed about Vietnam and what it was like to come home, and learn about the effects of trauma, including PTSD, co-dependence, and how the family system works.

Believing that Vietnam did not or should not have affected your family member is simply denial. If your interactions with your vet have been painful in the past, educating yourself about Vietnam and homecoming and PTSD will help you understand him better and perhaps help you interact with him with less pain on both sides. If you are married to or live with a vet, you may have been through all the experiences I've been through and more, or you may be suddenly faced with problems you never thought your vet would have. Either way, you can educate yourself now, and there is a lot of help and information out there that wasn't available in 1967.

Start with reading about Vietnam. I stick to personal narratives and novels written by vets, because I don't care what Kissinger or Nixon or Ky was doing. Histories can put things in perspective, but they don't change what happened to your vet over there, and they are often written as if napalming villages to save them was just fine and wouldn't *affect* anyone. Vietnam did not feel like history to him.

Information on PTSD is now widely available. Knowing the permanent effects trauma can have on rape and crime victims—knowing that even the families of crime victims, people not present at the event, can also develop PTSD symptoms, as recent research reveals—suddenly makes it obvious why someone who lived through a year of Vietnam has been permanently affected, too. And why we as co-survivors are affected.

Sha Linebaugh, who is married to a vet, said, "Education helped me the most. At the Vet Center they gave me a handout, and there it was in black and white, a statement of the problem. Yes. There is a problem with definable characteristics. It validated my feelings. Then I wanted to know, 'Can I expect him to get better, to change?' And they told me that it is definitely treatable."

This book provides more information than most mental-health professionals have about PTSD. Other things to read on PTSD are mentioned in the Appendix.

Many vets have some of the characteristics of PTSD, but not the diagnosable disorder. Reading about PTSD and understanding these normal reactions to stress will help both of you cope with them. According to one Vet Center counselor, sometimes just learning that their problems are a reaction to an identifiable catastrophic trauma can really help the vets. Identifying the traumatic incident lets them feel that if they can come to terms with that incident, they can come to peace with themselves. Often vets with PTSD do not relate it to Vietnam. They think they are crazy and just can't make it like everyone else can. They rebel at the thought that Vietnam could be affecting their lives. Remember the first stage of grief? Denial.

When these vets can identify what is uncomfortable and begin to work out possibilities for change, they begin to see themselves as survivors who can do something about it. As their co-survivors, we need to act, too, not just react. Acting is working on ourselves.

Beyond getting information on Vietnam and PTSD, you need to educate yourself on the family as a system so it will become clearer to you why changing has to involve you and may have to start with you. Learning the signs of dysfunction in the family—from indirect communication (telling your kid what bothers you so he'll tell Dad, telling your daughter, who then tells your son) to thinking that making mistakes is not okay—can help you see that your family system could work more smoothly and with less pain to family members. *Adult Children: The Secrets of Dysfunctional Families*, by John and Linda Friel, is the book for you if your family wasn't or isn't alcoholic, but perfectionism, workaholism, compulsive eating, or even compulsive TV watching or exercising is affecting the family. *The Dance of Anger*, by Harriet Lerner, talks about how to change family systems. *Families After Trauma* is aimed at the specific problems of families facing co-survivorship. Finally, I recommend reading T. Berry Brazleton's wonderful books on child-rearing and development if you have small kids (ask your librarian), and *Children of Trauma*, by Jane Middleton-Moz. These will help you begin to work on any dysfunctional child-rearing practices that may have evolved in your family.

Reading about co-dependence will make you aware of any dysfunctional patterns you may have developed that may need changing. Knowing about co-dependence will give you information to reinforce your new knowledge that you are not responsible for your vet's feelings or reactions. *Co-dependent No More*, by Melody Beattie, is the book I recommend.

When Bob was having a hard time with depression and "irritable heart" symptoms, we found great comfort in a book called *Feeling Good*, by David Burns, M.D. The book has a good self-test for detecting depression for people who have trouble identifying feelings. It also helped us think about and change the way we thought.

Feeling Good is about cognitive distortions. One of these, *all-or-nothing thinking*, is often very familiar to the families of troubled vets. *It's black or it's white. You're either for me or against me. There's one right way to do things. There is no middle ground. It's either right or it's wrong. He's good or he's bad. If I'm not perfect, I'm hopeless*. Bob and I thought like that most of the time.

Cognitive distortions include the tendency to *overgeneralize* so that we see any single "negative event as a never-ending pattern of defeat."

Distorted thinking gives us a *mental filter* that help us pick out all the negative details of anything and everything and dwell on them.

We disqualify the positive so that if we do anything good or something good happens it doesn't count.

Jumping to conclusions about how people will react combines both *mind reading* (knowing how other people feel without asking them—and it is usually negative) and the *fortune-teller error* (predicting bad outcomes and feeling as if they were "an already established fact").

We *magnify* (*catastrophize*) all the bad things and *minimize* all the good.

We *reason emotionally:* "I feel it; therefore, it must be true."

We try to motivate ourselves with *shoulds* and whip ourselves and everyone around who don't live up to our set of shoulds, oughts, and musts.

We *label:* "Instead of describing your error, you attach a negative label to yourself: 'I'm a *loser.*' " Or when someone else makes a mistake: "He's a bastard."

Finally, we *personalize:* We see ourselves as the cause of all our problems, when many of them, especially our vets' PTSD, have nothing to do with us. Our vets tend to see themselves as the cause of all our problems, too, when many derive from our upbringing or the ups and downs of everyday life. Stress invoked by that kind of guilt-provoking personalization helps keep us all stuck in unchanging, painful patterns of behavior.

Studying and understanding cognitive distortions can lift a great weight off you and your vet and your family. Doing automatic-thought/rational-response exercises from *Feeling Good* was very helpful to both Bob and me. Some PTSD groups use exercises from the book to work on feelings.

Cognitive distortions simply describe most of the ways co-dependent people think. Before we read *Feeling Good,* even though I could paraphrase and we were getting along better, my thinking was full of cognitive distortions. If I told Bob what to do rather than paraphrasing, I was no good (black-and-white thinking). I assumed he hated me (mind reading) *and* was just waiting for a good time to announce it and get a divorce (fortune-teller error). I was the worst wife in the world (magnification). When he got mad at me, I felt our whole marriage was a sham (reasoning emotionally). I made life really tough for myself, but I hadn't the slightest idea that I was thinking irrationally. I still struggle with the problem, but it's a lot easier now that I have a way to evaluate when my thinking is getting cockeyed.

Working on your thinking is important. "Do Optimists Live Longer?," an article by Nan Silver in the November 1986 issue of *American Health*, pointed out three characteristics of the way pessimists talk, which also happen to be cognitive distortions and characteristic of co-dependency:

• Pessimists overgeneralize. Their problems are eternal, stable, never-ending, and they are helpless: Life will always be lousy.

• Pessimists see problems everywhere (magnification and catastrophizing), ruining everything, "*global*," as the article stated, "rather than specific."

• Third, pessimists personalize problems by thinking they caused them.

The article went on to report that a study by Seligman, Peterson, and Vaillant, of ninety-nine Harvard veterans, concluded: "If you always go around thinking, 'It's my fault, it's going to last forever, and it's going to undermine everything I do,' then when you do run into further bad events, you become at risk for poor health."

Teaching ourselves that *sometimes* we are imperfect, and that the causes for things going wrong can be *external* and no one's fault, can be good for our health, our families, and our vets.

Changing helps you feel better about yourself just because you are taking control of your life. You are not helpless anymore. You don't just react to what happens to you like a helpless bit of fluff on the winds of life. You act!

Taking the focus off the veteran and his problems lets him have space to decide to work on himself. Admitting you have a problem, too, puts you in the same boat, and people in the same boat often can support each other. By taking pressure off your vet, his anxiety level will go down. Changing yourself sets a good example, especially if you don't rub it in! Finally, changing yourself will change the balance of your relationship, and your vet will find himself facing some sort of choice about changing, too.

As you begin to let go, you will also be able to feel better about your vet because he is no longer a reflection on you. He is a unique person who has been through a lot and you can respect him for that. His behavior is his own responsibility.

Mothers and siblings and friends and children of vets can feel just as helpless and guilty over their vets' problems as their wives and lovers. Changes they make in themselves—particularly in education about why their vet has been affected, and in learning new skills for interacting with their vet—will help them interact more effectively with everyone in their lives, a double bonus.

Another thing I learned to let go of was the idea that if I just tried harder, everything would be fine.

We have all been taught to "try harder" to improve our performance as wife, girlfriend, mother, sister, daughter. Try harder and then our men will be okay. We've already covered why this can't work, why we can't cure PTSD (or alcoholism or workaholism), but several other factors make effort alone ineffective.

For one thing, repeating a pattern that does not work will never make it work. Improvement comes only from a change in the pattern. If you can see how failure is often programmed into your vet's repetitive problems, you can deduce that your own patterns and reactions may be part of the problems, too. It's insane to expect different results from the same actions.

Instead of trying harder, deciding to change your patterns of relating means learning new skills and opening up new possibilities. You learn to distinguish between various patterns of action, and you learn to appreciate small differences and details you might never have noticed before. Figuring out which small changes might work for you, and how to implement them in your daily life without trying to transform yourself and your family into a new pattern of perfection overnight, can become a joyful exploration instead of co-dependent drudgery. Knowing you have choices and choosing which small actions to take will empower you and give you hope.

Forcing yourself to try harder as you repeat old patterns stresses you out, and stress destroys your ability to notice small changes (and all changes start out small). You can't learn from things you don't notice! If your vet makes a small change, and you're wrapped up in the stress of trying harder, you won't be able to see it and let him know you like it. Your vet also may not notice or may discount small changes in you because his stress level is high, so don't be surprised if you don't make much of an impression at first.

"Trying harder" also implies that there is only one right way to do things, and when you can't do them that way, you define yourself as a failure. Stuck in that old system again.

Finally, the habitual responses that grow from "just trying harder" eventually become compulsive and all alternatives are lost. Since our vets, especially ones with PTSD, face greater problems in beginning the process of change, we may be more able and more willing to lead the way.

If we don't change, the family won't change; family roles become rigid, family rules become engraved in stone, and the next generation suffers.

Reading this book shows you are already motivated to change. You recognize you have a problem—even if you think the problem is your vet—and are willing to learn. If you came to this book determined to find out what happened in Vietnam and how that affected your vet and how to fix him, the process of change is going to be very much like the process of grief discussed in the PTSD chapter.

I'm assuming that you are at least partway through the denial stage, since you recognize a problem and know it has something to do with Vietnam. If you still feel that the problem has nothing to do with you, here are some questions to ponder. You might want to write out your answers.

Key issues of people who have been affected by the dysfunction of a member of the family include:

Control Issues

- Do you feel tense and anxious when you don't like what your family members are doing? Do you want to talk, reason, explain, and straighten them out? Fix them? Do you want them to do it your way?
- Do you need to know where they are and what they are doing all the time?
- Do you check up on them?
- Do you want to keep them from making mistakes?
- Do you try to provide a perfect environment of positive experiences for your family?
- Do you try to provide negative experiences to "toughen them up"?
- Do you want them to think the way you do, like what you like,

hate what you hate, feel what you feel? Do they have to do things your way?
• Do you feel you must do everything and do it perfectly?

If you answered *yes* to some of these questions, one of your issues is control: of yourself, of others, of what you and they experience, and of your environment.

Issues of Responsibility

• If things go wrong for your family, do you feel it is your fault?
• If things go right, do you know it is because they listened to you?
• Do you feel that you can make things go right if people would just listen to you?
• Do you feel that you just aren't the responsible type? Or that you are fine but your family is really messed up and it has nothing to do with you?

Taking too much or too little responsibility is another issue for people in a denial stage or who need to change.

Issues of Trust

• Do you trust anyone?
• Do you trust people until they inevitably let you down (which is not trust—it's gullibility)?
• Do you trust your own feelings, or do you need to find out if other people have the same reactions?
• Do you think you always know what's right or best?
• Do you think you never know what's right or best?

Having too much or too little trust in ourselves, in others, or in our own judgment is an indication that working to change ourselves would be helpful to our families.

Avoidance of Feelings
List ten feelings you've had in the past twenty-four hours and the specific situations that caused them.

- Do you habitually say, "I'll think or worry about that tomorrow?"
- Do you feel you don't have time for feelings?
- Do you keep a stiff upper lip, button up your feelings, stifle them? Do you cover them with explosions of rage or sulking?
- Are you too ladylike to express negative emotions? Or too burnt-out to express hope?
- Do you have numerous aches and pains, including but not limited to headaches, stiff neck, backaches, and stomachaches?

These are ways of avoiding feelings that indicate that a change in you will be healthier for you and your entire family.

Personal Needs

- What are your personal needs right now?
- Do you have a plan for getting them met?
- Does your plan depend on getting other people to do things they have never done before, or is it realistically based on small steps you can take yourself?

If you can't list some needs, or never get them met, or make plans for changes that depend on other people, these are signs that working on yourself will help you and your family.

Letting go of denial that your vet's problems could have affected you (Does that sound familiar? Sort of like his saying, "Vietnam didn't affect me!") and working on yourself are hard and necessary tasks that will free your vet to work on his problems. Unfortunately, he may choose not to work on his problems, even to find himself another caretaker. He may be freed to grow, but choose not to. This is a very real and painful possibility, but one you can temper by changing yourself with a loving heart and by encouraging him to do the same without demanding changes or giving deadlines. Waiting for someone else to change when we are struggling to change ourselves can be absolutely maddening. It would be a lot easier if it worked out evenly.

If you start changing it's probably going to be at least six months before your vet even notices anything positive about it, much less becomes aware of the space you are giving him. The way I look at it, we have the rest of our lives to grow and change together, so I'm in no hurry.

As I've said twice before, not taking your vet's problems personally—thinking they're your fault or that you can cure them—is the first step. If you don't take it, all the other ones are infinitely more painful. But who am I to talk? I did it backward and you can, too, if you want.

When we admit we are powerless over the effects of Vietnam in our lives, it's similar to taking the First Step in the recovery programs of AA, NA, Al-Anon, or Adult Children. A great load is lifted off your shoulders. Maybe it is a load of guilt because your vet has been telling you for years that if you were a better wife, he wouldn't have any problems. If you've spent years trying to protect him from the results of his actions, letting go can be such a relief. If you've been looking for a cure for him, knowing that part is up to him can also be a relief. You don't have to push, nag, or pressure him to get therapy.

One of the sad parts about changing is that it is painful. A lot of grief is involved when we give up our caretaker roles, our certainty that we can find solutions for others, or that we already know what is right for everyone and everything in our lives, our surety, in effect, of our place in the universe. Think how this parallels the experience of our vets when they got to Vietnam and saw that saving Vietnam essentially seemed to involve destroying it, and that the people we were there to save didn't want us there. It wasn't exactly what they were brought up to believe would be their role as American fighting men. Many of them are still mourning this loss.

It says, in the pamphlet *Free to Care*, "The end of the anxious caretaking relationship is the end of this very important part of the lives of concerned persons. It is the death of a certain kind of relationship, a loss . . . Giving up the old role, it is important to realize, will necessarily involve a great deal of sadness." This is true whether you are wife or girlfriend, or mother, father, brother, sister, or daughter or son. If you've been taking responsibility for your vet, stopping will be hard and painful for you both. That's why you have to do it slowly, very slowly, one little step at a time.

"Why face the pain?," you may be asking. The only way out is through this pain—that's why. Change doesn't suddenly happen one bright April morning when you and your vet wake up transformed into Cinderella and Prince Charming. It happens through slow, painful everyday steps. It also happens in moments of deep happiness, when it suddenly sinks in that you are getting along better, that some of the pain is gone, that you've had three good days in a row, and he just hugged you for no special reason!

Thinking about the pain we face in changing is really important. Here are a few things to consider:

• List the feelings you have at the idea that you cannot cure your vet (helplessness, pain, sadness, anger, disbelief, grief, etc.).
• List how the possibility that you may lose him if you get better and he doesn't makes you feel.
• List the roles you play in your vet's life that you may have to give up; the predictable patterns you may miss even if you hate them.
• List the feelings about your roles—good and bad—that you will lose when you let go of those roles (I'm nice; I put up with so much; I'm such a good sport; etc. Or: I'm such a jerk to put up with him; There must be something wrong with me or he wouldn't treat me like this; This is what I deserve; etc.).
• List the roles your vet may be playing in your life that you may have to give up: scapegoat; macho man; someone to lecture to and straighten out; someone to pick on, someone more screwed up than you are.

These are the things you will be mourning if you decide to concentrate on becoming more healthy yourself.

You'll also have to mourn the time you've "wasted" doing the best you could at the time. You may be really angry at yourself because you "should have known" things that even the psychiatric community didn't know till last year. Let yourself feel what you feel. The pain means you need to learn something. Feel it, learn what it has to tell you—that you are human and feel human emotions and make mistakes and care deeply for your vet—and it will help you grow.

You may be very angry at first that *you* are the one who has to change. Remember, men are conditioned from childhood not to concentrate on relationships and interdependency but rather to compete and be independent. They haven't got the skills, the vocabulary, the practice, the habits of a lifetime of caring for other people's emotional well-being that we have. They're out of practice. Vietnam vets have an extra burden of numbness, impacted grief, and fear of intimacy laid on them by the conditions of war. After thirty or forty years of ignoring feelings and discounting their importance, the habit is hard to break.

People are always doing the best they can, and if you don't feel that your vet cares because he can't express it, or because he's honed his fighting skills, think about the terrible things you can hear coming out of youur mouth when you are hurting and afraid he doesn't love you. I can remember screaming at the top of my lungs that I was getting a divorce and I hated Bob and he was an asshole, when all I wanted was for him to love me. If you're the quiet type, think of all those times you've politely asked him to control his language, body posture, voice level, subject of discussion—in effect, told him everything about him was unacceptable to you and defective. Think how that must hurt.

Remember that anger is the second stage of grief. It's normal. "What have I done to deserve this?" is one of the questions many women ask themselves or their friends and family. The answer is nothing. It has nothing to do with you.

In their anger, many women believe that changing the man himself (making him shape up) or exchanging him for another man will fix everything, but experience and research have shown that people who get into one difficult relationship will get into another one unless they work on themselves first. If you don't believe this, read *Women Who Love Too Much* and *Letters from Women Who Love Too Much*, by Robin Norwood.

Use your anger to move you to the next question: "How can I take better care of myself?" The answer to that lies in changing yourself one step at a time, so you don't let the same things happen to you anymore.

Symptoms of the anger stage can include filing for divorce, kicking the vet out, running away, nagging, screaming, bitching, whining, telling people the truth about themselves, or stuffing endless grinding resentment. If you are burning dinner a lot lately, being sarcastic, cynical, flippant, habitually late, or overly polite, overeating, never eating, sighing frequently, having trouble sleeping, feeling really apathetic, clenching your jaw or tensing another part of your body, or are chronically depressed, these are some of the signs of hidden anger. Learn to check your body for signals—some people blush when they are upset, some breathe faster, some tap or drum their fingers, some people's voices rise, some yawn. If you need help with this, ask your family how they know you are getting upset.

Being unaware of hidden anger does a lot of damage to us and to our relationships. Because it doesn't just go away. We wind up expressing the anger we feel in inappropriate ways that hurt us and our families.

Recognizing our own anger, and realizing that anger is an appropriate emotion for us, is an important step. When you feel angry, ask yourself what you are feeling helpless about. If it's about the same old thing in relationship to your vet, take that anger and use it not to lash your vet or yourself, but to give you the energy to go out and buy *Co-dependent No More*, or to go to a vets' wives' group or Al-Anon or ACOA.

As mentioned earlier, in *PET*, Dr. Thomas Gordon said anger is a secondary emotion that usually covers another that is too painful or too scary to acknowledge consciously. That's why we're mad when our vets (or our kids) get home late and didn't call. We're afraid they are dead so we yell at them—and somehow expect them to read it as a sign of love! Working on recognizing the feelings under our anger is hard and painful: We may find scary stuff like fear of abandonment, fear of being engulfed by the other person, fear of what we might do if we did let go and get really angry.

Feeling angry is okay, but most of us have seen anger used inappropriately all our lives—screaming, distorted faces; physical violence; verbal razor blades slashing people's self-esteem to ribbons—so we don't know how to express it appropriately. We have no role models. Neither do our vets. Getting smashed or smashing things is not an appropriate way to deal with anger. Neither is verbal aggression.

Safe anger expression is discussed in a number of books about assertiveness and anger listed in the back of this book. One exercise that has always helped me is to write down the reasons why I am angry, then to list possible actions, and then to list why I should or shouldn't do them. This can get quite funny. "Reasons why I shouldn't punch Jack in the face when he finally gets here: It will hurt my hand. It won't make him want to come back. The satisfaction will be short-lived, not to say fleeting. It won't change his lateness." That's from a recent list I drew up. By the time I was done, I was in a better mood and able to tell Jack, kindly but firmly, "I was disappointed that you didn't get here when you said you would, because I had planned my day around your arrival and it messed up my plans." That is called a confrontive I-message in *Effectiveness Training for Women*, by Linda Adams.

The confrontive I-message is one of the safest ways to express anger, and it can help you identify the feelings under your anger as you get used to using it. There are three parts to a confrontive I-message: the specific feeling, the specific event that caused it, and the way it affected you.

How does this work? When someone yells at us, we may say, "You always yell at me, you jerk."

Think out how to make your feeling into a truthful I-statement—something like this: "I was angry, but it was really because it hurts so much when someone I love and who is supposed to love me yells at me and makes me afraid." Reframe it into an I-statement: "I am angry [feeling] when your voice gets loud and scary [specific event, specific details] because I become afraid of you [specific effect]." This is not a comfortable thing for any person to hear. For a stressed-out vet, it may increase his stress until he realizes that you'd just like him to find an alternative to scaring the shit out of you.

Confrontive I-messages, like counting to ten, give you a breather and help calm you down, while giving appropriate attention and respect to your feelings. Sometimes a confrontive I-message will result in an immediate and lasting change in behavior, but usually it has to become part of the broken-record repertory—you didn't know you'd be starting a broken-record collection to deal with your vet, did you?—before a stressed-out person like your vet can even notice what you are saying. When your vet does notice, he will probably be uncomfortable that he is causing you distress. Let him be. Don't give him directions; let him work through his discomfort to find his own way of meeting your needs. Neither of you needs to be yelled at.

PET mentions that one of the problems with I-messages is that they get ignored at first because "nobody likes to learn that his behavior is interfering with the needs of another." Since change is a slow process anyhow, that isn't really a big problem. The advantage of an I-message is that it's non-blaming, so eventually the person you are trying to get through to will hear it. "I miss our evenings out because I love you and going out together made me feel special to you" is a lot easier to hear than "You never take me out. You're no fun. You're a cheapskate. You're not the same person I married."

I-messages have a lot of other advantages for us as co-dependent co-survivors. They help us realize our own needs are legitimate, which is important if we've been putting our needs after those of our vets. They make us analyze our own feelings, an important step for people who find it easier to analyze their loved ones' defects. I-messages make us pay attention to what is under all that anger, the feelings we need to communicate for our own mental health, the feelings our vets need to hear so that they can start trying to grow and meet our needs.

You-messages and anger they already know how to deal with: They are experts at blocking and ignoring what we yell, experts at making us feel like emotional idiots, and experts at returning anger with interest and scaring the shit out of us.

I-messages are also truth-oriented: instead of saying "You always tell the same old bullshit stories," when you say "I'm too tired to listen" or "I don't enjoy listening to that story again," you are telling your vet the only thing you really know—what is inside of you. This can make your vet very uncomfortable. But as Dr. Gordon pointed out in *PET*, kids "can be responsive and responsible, if only grown-ups take a moment to level with them." If kids are often not aware of the effect their actions have on other people, how much more true may this be of a person wrapped in the pain of PTSD?

I-messages also place the responsibility *where it actually is*— within your vet (or your kids or your mom)—to modify this behavior. Letting your vet modify his behavior is much more healthy than trying to control his behavior by advising, whining, or blowing up. I-messages trust the hearer to find a solution; difficult for us co-dependents but absolutely vital if we are to get well ourselves. This can also be an empowering experience for your vet, and he may come up with a really neat solution.

I-messages teach honest identification and acceptance of feelings by example; not *you made me give up*, but *I feel so hopeless when we have these fights that it is hard to have faith that things will come out right between us*. This is an important example to set for men who have stuffed all feeling away as dangerous. I-messages show that feelings like hopelessness are part of the range of emotions that people can tolerate and live with and express. I-messages sometimes bring I-messages in return, and with your active listening skills, you may learn something of value from the exchange.

We can also use internal I-messages to remind us of the consequences of our own actions: "When I do too much, I get too tired, and the consequences for myself and my family are that I get cranky and I can't cope and I blow up"; Or: "When I know it all, I am perceived as boring and bitchy, and nobody listens to me anyhow."

Confrontive I-statements can lead to fights. Fights are a normal part of relationships, but many of us know only ugly, painful ways of fighting. Vet Centers teach the rules of fighting fairly, derived from *The Intimate Enemy*, which I mentioned in the last chapter. Recently I was telling someone about those rules and a friend laughed and said, "Yeah, but who uses them?" WE DO. The only way they will help your relationship is if you use them. If they don't work the first time, could you ride a bike the first time you tried? Wasn't the joy in trying and trying and finally succeeding?

One way to get in touch with your anger is to write down specific things your vet does that push your buttons, and how you usually react. Then write up some alternative ways of reacting that you could try.

If you think of an alternative and immediately say to yourself, "That wouldn't work because then he'll just—"; "Oh, I already tried that, and it didn't work"; or, "Yes, but . . ." followed by the reasons it won't work for you, you are stuck. People who are under a lot of stress often become very stuck, and that's normal. The alternatives you may come up with may not have worked in the past because you tried them under pressure—as we all have, hoping for an instant solution to all our vet's problems—or because you stopped trying the alternative because you didn't get immediate results—and you won't—or because you are not aware of how you come off to your vet or to other people. People who are feeling burdened find it hard to be aware of how they come across to other people. When they think they are being loving and reasonable, they often appear to others as anxious, angry, and blocked. You can check on this by taping yourself and listening to the tape, or asking a friend, or just listening to yourself as you talk. Are you blaming everyone around you, trying to get others to see "the truth" or "straighten them out"? Those are often signs of being stuck.

When you find your anger, especially if you were raised never to be angry, you can be frightened by just how angry you are. Accept this as part of a healing grief process. Bitch and moan and scream and rage, but not to *him*. When you have both gotten to a stage where you are communicating better and not fighting to win, use I-statements. When you have progressed from "You made me mad" to "I am angry," which may take years, you will know that you are changing and healing.

Letting go and learning new reactions is a hard, slow business. We have to remind ourselves that changes come slowly, step by step, one day at a time. Relax and know that you have the rest of your life to do this. And try alternative behaviors again and again: active listening, I-messages, letting go, slogans (see below), and broken records.

Another great alternative behavior, especially if your vet treats you to displays of rage or other inappropriate behavior, is to use a slogan. Repeat to yourself: "It has nothing to do with me. It has nothing to do with me." And don't rise to the bait. This puts the responsibility for his behavior where it belongs—within him. When you have control, say quietly, "Do you think it helps me when you ——— (fill in the blank)?" If this upsets him, let him be upset. Don't justify it, or explain it, or talk it into the ground. Repeat the questions quietly if you have to. Let him think about it. You may have to repeat this question a hundred times on a hundred different occasions (another addition to your broken-record collection), or you may have to ask it only once.

Other slogans that have been especially helpful to me are: "One day at a time," "Easy does it," and "What other people think of me is none of my business." My constant companions are a book of meditations that fits into my pocketbook, Liane Cordes's *The Reflecting Pond* (which is arranged by subject rather than having a reading for each day) and a tiny pamphlet called *Living "Easy Does It,"* both published by Hazelden. I also try to read a meditation every morning, currently either OA's *For Today,* or *Days of Healing, Days of Joy,* or *Reflections of the Light,* by Shakti Gawain, and say the serenity prayer whenever I think of it. Each of these helps me let go of the things I need to let go of for my own recovery, including the desire to bargain.

The next stage in the process of grief is the bargaining stage: "If he goes to the VA/Vet Center, I'll get help, too." This is an understandable effort to keep some feeling of control over what is going on, and you have to go through it. Sometimes it actually works and you get your vet to go to a place where he does receive good help.

After I gave up pushing books on him, Bob read *Don't Say Yes When You Want to Say No,* which helped him deal with other people. It may seem strange that a Vietnam vet could benefit from an assertiveness-training book, but Vietnam did not teach our vets assertion. It taught them *aggression.* That's why vets go from being fine to a rage, with no stages in between. The military didn't teach them how to make their needs known, but to have no needs. The military did not want to know their needs; it wanted them to kill whomever it said, whenever it said, however it said.

If you want to help your vet re-learn his feelings and needs, you have to know your own. No more "Oh, no, I don't mind" when you do. It's a risk, saying what you want. I still have trouble with it. Maybe you won't get it—a painful alternative you can lighten with the phrase "Experience is what you get when you don't get what you want." If neither of you is able to say what you want until you're so desperate that the other person has to say yes to avoid an ugly scene, the cure for this is to ask *more often.* Make a plan and talk it over. Try to ask for help more often and long before you are desperate. Practice asking often. Practice getting helped. Practice getting turned down. Practice turning your partner down in a kind and considerate way. Reverse the roles. Listen to each other. As you become used to doing this, you'll get to the point where you can hear each other's needs and often meet them—and give each other a break when the answer is "I can't right now," instead of playing "He never helps/she always nags."

When you are learning to change, don't discount your vet as a source. Always over fights long before I was, Bob taught me not to hold grudges. He even taught me to understand that everyone had fights, and it didn't mean it was all over between us whenever we had a big fight. It was really hard for me to learn that from him because, the way I saw it, Bob had the problems and I was fine. So if he thought our fights were normal, and I thought they were the end of the world, I must be right, right?

Bob also taught me to be less materialistic. Remember, though, that sometimes money and possessions are the emotional equivalent of love. If you're not getting love on a spiritual and emotional level because your vet can't show it, you may be very attached to possessions, and there is no reason not to be. We have to have something. Tell him that. "I need these things because I don't feel like you are there for me, and I have to have something." I often felt that my books and my ridiculous eight-legged Victorian table were the only things I had when I didn't have the certainty that Bob would be there for me.

Bob made some big changes in himself. He began hugging me. When I asked him about it one day in the course of thanking him for doing it (the principle behind that was trying to give good feedback because I liked the hugs), he said, "I am hugging you because I know you like it. It doesn't come naturally to me so I'm making a conscious effort to remember to do it. I like it, too. And you deserve it." That felt so good! He also began washing the dishes. After forty-four days of cooking and cleaning up on the boat, he didn't think one person should have to do both and work, too. It was really nice, and I hadn't *made* it happen.

If your vet decides to get help, it's doubly important to get help yourself, because if he comes back to the same family system, he may fall back into the same old patterns. Or he may move on to find someone with healthier patterns.

Bargaining never brought about changes in Bob. Long conversations in which we "worked out" our positions on stuff never helped us. They just pissed Bob off and encouraged my efforts at control, though lots of books recommend negotiation, so it must work for some people. I think actions speak louder than words. An example? As a remnant from the days when I took responsibility for everything, Bob always asks me where his tools are. It suddenly occurred to me that I can put my hand on every implement in the kitchen. I suppose we could have sat down and negotiated a deal whereby Bob would agree to take care of his tools and put them away and also agree that he wouldn't ask me where his things were before he looked for them, but what I did was simply start to say, "I don't know." If he's looked for half an hour and can't find something, I will help look because I have a knack for finding things, and he is a friend of mine whom I like to help out when he needs it. What this method does is leave out all the nagging (or negotiating, depending on your point of view).

Talking it over and deciding on a compromise solution works for us in some areas, such as picking a movie, but in changing deep-seated, habitual behaviors, talk is talk and doing is doing.

Feeling responsible for everything is no longer something I want to do. I used to want to because it gave me importance. I was the one who knew where everything was and I could find anything. Now that I don't feel like such a failure for not "curing" Bob, I don't need that importance anymore.

Maybe part of your recovery will be giving up similar responsibilities. Remember our slogan: It has nothing to do with me! Another slogan I use is: I don't have to straighten everything out. A third is: I don't have to do it, and if I don't do it and it doesn't get done, so what!

When you give up bargaining, you're going to feel really sad. I remember the exact moment in 1983 when I realized that nothing I ever did would change what had happened to Bob in Vietnam. It just about killed me, because I had always operated on the assumption that there was something I could do to fix it. I realized that he would never *get better*, that what he'd endured in Vietnam had left wounds that wouldn't heal, scars that would not go away. It sounds so dumb, but I wept, and I wept bitterly. Somehow, I had always been searching for the cure, and the realization that there wasn't one hit me hard. Real hard. I love him a lot, and I would have liked to be able to present him with a world unshadowed by the screams of dying men and the smell of those who died days ago, the remembered fear of swooping into a hot LZ in a huge, slow gaggle of helicopters, the nights alone in the dark.

I can't.

As I write, I still feel a terrible sense of grief and I assume this is similar to the grief vets feel when they remember the guys who died and the people who lost their homes or were maimed because of us. Or the grief many of them feel, without perhaps labeling it grief, when they contrast the homecoming they got with the homecoming they expected. When I felt that dreadful sense of loss, I didn't know what recovery was or that I was a co-dependent co-survivor. ACOA hadn't even been founded yet, and I had never read the Twelve Steps—which I knew I didn't need in any case, because they were for drunks—but I had just taken the First Step: admitted that I was powerless over the effects of Vietnam in my life and that my life had become unmanageable.

Most people have to be in a lot of pain before they take this step, and the step itself brings a lot of pain. Helplessness is not admired in America. Helplessness is not an easy position to take. It is reality, though.

The serenity prayer helps me: Grant me the serenity to accept the things I cannot change (what happened to Bob in Vietnam, PTSD, and how he reacts to stress), the courage to change the things I can (how I react to his reactions, as well as certain aspects of myself), and the wisdom to know the difference.

Bob still has bad days when he has feelings of impending doom, or deep depressions, or *irritable heart* symptoms. Because my stress level is lower, I can now detect that, on days when he is cold or irritable or acts like an asshole, he's having a bad day. He absolutely cannot tell me, cannot (yet) say the words "I am having a bad day." If I ask him, he can answer "Yes." Sometimes we talk, and if I listen actively it helps. Sometimes not. I don't take it personally if it doesn't. If he calls me stupid or an idiot, I tell him, "I'm willing to talk or listen, but I won't let you talk to me that way." On the second *stupid*, I'm out of the room. Maybe once a year now he forgets, which isn't bad for someone who used to fight to win.

If you join me in deciding to work on yourself instead of trying to fix your vet, we will have to grieve over the loss of that clear focus in our lives. We have to grieve for the loss of the ideas and ideals of relationships with which we grew up. We have to let go of the idea that "if I'm a good enough wife, he'll be okay." We have to give up the idea that we can control what happens to us by being good. And we have to turn our focus from outside to within ourselves.

We can't control how we feel, but we can learn to let some feelings fill us up and rush through us without reacting as we have in the past. With enough practice, we can let them do so without influencing our behavior, so that if in the past something our vet said would have had us shouting defensively, eventually we come to a point where we can say quietly, "How do you think it helps me when you say that?" Or even: "What an interesting idea!"

At this stage, crying is an emotional, biological, and physiological necessity. So is sharing your grief with a friend or a group that will *let you grieve*. As you examine yourself and your life, you will need the ability to be sad and to mourn the failures of the past, the problems of the present, and your fears about the future. Crying will help you let those things go and get on with your life. You may feel angry again. If you look beneath your anger, you will find feelings of loss and fear and pain that are really hard to face. Face them and cry your way through and you will be free of them for a while. When they come back, you'll know how to free yourself of them for another while. You'll also be more confident of your ability to survive pain.

I learned how to repress pain when Bob was in Vietnam. When he went, I tried to keep a stiff upper lip, and the closest I've ever been able to come to that still-buried pain was starting to scream one day at the shrink. I know why vets don't want to face their pain. I don't, either, and I have no deaths to mourn.

Accepting the death of the caretaker role and beginning to work on ourselves is a giant step for most of us, and yet it is only the beginning. This idea can be really daunting. If your mindset is like mine was, you instantly start trying to change, perfectly and completely. Well, that just isn't possible, no matter what fairy tales you were raised with. Some of my family fairy tales were: If it's worth doing, it's worth doing well; if you can't do something right, don't do anything at all; a stitch in time saves nine. All of them implied (quite incorrectly) that everyone else had no trouble doing everything right. People act that way all the time. That's just what it is, too—an act.

My current ideas run more along the lines of: If it's worth doing, it's worth doing badly: if I can't do it right, I'll do it the best I can; a stitch in time may save nine, but I'd just as soon do the nine when I have the time as try to force myself to do one stitch when I don't. I have the rest of my life to work on my recovery. I'll be in recovery for the rest of my life, recovering, not recovered. I'll go on working on me and trying to change what I don't like in myself. I'll make tiny changes, baby steps.

Changing is a process. I'm not trying to become changed, done, finished, perfect, dead. I think of my life as a long, slow journey, one step at a time, in which the pleasure will often come from the steps themselves, from the sunlight on the leaves, from a smile, a book, a warm moment with Bob. Life is a process, and it's not over till you're over. When I stop, I'll be dead.

Recovery, like life itself, is a process that I am planning to enjoy. I know it will be painful at times, but I've survived pain before. Nothing could be worse than when Bob went to Vietnam. Nothing could be worse than when he didn't seem to love me anymore and when I couldn't do anything right. Nothing could be worse than when he went to jail. Nothing could be worse than believing I had the power to fix him but just wasn't a good enough wife or person to do it.

If your vet seems stuck in time, you can see how painful it is for him. Your little steps can help you out of the co-dependent co-survivor trap, and blaze a trail for him.

So what are some good ways to change ourselves?

Write down something specific you want to change.

If your major issue is your vet's depressions, you'll probably write: "I want him to be less depressed." Nothing you do will fix his depressions, but with your new angle of vision, maybe you could reframe it. In *PET* and *EWT* it is called figuring out who owns the problem. You can't solve problems that your vet owns.

Reframe. Maybe you'll write: "I want to change so that when he is depressed, I don't feel responsible for the depression and for fixing it. This will let me be supportive without the guilt I now feel from assuming it's my fault he's depressed."

What can you do today if he comes home depressed? Start with repeating to yourself the slogan "It has nothing to do with me." If you start to feel that you just have to do *something* to fix him, it is a sure indication that you are used to trying to control situations in which you feel—and are actually—helpless. Sit down and write out just how you feel, list the advantages and disadvantages of repeating steps that haven't worked in the past. Then perhaps you can say, "I wish I knew how to help you," instead of feeling responsible for cheering him up. If he says he wouldn't be depressed if you were nicer, and you say, "I know you feel that way, but you seem to get depressed whether I am nice or not. I don't think it's me at all," you are taking a small step on the long road to healing.

Have a plan for the short term that fits you. Have one for the long term, too.

Part one of your plan is learning new skills—I-messages, active listening, slogans, detaching, broken records. You can learn from books or with a friend, learn in group or from tapes. Find a way that suits you and practice it. Somewhere out there are the techniques that will help you, but it is up to you to find them.

Another part of your plan has to involve practicing new skills. Knowing about them isn't the same as using them—talk is talk, and doing is doing. You can practice in a group, with a friend, on tape, in front of a mirror, and with your family.

A third part of your plan has to be taking care of yourself (time alone, eating right, not getting too tired, and especially forgiving yourself for slips). "Whoops!" is a good slogan to use for slips.

You may tend to put everything and everyone before yourself. Analyze your needs. This will help you focus on yourself. I'm not talking about new curtains or a new house. I mean needs for love and respect and attention, which are things you can give yourself. Surprisingly, when you do love and respect yourself, and give yourself attention, others will sense it and treat you better.

Even when you try to love yourself and do things for yourself you may be stuck. I had that problem. I was trying to use affirmations to help me start to take care of myself and forgive myself for all those wasted years. The book said to write, "I, Patience, love myself," and then write down my mind's reaction, which was, "Bullshit! You idiot! Why are you writing this?" I wrote the affirmation twenty times the first day and wound up not able to write any affirmations for weeks. Then I went to see Janet Woititz, the author of *Adult Children of Alcoholics*, speak. At the end of her talk she had us relax and close our eyes. We breathed evenly and deeply as she led us quietly into a relaxed state. Then she had us each picture ourselves as a child. When we had that picture, she had us go over to that child and hug her and tell her we loved her and would always be there for her. Men and women had tears running down their faces. Since then I've been able to write that affirmation, "I, Patience, love myself," and for the first time in my life to feel it. If you are having trouble taking care of yourself instead of others, get a book or tape or take a course on relaxation or visualization. When you are relaxed, visualize yourself as a child—or at any point in your life when you needed love and support, even right now—and go over and hug yourself and tell yourself you love her and will always be there for her.

Rewarding yourself is an equally important part of a plan for changing (anything from a long, warm bath to a day in the mountains, from a new blouse to a new book). Schedule these into your week to remind yourself that you are important and deserve rewards. If you've been dealing with bad feelings with food or shopping binges or some other behavior you'd as soon let go of, plan out rewards that don't involve those behaviors. The harder it is to think of rewards, the more important it is that you work on figuring out such rewards.

Another important element in any plan for changing is to pay attention to interactions between you and your vet. This includes analyzing how and what happens, rather than focusing on who was right—and looking for circumstantial evidence of co-dependence, co-survivorship, and caring, all of which may be masked by stress. Notice what kinds of things you say to each other, and how you say them.

Paying attention to your own feelings is important, too. Can you identify them? Are there physical symptoms that are associated with some feelings? Are you feeling your feelings instead of stuffing them away for a "later" that never comes? Analyzing your feelings will also give you valuable information: *What is this anger hiding from me? Why do I feel it now?*

Finally, your plan should include a way to slow down automatic reactions. These can keep us as stuck as our vets. *Families After Trauma* gives a good outline for both vet and partner, called "The Process of Becoming Aware." The goals of this process are to move beyond automatic "anxiety, tension, emotional pain" and to "enrich and enhance the relationships with my partner, family, and friends." When you "slow down the process of automatic behavior used for survival," whether in Vietnam or in the emotional climate of the co-survivor family, you can decide whether to try out new behaviors.

The Process of Becoming Aware:

- *Check Feelings* and tensions in the body.
Where are they located?
What has this meant in the past in terms of behavior for me?
- *Check* the *time* frame.
What has occurred to trigger this response in the last 24 to 48 hours?
Or is the fear in the future?
What's coming up?
- *Listen to self-talk.*
What am I telling myself about the situation?
Am I predicting pain, broken trust, failure, rejection, or abandonment?
- *Watch and listen to others.*
How are they responding to me?
How am I responding to them?
- *Get feedback* from others.
Do they see the situation the same way? Why? Why not?
Do they feel the tension? How and where?
- *Decide* what I believe about my own tension.
- *Decide* to act or not to act, based upon the current information I have gathered.

No one can incorporate all these new suggestions into her life at once. Your weekly plan could read something like: *I will paraphrase one thing my vet says or does every day this week (practicing new skills). I will notice when I am upset and analyze the reason without blaming two times this week (paying attention to myself). I will make a list of good things that happened to me this week at lunch on Friday. This will help me be in a better mood for the weekend (rewarding myself).* Three goals per week are enough.

Your daily plan could read: *I will read (whatever self-help book is helpful) today.* Do this even if you read only one page. *I will para-phrase my vet once today. I will take a long, quiet bath while the kids watch TV.* And if you do only one thing on the list, that's okay, too. You're working on your perfectionism.

Self-help books can teach you many of the skills of having a good relationship. I read as many self-help books as I can, and often learn something new to incorporate into my life. I take what I need and leave the rest, an old AA slogan. With the current explosion of self-help books, there are plenty of options. I've mentioned some of my favorites and there are more listed in the section on Suggested Fur-ther Reading. When you are looking for a self-help book, look for ones that do not offer instant fixes. There are no quick cures for behaviors that have been learned over the course of a lifetime.

As time passes and you learn new skills, putting them into practice becomes easier. Suppose your issue is "I want to have fewer fights." This is a problem both you and your vet own, since it takes two to fight. Try to use "The Process of Becoming Aware" when you start to react to your vet. Instead of becoming numb, yelling, nagging, or whatever, you can check your feelings, then check the time frame for added stresses, then listen to yourself to identify black-and-white thinking, or overgeneralizing, or any other cognitive distortion. Just taking that time will delay the onset of an argument. Ask how your vet is feeling, and notice if his emotions are evoking reactions in you. Perhaps you can actively listen to him, send him I-messages, and then both analyze what is going on. Slow down the process and you give him room to change, because he doesn't have to pour energy into defending himself or shutting out your words by becoming numb and absent.

Notice how you do say things. "You made me mad" indicates that you are letting him control you. It's a good place to start from since most of us are there, but it isn't a healthy place. Suppose the rest of it was: ". . . when you said I have no problems." When you can turn that into a healthy, confrontive I-message—"I feel angry when my problems are discounted, because even though I never fought in Vietnam, I'm still a co-survivor of those events and live with the problems they've caused"—you are on the road to healing.

Further recovery will enable you to add clear statements of your needs. Instead of "You never listen to me," which is a vague and *global* (meaning the opposite of specific) complaint, you'll be able to say, "I need my problems at work today to be acknowledged. I need your support, and that support can just be letting me complain this evening without trying to solve my problems or belittle them." If your vet immediately wants to fix the problem or point out that it shouldn't be a problem, remember that co-dependency cuts both ways.

Relationships are an art, not a science. If you paraphrase accurately but with a knife's edge in your voice, or wait with a tapping finger, or get so anxious to make it all right that you can't give your vet time to work through something painful, the techniques you are trying to develop won't work. Nor will they if you state your authentic feelings and needs in such a wishy-washy voice that you can't be taken seriously.

You can balance what you need with what your vet can tolerate at this time. Remember, he does have a real problem but it will get better if he gets therapy, and you can get better whether he does or not. Sense what is working and what isn't. Work on being assertive without being aggressive; change your perspective; listen without accepting abuse. Forgive yourself when you backslide, and your vet when he does, too.

One of the reasons you should be accepting of human frailty is because you, too, have flaws and faults. If you didn't, you'd be intolerable. (Do you like anyone who thinks he or she is perfect? Is he or she?) Flaws and faults are really useful. Forgiving yourself for having them and seeing them as a natural outgrowth of your upbringing and experience will help you live with your partner's flaws—particularly those that may arise out of the experience of Vietnam—without resentment. He does have a right to be imperfect, too, but *it would be nice if* he were less so.

When I began to examine myself for flaws and faults (Who, me?), I ran into things I didn't want to see: selfishness (*Bob had to change for me*); materialism (*I acted as if my possessions were more important than people*); self-satisfaction (*look at how nobly I put up with him*); dishonesty (*believing I knew what other people needed, wanted, or should do; the inability to say what I needed or wanted; denying that we had a problem; saying I didn't mind Bob's affair; overlooking increasingly inappropriate behavior such as reckless driving and heavy drinking; keeping a positive attitude*); mixed motives (*I wanted him to change but did everything to keep him the same*); the desire to control (*being helpful*); conceit (*I'm so loyal, so undemanding, so accepting, so wonderful; I deserve someone just like me and he's no good*); manipulation (*I'll do it even though I don't want to and then he'll owe me*).

If you see such faults in yourself, what are you going to do? If you continue to deny them, you will still *have* them and you'll still be stuck. Believe me, everyone has faults. It's okay. It's nice if you can see them, though, because then you can allow other people to be imperfect, and you can work toward letting go of the faults you don't want to keep.

One of the most destructive forms of dysfunctional thinking is perfectionism. Trying to be perfect is a dead end. Trying to be alive and human is more worthwhile. So keep a few faults. It'll be easy. Believe me, I know.

We can also stop enabling our vets to say "Vietnam didn't affect me." Privately and quietly you can ask your vet a question that deals with those effects of Vietnam that affect you.

If your husband is a perfectionist, and is trying to force perfection on you and the kids, ask: "Would it be as important to you that we be the perfect family if you hadn't been to Vietnam? Sometimes it seems to me that *that's* how Vietnam affected you."

If your husband works all the time and never has time for you and the kids, or if your son or brother or father has no time for anything but work, ask: "Would you have been this much of a workaholic if you hadn't been to Vietnam? Sometimes I feel that in trying to prove Vietnam didn't affect you, you forget *us*." Or: "You forget there are other things in life besides success."

If your vet is having PTSD symptoms, you can point out quietly and kindly the effect they have on you and the kids. "I don't 'think rage is an appropriate reaction to a later supper/the kids' report cards/a birthday party. I know that combat vets often find themselves in a rage." You can even add the suggestion, "I wonder if getting some help would be appropriate."

"Are you aware that when you talk about Vietnam and how bad it is all the time, I am filled with a sort of hopeless misery because I can't fix it for you?" Suggest: "Help is now available that wasn't in the bad old days."

"Do you realize why I don't want to hear about Vietnam anymore? Because then you have no motivation to get the therapy these stories indicate you need, so although I go through the pain of hearing about it, I get no benefit." If you can manage a loving tone, add, "I need you to get better."

You could even say as a broken record, "I need you to get some help because I cannot bear the burden of being the only parent, the only one with a job, the only one who does housework or runs our social life, anymore. It's too much for me. I need your help, and I think you need help to be able to give as well as receive."

"When you're so depressed, it makes me very sad, because I want to make it better but I can't."

"Are you aware that being a co-survivor can be traumatic, too, that flashbacks and rages affect the people who witness them, just as events in Vietnam still affect you?"

A kind and concerned broken record, letting your vet know how his problems are affecting you, cuts right through denial and confronts him—without blame or accusation—with the results of his behavior. It may be months before your vet can hear what you are saying. People with high stress levels simply can't hear things the first time you say them. And when they do, they may hear blame and criticism, which is not what you are actually offering, either. Keep your broken record going, quietly and caringly. Eventually, sometimes after months, they hear what you are saying. "You mean it makes you depressed when I'm depressed? I didn't know that!"

One of the big questions women have is: What do I tell the kids? If your vet has rages, or wakes up screaming, or sits in the cellar depressed, you can tell them that these are symptoms of having been through a trauma in which you think you are going to die or have seen friends die, and that it has nothing to do with them. Tell them it isn't their fault and nothing they (or you) do will have any effect in the long term, although sometimes bringing home a good report card or making the football team will seem to help. You can explain the symptoms to them, simply and at their level. "Daddy has nightmares because he was in the war," for little kids. And: "One of the symptoms combat vets often have is severe depressions, etc.," for the older ones. Above all, don't ignore what is going on. Kids do notice it, and they simply assume it is their fault. Things the vet may say when he's upset ("If we didn't have those kids, I'd be fine") can contribute to this.

Kids may also assume it's *your* fault, because of things your vet may say, or because of the assumptions that seem to permeate our society. We need a book like the one for kids of alcoholics, *My Dad Loves Me, My Dad Has a Disease*, for the children of all PTSD sufferers.

Charles Figley, Ph.D., a combat veteran and pioneer in the recognition and treatment of PTSD, said on October 11, 1988, on National Public Radio's "Morning Edition": "Combat-related PTSD is not very easy to cure. It is a long-term recovery process. The thing that's necessary is that not only the clinicians are aware of the course, but that they need to educate the men and women they work with that this is a normal reaction to an abnormal situation."

We are the pioneers in the understanding and treatment of the effects of PTSD on families. We are developing treatment methods for ourselves. At first no one knew what was wrong with our vets. Later the helping professions understood only too well what had happened to our vets, but couldn't figure out why that should affect us or our children.

With time and work and waiting for each other, families can reach new levels of relating in which they are able to appreciate the pain and the strengths and the joys of other members of the family. Nothing will erase the experiences of Vietnam for our vets, nor the experience of helplessness to help them many of us and our kids have faced, but we can use that pain to propel us into a future that has sunlight as well as the shadows of the past. On the shadowed days, instead of trying to control and mask and numb our pain as we—very humanly—did in the past, we can learn to comfort each other. Finally, we can use our pain to try to make the world a better, safer, more peaceful place.

Recovery is not for sissies.

Sources

INTRODUCTION

Discussion of the working through process: John P. Wilson, Ph.D., and Gustave E. Krause, M.A., "Predicting Post-Traumatic Stress Disorders Among Vietnam Veterans," in William E. Kelley, M.D., *Post-Traumatic Stress Disorder and the War Veteran Patient* (New York: Brunner/Mazel, 1985), 107, and John P. Wilson, Ph.D., *The Forgotten Warrior Project* (Cleveland: Disabled American Veterans, 1978), 157.

Veteran suicide: Joel Osler Brende and Erwin Randolph Parson *Vietnam Veterans: The Road to Recovery* (New York: Plenum, 1985), 75. Norman Hearst, Thomas B. Newman, and Stephen Hulley, "Delayed Effects of the Military Draft on Mortality: A Randomized Natural Experiment," in the *New England Journal of Medicine*, 314.10 (March 6, 1986): 620–24. Also see Michael D. Kogan and Richard W. Clapp, "Mortality Among Vietnam Veterans in Massachusetts, 1972–1983," a report dated January 25, 1985 and published by the Massachusetts Office of the Commissioner of Veterans Affairs Services and The Agent Orange program, Massachusetts Department of Public Health Statistics and Research.

PART ONE. VIETNAM: WHAT IT WAS

Chapter 1: Who Went

The information in this chapter and the following chapters came from interviews with veterans. Some asked that their names not be used, or first names only, and that their unit not be identified, and I have followed their wishes.

The Draft
Some statistics are from Colonel Harry G. Summers, Jr.'s, *The Vietnam War Almanac* (New York: Facts on File Publications, 1985), 146.

Randy Martin, "Who Went to War," in Ghislane Boulanger and Charles Kadushin, *The Vietnam Veteran Redefined, Fact and Fiction* (Hillsdale, N.J.: Lawrence Erlbaum Associates, 1986), 13–24. Myra McPherson, *A Long Time Passing* (New York: Doubleday, 1984), 98.

G. David Curry, *Sunshine Patriots* (Notre Dame, University of Notre Dame Press, 1985), 74.

James Fallows, "What Did You Do in the Class War, Daddy?" in A. D. Horne, *The Wounded Generation* (Englewood Cliffs: Prentice Hall, 1981), 15–29.

Christopher Buckley, "Viet Guilt," *Esquire*, 100 (September 1983), 68–72.

For an overview of who served and who didn't, see the diagram in Lawrence M. Baskir and William A. Strauss's article "The Vietnam Generation," A. D. Horne, *The Wounded Generation*, 6.

Corson's quote: MacPherson, *A Long Time Passing*, 94.

Statistics on WIA and KIA and on the Project 100,000 men: Dean K. Phillips, "The Case for Veteran's Preference" in Charles R. Figley and Seymour Leventman's *Strangers at Home: Vietnam Veterans Since the War* (New York: Praeger, 1980), 346 and 348. See also David Curry, *Sunshine Patriots*, on Project 100,000, 23.

Training

Erik H. Erikson's *Identity, Youth and Crisis* (New York: W W Norton and Co., 1968). Erikson first heard the term "identity crisis" at the Mt. Zion Veterans' Rehabilitation Clinic during World War II. "Most of our patients . . . had through the exigencies of war lost a sense of personal sameness and historical continuity," he reported on page 17. Working with them led eventually to his theory of developmental crises and the realization that at around eighteen people go through a major identity crisis as they decide who they are.

William Barry Gault, M.D., "Some Remarks on Slaughter," *American Journal of Psychiatry*, 128.4 (1971): 450–454.

The Career Military Dilemma

William P. Mahedy, *Out of the Night* (New York: Ballantine, 1986), 27 and 42–43.

John Del Vecchio, *The 13th Valley* (New York: Bantam, 1982).

On the Way

The material in this part is all from interviews.

Joe Pearson, who served in Vietnam when he was seventeen, eighteen and nineteen, (a partial tour, a full tour, and an extension) died of smoke inhalation on September 29, 1987. His brother wrote me, "You might want to make a note that Joe died as a result of his drinking and drug problem."

Chapter 2: In the Rear

Much of the information in this chapter is from personal interviews or correspondence.

Signs of the Tet Offensive were evident in the preceding year as reported not only in the CBS documentary "The Uncounted Enemy: A Vietnam Deception," but by personal communication from a veteran of U.S. Army intelligence who was there at the time, and the report of intelligence analyst Doris Allen in Keith Walker, *A Piece of My Heart* (New York: Ballantine, 1985), 312–13.

Reports about the government-sponsored whorehouses: Susan Brownmiller's *Against Our Will* (New York: Simon and Schuster, 1975), 94–97. Bob told me about one built for the First Cav enlisted men when he was there in 1965–66.

John Ketwig, . . . *and a hard rain fell* (New York: Pocket Books, 1985), 42, 39, and 107.

Chapter 3: In the Pipeline and Forward Bases

On the Road
, Ketwig, . . . *and a hard rain fell*, 50–53.

In the Air
Statistics on the C-130: Anthony Robinson, *Weapons of the Vietnam War* (Greenwich, CT.: Bison Books, 1983), 126.

Forward Bases
Quote about racism is from Samuel Hoard, *Almost a Layman* (Orlando, FL.: Drake's Publishing, 1981), 55.

Don Bodey, *FNG* (New York: Viking, 1985), 178.

Chapter 4: Going Forth: Aviation and Mechanized Combat

Helicopters
Phillips, "The Case for Veteran's Preference," Figley and Leventman, *Strangers at Home*, 347, reports the statistics on wounds. John Keegan falls for the U.S. government statistic of fifteen minutes from wound to hospital in *The Face of Battle* (New York: Penguin, 1978), 275.

Huey gunships: Matt Brennan, *Brennan's War* (New York: Pocket Books, 1986, 203).

Fixed Wing
Statistics on fixed-wing sorties: Robinson, *Weapons of the Vietnam War*, 108.

Mike Geokan's unpublished manuscript, *Aces of Iron*, is an ironical, moving view of the war from inside a tank.

Yeager quote: Chuck Yeager, and Leo Janos, *Yeager* (New York: Bantam, 1985), 292.

Mechanized Combat
John A. Cash, John Albright and Allan W. Sandstrum, *Seven Firefights in Vietnam* (New York: Bantam, 1985), 63.

Mike Geokan, *Aces of Iron*.

Chapter 5: In the Field

Statistics on blacks in the field: Phillips, "The Case for Veteran's Preference," Figley and Leventman, *Strangers at Home*, 348.

Regarding the M-16: Summers, *The Vietnam War Almanac*, 234, and Robinson, *Weapons of the Vietnam War*, 32. Robert Pisor, *The End of the Line: The Siege of Khe Sanh* (New York: Ballantine Books, 1982), 6.

Joe Haldeman's poem "D/X" appears in a science fiction anthology about Vietnam, *In the Field of Fire*, Jeanne Dann and Jack Dann, ed. (New York: Tor, 1987), 394–401.

Frederick Downs, *The Killing Zone* (New York: Berkley, 1983), 259–61.

Spencer J. Campbell, M.S.W., *Reflections of a Vietnam Veteran*, pamphlet for the New Jersey State Commission on Agent Orange (Trenton: The Image Factory, 1983).

Chapter 6: Back in the World

Joel Osler Brende and Erwin Randolph Parson, *Vietnam Veterans: The Road to Recovery* (New York: Plenum, 1985).

Quotes on homecoming from interviews and from Clark Smith's "Oral History as 'Therapy': Combatants' Accounts of the Vietnam War," Figley and Leventman, *Strangers at Home*, 14, and Campbell, *Reflections of a Vietnam Veteran*.

FBI training video seen at the presentation, "Co-Worker Harm, Injury, and Death," a panel at the Third Annual Meeting of the Society for Traumatic Stress Studies, Baltimore, MD, October 25, 1987.

Quote from Wilson and Krauss, "Predicting Post-Traumatic Stress Disorders Among Vietnam Veterans," in Kelley, *Post-Traumatic Stress Disorder and the War Veteran Patient*, 140.

Quote from Ketwig, . . . *and a hard rain fell*, 303–4.

Negative TV stereotyping discussed in Paul Camacho's article, "From War Hero to Criminal: The Negative Privilege of The Vietnam Veteran," Figley and Leventman, *Strangers at Home*, 267–78.

Quote from Ketwig, . . . *and a hard rain fell*, 259–60.

Quote from Smith, "Oral History as 'Therapy': Combatants' accounts of the Vietnam War," Figley and Leventman, *Strangers at Home*, 15.

Sarah Haley, "Some of My Best Friends Are Dead," Kelley, *Post-Traumatic Stress Disorder and the War Veteran Patient*, 64.

Rick Eilert, *For Self and Country* (New York: William Morrow & Co, 1983). Intensely moving, as is Frederick Downs's, *Aftermath* (New York: Berkley, 1985).

Hourly wage statistics from Andrew I. Kohen and Patricia M. Shields, "Reaping the Spoils of Defeat: Labor Market Experiences of Vietnam-Era Veterans," Figley and Leventman, *Strangers at Home*, 181–209.

Unemployment: Fred Milano's "The Politicization of the 'Deer Hunters,' " Figley and Leventman, *Strangers at Home*, 229–46.

Information about Spin numbers: Lawrence M. Baskir and William A

Strauss's *Chance and Circumstance* (New York: Alfred A. Knopf, 1978), 154–157.

Regarding the military's treatment of returning vets with time to serve: Baskir and Strauss, *Chance and Circumstance*, 1978, 148.

Downs, *The Killing Zone*, preface.

On the GI Bill: Charles Moskos, "Surviving the War in Vietnam," Figley and Leventman, *Strangers at Home*, 83.

Sidney E. Cleveland and Fred Lewis, "Attitudes of Vietnam vs. WWII-Korean Era Veteran Employees toward VA Hospital Practices," *The Vietnam Veteran in Contemporary Society* (Washington D.C.: Veterans Administration, May 1972), IV-113.

Percent of vets using the VA: Ronald Bitzer's "Caught in the Middle: Mentally Disabled Vietnam Veterans and the Veterans Administration," Figley and Leventman, *Strangers at Home*, 314. Amputations: Phillips, "The Case for Veteran's Preference," Figley and Leventman, *Strangers at Home*, 348.

Robert Muller's words are from "A Symposium," the round table discussion by Philip Caputo, James Fallows, Robert Muller, Dean K. Phillips, Lucian Truscott IV, James Webb, and John P Wheeler III with Richard Harwood as moderator in A. D. Horne, *The Wounded Generation*, 123.

VETERAN KICKS AUNT is the headline on the newspaper the vet is reading in the cartoon on page 54. The caption reads, "There's a small item on page 17 about a triple ax murder. No veterans involved." Bill Mauldin, *Back Home* (New York: William Sloan Associates, 1947), 54.

Quote on support: Wilson and Krauss, "Predicting Post-Traumatic Stress Disorders Among Vietnam Veterans," in Kelley, *Post-Traumatic Stress Disorder and the War Veteran Patient*, 113.

PART TWO. THE AFTEREFFECTS

Chapter 7: So What's So Different About Vietnam?

Age

McPherson, *Long Time Passing*, 52.

Had to be nineteen to go overseas: in Keith Winston *V-Mail: Letters Home From a Combat Medic* (Chapel Hill: Algonquin Books, 1985).

Shared Burden

William Manchester, *Goodbye, Darkness* (Boston: Little, Brown, 1979, 1980), 393.

Ross S. Carter, *Those Devils in Baggy Pants* (New York: Signet, 1951), viii.

Tour of Duty

Quote from Carter, *Those Devils in Baggy Pants*, vii.

Quote from Manchester, *Goodbye, Darkness*, 398.

The change from serving for the duration to point system to one year tour is explained in Jim Goodwin, Psy.D., *Readjustment Problems Among Vietnam Veterans*, a pamphlet published by the Disabled American Veterans, PO Box 14301, Cincinnati, OH, 45214, 6.

Unit Solidarity

General Sir John Hackett, *The Profession of Arms* (New York: Macmillan, 1983), 215.

Herbert Spiegel, M.D., "Psychiatry With an Infantry Battalion in North Africa," *Neuropsychiatry in World War Two*, Vol II (Washington Office of the Surgeon General, Department of the Army, 1966–73), 111–126.

Barbaric rites for FNG's: Mark Baker, *Nam* (New York: Berkley Books, 1983), 59.

Quote from Carter, *Those Devils in Baggy Pants*, 123.

Periods of Retraining

Farley Mowat, *And No Birds Sang* (New York: Bantam, 1983), 121.

Support of the Population

See W. D. Ehrhart, *Going Back: An Ex-Marine Returns to Vietnam* (Jefferson, N.C.: McFarland & Company, 1987). On pages 4 and 5, Ehrhart gives the best precis of what was going on—as opposed to what he as an idealistic enlistee was told was going on—that I've read.

Further information about South Vietnamese corruption is in William J. Lederer, *Our Own Worst Enemy* (New York: W W Norton & Co, 1968).

The last quote is from Smith, "Oral History as 'Therapy': Combatants' Accounts of the Vietnam War," Figley and Leventman, *Strangers at Home*, 14.

Support at Home

Farley Mowat, *And No Birds Sang*, 120.

Wilson and Krauss, "Predicting Post-Traumatic Stress Disorders Among Vietnam Veterans," Kelley, *Post-Traumatic Stress Disorder and the War Veteran Patient*, 142.

Declaration of War

John Trotti, *Phantom Over Vietnam* (New York: Berkley, 1985), 102.

"You think of the lives which would have been lost in an invasion of Japan's home islands . . . and you thank God for the atomic bomb," Manchester, *Goodbye, Darkness*, 250.

Discussion of interpreters: William J. Lederer, *Our Own Worst Enemy*, 19–22.

Doing research for *Chickenhawk* in the deposit of declassified documents at the University of Florida library, Bob discovered that the Kennedy and Johnson administrations often asked major newspapers like *The New York Times* or *Washington Post* to suppress reports of things like 80 percent support for the VC in South Vietnam. The newspapers suppressed stories that might have kept us out of Vietnam.

Story of our involvement in provoking the Gulf of Tonkin incident in Stanley Karnow's *Vietnam* (New York: Viking, 1983), 359–76.
Lionel Chetwynd's movie, *Hanoi Hilton*, 1987.

Fighting for Freedom
Seymour Leventman and Paul Camacho, "The 'Gook' Syndrome: The Vietnam War as a Racial Encounter," Figley and Leventman, *Strangers at Home*, 68.
Goodwin, *Readjustment Problems Among Vietnam Veterans*, 8.
Mahedy, *Out of the Night*, 27.
Quotes from Smith, "Oral History as 'Therapy': Combatants' Accounts of the Vietnam War," Figley and Leventman, *Strangers at Home*, "the regular military was fucked up . . ." 33; the quote on embezzlement, 69.

Consistent, Experienced Officers
Matthew Brennan, *Brennan's War*, wounds quote, 255, officer after souvenirs, 73.
Ketwig, . . . *and a hard rain fell*, 107.
Two years in a British Army unit: Hackett, *The Profession of Arms*.

Clear Combat Zones and Visible Progress on the Ground
Farley Mowat, *And No Birds Sang*, 174–76.
Wilson and Krauss, "Predicting Post-Traumatic Stress Disorders Among Vietnam Veterans," in Kelley, *Post-Traumatic Disorder and the War Veteran Patient*, 140.
Wastage: Paul Fussell, *The Great War and Modern Memory* (London: Oxford University Press, 1975), 41.
Leventman and Camacho, "The 'Gook' Syndrome: The Vietnam War as a Racial Encounter," Figley and Leventman, *Strangers at Home*, 64.

Clear-cut enemy
See the waifs in Bill Mauldin, *Up Front* (New York: Henry Holt and Co., 1945).
The whore story: Ketwig, . . . *and a hard rain fell*, 79.
World War II atrocities: Manchester, *Goodbye, Darkness*, 439 and 447, Carter, *Those Devils in Baggy Pants*, 41, and Mowat, *And No Birds Sang*, 159–60.
On atrocities in Vietnam: Mahedy, *Out of the Night*, 17 and 42.

Casualties
Summers, *The Vietnam War Almanac*: 1st Cavalry, 163; 1st Infantry Division, 165; 4th Infantry Division, 172; III Marine Amphibious Force, 339; 25th Infantry Division, 346; Americal Division, 78; 101st Airborne, 272.
World War I artillery casualty figures from "Soldiers," documentary shown on PBS, Artillery episode called "Gunner."
Casualty figures by cause: Summers, *The Vietnam War Almanac*, 112.
Casualty figures exceed WW II: Summers, *The Vietnam War Almanac*, 112.

Psychological Casualties

Psychological casualty figures: Goodwin, *Readjustment Problems Among Vietnam Veterans*, 6.

Ronald Bitzer, "Caught in the Middle: Mentally Disabled Vietnam Veterans and the Veterans Administration," Figley and Leventman, *Strangers at Home*, 305–21.

The quote from the U.S. Government report, "Combat Exhaustion" is in John Keegan's, *The Face of Battle* (New York: Penguin, 1976), 335–36. Interestingly enough this report agrees with the "subjective opinions and timings" of World War I combat veterans as reported in Denis Winter, *Death's Men* (New York: Penguin, 1978), 133.

DSM II was published by the American Psychiatric Association in 1968.

Why the symptoms of PTSD were ignored: Steven Silver, Ph.D., "Post-Traumatic Stress and the Death Imprint," Kelley, *Post-Traumatic Stress Disorder and the War Veteran Patient*, 45.

Morale

Spiegel, "Psychiatry With an Infantry Battalion in North Africa," *Neuropsychiatry in World War Two*, 116–17.

Drugs

See the booze and cigarettes in Mauldin, *Up Front*.

Quotes on marijuana and on drinking both in Keegan, *The Face of Battle*, 333.

Supportive Re-entry into Society

Quote from Wilson and Krauss, "Predicting Post-Traumatic Stress Disorders Among Vietnam Veterans," in Kelley, *Post-Traumatic Stress Disorder and the War Veteran Patient*, 141.

Willard Walker, "The Victors and the Vanquished," Figley and Leventman, *Strangers at Home*, 45.

Time Bombs

Fred Wilcox, *Waiting for an Army to Die*, New York, Vintage, 1983, *xii*.

This paragraph is quoted in Erwin Randolph Parson, Ph.D., "The Reparation of the Self: Clinical and Theoretical Dimensions in the Treatment of Vietnam Combat Veterans," *Journal of Contemporary Psychotherapy*, 14.1 (Spring/Summer 1984), 9, from a paper presented by Dr. Parson at "the St. Georges/Stapleton and the New Brighton Service Providers Network, Staten Island, New York, 1982." Dr. Parson was a medic in Vietnam. A small part of his story is in Al Santoli, *To Bear Any Burden* (New York: E. P. Dutton, Inc., 1985), 310.

Craig Kubey, David F. Addlestone, Richard E. O'Dell, Keith D. Snyder, Barton F. Stichman, and The Vietnam Veterans of America, *The Viet Vet Survival Guide* (New York: Ballantine Books, 1985). Agent Orange information is on pages 81–98.

The Whiners

See H. C. Archibald and R. D. Tuddenham, "Persistent Stress Reaction Following Combat: A Twenty-year Follow-up." *Archives of General Psychiatry*, 12:475–481, (1965). Notice the date—the first year American troops went to Vietnam to fight for the South Vietnamese, instead of just advise. See also R. Pary, M.D., D. Turns, M.D., C. Tobias, M.D., "A Case of Delayed Recognition of Posttraumatic Stress Disorder," *American Journal of Psychiatry*. 143.7:941, (1986).

Manchester, *Goodbye, Darkness*, 23 and 284.

Quote from Mauldin, *Back Home*, jacket copy and 69.

Harry Truman, *Dear Bess: The Letters from Harry to Bess Truman, 1910–1959*, Robert H Ferrell, ed. (New York: W W Norton & Co., 1983), 390.

Chapter 8: Post-Traumatic Stress Disorder

Jane Smiley "Long Distance," *The Atlantic Monthly*, January 1987, 75.

Bruce Beresford's 1979 Australian movie, *Breaker Morant*. The quote is from the defense lawyer during the trial.

Speech by Lady Percy mentioned in Michael Trimble, "Post-Traumatic Stress Disorder: History of a Concept," *Trauma and Its Wake*, Charles Figley, Ph.D., ed. (New York: Brunner/Mazel, 1985), 6–7. My own listing of the symptoms.

John Russell Smith, "A Review of One Hundred and Twenty Years of the Psychological Literature on Reactions to Combat," unpublished dissertation submitted to Duke University 1981, 27.

Civil War vets: Herbert Hendin and Ann Polliger Haas, *The Wounds of War* (New York: Basic Books, 1984), 16–17 and 19.

Irritable heart: 1871. Dr. Jacob Mendes DaCosta, "On Irritable Heart: A Clinical Study of a Form of Functional Cardiac Disorder and Its Consequences," *American Journal of Medical Sciences*, 61:17–52.

Dr. Albert Wilson is quoted in Winter, *Death's Men*, 129, bodies on the battlefields, 132–33. Also read Fussell, *The Great War and Modern Memory*, for general information on combat in World War I. Both books contain lists of titles of memoirs from the period.

Shell shock discussed in Trimble, "Post-Traumatic Stress Disorder: History of a Concept" in *Trauma and Its Wake;* Smith, "A Review of One Hundred and Twenty Years of the Psychological Literature on Reactions to Combat"; Winter, *Death's Men*, 129; Fussell, *The Great War and Modern Memory:* the chapter by Ghislane Boulanger, Ph.D., "Post-Traumatic Stress Disorder: An Old Problem with a New Name," in Stephen M. Sonnenberg, M.D., Arthur S. Blank, M.D., and John A Talbott, M.D., *The Trauma of War: Stress and Recovery in Vietnam Veterans* (Washington: D.C.: American Psychiatric Press, 1985); and the excellent chapter "From Shell Shock to PTSD," in Brende and Parson, *Vietnam Veterans: The Road to Recovery* among other places.

Discussion of treatment for shell shock in Smith, "A Review of One Hundred and Twenty Years of the Psychological Literature on Reactions to Combat" and the chapter "From Shell Shock to PTSD," in Brende and Parson, *Vietnam Vets: The Road to Recovery*.

Pensions: Winter, *Death's Men*, 140.

Freud's opinions quoted in Brende and Parson, *Vietnam Veterans: The Road to Recovery*, 67, and Henry Krystal, M.D., *Integration and Self-Healing: Affect, Trauma, Alexithymia*, (Hillsdale, N.J.: The Analytic Press, Lawrence Erlbaum Associates, 1988), 201.

Quote on frailties of psychiatrists: Boulanger, "Post-Traumatic Stress Disorder: An Old Problem with a New Name," in Sonnenberg, Blank, and Talbot, *The Trauma of War*, 18.

Quote on Audie Murphy: Thomas B. Morgan, "The War Hero" *Esquire*, December 1983 (Golden Anniversary Collector's Issue), 597–604.

First psychiatric definition of stress reaction: American Psychiatric Association, Committee on Nomenclature and Statistics (1952): *Diagnostic and Statistical Manual, Mental Disorders* (DSM I), Washington, D.C. 1952.

American Psychiatric Association, Committee on Nomenclature and Statistics (1968): *Diagnostic and Statistical Manual, Mental Disorders* (DSM II), Washington, D.C., 1968, VIII 307* 48–49.

Follow-up studies on World War II vets: Archibald and Tuddenham, "Persistent Stress Reaction Following Combat: A Twenty-year Follow-up," *Archives of General Psychiatry*, 12 (1965) 475–481.

Discussion of the grief process in Elizabeth Kubler-Ross, M.D., *On Death and Dying* (New York: Macmillan, 1969).

First recognition of PTSD: American Psychiatric Association, Committee on Nomenclature and Statistics, (1980): *Diagnostic and Statistical Manual, Mental Disorders* (DSM III), Washington, D.C., 1980.

Dr. Dondershine speaks on the video about PTSD: "The War Within," Jonathan Dann, Producer, KRON-TV News, Chronicle Broadcasting Co, 1982.

Arthur Blank, M.D., "Irrational Reactions to Post-Traumatic Stress Disorder and Vietnam Veterans," Sonnenberg, Blank, and Talbot, *The Trauma of War*, 69–98.

The definition of PTSD I have quoted is from American Psychiatric Association, Committee on Nomenclature and Statistics, (1987): *Diagnostic and Statistical Manual, Mental Disorders*, (DSM IIIR), Washington, D.C., 1987, 247–251.

Quote on intrusions from Wilson and Krauss, "Predicting Post-Traumatic Stress Disorders Among Vietnam Veterans," in Kelley, *Post-Traumatic Stress Disorder and the War Veteran Patient*, 105.

The intrusive memory is quoted from: Sam R. Watkins, *Company Aytch*, (New York: Collier, 1962), 247–88.

Quote from Robert Apley on "The War Within."

Shadows of Vietnam: Campbell, *Reflections of a Vietnam Veteran*.

Erich Vierthaler, Ph.D., "Vietnam-Era Veteran Contacts with the Criminal Justice System: A Legacy of Wartime Military Service, Military Experience, of the Vietnam War? A Call for Research to Compare Veteran and Civilian

Cases," Paper presented at the Annual Meeting of the Academy of Criminal Justice Sciences, March 17–21, 1986, Orlando, FL, 7.

Problems with kids: Sarah Haley, "The Vietnam Veteran and His Preschool Child: Child Rearing as a Delayed Stress in Combat Veterans," *Journal of Contemporary Psychotherapy*, 14.1 (Spring/Summer 1984), 114.

Diagram of healing a memory: Dennis and Matthew Linn, S.J., *Healing Life's Hurts* (New York: Paulist Press, 1978), 11.

Impacted grief is a phrase used by Chaim Shatan, M.D., "The Grief of Soldiers: Vietnam Combat Veterans' Self-Help Movement," *American Journal of Orthopsychiatry*, 43, (1973), 640–53.

Parson, "The Reparation of the Self," 28.

Norma Winkler, "Hidden Injuries of War," Figley and Leventman, *Strangers at Home*, 87–107.

Robert Muller quote: A. D. Horne, *The Wounded Generation*, 119.

Stephen M. Sonnenberg, M.D., "Introduction: The Trauma of War," Sonnenbereg, Blank, and Talbott, *The Trauma of War*, 6.

Chaim Shatan, M.D., "Have You Hugged a Vietnam Veteran Today?" Kelley, *Post-Traumatic Stress Disorder and the War Veteran Patient*, 15–16.

John Wilson, Ph.D., "Predicting PTSD Among Vietnam Veterans," Kelley, *Post-Traumatic Stress Disorder and the War Veteran Patient*, 143.

Helene Jackson, "The Impact of Combat Stress on Adolescent Moral Development in Vietnam Veterans," submitted in partial fulfillment of the requirements for the degree of Ph.D., Smith College School for Social Work, 1982, 92, and 112.

Condensed from "Insensibility," *The Poems of Wilfred Owen*, Jon Stallworthy, ed. (New York: W W Norton & Co., 1986), 122–23.

Walker, "The Victors and the Vanquished," Figley and Leventman, *Strangers at Home*, 45.

Helen DeRosis, M.D., *Women and Anxiety* (New York: Delacorte Press, 1979), 43.

Quotes from Shatan, "Have You Hugged a Vietnam Veteran Today?" Kelley, *Post-Traumatic Stress Disorder and the War Veteran Patient*, 19–20 and 14.

Lawrence C. Kolb, M.D., B. Cullen Burris, M.D., Susan Griffiths, R.N., "Propranolol and Clonidine in Treatment of the Chronic Post-Traumatic Stress Disorders of War," *Post-Traumatic Stress Disorder: Psychological and Biological Sequelae*, Bessel A. van der Kolk, M.D., ed. (Washington D.C.: American Psychiatric Press, 1984), 100.

Chaim Shatan, M.D., "Have You Hugged a Vietnam Veteran Today?" Kelley, *Post-Traumatic Stress Disorder and the War Veteran Patient*, 19.

Emmanuel Tanay, M.D., "The Vietnam Veteran—Victim of War," Kelley, *Post-Traumatic Stress Disorder and the War Veteran Patient*, quote on acquired talents, 30, quote about guilt, 32.

Veteran suicide: Brende and Parson, *Vietnam Veterans: The Road to Recovery*, 75; Hearst, Newman, and Hulley "Delayed Effects of the Military Draft on Mortality: A Randomized Natural Experiment," 620–24. Also see Kogan and Clapp, "Mortality Among Vietnam Veterans in Massachusetts, 1972–1983."

Types of guilt: Parson, "The Reparation of the Self," 15.

Janet Woititz, Ed.D., spoke at a conference on family violence sponsored by the Gainesville Committee on the Status of Women, May 1988.

Who needs therapy: Smith, "Individual Therapy with Vietnam Veterans," Sonnenberg, Blank, and Talbott, *The Trauma of War*, 129.

Goodwin, *Readjustment Problems Among Vietnam Veterans*, 6.

White collar PTSD: Ray Scurfield, phone conversation with author, April 4, 1988.

Richard A. Kulka and William E. Schlenger, "Tables to Accompany: The Unforgotten Warrior Project: Annual Update of the *National Vietnam Veterans Readjustment Study*," Research Triangle Institute, PO Box 12194, Research Triangle Park, NC, 27709. Presentation for the Pre-Meeting Institute on "The Unforgotten Warrior Project: Annual Update on Current Research and Treatment of Vietnam Veterans with PTSD," for the Fourth Annual Meeting of the Society for Traumatic Stress Studies, Dallas, October 23, 1988, Table 10.

Time "in the field": Sarah Haley, "When the Patient Reports Atrocities," *Archives of General Psychiatry*, 30 (February 1974), 195.

Chronic pain: Richard A. Benidilet, and Lawrence C. Kolb, M.D., "Preliminary Findings of Chronic Pain and Post-Traumatic Stress Disorder," *American Journal of Psychiatry*, 143.7, 908.

Visible tension: ". . . in working with one extremely blocked veteran . . . his overall muscular tension would visibly increase . . ." Lee D. Crump, "Gestalt Therapy in the Treatment of Vietnam Vets Experiencing PTSD," in *Journal of Contemporary Psychotherapy*, 14.1 (Spring/Summer 1984), 93.

Walking time bomb and sensitive to slights: Parson, "The Reparation of the Self," 15 and 30. Helene Jackson, "The Impact of Combat Stress on Adolescent Moral Development in Vietnam Veterans," 155.

Depression: Goodwin, *Readjustment Problems Among Vietnam Veterans*, 11, 13, and 14.

Withdrawal: Wilson *Forgotten Warrior Project*, 30.

Deflection of aggression: Victor J. Defazio and Nicholas J. Pascucci, "Return to Ithaca: A Perspective on Marriage and Love in Post-Traumatic Stress Disorder," *Journal of Contemporary Psychotherapy*, 14.1 (Spring/Summer 1984), 87.

Passivity: Smith, "Individual Therapy with Vietnam Veterans," Sonnenberg, Blank, and Talbott, *The Trauma of War*, 137–38., Haley, "Some of My Best Friends Are Dead," Kelley, *Post-Traumatic Stress Disorder and the War Veteran Patient*, 61. Robrert Marrs, M.A., "Why the Pain Won't Stop and What the Family Can Do to Help," Kelley, *Post-Traumatic Stress Disorder and the War Veteran Patient*, 88.

Giving up sex: Defazio and Pascucci, "Return to Ithaca: A Perspective on Marriage and Love in Post Traumatic Stress Disorder," 86–87.

Chapter 9: Our Problems

Candis M. Williams and Tom Williams, "Family Therapy for Vietnam Veterans," in *Post-Traumatic Stress Disorders: a handbook for clinicians*, Tom Williams, Psy. D., ed. (Cincinnati: Disabled American Veterans, 1987), 222. Available from the DAV National Headquarters, PO Box 14301, Cincinnati, OH, 45214, this book also contains information on PTSD from family violence, sexual assault, community disasters, and "Peacetime Combat" (police officers).

Ray Scurfield, phone interview with author, April 4, 1988. Ray is a Vietnam vet who says he was a REMF-O (rear echelon mother-fucking officer)—a psychologist—who has spent his life since Vietnam working with vets and is now head of the PTSD in-patient unit at the VAMC in Tacoma, WA.

What is normal? Adapted from Janet Woititz's *Adult Children of Alcoholics* (Deerfield Beach, FL: Health Communications, 1983), 55–95.

Linda Flies Moffat and James Moffat, *Families After Trauma*, 1984, available from Minnesota Curriculum Services Center, 3554 White Bear Ave, White Bear Lake, MN 55110, 47–49.

Earnie Larsen and Carol Larsen Hegarty, *Days of Healing, Days of Joy: Daily Meditations for Adult Children* (New York: Harper/Hazelden, 1987) (no page numbers) reading for March 30.

Sarah Haley, personal communication with author, Baltimore, October 24, 1987.

Anne Wilson Schaef, *Co-Dependence: Misunderstood-Mistreated* (San Francisco: Harper & Row, 1986), 69.

Don't talk, don't trust, and don't feel: The title of Chapter 3 of Claudia Black's *It Will Never Happen to Me* (Denver: M.A.C., 1981), 30.

Characteristics of families of combat vets with PTSD: Linda Reinberg, Ph.D., "Follow-Up Report on Research with Fifty-six Families of Combat Survivors," a paper presented at the Fourth Annual Meeting of the Society for Traumatic Stress Studies, Dallas, TX, October 24, 1988

Dual survivor families: Ross L. Mayberry, Ph.D., "Evolutions in the Treatment of Vietnam Veteran Families," paper presented at the Society for Traumatic Stress Studies, Dallas, TX, October 24, 1988.

Ray Scurfield, phone interview: April 4, 1988.

PART THREE. HELP YOURSELF

Chapter 10: First Aid

Sharon Wegscheider-Cruse, *Choicemaking* (Deerfield Beach, FL: Health Communications, 1985), 182–83.

The pain of being unable to help: Charles R. Figley, "A Five-Phase Treatment of Post-traumatic Stress Disorder in Families," in *The Journal of Traumatic Stress* (New York: Plenum Press) 1.1 (January 1988), 134. Charles Figley was a marine in Vietnam and has worked in the fields of PTSD and family therapy for years.

Linda Flies Moffat and James Moffat, *Families After Trauma*, 53.

Judith Jobin, "Lifting Someone Out of the Dumps," *Self*, February 1986.

Mahedy, *Out of the Night*, 124.

Coping with Signals for Help

Veteran suicide: Brende and Parson, *Vietnam Veterans: The Road to Recovery*, 75. Hearst, Newman, and Hulley, "Delayed Effects of the Military Draft on Mortality: A Randomized Natural Experiment," 620–24. Aso see Kogan and Clapp, "Mortality Among Vietnam Veterans in Massachusetts, 1972–1983."

Help

Ray Scurfield, phone conversation: April 4, 1988.

The VA Hospital

World War II POW's and the VA: Donald Knox, *Death March* (New York: Harcourt Brace Jovanovich, 1981), 476–77.

"Besides the San Francisco office, the Washington regional office, St. Petersburg, Philadelphia, Baltimore, Los Angeles, and Winston-Salem offices have *repeatedly* been found to administratively deny claims without proper processing." The VVA Staff, "Scandal Hints Plague VA," *The Veteran*, November 1986, 6.

On the VA interview: Arthur L. Arnold, M.D., "Diagnosis of Post-Traumatic Stress Disorder in Vietnam Veterans," Sonnenberg, Blank, and Talbott, *The Trauma of War*, 102, and Parson, "The Reparation of the Self," 18.

Treatment

The World War II vet with the Silver Stars: See Pary, Turns, and Tobias, "A Case of Delayed Recognition of Posttraumatic Stress Disorder," 941.

Vet Rap Groups

Joel Osler Brende, M.D., "Twelve Themes and Spiritual Steps for Combat Veterans," Paper presented at the Fourth Annual Meeting of the Society for Traumatic Stress Studies, October 25, 1988, Dallas, TX.

Other Sources

Books to consult: Otto and Miriam Ehrenberg, *The Psychotherapy Maze* (New York: Simon and Schuster, 1986 revised and updated), and Emily Marlin, *Hope* (New York: Harper & Row, 1987). See also Aphrodite Matsakis, Ph.D., *Vietnam Wives* (Kensington, MD: Woodbine House, 1988).

Betty Ford, *Betty: A Glad Awakening* (New York: Doubleday, 1987).

Mahedy, *Out of the Night*, 180 and 189.

MacNutt, Francis, OP, *Healing* (New York: Bantam, 1974), 166.

Linn and Linn, *Healing Life's Hurts*, 24.

MacNutt, *Healing*, 166–8.

Ray Scurfield, phone interview: April 4, 1988.

Matsakis, *Vietnam Wives*, 326–30.

Description of family therapy in Terence Williams, *Free to Care* (Center City, MN: Hazelden, 1975), 4. Quote is from Murray Bowen, "A Family Systems Approach to Alcoholism," in *Addictions:* Summer 1974.

Virginia Satir, *Peoplemaking* (Palo Alto, CA: Science and Behavior Books, 1972), 19.

Charles R. Figley, "A Five-Phase Treatment of Post-Traumatic Stress Disorder in Families," *The Journal of Traumatic Stress*, January 1988.

Chapter 11: Listening

Larsen and Hegarty, *Days of Healing, Days of Joy: Daily Meditations for Adult Children*, reading for August 14.

Communication Outline for Family and Friends of Vietnam Veterans, in Marrs, "Why the Pain Won't Stop and What the Family Can Do to Help," in Kelley, *Post-Traumatic Stress Disorder and the War Veteran Patient*, 93.

Dr. George R. Bach and Peter Wyden, *The Intimate Enemy: How to Fight Fair in Love and Marriage* (New York: Avon, 1970).

Eric Berne, M.D., *Games People Play* (New York: Grove Press, 1964).

Dr. Thomas Gordon, *PET: Parent Effectiveness Training* (New York: Peter H Wyden, Inc.), 1970.

Robert Bolton, Ph.D., *People Skills* (Englewood Cliffs: Prentice Hall, 1979), 14–26.

Frank Herbert, *Dune* (New York: Berkley, 1977), 8.

Dalma Heyn, "5 Ways to Get Closer to Your Husband," *McCall's*, November 1986, 63.

Common Concern Program, audio cassette tapes developed by the California Department of Mental Health (Oakland: New Harbinger Publications, Inc., 1985). Session One talks about types of questions.

Suzette Hadin Eglin, *Gentle Art of Verbal Self-Defense* (Englewood Cliffs: Prentice Hall, 1980).

Ray Scurfield, phone interview: April 4, 1988.

Chapter 12: Changing

Larsen and Hegarty, *Days of Healing, Days of Joy*, reading for August 16.

Harriet Goldhor Lerner, Ph.D., *The Dance of Anger* (New York: Harper & Row, 1985), 33–34.

Definitions of Cognitive Distortions: David Burns, M.D., *Feeling Good* (New York: William Morrow & Co. 1980), 49–50.

Nan Silver, "Do Optimists Live Longer?" *American Health*, November 1986.

The ideas about trying harder came from a book on physical healing. Yochanan Rywerant, *The Feldenkrais Method* (San Francisco: Harper & Row, 1983), 214–15.

Williams, *Free to Care*, 6.

Anger: Gordon, *PET*, 125–29.

Linda Adams with Elinor Lenz, *Effectiveness Training for Women* (New York: Wyden Books, 1979), discussion of anger and I-messages in Chapter 7, "When You Own the Problem," 63–72.

Ignoring I messages: Gordon, *PET*, 135.

Responsive and responsible: Gordon, *PET*, 132.

"The Process of Becoming Aware," is Unit II, Handout D, Moffat and Moffat, *Families After Trauma*.

Charles Figley, Ph.D., October 11, 1988, interview on National Public Radio's "Morning Edition."

Suggested Further Reading

PART ONE. VIETNAM: WHAT IT WAS

Baker, Mark. *Nam*. New York: Berkley Books, 1983. A variety of experiences told in the vets' own words. Gave me a lot to think about.

Bodey, Don. *FNG*. New York: Viking, 1985. The everyday horrors of being a grunt. I couldn't put it down.

Brennan, Matt. *Brennan's War*. New York: Pocket Books, 1986. An intense memoir by a three-tour veteran. His second book, *Headhunters*, New York: Pocket Books, 1988, consists of stories from the legendary 1st of the 9th Cav of the 1st Cavalry Division.

Caputo, Philip. *A Rumor of War*. New York: Holt, Rinehart and Winston, 1977. Superbly written memoir of a Marine LT in 1965 through 1966.

Costello, Michael. *A Long Time From Home* New York: Zebra Books, 1984. Intense, moving novel set during the Tet Offensive.

Crapser, William. *Remains*. Old Chatham, N.Y.: Sachem Press, 1988. A series of powerful stories of Vietnam.

Del Vecchio, John. *The 13th Valley*. New York: Bantam Books, 1982. A stunning novel of warfare in the mountains and valleys of northern Vietnam (I Corps) in 1970.

Donovan, David. *Once a Warrior King*. New York: McGraw-Hill, 1985. Excellent memoir about living with the Vietnamese as an advisor.

Downs, Frederick. *The Killing Zone*. New York: W W Norton & Company, 1978. A moving memoir: "This is the way it was for us, the platoon of Delta One-six." I love this book and this guy.

Durden, Charles. *No Bugles, No Drums*. New York: Avon Books, 1984. Best opening line. Intense novel.

Edelman, Bert, ed. *Dear America: Letters Home from Vietnam*. edited for the New York Vietnam Veterans Memorial Commission. New York: Pocket Books, 1985. The title says it all.

Ehrhart, W. D., ed. *Carrying the Darkness*. New York: Avon Books, 1985. The latest and best anthology of Vietnam poetry.

————. *Marking Time*. New York: Avon Books, 1986.

————. *Vietnam/Perkasie*. New York: Zebra Books, 1985. Wonderful books by a Marine intelligence assistant who went out with the grunts.

Floyd, Brian Alec. *The Long War Dead*. New York: Avon Books, 1976. Poems about a marine platoon. Intensely moving.

Glasser, William J, M.D. *365 Days*. New York: Bantam Books, 1972. A doctor tells the stories of some of his patients.

Glick, Allen. *The Winter Marines*. New York: Bantam Books, 1987. A moving novel about a marine unit living in a village to protect it.

Haldeman, Joe. *War Year*. New York: Avon Books, 1984. A great book with a devastating ending. First published in hardback in 1972 by Holt, Rinehart and Winston, New York, with a different ending.

Heinemann, Larry. *Close Quarters*. New York: Farrar, Straus, & Giroux, 1977. Also a Penguin paperback. III Corps. Tracks. Best war novel ever written. Reading it is like going through hell, but worth it.

Ketwig, John. . . . *and a hard rain fell*. New York: Pocket Books, 1985. Another tremendous book. John was "just" a mechanic, and the experiences he relates show that there was no "just anything" in Vietnam.

Marshall, Kathryn. *Combat Zone*. Boston: Little, Brown, 1987. Excellent. Women's own stories in Vietnam.

Mason, Robert. *Chickenhawk*. New York: Viking, 1983. Memoir of a helicopter pilot's tour with the First Cav in 1965–66. Also available as a Penguin paperback.

Parrish, John A., M.D. *12, 20 and 5: A Doctor's Year in Vietnam*. New York: Bantam Books, 1986. A doctor's moving memoir about his tour.

Rottmann, Larry, Barry, Jan, and Paquet, Basil T., ed. *Winning Hearts and Minds*. Brooklyn: 1st Casualty Press, 1972. Very moving Vietnam poetry.

Santoli, Al. *Everything We Had: Oral History of the Vietnam War*. New York: Ballantine, 1985.

————. *To Bear Any Burden*. New York: E. P. Dutton, 1985. Personal stories of a number of vets and refugees.

Terry, Wallace. *Bloods*. New York: Random House, 1984. Personal narratives about the black experience. Excellent.

Trotti, John. *Phantom Over Vietnam*. New York: Berkley Books, 1985. Fascinating memoir of a jet jockey.

Van Devanter, Lynda. *Home Before Morning*. New York: Beaufort Books, 1983. Intense, honest story of what happened to one nurse and the aftereffects.

Walker, Keith. *A Piece of My Heart*. New York: Ballantine Books, 1985. Excellent. More stories from women in Vietnam.

Webb, James. *Fields of Fire*. New York: Bantam Books, 1982. Another great novel.

Wizard, Brian. *Permission to Kill*. Starquill Publisher, PO Box 6, Port Douglas, North Queensland, Australia, 4871 or Brian Wizard, 1579 Farmer's Lane, Suite 66, Santa Rosa, CA, 95405. A doorgunner's self-published story.

AFTERWARD

Broyles, William Jr. *Brothers in Arms*. New York: Alfred A. Knopf, 1986. Moving, interesting, amusing, healing narrative of returning to Vietnam.

Downs, Frederick. *Aftermath*. New York: Berkley Books, 1985. In the hospital and after. Very moving.

Ehrhart, W. D. *Going Back: An Ex-Marine Returns to Vietnam*. Jefferson, N.C.: McFarland & Company, 1987. Wonderful day-by-day account of a trip back. Ehrhart always gets to the heart of things.

Eilert, Rick. *For Self and Country*. New York: William Morrow & Company, 1983. A tremendously moving account of what one vet went through after he was wounded.

Heinemann, Larry. *Paco's Story*. New York: Penguin Books, 1987. Winner of the National Book Award for fiction. The aftereffects for the sole survivor of Alpha Company.

McMullen, James P. *Cry of the Panther*. Englewood, FL: Pineapple Press, 1984. Florida everglades with Vietnam flashbacks. A painful, beautiful, moving book.

Palmer, Laura. *Shrapnel in the Heart*. New York: Random House, 1987. Stories of people who lost someone in Vietnam and left poems, letters, et cetera, at the Wall.

Scruggs, Jan C, and Swerdlow, Joel L. *To Heal a Nation*. New York: Harper & Row, 1985. Story of the struggle to get the Vietnam Veterans Memorial built. Contains all the names on the Wall.

POST-TRAUMATIC STRESS DISORDER

Brende, Joel Osler, M.D. and Parson, Erwin Randolph, Ph.D. *Vietnam Veterans: The Road to Recovery*. New York: Plenum Publishing, 1985. An excellent explanation of Vietnam and PTSD for the general reader.

Campbell, Spencer. *Reflections of a Vietnam Veteran*. pamphlet, The New Jersey State Commission on Agent Orange, 1983, The Image Factory, Trenton N.J. A marine explains the aftereffects of war.

Goodwin, Jim, Psy. D. *Readjustment Problems Among Vietnam Veterans*. Pamphlet published by the Disabled American Veterans, PO Box 14301, Cincinnati, OH, 45214. Simple clear explanation of the problem.

Mahedy, William P. *Out of the Night*. New York: Ballantine Books, 1986. Discusses the spiritual aftereffects of Vietnam. A favorite.

POST-TRAUMATIC STRESS DISORDER BOOKS
FOR PROFESSIONALS

Figley, Charles, Ph.D., ed. *Trauma and Its Wake, The Study and Treatment of Post-Traumatic Stress Disorder*. New York: Brunner/Mazel, 1985.

———. *Trauma and Its Wake*, Vol II, *Traumatic Stress Theory, Research, and Intervention* New York: Brunner/Mazel, 1986. Excellent books which cover all types of PTSD including Vietnam veterans'.

———. *The Journal of Traumatic Stress*, editor. Plenum Press, 233 Spring St, New York, NY 10013-1578. Latest research and treatment: articles on all forms of traumatic stress. Individual subscription $29.50 per year. Will also be received as part of membership in the Society of Traumatic Stress Studies, POBox 1564, Lancaster, PA, 17603-1564. Regular membership in the society is $70 a year. It is $40 for full-time students and retirees.

Journal of Contemporary Psychotherapy, Vol. 14, No. 1, Spring/Summer 1984. Issue devoted to Vietnam veterans and full of excellent articles on treatment.

Kelley, William E., M.D., ed. *Post-Traumatic Stress Disorder and the War Veteran Patient*. New York: Brunner/Mazel, 1985. Another excellent book—focused on Vietnam veterans.

Sonnenberg, Stephen M., M.D., Blank, Arthur S., M.D., and Talbot, John A., M.D. *The Trauma of War: Stress and Recovery in Vietnam Veterans*. Washington, D.C.: American Psychiatric Press, 1985. Required reading for all health-care professionals who work with veterans.

van der Kolk, Bessel A., M.D., ed. *Post-Traumatic Stress Disorder: Psychological and Biological Sequelae*. Washington, D.C.: American Psychiatric Press, 1984.

———. *Psychological Trauma*. Washington, D.C.: American Psychiatric Press, 1987. Lots of different angles ono PTSD in these two books. *Psychological Trauma* focuses on childhood trauma and intergenerational effects.

Williams, Tom, Psy. D. *Post-Traumatic Stress Disorders: a handbook for clinicians*. Cincinnati: Disabled American Veterans, 1987. Second edition of a tremendously helpful book (available from the DAV National Headquarters, PO Box 14301, Cincinnati, OH 45214). It contains information on family violence, sexual assault, community disasters, and "Peacetime Combat" (police officers), as well as Vietnam veterans.

Wilson, John P., Ph.D. *The Forgotten Warrior Project*. Cleveland: Disabled American Veterans, 1978. Required reading for health-care professionals working with Vietnam vets.

SELF-HELP FOR VETS

Crapser, William. *Returning from Vietnam*. Old Chatham, NY: Sachem Press. A wonderful essay about healing by a Vietnam vet. For additional free copies write to: B. Cullen Burris, M.D., Mental Hygiene Clinic, Albany, VAMC, 113 Holland Ave, Albany, NY, 12208.

Moffat, Linda Flies and James. *Families After Trauma*. White Bear Lake, MN: Minnesota Curriculum Services Center. Educational program about why Vietnam affects the whole family. Written by a vet and his wife for Vietnam vets and their families, and although it is expensive—over thirty dollars if you live outside Minnesota—I'd like to see it used as an educational tool by vet groups. If you can't afford it, get the public library to buy it, or get the local adult education program to sponsor a group using it.

Kubey, Craig, Addlestone, David F., O'Dell, Richard E., Snyder, Keith D., Stichman, Barton F., and the Vietnam Veterans of America. *The Viet Vet Survival Guide.* New York: Ballantine Books, 1985. Information on dealing with the VA and your rights.

HELP YOURSELF

Co-dependency and Dysfunctional Families

Friel, John and Linda. *Adult Children: The Secrets of Dysfunctional Families.* Deerfield Beach, FL: Health Communications, 1988. Most comprehensive book on family dysfunction, workaholism to alcoholism.

Gil, Eliana Ph.D. *Outgrowing the Pain.* Walnut Creek, CA: Launch Press. If you're not sure whether you or your children were abused, here is a good place to start.

Matsakis, Aphrodite, Ph.D. *Vietnam Wives.* Kensington, MD: Woodbine House, 1988. Excellent book on the lives of women whose husbands have severe PTSD problems. Good advice, too.

Middleton-Moz, Jane. *Children of Trauma.* Deerfield Beach, FL: Health Communications, 1989. Tremendously healing book about childhood trauma. Read it for yourself or your kids.

Schaef, Anne Wilson. *Co-Dependence: Misunderstood-Mistreated.* San Francisco: Harper & Row, 1986. Excellent book on the theoretical underpinnings of co-dependency and how it permeates our society.

Woititz, Janet, Ed. D. *Adult Children of Alcoholics.* Deerfield Beach, FL: Health Communications, 1983. Anything by Dr. Woititz is worth reading. Defines some of the problems we develop living in dysfunctional family systems, alcoholic or not.

COMMUNICATION

Adams, Linda, with Lenz, Elinor. *Effectiveness Training for Women.* New York: Wyden Books, 1979. Skills from *PET* rewritten for women. Excellent.

Bolton, Robert, Ph.D. *People Skills.* Englewood Cliffs, NJ: Prentice Hall, 1979. Listening and communication skills. Also excellent.

Eglin, Suzette Hadin. *Gentle Art of Verbal Self-Defence.* Englewood Cliffs, NJ: Prentice Hall, 1980. How to identify and deal with the "sweet" or "reasonable" things people say that leave you angry or hurt.

Gordon, Dr. Thomas. *PET: Parent Effectiveness Training.* New York: Peter H. Wyden, Inc., 1970. My old favorite. Helpful if you have kids.

McKay, Matthew, Ph.D., Davis, Martha, Ph.D., and Fanning, Patrick. *Messages, the Communication Book.* Oakland, CA: New Harbinger, 1983. Another terrific book on learning to communicate.

Miller, Sherod, Ph.D., Wackman, Daniel, Ph.D., Nunnally, Elam, Ph.D., and Saline, Carol. *Straight Talk.* New York: Signet, 1982. Great book derived from a couple's communication course.

MEDITATION BOOKS

Borysenko, Joan, Ph.D., with Rothstein, Larry. *Minding the Body, Mending the Mind*. Reading, MA: Addison-Wesley Publishing Co., 1987. Wonderful book combining physical, psychological, and spiritual healing. Chapter 5 (Mind Traps: Outwitting the Dirty Tricks Department of the Mind), is superb.

Cordes, Liane. *The Reflecting Pond*. Center City, MN: Hazelden, 1988. A meditation book arranged by subject rather than having a reading for each day, and small enough ot fit in your purse or pocket.

Fishel, Ruth. *The Journey Within: A Spiritual Path to Recovery*. Deerfield Beach, FL: Health Communications, 1987. A book on learning to meditate.

Gawain, Shakti. *Reflections of the Light*. San Rafael, CA: New World Library, 1988. Contains really excellent healing exercises and ideas. Take what you like and leave the rest.

Larsen, Earnie, and Hegarty, Anne Larsen. *Days of Healing, Days of Joy*. New York: Harper/Hazelden, 1987. This little book, another Hazelden gem, is one of the foundation stones of my recovery program. When I'm too tired to do anything else, I can usually find the energy to read the daily meditation from this book and be comforted.

Lerner, Rokelle. *Daily Affirmations*. Deerfield Beach, FL: Health Communications, 1985. Daily positive thought to ponder.

CHANGING

Ann M. *Letting Go of the Need to Control*. Center City, MN: Hazelden, 1987. Order No. 5322. A very helpful analysis of controlling behavior by a woman who thought of herself as selfless, not controlling. I identified.

Beattie, Melody. *Co-dependent No More*. New York: Harper/Hazelden, 1987. It might help to substitute "PTSD" or "the effects of Vietnam" for drinking and drugs if those are not problems in your family. Good exercises for your journal.

Burns, David, M.D. *Feeling Good*. New York: William Morrow & Co., 1980. Deals with depression and how we twist up our thinking. The exercises helped Bob and me a lot and are used in some PTSD programs.

Cermak, Timmen L., M.D. *A Time to Heal: The Road to Recovery for Adult Children of Alcoholics*. New York: Avon Books, 1988. The chapter on PTSD and adult children is required reading. It may apply to you or your children even without alcoholism in the family.

Common Concern Program, audio cassette tapes developed by the California Department of Mental Health, 1985, published by New Harbinger Publications, Inc., 5674 Shattuck Ave, Oakland, CA, 94609. Useful for starting your own non-12 Step group.

Do's & Don'ts from the Hazelden Family Center. Hazelden, Center City, MN, 1982. Order No. 1235. An extremely helpful short pamphlet that helped me organize some ideas for a healing program for myself. Substitute PTSD for alcoholism where necessary.

Fensterheim, Herbert, Ph.D., and Baer, Jean. *Don't Say Yes When You Want to Say No.* New York: Dell Publishing, 1975. How to become more assertive.

Hayes, Jody. *Smart Love.* Los Angeles: Jeremy P. Tarcher, Inc., 1989. An excellent workbook for co-dependents or anyone who wants to change.

Julia H. *Letting Go with Love.* Los Angeles: Jeremy P. Tarcher, Inc., 1987. Although aimed at the co-dependents of substance abusers, this book was tremendously helpful to me in letting go of Bob's problems and working on mine.

Kathleen W. *Healing a Broken Heart: 12 Steps of Recovery for Adult Children.* Deerfield Beach, FL: Health Communications, 1988. My favorite book about working the 12 Steps.

Klass, Joe. *The 12 Steps to Happiness.* Center City, MN: Hazelden, 1982. Order No. 1053. A favorite on how to do the 12 Steps.

Kritsberg, Wayne. *The Adult Children of Alcoholics Syndrome.* New York: Bantam Books, 1988. You don't have to have alcoholism in your family to benefit from Chapters 9–20 of this book, the Family Integration System. Excellent for working on patterns you learned as a kid that may interfere with happiness now.

Larsen, Earnie. *Getting Control of Your Life: A Survival Kit for Adult Children of Alcoholic and Dysfunctional Families.* Earnie Larsen Publishing, PO Box 33, Waconia, MN, 55387-0033, 1987. Series of pamphlets with lots of useful exercises.

————. *I Should Be Happy, Why Do I Hurt?* St. Paul, MN: International Marriage Encounter, 1986. A series of five pamphlets on personal growth. A favorite.

————. *Stage II Recovery.* San Francisco: Harper & Row, 1985. A book about recovery from dysfunctional patterns—whatever the source. Good exercises included.

————. *Stage II Relationships.* San Francisco: Harper & Row, 1987. Equally wonderful book about building relationships. Good exercises.

Lerner, Harriet Goldhor, Ph.D. *The Dance of Anger.* New York: Harper & Row, 1985. Excellent ideas on how to change a stuck relationship.

Living "Easy Does It." A pamphlet in the Rich Rewards series, Hazelden, Center City, MN, 1987. Order No. 5326. I keep this one in my pocketbook for those desperate moments when I need to remind myself, "progress, not perfection."

Marlin, Emily. *Hope.* New York: Harper & Row, 1987. Tremendously healing book aimed at ACOA's but useful to us.

Moffat, Linda Flies and James. *Families After Trauma.* Minnesota Curriculum Services Center, 3554 White Bear Ave, White Bear Lake, MN, 55110. Educational program aimed specifically at the family affected by trauma or PTSD.

Norwood, Robin. *Women Who Love Too Much.* New York: Pocket Books, 1985. One of the best. Janice's story on page 161 really hit me.

Rainer, Tristine. *The New Diary.* Los Angeles: Jeremy P. Tarcher, 1978. Lots of varied techniques to make your journal an instrument of healing. A favorite of mine.

Ray, Veronica. *Design For Growth, Twelve Steps for Adult Children.* San Francisco: Harper/Hazelden, 1988. Every 12 Step book I read offers new perspectives on healing and recovery. This one had a lot to say to me about being gentle with myself.

Rosellini, Gayle and Worden, Mark. *Of Course You're Angry.* San Francisco: Harper/Hazelden, 1985.

Rowe, Kathleen. *Women's Issues.* Center City, MN: Hazelden, 1986, Order No. 5498. Wonderful discussion of some of the issues for women in recovery.

Scarf, Maggie. *Intimate Partners: Patterns in Love and Marriage.* New York: Random House, 1987. Excellent book. Has some good exercises.

Shroeder, Melvin. *Hope For Relationships.* Center City, MN: Hazelden, 1980. Order no. 1335. A very helpful pamphlet describing the stages in relationships and how to work through them.

The Twelve Steps for Everyone . . . who really wants them. Revised edition. Minneapolis: CompCare Publishers, 1987. First and second editions contained "new pronouns" which made 'em hard to read. Another useful book on how to do the 12 Steps.

Wegscheider-Cruse, Sharon. *Choicemaking.* Deerfield Beach, FL: Health Communications, 1985. Chapter 1 (Varieties of Co-dependency) is invaluable.

Weisenger, Hendrie, Ph.D. *Dr. Weisenger's Anger Work Out Book.* New York: Quill, 1985. Recommended by Ray Scurfield.

Williams, Terence. *Free to Care.* Center City, Mn.: Hazelden, 1975. Helpful pamphlet on letting go.

Woititz, Janet. *Guidelines for Support Groups.* A pamphlet. Deerfield Beach, FL: Health Communications, Inc, 1986. Useful guidelines if you are starting a group.

Some Further Sources of Help

AA World Service (Alcoholics Anonymous), PO Box 459, Grand Central Station, New York, NY 10163. (212) 686-1100. Check your local phone book, too.

Al-Anon Family Group Headquarters, World Service Office, PO Box 862, Midtown Station, New York, NY 10018-0862, or 1372 Broadway (at 38th St.), 7th Floor, New York, NY 10018. (212) 302-7240. Check your local phone book, too.

Alliance of Information and Referral Services (AIRS), PO Box 3456, Joliet, IL 60434. Send a self-addressed stamped envelope for the nearest information and referral service—which should list whatever help is available in your area.

CompCare, 2415 Annapolis Lane, Minneapolis, MN 55441, (800) 328-3330. Free catalog on request. Books on compulsive behavior (including alcoholism, drug-addiction, sexual addiction, and compulsive eating) and recovery.

Disabled American Veterans, National Headquarters, PO Box 145550, Cincinnati, OH 45250-5550. Published *Readjustment Problems Among Vietnam Veterans*, and *Post-Traumatic Stress Disorders: a handbook for clinicians*. This group also funded the *Forgotten Warrior Project*, and had storefront vet centers before the government did. Has a network of service officers to help with claims.

Hazelden Foundation is one of the best sources in the country for literature that can be adapted to our needs in dealing with the effects of Vietnam on our families. Free catalog upon request. Hazelden Educational Materials, Pleasant Valley Rd., Box 176, Center City, MN 55012-0176. Toll free: (U.S. only) 1-800-328-9000, (MN only) 1-800-257-0070.

Health Communications, Inc., Enterprise Center, 3201 Southwest 15th Street, Deerfield Beach, FL 33442. (800) 851-9100. Publishes a series of wonderful books for ACOA's and other co-dependents. I would not be comfortable recommending them, however, without saying that, in my opinion, one recent book, *Recovery from Rescuing*, blots an otherwise find publishing record.

Nar-Anon Family Group Headquarters, PO Box 2562, Palos Verdes, CA 90274, (213) 547-5800.

Narcotics Anonymous, World Service Office, PO Box 9999, (16155 Wyandotte

St.), Van Nuys, CA 91406. Check your phone book or contact the World Service Office.

National Association for Children of Alcoholics, 31582 Coast Highway, Suite B, South Laguna, CA 92677-3044. (714) 499-3889.

National Coalition Against Domestic Violence, PO Box 15127, Washington DC 20003-0127. If you are in crisis or need a referral, call 1-800-333-7233. You may have to hold.

National Self-Help Clearinghouse, 25 W. 43rd St., Rm. 620, New York, NY 10036, (212) 840-1259. Puts you in touch with one of sixty regional clearinghouses for self-help groups.

Overeaters Anonymous, World Service Office, 4025 Spencer, Suite 203, Torrance, CA 90503, (213) 542-8363, or PO Box 92870 Los Angeles, CA 90009.

Paralyzed Veterans of America, 801 18th St, NW, Washington, DC, 20006, (202) 872-1300. Has a network of service officers who handle VA claims for all veterans including paralyzed ones.

Sex and Love Addicts Anonymous Fellowship Wide Services, Inc., PO Box 88, Newton Branch, Boston, MA 02158.

Veterans Education Project, PO Box 42130, Washington, DC 20015. Publishes *The Veteran's Self-Help Guide on Stress Disorder*. Provides other resources on dealing with the VA system.

Vietnam Veterans of America, 2001 S Street, NW, Suite 700, Washington DC 20009, (202) 332-2700. Publishes *The Veteran*, a monthly newspaper focused on veterans' issues, and offers legal services for discharge upgrades, et cetera, and service officers to help with claims. Also lobbies Congress for veterans interests. Twenty dollars annual dues includes the paper. Help is free.

I have included only the veterans organizations with which I've had personal experience. Many others exist.

Suggested Guidelines for a Twelve Step Support Group for Families of Veterans

Welcome

My name is _____. I am a family member of a veteran. We want to welcome you to the _____night meeting of the Families of Veterans Support Group. Would you join me in a moment of silence to compose ourselves.

Let us join hands while I read the statement of purpose:

Look around you and you will see people who have experienced many of the same things you may have experienced. Veterans of war develop certain characteristics. One may be reexperiencing the trauma through obsessive thoughts, nightmares, flashbacks, sudden reemergence of survival behaviors, and emotional overloads, rages, or deep depressions. Another characteristic, emotional numbing, may include a sense of not really being a person, feelings of not fitting in, feeling that one has no emotions, and not being able to feel emotions in situations calling for intimacy, tenderness, sexuality, or grief. Hypervigilance includes being unable to relax, having frequent startle responses, continual feelings of anxiety, and attacks of panic. Survivor guilt includes self-destructive behaviors, depression, and a feeling of guilt at surviving when others did not. Each of these normal reactions to traumatic experiences can have a profound and painful effect on the family, especially if family members do not understand that they are normal.

If these issues have caused us time and again to put aside our own needs and concerns to try to help our veterans, we may have developed patterns for coping which are not working in the way we hoped they would.

At this time I have asked _____to read the preamble.

Preamble

We are a fellowship of people who share experience, strength, and hope with each other in order to deal with the effects of war on our lives. The only requirement for membership is the sincere desire to make life better for ourselves and our families. We do not wish to blame, but rather to understand the effects of war on people and how those effects can affect the family members, thereby becoming free to grow and accept responsibility for our own lives. We are a self-supporting group through our own contributions. We are not allied with any sect, denomination, politics, organization, or institution. We do not wish to engage in any controversy or endorse or oppose any cause.

The primary purpose of our group is to learn to deal with the effects on our lives of our veterans' experiences and survivor skills, and to develop healthy patterns to cope with these.

I have asked _____to read the 12 Steps.

The 12 Steps

Here are the steps we took which are suggested as a program of recovery:

1. We admitted we were powerless over the effects of war on ourselves and our families—that our lives had become unmanageable.
2. Came to believe that a power greater than ourselves could restore us to sanity.
3. Made a decision to turn our will and our lives over to the care of our Higher Power as we understood our Higher Power.
4. Made a searching and fearless moral inventory of ourselves.

5. Admitted to our Higher Power, ourselves, and to another human being the exact nature of our wrongs.

6. Were entirely ready to have our Higher Power remove our shortcomings.

7. Humbly asked our Higher Power to remove our shortcomings.

8. Made a list of all people we had harmed, and became willing to make amends to them all.

9. Made direct amends to such people wherever possible, except when to do so would injure them or others.

10. Continued to take personal inventory and, when we were wrong, promptly admitted it.

11. Sought through prayer and meditation to improve our conscious contact with our Higher Power as we understood our Higher Power, praying only for knowledge of our Higher Power's will for us and for the power to carry that out.

12. Having had a spiritual awakening as the result of these steps, we tried to carry this message to others, and to practice these principles in all our affairs.

The following are the original Twelve Steps reprinted and adapted with permission of AA World Services, Inc.

1. We admitted that we were powerless over_____that our lives had become unmanageable.

2. Came to believe that a power greater than ourselves could restore us to sanity.

3. Made a decision to turn our will and our lives over to the care of God, *as we understood God.*

4. Made a searching and fearless moral inventory of ourselves.

5. Admitted to God, to ourselves, and to another human being the exact nature of our wrongs.

6. Were entirely ready to have God remove all these defects of character.

7. Humbly asked God to remove our shortcomings.

8. Made a list of all persons we had harmed, and became willing to make amends to them all.

9. Made direct amends to such people wherever possible, except when to do so would injure them or others.

10. Continued to take personal inventory and when we were wrong promptly admitted it.

11. Sought through prayer and meditation to improve our conscious contact with God *as we understood God*, praying only for knowledge of God's will for us and the power to carry that out.

12. Having had a spiritual awakening as the result of these steps, we tried to carry this message to_____and to practice these principles in all our affairs.

. . . No one among us has been able to maintain anything like perfect adherence to these principles. We are not saints. The point is we are willing to grow along spiritual lines. The principles we have set down are guides to progress. We claim spiritual progress rather than spiritual perfection.

—Adapted from "The Big Book of AA," pages 59–60.

After the opening readings, it is suggested that each person introduce him or herself, first names only, and, if willing, give a brief statement about what brought him or her to the meeting. Following any announcements, the leader then announces the topic (leader and topic selected the previous week) and tells how the topic has affected his or her life and any ways he or she has found to cope with these effects. Then the next person in the circle talks about his or her experience with the subject and so on around the circle. Blaming and dumping are to be avoided. (Dumping means describing all the awful things that happened this week.) We share experience, strength, and hope. It is suggested that no one be interrupted with suggestions or advice. We do not come to the meeting to take care of more people, but to find support and learn ways of taking care of ourselves.

After the discussion period closes the leader says:

We are a self-supporting group. There are no dues or fees, but we buy literature and pay for the use of the room. The usual contribution is a dollar.

We need to select a topic and a leader for next week. Are there any pressing concerns? Who will volunteer to lead?

We use anonymity to protect the group. What you have heard

here and whom you have seen here is confidential. Keep it within the walls of this room or the confines of your mind.

Would all who care to join me in the Serenity Prayer (in a circle holding hands):

Grant me the serenity to accept the things I cannot change, the courage to change the things I can, and the wisdom to know the difference.

Keep coming back!

Suggested topics: Symptoms of PTSD. What co-dependency is. Boundaries between people. Detaching with love. Acting vs. reacting. Assertion rather than aggression. Criticism. Multiple roles. . . .

Suggestions for Doing the Steps

Read a book about doing the steps, substituting "the effects of war" for "alcohol." Five are listed in Suggested Further Reading.

1. Make a list of the things you are powerless over.
2. Find a higher power you can accept. Accepting a God named Him is not necessary. This may involve exploring religions, philosophies, nature, your group, or your glove compartment.
3. Practice turning things over. This may be as simple as writing down your worries and putting them in the glove compartment of your car. I turned mine over to Lee Iacocca for the first six months I was doing the steps. It worked.
4. An inventory is just what is there in the store *now*, good and bad. We need to know our present characteristics if we want to change. We can't change what we don't know we are doing.
5. We share our inventory with ourselves because we need the awareness. We share it with our Higher Power because that is the safest other to share with. We share it with another carefully chosen person, one who is nonjudgmental and accepting, to release ourselves from the tyranny of our secrets. They are never as bad—spoken out loud—as they loom in our minds.
6. Becoming willing to let go of some characteristics that feel good but don't necessarily work (like being right—one of my specialties) is often harder than acknowledging their existence.
7. Ask your higher power to help you let those characteristics go. Asking out loud and saying each characteristic out loud helps.
8. Painful work, to realize we may have harmed others, and it is sometimes painful becoming *willing* to make amends to people who have hurt us as much or more than we have hurt them. Make a list of right-aways, laters, and nevers, and work on the ones you can do now.
9. Amends are not apologies. Amends can be as simple as beginning to take care of yourself so your family isn't always guilt-tripped by how much you do for them. Amends involve

changing behavior. Amends are made without long explanations of why you did something, and without pointing out how the other person was wrong, too. "I am sorry for my part in this," is a good way to put it. All you are responsible for is making the amends, not how the other person receives it.

10. Doing a spot check inventory when you notice you are upset or reacting (instead of acting) during the day, or looking over your day in the evening, are two ways of doing this. Promptly admitting when I am wrong has been the most freeing step for me. I make mistakes because I am human. It's okay as long as I don't deny that I made a mistake.

11. I read somewhere that praying is not asking but listening.

12. It's easier to carry the message than it is to practice these principles in all our affairs. I prefer to listen to people and, if they are interested, tell them what has worked for me, rather than advising everyone to do what I did.

Index

431